FOR REFERENCE

Do Not Take From This Room

Creative and Performing Artists

for Teens

Creative and Performing Artists

for Teens

volume 3: l - p

Thomas McMahon
editor

GALE GROUP

Detroit
San Francisco
London
Boston
Woodbridge, CT

S

Creative and Performing Artists for Teens

Staff

Project Editor: Thomas McMahon
Editorial Staff: Catherine Goldstein, Alan Hedblad, Karen Uchic, Erin White
Managing Editor: Joyce Nakamura
Publisher: Hal May
Project Coordinator: Cheryl Warnock
Research Specialists: Andrew Guy Malonis, Barbara McNeil, Gary Oudersluys, Maureen Richards
Research Associates: Patricia Tsune Ballard, Corrine A. Boland, Wendy K. Festerling, Tamara C. Nott, Tracie A. Richardson
Research Assistants: Tim Lehnerer, Patricia L. Love
Research Manager: Victoria B. Cariappa
Permissions Associates: Sarah Chesney, Edna Hedblad, Michele Lonoconus
Image Database Supervisor Randy Bassett
Imaging Specialists Robert Duncan, Michael Logusz
Imaging Coordinator Pamela A. Reed
Senior Art Director: Pamela A. E. Galbreath
Product Design Manager: Cynthia Baldwin
Typesetter: Casey Roberts

Library of Congress Cataloging-in-Publication Data

Creative and Performing Artists for Teens
    v. cm.
    Includes bibliographical references and index.
    Contents: v. 1. A-C — v. 2. D-K — v. 3. L-P — v. 4. Q-Z.
    Summary: Biographical entries of approximately 300 creative and performing artists from the fields of literature, music, the visual arts, and film and television.
    ISBN 0–7876–3973–7 (set : hardcover : alk. paper). — ISBN 0–7876–3974–5 (v. 1. : hardcover : alk. paper). — ISBN 0–7876–3975–3 (v. 2. : hardcover : alk. paper). — ISBN 0–7876–3976–1 (v. 3. : hardcover : alk. paper). — ISBN 0–7876–3977–X (v. 4. : hardcover : alk. paper)
    1. Arts, Modern—20th century Bio-bibliography Dictionaries Juvenile literature. [1. Arts. Modern—20th century—Biography.] I. Gale Group. Title: Creative and performing artists for teens.
NX90.C74 1999   [B]99–35562
700' .92'2-dc21   CIP

volume 1: a-c

Table of Contents

volume 2: d-k

volume 3: l-p

volume 4: q-z

Artists by Field

Animators and Cartoonists

Authors

Comedians

Designers and Sculptors

Directors and Screenwriters

Painters

Photographers

Singers and Musicians

Creative and Performing Artists for Teens is a reference work designed to provide biographical profiles on a wide range of creative artists who appeal to junior high and high school students. This four-volume set features an eclectic mix of twentieth-century artists, including singers, musicians, cartoonists, novelists, poets, painters, sculptors, directors, and film and television personalities. Their artistries range from the classic to the contemporary, the lighthearted to the serious, the mainstream to the fringe. The goal of *Creative and Performing Artists for Teens* is to present this great diversity of artists in a format that is entertaining, informative, and understandable to the young adult reader.

Format

The biographies of the artists are arranged alphabetically over four volumes. Artists are listed according to the names by which they are best known to their audience. Each entry begins with the artist's name, principal occupations, birth and death information, and a quote by or about the artist. A typical entry also includes:

- A personal data section with information about the artist's marriage, children, and education.

- A distinctive essay offering detailed comments on the artist's life, career, artistic intentions, world views, and controversies.

- A list of sources for further reading.

- Boxed sidebar listings of the artist's major works—both popular and critical favorites.

A cumulative index to featured artists and titles of their works appears in each volume.

Advisory Board

The final list of entrants for *Creative and Performing Artists for Teens* was compiled with the help of an advisory board of librarians, educators, and students. We would like to thank our board once again for their efforts and acknowledge them here:

Mary Arnold, Librarian
Cuyahoga County Public Library
Maple Heights, Ohio

Joan Eisenberg, Librarian
and ''The Bookies'' Reading Group
Cambridge Public Library
Cambridge, Massachusetts

Francisca Goldsmith, Librarian
and ''Feedback'' Teen Advisory Board
Berkeley Public Library
Berkeley, California

Jim Marshall, Educator
and students from the
Minnesota Center for Arts Education
Golden Valley, Minnesota

Caryn Sipos, Librarian
North Bend Library
North Bend, Washington

Kay E. Vandergrift, Professor
Rutgers University
New Brunswick, New Jersey

Comments and Suggestions

We welcome your comments and suggestions about *Creative and Performing Artists for Teens.* Please contact:

The Editor
Creative and Performing Artists for Teens
Gale Group
27500 Drake Rd.
Farmington Hills, MI 48331–3535
Phone: (800) 357–GALE
Fax: (248) 699–8054

Mercedes Lackey

Fantasy novelist
(1950–)

Born June 24, 1950, in Chicago, IL; daughter of Edward George and Joyce (a homemaker; maiden name, Anderson) Ritche; married Anthony Lackey, June 10, 1972; married Larry Dixon (a science fiction/fantasy artist and author), December 10, 1990. Education: Purdue University, B.S., 1972.

"Love, freedom, and the chance to do some good—they're the things worth living and dying for. . . ."

Since the publication in 1987 of *Arrows of the Queen,* Mercedes Lackey has become known as one of the most popular and prolific authors of fantasy writing today. Her works, particularly those set in the world of Valdemar, are especially enjoyed by young adults for their themes of personal growth, self-discovery, and coming of age. Her involving plots—featuring intelligent animals, fantastic creatures, and psychic and magical abilities—and complex characters have led *Booklist* reviewer Roland Green to call her "an above-average fantasy writer" with the capacity to develop into a "major figure in the field."

Lackey discovered science fiction and fantasy at a young age and began writing her own stories when genre grand master Andre Norton "wasn't turning out books at a fast enough rate to suit me," as she told Bradley H. Sinor in *Starlog.* After moving to Tulsa, Oklahoma, in 1982, Lackey began writing stories for science fiction and fantasy fan magazines while working at American Airlines. "Whenever I wasn't at work, I was bored out of my mind and needed something to do," she told Sinor. In addition to writing for the magazines, Lackey attended science fiction fan conventions. It was at one such convention that she met writer C. J. Cherryh, who encouraged her to move her work into the professional arena; at another, she met with Betsy Wollheim of DAW Books, who eventually bought Lackey's first book.

World of Valdemar

That first novel was *Arrows of the Queen,* the story of Talia, a thirteen-year-old girl from a controlling Hold family living in the ultra-conservative Borderlands of Valdemar. Unlike most Holdgirls, Talia rebels; she learns to read, her only escape from a life of unending chores and obedience to male members of the family. When she is confronted with the prospect of marrying, she flees the house to wander a nearby road and contemplate running away. But before she can make a decision, she encounters a Companion, one of the magical, intelligent, and clairvoyant beings in horse form who choose those who will be Heralds, the respected and admired administrators of justice throughout Valdemar. Talia learns about her new life as not only a Herald but also special advisor to the Queen, the "Queen's Own."

Fantasy Review contributor James T. Crawford called *Arrows of the Queen* an "absorbing book that really puts the reader in Talia's place" by focusing on themes of "personal growth and discovery." The next two "Queen's Own" books, *Arrow's Flight* and *Arrow's Fall,* continue these themes as Talia takes up the duties of a Herald, faces the responsibilities imposed by her empathic talents, and discovers an evil threat to the queen's kingdom. In another *Booklist* review, Green characterized the former as "a page-turner" and praised the author for improving her narrative technique.

"Mage Winds" Novels

The "Mage Winds" trilogy begins where *Arrow's Fall* leaves off. In the first book, *Winds of Fate,* Elspeth, heir to the throne, has become a Herald. The evil prince Ancar, previously thwarted by Talia, is causing more magical trouble, and Elspeth volunteers to go in search of an Adept mage who can train the people of Valdemar in the magic they need to protect the kingdom. Eventually she finds Darkwind, of the Tayledras Clan in k'Sheyna, who has renounced his own powers until he meets Elspeth and learns her troubles. But Darkwind's clan has their own evil enemy. The two team up with others to combat the evil Adept Mornelithe Falconsbane in *Winds of Change.* In the final novel of the series, *Winds of Fury,* Elspeth and Darkwind travel to Valdemar to take care of the threat Prince Ancar presents.

In this series Lackey presents a number of non-human characters in addition to the Companions. Gryphons, changechildren, and hertasi share this world with human characters in interesting ways; all are "strong and believable," according to a *Publishers Weekly* reviewer. Other reviewers have noted the coming-of-age focus in the series; in describing Lackey's "essential themes," Rebecca Sue Taylor and Margaret Miles stated in *Voice of Youth Advocates:* "Becoming an adult is scary, hard work; finding the right person to share your life with is never as simple as it seems; and honesty and honor are the best one can strive for."

The "Last Herald-Mage" series depicts people and events in Valdemar about six hundred years before those in the "Queen's Own" and "Mage-Winds" trilogies. At fifteen, Vanyel is heir to the throne in Valdemar but would rather be a Court Bard, a musician for one of the Great Courts of Valdemar, than a warrior. His disappointed father sends him to live with his Aunt Savil, a Herald at Valdemar's High court. There he discovers his mage gift and trains it until he becomes the most powerful mage in Valdemar. He also faces the challenge of his homosexuality; by the third book, *Magic's Price,* his parents finally accept their son for who he is. Throughout the trilogy Vanyel is haunted by dreams of his own death, which comes about in the third book. Ironically, from the point of view of the first novel, *Magic's Pawn,* he dies heroically, defending Valdemar by holding off the Dark Servants' approach. In *Voice of Youth Advocates,* P. A. Timko lauded Lackey's "broad array of meticulously crafted characters," while Green wrote of *Magic's Promise* that Lackey's "characterization, plotting and wit are all of a high order."

Lackey has fleshed out the history of Valdemar in several other works, leading Scott Winnett in *Locus* to observe that her world is becoming "a major creation" along the lines of Anne McCaffrey's Pern or Marion Zimmer Bradley's Darkover. *The Black Gryphon,* written with her husband Larry Dixon, is a prehistory set centuries before the other books and features a race of birds approaching intelligence. The ''Vows and Honor'' novels, *The Oathbound* and *Oathbreakers,* feature the Shin'a'in swordswoman Tarma and the sorceress Kethry, a wandering oathbound pair who battle demons—both monstrous and human. In the ''Mage Storms'' trilogy, Lackey ''continues to expand upon her world's rich history and cultures,'' according to a *Library Journal* critic.

Working with Other Authors

Lackey has written many novels in collaboration with other authors, including her childhood favorite Andre Norton (*The Elvenbane*) and early mentor C. J. Cherryh (*Reap the Whirlwind*). On writing novels with others, she told Taylor, Gayle Keresey, and Miles in a *Voice of Youth Advocates* interview: ''I can, now that I have my 'own' style, chameleon anyone I can work with,'' in order to produce a blended book. In addition, Lackey's husband Larry Dixon has often served as an uncredited collaborator for many of her novels. Other joint projects include works with established genre authors such as Marion Zimmer Bradley, Anne McCaffrey, and Piers Anthony.

''I'm a storyteller; that's what I see as 'my job,''' Lackey once commented. ''My stories come out of my characters; how those characters would react to the given situation. Maybe that's why I get letters from readers as young as thirteen and as old as sixty-odd.'' Music is another important element in Lackey's work. She writes lyrics for songs, sometimes making it part of the novel-writing process. As she once revealed, ''I frequently will write a lyric when I am attempting to get to the heart of a crucial scene. . . . When I write the 'folk music' of these peoples, I am enriching my whole world, whether I actually use the song in the text or not.'' Lackey is known as a leading songwriter in the ''filk'' (folk music set in science fiction or fantasy worlds) genre, and has had many of her songs recorded by various artists.

Responsibility and social consciousness are significant themes in Lackey's work. Her inventions of non-human intelligent beings to populate her worlds with humans and how they do and don't get along are reflective of ethnic problems in our own world. Her protagonists are more often than not abused children and adolescents finding ways to live better lives. As the years have passed, Lackey has been hampered in her writing by a kind of dyslexia that makes typing very difficult, but she has no plans of ending her career. She once remarked that ''in everything I write I try to expound the creed I gave my character Di Tregarde in *Burning Water*—there's no such thing as 'one, true way'; the only answers worth having are the ones you find for yourself; leave the world better than you found it. Love, freedom, and the chance to do some good—they're the things worth living and dying for, and if you aren't willing to die for the things worth living for, you might as well turn in your membership in the human race.''

Sources for More Information

Books

Authors and Artists for Young Adults, Volume 13, Gale, 1994.

St. James Guide to Fantasy Writers, St. James Press, 1996.

St. James Guide to Young Adult Writers, St. James Press, 1999.

Don't Miss ...

''Queen's Own'' Trilogy
Arrows of the Queen, DAW, 1987
Arrow's Flight, DAW, 1987
Arrow's Fall, DAW, 1988

''Last Herald-Mage'' Trilogy
Magic's Pawn, DAW, 1989
Magic's Promise, DAW, 1989
Magic's Price, DAW, 1990

''Mage Winds'' Trilogy
Winds of Fate, DAW, 1991
Winds of Change, DAW, 1992
Winds of Fury, DAW, 1993

k.d. lang

**Singer and songwriter
(1961–)**

*"I've always been one for melding
genres together. . . ."*

*Born Katherine Dawn Lang, November 2, 1961, in
Edmonton, Alberta, Canada; companion of Leisha Haley.*

Her music has been called cow-punk or new
wave country. While Canadian singer k.d.
lang transcends easy labelling, her expressive voice
and wild stage shows are bringing a whole new
generation of listeners back to country music.
With the release of her third album, *Shadowland,*
k.d. lang joined young singers like Dwight Yoakam
and Randy Travis as new stars in the country
music firmament. But unlike Yoakam, a country
purist who rejects Nashville "schmaltz," lang
embraces both the old and the new. While some
have called her unusual renderings of classic tunes
campy or even sarcastic, lang insists her music
is sincere.

lang seems to have a broad appeal. She has
garnered standing ovations everywhere from
Vancouver punk clubs to the Grand Ole Opry. The
Nashville Banner called her "one of the most
exciting new artists to come around in a while."
At the same time, *Rolling Stone* applauded her
already "legendary" live performances. Among
her many influences, lang lists Patsy Cline and
Boy George.

Small Town Upbringing

k.d. lang has country roots. She was born Katherine Dawn Lang in 1961 and was raised in the tiny town of Consort (pop. 672), Alberta, Canada. As a teenager, k.d. earned summer money driving a three-ton grain truck for local farmers. Despite her rural surroundings, lang's early musical influences were not country. She trained on classical piano and listened to her older sister's rock music collection. "I grew up not liking country music," she told Jay Scott in *Chatelaine*. "I was brought up in a family that studied classical music, at the piano. We also listened to Broadway shows. And I listened to Janis Joplin and the Allman Brothers." Later, in college, she dabbled in performance art.

But music remained her first love. As a teenager, she was a would-be professional, doing numbers like "Midnight Blue" and the "Circle Game" on her acoustic guitar at weddings and other functions. At college, she discovered the music of Patsy Cline, whose emotional approach drew lang back to the golden age of country, when singers like Johnny Horton and Hank Williams sang simple tributes to the everyday life of ordinary people.

In 1982 she answered an ad in an Edmonton newspaper for a singer for a Texas swing fiddle band. Her future manager, Larry Wanagas, was at the audition. He knew immediately that a unique talent was ready to be developed. "The first show she did," he told Perry Stem in *Canadian Musician* magazine, "surprised herself as well as me. I knew she could sing, but what she brought to the stage was this undeniable presence."

Unique Stage Persona

For the next two years, lang and her band, the Declines, toured throughout Canada. They played country, college, and rock bars. k.d. would stomp out wearing ugly, rhinestone-studded glasses (without lenses) and cowboy boots with the tops sawn off. She would fling herself to the stage in the middle of her version of the 1960s girl-pop classic "Johnny Get Angry." But no matter how contorted her hijinks, her voice rang deep and melodious. It didn't take long for the word to spread—this weird-looking woman from the plains of Alberta was singing country tunes like they had never been sung before.

Her first album, *A Truly Western Experience,* was recorded during this period on an independent Edmonton label. It showed that her voice could be transposed successfully to vinyl, but it didn't sell well. Then, in the spring of 1985, after playing a gig at New York's Bottom Line club, the head of Sire Records signed her to his label. Seymour Stein was already recording the Talking Heads, Madonna, the Pretenders, and the Ramones. After witnessing her Bottom Line show, he decided she was ready for big-time exposure. "You are what should have happened to country music 30 years ago," he told her at the time.

Her star was on the rise. In November, she was named Canada's "most promising female vocalist." But in 1986, lang disappeared from the concert circuit. When she reappeared, she had abandoned the persona that had won her headlines. A restrained, new Kathy Dawn lang emerged, without the cat glasses and the studied attempts to make herself ugly. "The reason I've tempered my style is because I'm taking my music more seriously," lang told *Western Report*. "I'm tired of being written about as some zany, crazy kid. I think the gap between k.d. and Kathy has lessened to the point where I'm almost completely Kathy on stage now." lang clearly sought to defy the critics who doubted her artistic commitment.

A More Mature Vision

lang's second album, but first major release, *Angel With a Lariat,* was the product of k.d.'s new devotion to her music. It was a complex collection of lang's own pieces and country classics, like Patsy Cline's heartbreaker "Three Cigarettes in an Ashtray." Produced in England by rocker Dave Edmunds, it featured the spontaneity of a live performance. And at the same time, it strove to recapture the honesty and purity that lang found lacking in contemporary country music. The reviews were generous. The Toronto *Globe and Mail,* for example, called the production "a breathlessly paced, musically adventurous album that's unlike anything in contemporary or rock music."

With the release of her first major commercial effort, k.d. began to look south of the Canadian border. In May 1987, she made her television

k.d. lang in concert

debut on *The Tonight Show*. Johnny Carson was so impressed that he invited her back three times. She quickly became a television regular, appearing on *Late Night with David Letterman, Hee Haw,* and on pay-TV alongside Bruce Springsteen and Elvis Costello. She also teamed up with music legend Roy Orbison to record a stirring version of the rock veteran's classic ballad "Crying." Their co-production sold more than 50,000 copies in the United States. Nonetheless, major radio airplay still seemed to elude lang.

In the summer of 1988, lang released the album that was to feature her vocal talents in a way that *Angel With a Lariat* never did. *Shadowland* was produced by country legend Owen Bradley, the man who developed Patsy Cline's talent. Indeed, *Shadowland* seemed to be a coming-to-terms of lang's long-time obsession with her mentor and role model. None of the songs on the album are her own. Instead, they are nostalgic, sincere interpretations of emotional ballads known in the country music business as "weepers." The album did well, garnering respectable sales and laudatory reviews.

Her 1989 release, *Absolute Torch and Twang,* "splits the difference between the unbridled high spirits . . . of *Angel With a Lariat* and the more studied, Patsy Cline-influenced studioscapes crafted by legendary country producer Owen Bradley on *Shadowland,*" noted Holly Gleason in a *Rolling Stone* review. "There are more obvious records

lang could have made," Gleason continued, "ones designed to make her a country queen. Instead, she opted for songs that challenge her abilities and make a case for artistic vision."

Going Public

lang released another successful album in 1992. *Ingenue* went multi-platinum and garnered lang a Grammy nomination for Album of the Year. It was during interviews promoting *Ingenue* that lang went public with her lesbianism. In an interview with *Mademoiselle,* lang called her new openness "an incredible change for the better. Not that I ever hid anything. But it's still a deep feeling of emancipation." Fascination with lang continued among the masses. Her 1993 *Vanity Fair* cover shot with supermodel Cindy Crawford and her controversial "Meat Stinks" ad campaign for PETA (People for the Ethical Treatment of Animals) brought her further into the limelight.

Another hit came with lang's 1995 album, *All You Can Eat.* Its soulful sound explored yet another facet of lang's repertoire. She told *People,* "I've always been one for melding genres together, but I think that's because I'm really honestly interested in, and have been influenced by, such a broad spectrum of music that it can't help but come out that way. I couldn't see myself just doing something pure because to me that's in a way only regurgitating and recycling, and not evolving."

With the 1997 release of her sixth album, *Drag,* (a title having nothing to do with lang's fashion preferences), the world recognized that lang had clearly outgrown cow-punk style. Many critics announced that her singing and songwriting had matured to take on a more seductive, cabaret quality. Songs such as "Love is Like A Cigarette" and "Don't Smoke in Bed" were part of a theme that uses cigarette-smoking (hence the title, *Drag*) as a metaphor for unhappy relationships. Considered by many critics as one of the best interpretive singers of the day, lang also recorded cover songs by Roy Orbison, the Steve Miller Band ("The Joker"), and a rendition of "Theme From the Valley of the Dolls."

In a small leap from the music industry to television, lang took part in a ground-breaking television event in April 1997, when ABC aired the controversial coming-out episode on the sitcom

Ellen, in which actress Ellen DeGeneres's title character declared herself a lesbian and became the first openly gay character on TV. A friend of DeGeneres's, Lang participated in the event with a guest role as a singing waitress in a gay bar.

Avoids Easy Labels

lang continues to defy the easy labels. Even without her spiked hair, k.d. lang stands in stark contrast to the pronounced femininity of Nashville's female country artists. She may mimic country music's golden years, but her mannish looks do not fit in with the bouffant hairstyles of earlier times. When *Chatelaine* magazine chose lang as its 1988 Woman of the Year, she defiantly posed for the magazine cover without make-up. Yet in July 1997 lang uncharacteristically appeared in *Vogue* wearing evening gowns. The fashion switch, however, didn't reflect a complete change of heart. Lang told Julie Klam in *Rolling Stone* that she saw wearing the gowns as "spiritual" experience, rather than a glamorous one.

If lang's fashion can no longer be pegged, neither can her music. She has admitted to not wanting to be categorized musically. Her more recent albums have more of a pop sound than a country one. She told *Interview* that switching styles isn't meant to confuse her fans, but she wants to remain "contemporary and progressive." lang said to Klam, ". . . I worship my differences.

Choice Cuts

Angel With a Lariat, Sire, 1987

Shadowland, Sire, 1988

Absolute Torch and Twang, Sire, 1989

Ingenue, Sire, 1992

All You Can Eat, Warner Bros., 1995

Drag, Warner Bros., 1997

The fact that I'm an anomaly and my career has been a struggle is much more rewarding."

Sources for More Information

Periodicals

Entertainment Weekly, June 13, 1997.

Interview, September, 1997.

Maclean's, April 28, 1997.

People, July 7, 1997.

Rolling Stone, November 13, 1997.

On-line

The *Rolling Stone* Network, located at http://www.rollingstone.com.

Dorothea Lange

**Photographer
(1895-1965)**

*"Lange lived instinctively, but . . .
always found herself in the right
place at the right time."*

—Christopher Cox

*Born in 1895 in Hoboken, NJ; died October 11, 1965, in
San Francisco, CA; married Maynard Dixon (an artist and
illustrator), 1920 (divorced October, 1935); married Paul
Schuster Taylor (an economist), December, 1935; child-
ren: John and Daniel Dixon. Education: Seminar with
Clarence White at Columbia University, 1917.*

Dorothea Lange used to say that she decided
to become a photographer in an effort to
"maintain myself on the planet," according to
Christopher Cox in the introduction to Aperture's
Dorothea Lange. Whether she meant that she
thought photography would earn her a living or
satisfy her intellect or both, it is clear that Lange's
work has done much to physically and spiritually
sustain countless Americans. Her photographs influenced the United States government in its decision to aid those most affected by the Great
Depression.

The view through the lens of Lange's camera
alerted Americans to the plight of the Dust Bowl
migrants during the same time. It was Lange's
work that sensitively recorded the inhumanity of
the relocation of Japanese-Americans during World
War II. Lange is remembered today for the fact
that, as she documented history, she helped determine the future.

Lange was born in Hoboken, New Jersey, to a
family that, in the words of Lange's son Daniel

Dixon in *Celebrating A Collection,* "was shattered" by the later desertion of her father. Nevertheless, Lange's mother Joan was hard-working and capable. Soon after her husband abandoned the family, she saw Lange through the bout of polio that left the young girl with a permanently lame leg.

A Bold Decision

After Lange had completed high school and was studying to become a teacher, she made what seemed to be an abrupt decision to become a photographer. Despite the fact that she had never taken a photograph and didn't own a camera, she sought work at the best studio portrait salons in New York City and found it. Lange took advantage of her position at a studio owned by Arnold Genthe, a promoter of the "candid" portrait and the most famous of her employers, and began to learn about photography, developing film, and running a studio.

During the time she worked for Genthe, Lange became educated about the work and theories of other prominent photographers. She attended a Clarence White seminar at Columbia University. White, according to Cox, was one of those "struggling to overturn" the Romantic photography that Genthe epitomized. Lange was inspired by White's work and philosophy. After taking his seminar, she was ready to begin her own work as a photographer. She bought a camera and equipment and began to experiment by taking photos of friends and relatives.

At the age of 22, Lange decided to leave New York and travel around the world with a friend. Their journey ended in San Francisco, when a pickpocket stole the young women's money. Lange immediately found a job at a dry-goods store with a photo-finishing department on Market Street. Cox notes that "Lange lived instinctively, but . . . always found herself in the right place at the right time."

A Studio of Her Own

Lange's job in San Francisco allowed the charismatic young woman to make friends with bohemian photographers, path-breaking woman photographers, and the fashionable set which patronized them all. Lange soon met Jack Boumphrey, who financed the opening of Lange's own portrait studio just one year after she had arrived in the city. Lounging around her studio at tea-time each day, Lange was a striking character—her place of business became a trendy social spot.

Those viewing Lange's portraits from this stage in the photographer's career will not find the work she is known for now. Lange's efforts then were focused on providing quality, commissioned portraiture that flattered her fashionable clients in a meaningful way. She would either stage the portraits she took in her studio or follow her subjects around their homes or at parties with her cumbersome cameras.

Less than a year after Lange met Maynard Dixon, a famous artist and illustrator of Western scenes, they were married. Lange was just twenty-four years old; Dixon, who was forty-five, had a daughter. The couple had two children together, John and Daniel. Until the beginning of the Great Depression, the marriage seemed solid. Lange appreciated Dixon's work as an artist and especially enjoyed taking trips with him to the southwest, where he did much of his work.

Out of the Studio and into the Street

When the stock market crashed in 1929, Lange's life was transformed. Her business survived, but she and Dixon moved into their separate studios and the boys were sent to boarding school to save money. In spite of the problems in her personal life, and because of the troubles caused by the Depression, the inspiration for and character of Lange's work dramatically changed at this time. Lange recalled one particular event: "One morning, as I was making a solio proof at the south window, I watched an unemployed young workman coming up the street. He came to the corner, stopped, and stood there a little while. Behind him were the waterfront and the wholesale districts; to his left was the financial district; ahead was Chinatown and the Hill of Justice; to his right were the flophouses and Barbary Coast. What was he to do? Which way was he to go?" The man's plight and his indecision captivated Lange. She took her large camera out into the street and began photographing the people she saw there.

Masterworks

White Angel Breadline, 1933

Man beside Wheelbarrow, 1934

Ditched, Stalled, and Stranded, 1935

Migrant Mother, 1936

Jobless on Edge of Pea Field, 1937

Cotton Picker, 1940

Like her decision to stop studying to be a teacher and learn the art of photography, Lange's decision to take her camera out of the studio and into the street was a critical one. Yet once Lange had taken her first street photographs, she did not know what to do with them. Work of this kind was rare, and her customers were unlikely to appreciate it or support it financially. Nevertheless, Lange knew that there was something special about these photographs.

These first photographs taken by Lange in San Francisco during the Depression years are consistently thought-provoking, and often haunting. In "White Angel Breadline" (1933), a man in the center of the photograph supports himself on a the bar of a wooden rail fence as if he is waiting for an order at a lunch counter. Yet his face, with his eyes hidden by a hat, is grim, and his empty metal cup captures the eye's attention. The remainder of the picture is filled with hatted men, their backs to the photographer—they are also waiting in the line to receive food from the "White Angel."

Lange's Photographs Make a Difference

Images like these, displayed in Willard Van Dyke's Oakland gallery, won the immediate attention of Paul Taylor. Taylor was a professor of economics who had used photographs to illustrate the social and economic problems he had been studying. Taylor was attempting to gain funds for the refugees streaming into California. He requested that Lange work on his team, which was conducting a study for the California affiliate of the Federal Emergency Relief Administration. The work Lange conducted with Taylor was effective. As Therese Thau Heyman notes, "Because of it, government budgets were approved; substantial sums for food and camps were voted; articles in the 1935–36 San Francisco News brought action immediately."

Heyman observes that, given this success, it is not surprising that Lange ended her marriage to Maynard Dixon. In 1935, Taylor and Lange were married in Albuquerque. They toured the country during the summers from 1935 to 1939 with the hope that, in the words of Heyman, "social conditions would change for the better, in part because of their reporting." During this time, Lange took the photograph that would remain in the American consciousness for years, "Migrant Mother." It happened when Lange made a quick decision to stop at a camp in Nipomo, which she had already passed on her way home to Berkeley. As Heyman relates, this picture was published in the San Francisco News and aid was sent to the camp soon after. The photo, as Cox writes, is an "icon" of the 1930s. At home in Berkeley, Lange and Taylor worked to put together the book which emerged in 1939 as An American Exodus: A Record of Human Erosion in the Thirties.

Lange's Last Years

Lange occupied herself with domestic people and problems during the war years. Lange and her husband became interested in the plight of relocated Japanese Americans in California in 1942. While many of her photographs of the internment were not released to the public during those years, Maisie and Richard Conrat (who worked for Lange during this period) collected some of them and, along with other photographs and contributions, published the work as Executive Order 9066: The Internment of 110,000 Japanese Americans.

Among the moving photographs in Executive Order 9066 made by Dorothea Lange are many

images of parents and grandparents with small children. One taken on May 8, 1942, in Hayward, California, displays an upright and prosperous-looking grandfather, waiting somberly yet proudly for an evacuation bus with his grandchildren. Long white tags dangling from their coats betray their destination. Lange also made some thought-provoking photographs of signs concerning the evacuations and relocations or bearing overtly racist statements. One of the most striking of these was taken in April, 1942, in Oakland, California. A large white ''SOLD'' sign looms above the

Wanto Grocery, but pasted across the windows of the market is an even more prominent sign which states ''I AM AN AMERICAN.'' A note with the picture explains that the owner of the store placed the sign on the store the day after the attack on Pearl Harbor in December, 1941, and that he was later forced to close his store and evacuate.

After the war, Lange photographed the original meetings of the United Nations. Heyman relates that the stressful experience of working among fast-paced, often indifferent and unscrupulous press photographers contributed to stomach ulcers and Lange's physical collapse. It was eight years before she would work again, and when she did, it was on occasional assignment for *Life* magazine.

In her last years, Lange began to spend more time photographing subjects close to home. She was especially enthusiastic about making photos of the beautiful oak trees at her Berkeley home and of family members enjoying themselves at their cabin. These latter photos were collected and arranged with poems by Margaretta K. Mitchell in the volume *To a Cabin* after Lange's death.

When Lange was told that she had terminal cancer in 1964, she faced her impending death with courage and worked as hard as she could to finish various projects, including a retrospective exhibit of her work for the museum of Modern Art in New York and *The American Country Woman.*

Lange died in Berkeley in 1965. She remains, in the words of Sanford Schwartz, a critic for the *New York Times Book Review,* "a special and beloved figure in the history of photography."

Sources for More Information

Books

Conrat, Maisie, and Richard Conrat, *Executive Order 9066: The Internment of 110,000 Japanese Americans,* photographs by Dorothea Lange and others, California Historical Society, 1972.

Dorothea Lange, Aperture, 1981.

Heyman, Therese Thau, *Celebrating a Collection: The Work of Dorothea Lange,* Oakland Museum, 1978.

Lange, Dorothea, *Dorothea Lange Looks at the American Country Woman,* Amon Carter Museum, 1967.

Gary Larson

**Cartoonist
(1950–)**

Born August 14, 1950, in Tacoma, WA; son of Vern (an automobile dealer) and Doris (a secretary) Larson; married, September, 1988. Education: Washington State University, B.A., 1972.

"I realize that some of my cartoons go over people's heads."

Before his retirement in 1995, cartoonist Gary Larson presented an unconventional and surreal world in his daily one-panel comic feature *The Far Side;* in the strip, animals are always smarter than humans and the humans themselves are always very strange. Syndicated in more than 300 newspapers throughout the United States, *The Far Side* was also collected into numerous best-selling cartoon anthologies. James Kelly, writing in *Time,* asserted that "if a single theme animates [Larson's] work, it is that man, for all his achievements, is just one species on earth, and not always the wisest or strongest one." Larson related to Kelly: "It's wonderful that we live in a world in which there are things that can eat us. It keeps us from getting too cocky."

This attitude is reflected in Larson's creations, which present such odd juxtapositions as a movie theater crowded with insects waiting to watch *Return of the Killer Windshield;* campers slumbering in sleeping bags while bears examining them exclaim, "Sandwiches!"; and a pilot mildly puzzling over the appearance of a mountain goat in the cloud bank directly ahead. Commenting on this brand of humor, *Detroit News* book critic Beaufort Cranford declared that *The Far*

623

Side is, "radically dependent on twists of perception," adding that Larson's humor is "so black that it can only have come from the eerie corridors of a very bizarre mind. . . . Clearly it is also the stuff of a demented imagination." Other reactions to Larson's work include *Washington Post* contributor Richard Harrington's announcement that *The Far Side* is nothing short of "macabre, weird, zany, twisted, whimsical, fiendish, bizarre, odd, strange."

Larson's Training Ground

Larson began cartooning in an offhand way while working at a series of diverse jobs. After performing as a jazz guitarist in a duo called "Tom and Gary," he worked at a music store in Seattle, Washington. Larson recounted that in the late 1970s, while working at the music store, he drew several cartoons and offered them to *Pacific Search,* a nature magazine. "They bought all six," he related in his interview with Harrington. "I was shocked." This sale, explained Larson, encouraged him to continue cartooning after he began working for the Humane Society in 1978. During an investigation of animal abuse, Larson met a *Seattle Times* reporter who saw his cartoons and urged him to submit them to her paper. Soon the *Seattle Times* was running a weekly cartoon, "Nature's Way," that the cartoonist referred to as his "training ground." Shute related that "Nature's Way" was canceled within a year "after complaints about the unnatural selection of the subject matter."

Heeding a suggestion, Larson submitted his material to the *San Francisco Chronicle* and eventually signed a five-year contract with Chronicle Features syndicate, which nationally introduced Larson's daily cartoon as *The Far Side.* The subject matter of the strip remained under fire, however. "I lived in terror of cancellation," revealed Larson in an interview with Tim Appelo for *Pacific Northwest.* "I was always being cancelled by newspapers, and I was horrified every time. All these 'Nancy' readers would see this hideous thing and cry out. But the people on the news staffs enjoyed the strip. I think that's the single thing that saved me."

The Far Side, syndicated by Universal Press Syndicate beginning in 1984, came in its first seven years to appear as a regular feature in more than 300 American dailies. By the time Larson retired in 1995, the cartoon was appearing in almost 1,900 newspapers. In addition to his highly successful cartoon, Larson also had a number of best-selling anthologies of his work, including *The Far Side, In Search of the Far Side, Valley of the Far Side, Night of the Crash-Test Dummies, Wildlife Preserves,* and *Cows of Our Planet.*

A Taste for the Bizarre

Larson also explained to Cranford that he believed his strip "touches a sense of humor that's always been out there somewhere. Television and other media have reflected that kind of humor, but it had never found its way into the newspapers. I think there was an oddness out there that made people ready to accept and enjoy it." Fans delighted, for example, in a panel depicting a boat full of headhunters staring incredulously at two tourists with enormously large heads as they paddle by. And another favorite has a pack of dogs disguised as humans sneaking into a post office and attacking the workers.

Committed to the single-panel format, Larson described his work in an interview for *People* as "basically sitting down at the drawing table and getting silly." He informed Harrington: "I think very visually and I think a single panel lends itself to that one instant visual image. . . . It all kind of comes to me at once, more or less simultaneous. Sometimes a caption will hit me first, but that's rare. Usually it's the image that will come first, this one hideous moment that just lands on me." Such moments resulted in cartoons like the one in which a lemming trailing a suicidal group at the water's edge glances furtively to determine if his life preserver will be detected; or one that depicted Reuben, the hospital worker, caught rubbing newborns on his clothes for static electricity and sticking them to the walls like balloons. For Larson, humor captured in single images like these depended on subtleties.

"I really sweat over the nuances in a face or I try to think what is the focus of this cartoon," Larson told Krucoff. This focus can sometimes be slightly blurred, however; not every reader always gets the joke. "I realize that some of my cartoons go over people's heads," admitted Larson in an interview with Sheridan Warrick for *Pacific Discovery.* "But if out of ten people, I think that

Illustration from
***There's a Hair in My
Dirt: A Worm's Story***

one will bellylaugh and the other nine will be dumbfounded, I'll go for it. The one thing I try not to do is condescend to people. If you start doing cartoons that are too universal, you end up with something milked out and uninteresting. I'd rather be misunderstood.''

Animals Steal the Scenes

A variety of characters filled Larson's subtle and sometimes ''misunderstood'' cartoons, but more often than not the starring roles were given to animals. ''Mostly I think of animals as a vehicle for my own particular sense of humor,'' explained Larson in a *San Francisco Chronicle* interview with David Perlman. ''A lot of the time I end up exploring the weird prejudices we humans have toward some animals. If a real animal starts adding

too many legs or too many eyes, it seems to become too alien for most of us to stand.''

Among the many animals that were fodder for Larson's work were cows—one of his personal favorites. ''I particularly enjoy drawing cows,'' Larson related to Harrington. ''I'm not exactly sure why. They seem to be some kind of absurd, almost non sequitur animal to put into certain situations. I even find humor in the name.'' Larson's use of other creatures included kangaroos, dinosaurs, amoebas, warthogs, and a *Far Side* shark who approaches another with the line, ''Say honey, didn't I meet you last night at the feeding frenzy?''

In *The Far Side* Larson's pursuit of fun and silliness met with enormous success, a circumstance the cartoonist found difficult to trust. He told Krucoff: ''Sometimes I have a hard time shaking the feeling that there's been a big mistake.

Gary Larson   **625**

Popular Works

Comic Strips
The Far Side, syndicated, 1984–95

Books
The Far Side, Andrews & McMeel, 1982

The Far Side Gallery, Andrews & McMeel, 1984

Last Chapter and Worse: A Far Side Collection, Andrews & McMeel, 1986

There's a Hair in My Dirt: A Worm's Story, HarperCollins, 1998

It's taken me by surprise that things have happened the way they have. . . . I have a sense of not wanting to really give myself over to it entirely, a sense that it could all suddenly turn to smoke or I'm going to hear my mother's voice in the distance saying, 'Gaaaaary, time for school!' and there I am, 12 years old." Larson echoed this skeptical outlook in an interview for *People:* "I keep thinking someone's gonna show up and say, 'There's been a mistake. The guy next door is supposed to be drawing the cartoon. Here's your shovel.'"

Despite Larson's fear, it was not "the guy next door" but Larson himself who ended his stint producing one of the nation's most beloved cartoons. Citing fatigue and "dread that his work might 'ease into the Graveyard of Mediocre Cartoons,'" as quoted by *Newsweek*'s David Gate, Larson announced in late 1994 that he was retiring. His announcement was similar to one he made in 1988, when he took a sabbatical of fourteen months from writing the cartoon, but in this case Larson's work stoppage was for good. Honoring Larson's fifteen-year achievement in the *Nation,* Alexander Cockburn wrote: "Larson is not the first satirist of the human condition to tell parables through beasts. But before him cows never had the sensitivities of Proust, nor dogs the wisdom of Solomon."

When Larson stopped writing *The Far Side,* he didn't retire from working. "I didn't expect to go fishing for the rest of my life," he told an interviewer from *Editor and Publisher.* Since retiring the cartoon, he's been involved in an animated movie, *Tales From the Far Side II* (a follow-up to his 1994 feature *Tales From the Far Side*) and an illustrated book, *There's a Hair in My Dirt: A Worm's Story.* Larson notes that producing an animated cartoon is very different from drawing a newspaper comic. In addition to having the ability to show characters moving and turning 360 degrees, it also allows the writer to tell an entire story. "Far Side comics were the first part of the stories," Larson told *Editor and Publisher.* "This is more than the first part of the stories, although everything once again ends disastrously!"

"I can't honestly say that I miss it," he told an interviewer from *Editor and Publisher* about the comic strip, "although I do have some wistful feelings. It was just a wonderful experience for me. . . . But I just kind of sensed that the comic had this lifetime. It was time to move on and try other things. One of those 'been there, done that' feelings came over me." Reruns of the cartoon are still distributed by Creators Syndicate to about 250 publications outside the United States, and it remains popular. About his future plans, Larson said, "I have several things on the back burner. I have to decide whether to turn the heat up or let them sizzle away!"

Sources for More Information

Periodicals
Editor and Publisher, March 21, 1998.

New York Times, April 28, 1998.

Publishers Weekly, August 25, 1997, p. 25.

Time, January 20, 1997, p. 19.

U.S. News & World Report, June 15, 1998, p. 14.

On-line
Creators Syndicate Web site, located at http://www.creators.com.

The Ink Group, located at http://www.inkgroup.com/artist/larson.html.

Lucy Lawless

**Actress
(1968-)**

Born Lucy Ryan, March 28, 1968, in Mount Albert, Auckland, New Zealand; daughter of Frank (a politician) and Julie (a homemaker) Ryan; married Garth Lawless, 1987 (divorced, 1995), married Rob Tapert, March 28, 1998; children: (first marriage) Daisy. Education: Attended Auckland University, New Zealand, 1986–87; attended William Davis Center for Actors Study, Vancouver, British Columbia, Canada.

"Never in my wildest dreams did I ever think that I'd one day be a female action hero."

As the star of the syndicated action-adventure television series *Xena: Warrior Princess,* Lucy Lawless became an overnight sensation accidentally and unexpectedly. "Never in my wildest dreams did I ever think that I'd one day be a female action hero. I thought I'd be doing Shakespeare," Lawless told interviewers at the National Association of Television Program Executives in 1996. Nevertheless, Xena's success can be fully attributed to Lawless—who *is* Xena to her fans and colleagues. Ironically, Lawless was the last choice to play the role of Xena on *Hercules: The Legendary Journeys,* whose viewer-raved performance led to the *Xena* spin-off series. In its first two seasons, the show outperformed most other syndicated shows in the ratings, including *Baywatch,* and beat many network programs in competing time slots. Not since actress Linda Carter played *Wonder Woman* in the 1970s has television featured a female superhero in her own show. "Now's the right time for a woman hero," Lawless further commented.

Lawless's legion of Xena fans don't fit any one mold. Appealing to feminists, computer nerds, lesbians, straight men, children, and sword-and-sorcery lovers alike, Lawless/Xena quickly developed a cult following and amassed a presence in pop culture with a multitude of fan Web sites, trading cards, fanzines, action figures, and CD-ROMs. Even other network television programs paid homage to Lawless's character, with episodes featuring their own versions of Xena. In January 1997 Lawless appeared at the first official Hercules/Xena convention at the Burbank (California) Airport Hilton to a sold-out crowd of hundreds of fans dressed in medieval costumes. "I can't believe all the fuss," remarked Lawless, who signed autographs and posed for pictures.

New Zealand Roots

Despite her Americanized accent on the show, Lawless was born and raised in Mount Albert, Auckland, New Zealand. In 1968, the year she was born, her dad became the town mayor. The fifth of seven children and the oldest daughter, Lawless was a tomboy who attended Catholic schools. She developed an interest in singing and acting at a fairly young age. "She used to get up on the coffee table with a seashell for a microphone and sing away," her mother told Karen Schneider and Kirsten Warner in *People.* In high school she performed in several musicals and plays. After graduation in 1986 she studied opera and languages at Auckland University for a year, until her adventurous nature led her to roam Europe with her boyfriend, Garth Lawless.

When money ran out in Europe, the couple traveled to Australia and both got jobs at a remote outback gold-mining company working as miners. As one of the few female miners, Lawless performed the same strenuous work as the men—digging, driving trucks, mapping the ground, and pushing massive amounts of earth through a diamond saw. "I don't know what we were thinking," she recalled. During her time in Australia, Lawless became pregnant, and she and her boyfriend quickly married and moved back to New Zealand. After the birth of their daughter, Daisy, Lawless renewed her interest in an acting career, appearing in television commercials until she landed a part with a television comedy troupe on a show called *Funny Business* at age 20. In 1989 Lawless was crowned Miss New Zealand.

Lawless acted in episodic guest roles on various television shows before she, her husband and daughter moved to Vancouver, British Columbia, for eight months so she could study drama at the William Davis center for Actors Study. Returning to New Zealand in 1992, Lawless became the co-host for *Air New Zealand Holiday,* a broadcast travel magazine program that allowed her to travel around the globe. After two seasons working as co-host, she was cast in the television movie, *Hercules and the Amazon Women* as Lysia, a renegade Amazon enforcer. The movie was part of a series that launched the weekly, one-hour syndicated *Hercules* program.

Lawless soon appeared in yet another role on the *Hercules* series, this time as Lyla, the bride of Derc the Centaur. In 1994 producers at Universal came up with a show idea in which Hercules would meet his greatest enemy, Xena, a fierce warrior princess. The three-episode show was to be aired during an important sweeps month. The studio considered several "name" actresses for the part, but all refused, finding the New Zealand set location too distant. An American actress was eventually cast for the role, but she fell sick at the last minute. The show's producers needed someone to fill the role fast, but Lawless, who had already featured in two separate roles on the show, wasn't an option. "Since she already played two different parts in Hercules, the studio wanted another actress," explained executive producer Rob Tapert to the *Los Angeles Times.* Then Tapert and crew changed her appearance, dying the naturally blond Lawless brunette. Satisfied with her transformation, the episodes began shooting within a week. The studio was very impressed with Lawless's new look and her performance during the filming. "The rest is history," Lawless remarked: she was on her way to her own series. Producers reformed Hercules's nemesis into a heroine and *Xena: Warrior Princess* debuted in September 1995.

Her Own Show

With her sidekick Gabrielle, Lawless's Xena battles for good in a mythical, barbaric land that spans no particular time period or location, taking many historical liberties: a show may feature Helen of Troy, while another David and Goliath. Lawless commented to David Sheff in a Yahoo

Still from **Xena: Warrior Princess**

Internet Life interview: "We don't care much about chronology. We have Julius Caesar one week and Jesus Christ the next. People mustn't worry their pretty little heads about it." The show also offers a lot of humor.

Through fancy kicking, punching, sword-fighting, and other use of weaponry, Xena fights giants, monsters, gods, immortals, warlords, and plain-old evil. The role demands a lot of athletic ability from the nearly six-feet tall Lawless, who initially doubted her abilities. "Action-adventure scared me. I'd never been physically inclined. My nickname [as a child] was Unco [for uncoordinated]," she said in the *Los Angeles Times*. Her skillful battle scenes were honed by her study in Los Angeles with a martial arts master. At the beginning of 16-hour days, she gets up in the early hours of the morning to train at the gym before shooting.

Lawless's series is popular for more than just its fight scenes. The show often pushes the envelope in matters involving sexuality and nontraditional relationships. Lawless is one of the few white women in television history to passionately kiss an African American man on screen—and more than once. Even more controversial is the speculation about the nature of Xena's close relationship with the Gabrielle character, particularly whether or not the two are lovers. "They have love for each other," explained supervising producer Steve Sears of the two characters. "It's up to the audience to determine what that love is." When questioned about the subject, Lawless responded, "We do have fun with that aspect, but I never want to shove it down people's throats because it can also be alienating and we don't want to do that to any sector of our audience. But we don't want to alienate our lesbian following. We love 'em all equally. . . ."

While many enjoy Lawless's character for her looks, her mystique, her fighting abilities, or her body-hugging leather and metal outfit, feminists enjoy the show for Lawless's role as a powerful, independent woman. Appearing on the cover of the July/August 1996 edition of *Ms.*, the magazine said of Lawless's alter ego: "Many feminists have been dreaming of mass-culture moments like this since feminism came into being. . . . No woman television character has exhibited the confidence and strength of the male heroes of archetype and fantasy [as Xena]. . . ."

Popular Works

Television

Hercules: The Legendary Journeys, MCA Television Entertainment, 1994–95

Xena: Warrior Princess, MCA Television Entertainment, 1995–

Feminist Leanings

Lawless was initially reluctant to be considered a feminist role model, but later felt more comfortable. "I met so many women and young girls who feel ... empowered, by watching. I realized this isn't a burden, this is an honor." She told Sheff, "I'm thrilled that women are encouraged to follow their dreams and I am equally pleased that young men are getting a new view of women: an unapologetic woman." As far as Lawless herself being a role model (as opposed to Xena), she said, "I try not to behave in a way that could encourage someone else to do anything they shouldn't. ... At the same time, I can't imagine why anybody would want to be like me. ... I guess I do see why they might like to be like Xena. So I do take it as seriously as I should but no more than that. I'm not letting it dominate my life. If I did, I'd be an unhappy woman. [I'd] be too self-conscious to make mistakes and experience life."

In October 1996 Lawless was injured while taping a skit on horseback for *The Tonight Show* with Jay Leno, suffering multiple fractures in her pelvis after a fall. She was hospitalized for two weeks and was unable to work for two months. Stunt doubles were brought in for taping until she was physically fit. Psychologically, it took her a while to ride a horse again. She did return to *The Tonight Show* to joke about the incident with Leno. In May 1997 Lawless made the news again for another accident—this time exposing her breasts while singing the national anthem during a sold-out Detroit Red Wings/Anaheim Mighty Ducks play-off game at the Anaheim Arena. She unknowingly popped out of her form-fitting, bustier-style costume when she lifted her arms while trying to hit the concluding high note. Viewers watching the game live on television in Detroit got a full, unobstructed view, and censored clips were broadcast on sports highlights shows everywhere. Lawless was embarrassed by the incident, but kept a good sense of humor. "I'm a goofy sort of person. In fact, people always say they can't believe I play [Xena]," she once commented.

Despite her perceived goofiness, Lawless is fluent in German, French and Italian, and studied opera for several years. She sings her own songs for *Hercules* and *Xena—The Animated Movie: The Battle for Mount Olympus* (1997). Starting in September 1997 she starred in the Broadway production of *Grease!* in the role of "Rizzo," which was previously played by Brooke Shields and Rosie O'Donnell. The seven-week performance was Lawless's first musical since high school.

Lawless divorced her husband in 1995, but kept his unique last name. She remains a devoted mom to Daisy, who stays with her during weekends at their home in Mount Albert. Lawless is happy to live near her family. "People who have always known you are not going to let you get too big for your boots," she joked to Sheff.

Lawless is grateful for and proud of the show's popularity, but despite her sudden international fame, she tries to remain grounded. She once commented about her celebrity-status, "It's not real to me. ... It has nothing really to do with my daily life. You get up and put your pants on one foot at a time like everybody else. Then you go out and water the garden or clean up the dishes from the night before."

Sources for More Information

Periodicals

Advocate, March 2, 1999.

Entertainment Weekly, March 7, 1997, p. 38.

Los Angeles Times, November 8, 1995, p. B69.

Ms., July/August, 1996, pp. 74–77.

People, April 8, 1996, p. 93; December 29, 1997.

TV Guide, April 10, 1999.

Us, October, 1997.

USA Today, February 14, 1996; January 15, 1997, p. 3D.

On-line

Xena Web site, located at http://www.mca.com/tv/xena/cast/lawless.html.

Jacob Lawrence

**Painter
(1917–)**

Born September 7, 1917, in Atlantic City, NJ; son of Jacob Armstead Lawrence (a railroad worker) and Rose Lee; married Gwendolyn Knight (an artist). Education: Took art classes under Charles Alston.

Jacob Lawrence was one of the first African American artists to rise to prominence in the mainstream American art world. He was encouraged by teachers and fellow artists during his teenage years to study both art and African American history. He combined these interests to produce works unique in both their subject and style. Many of these comprise series of panels that join together to create a narrative. Lawrence is also known as an illustrator of books for adults and children.

In the early part of the twentieth century, huge numbers of African Americans migrated from the rural South to the cities of the North. They hoped to find jobs in growing industries, particularly on the automobile assembly lines of Detroit, Michigan. Lawrence's parents, Jacob Armstead Lawrence and Rose Lee, were among these migrants. They met and married in Atlantic City, New Jersey. The oldest of their three children, Jacob, was born there on September 7, 1917. During Lawrence's childhood, his family was forced to relocate many times as his parents looked for work. Steady jobs were hard to find, especially for African Americans. Racial prejudice prevented them from pursuing certain jobs or professions.

"I paint the things I know about, the things I have experienced. The things I have experienced extend into my national, racial, and class group. So I paint the American scene."

These many moves had a disruptive effect on Lawrence, who was a quiet and sensitive boy; he found it difficult to constantly adjust to new neighborhoods and schools.

Moved to Harlem during Renaissance

The hardest adjustment of all came when he was 13. It was then that he went to live with his mother in Harlem, the mostly African American section of New York City. It was a crowded, teeming place, and the public school Lawrence attended was considered among the roughest in the area. But Harlem in the 1930s was also the center of what became known as the Harlem Renaissance. Many African American artists, writers, musicians, and scholars lived there. It was a time of great creativity and excitement.

To keep her son out of trouble, Rose Lawrence enrolled him in an after-school arts and crafts program at a local community center. It was taught by a young African American artist named Charles Alston. Alston liked the serious, quiet Lawrence and made sure he had lots of materials for his efforts: soap to carve, reeds to make baskets, crayons and pencils for drawing, wood for construction. "I decided then that I wanted to be an artist," Lawrence later wrote. He found that drawing geometric designs in bright colors satisfied him greatly. He soon moved on to elaborate patterns and developed his own method of painting in which particular shapes were rendered in corresponding colors, one at a time; he would paint all the triangles in red, then do all the squares in yellow, and so on. Lawrence continued in this mode through much of his career. This notable consistency of color is apparent in the artist's later series of story panels.

Quickly Gained Notice among Artists

Alston recognized that the young Lawrence was a significant talent. He remarked in later years that Lawrence never asked like the other children, "What should I do next?" He always had a project in mind and simply needed information to help him complete it. Alston told many of his artist friends about this gifted young man. They frequently visited the class to see his work and encourage him. Lawrence quickly became known among the artistic circles of Harlem.

Lawrence got many of his ideas from the books and magazines he found at the center where the classes were held. He once came across an article about a famous artist who made papier-mâché masks. Lawrence had Alston show him how to mix papier-mâché, and he went on to create many colorful, life-size masks. He also used cardboard boxes to fashion three-sided scenes depicting locales in Harlem—stores, barbershops, houses, and newsstands. These were like miniature theater sets, though Lawrence had never been to the theater.

During the time he worked with Alston, Lawrence found little at school to interest him. After two years of high school he dropped out, despite his mother's protests. This was during the Great Depression, and jobs were extremely scarce. Lawrence was able to earn only meager funds by selling old bottles and running errands. He continued to paint whenever he could, but times were hard. Then, in 1936, Lawrence was accepted into the Civilian Conservation Corps (CCC), a government program designed to get young men out of the cities to work on projects such as planting trees and building roads and dams. Lawrence's CCC service taught him many new skills and made him think that perhaps painting should be only a hobby.

Enters Depression-era Funding Program

He returned to New York but still could find no work besides odd jobs. He again began attending art classes at various community centers, including one offered by the acclaimed sculptor Augusta Savage. Like Alston, Savage recognized Lawrence's talent and took him under her wing. She soon realized that Lawrence was having difficulty earning money. She took him to a government office to enroll him in a project that helped support artists. But Lawrence was not eligible because he was only 20 years old and not the required 21. Lawrence was extremely disappointed and continued looking for other work. Savage did not give up, however. She waited a year and on Lawrence's twenty-first birthday, she took him back to the government office to sign him up. He

was accepted and offered $25 a week, a comfortable living in those days. He was free to do what he wanted as long as he produced two paintings every six weeks. Lawrence later stated, "If Augusta Savage hadn't insisted on getting me on the project, I would never have become an artist. It was a real turning point for me."

For about a year and a half, Lawrence was able to take classes, hone his painting skills, and put concerns about money out of his mind. Through the funding project he met many other artists and writers. They gathered in each other's studios to exchange ideas about art, literature, and life in general. Lawrence's paintings from this period are mostly scenes of Harlem, among them *Clinic* and *Bar 'N Grill*. He was able to keenly illustrate how hard it was to survive during the Depression years. Through color, pattern, and exaggerated form, he expressed weariness and despair.

Studied African American History

During these years Lawrence regularly attended a discussion group focusing on African and African American history held at the local public library. It was led by a prominent scholar, Charles Seifert. Seifert applauded Lawrence's interest and encouraged him to study American history in depth, especially the role of African Americans. The artist had never learned this history in school. Now he uncovered many critical events and heroes forgotten by the public school system. These discoveries provided him with subjects for many of his works.

Lawrence was particularly drawn to the life story of Francis Dominique Toussaint, known as Toussaint L'Ouverture, the military leader of eighteenth-century Haiti, who overthrew the slave system and liberated the Caribbean island nation from French domination. Lawrence read everything he could about Toussaint and decided to paint a record of his achievements. But one painting was not enough. Lawrence ultimately unveiled a series of 41 panels, beginning with Christopher Columbus's "discovery" of Haiti and then outlining Toussaint's childhood, battles, and death in a French prison. The settings of the scenes employed a great measure of realism, but Lawrence used intense color and exaggeration to express the emotional power of this hero.

This series and later ones have been compared to movie stills or slides that narrate a story as the he gathered from family members, his own childhood experiences, and exhaustive research. Painted in Lawrence's bold, geometric style, with many vivid colors, they depict the hard life of the migrants, but also their courage and dignity. In 1992 Lawrence published a book, *The Great Migration*, using many panels from the series. In the introduction he wrote, ''Uprooting yourself from one way of life to make your way in another involves conflict and struggle. But out of the struggle comes a kind of power, and even beauty. I tried to convey this in the rhythm of the pictures, and in the repetition of certain images.'' The Migration series was another triumph.

viewer progresses through them. Lawrence continued in this method, portraying the lives of several African American heroes, including Harriet Tubman, a leader of the Underground Railroad of antislavery forces who smuggled slaves North; writer and abolitionist Frederick Douglass; and John Brown, a white abolitionist who led a slave revolt in Virginia. In all of these works, he used his formidable artistic skills to conjure the struggle for freedom and justice, forcefully representing the strength of character of his subjects.

Exhibited L'Ouverture Series at 22

Lawrence was only 22 when he completed the Toussaint L'Ouverture series in 1938. It received much attention for its unusual subject matter and praise for its artistry. Two acquaintances of Lawrence prominent in the art world arranged for the panels to be included in an exhibition at the Baltimore Museum of Art. This was the first major museum to feature an exhibition by African American artists. An entire room was devoted to Lawrence's panels. The exhibition won him great recognition and several fellowships.

Lawrence was encouraged by his success to begin work on still another series. This one told the story of the many African Americans who migrated to the cities of the North around World War I. The 60 panels were created from accounts

Wife Offered Needed Support

About this time Lawrence married a young painter he had met through Savage named Gwendolyn Knight. She became indispensable to his career, frequently helping him prepare his panels. But more important, Knight offered unflagging support when Lawrence encountered various artistic and emotional obstacles in later years.

Lawrence served in the Coast Guard during World War II, from 1943 to 1945. He was a steward's mate, the only rating available to African Americans because the military was segregated by race in those days. Lawrence was lucky to be selected for the Coast Guard's first racially integrated crew. The crew commander knew of his artistic career and secured Lawrence a position as a public relations officer. He was assigned to paint a record of life in the Coast Guard. The troopship he served on sailed to Italy, Egypt, and India. Lawrence's Coast Guard paintings were shown at several museums after the war.

Doubts of America's ''number one'' Black Painter

Lawrence's reputation grew quickly in the postwar years. He was called ''America's number one black painter.'' But this phrase troubled him because it seemed to suggest two different criteria of value, one for black artists and a different one for ''real'' artists. During this time Lawrence also found it difficult locating new subjects for his paintings. Trends in art were changing, too. Abstract art, that which focused on the emotional rather than the physical realm, was beginning to dominate the art world.

These forces combined to create doubt in Lawrence's mind about his talents and abilities; he began to question his success and wonder if it were not just luck that got him where he was. His anxiety became so severe that in 1949 he entered a hospital to seek treatment. Lawrence felt that his two years there greatly helped him reconcile his feelings and increase his understanding of his place in the world. His work of the 1950s reflects this new peace. Perhaps the most important series from these years is *Struggle: From the History of the American People*. These 30 paintings display key events in U.S. history, emphasizing the role of ordinary people of all races and heritages.

Received Numerous Awards

Despite Lawrence's doubts, the art world continued to honor him. In 1953 he was the first African American artist to receive a large grant from the National Institute of Arts and Letters and the first elected a member of the Institute in 1965. In 1983 he was only the second African American elected to the 50-member American Academy of Arts and Letters. He also received the National Medal of Arts from President George Bush in 1990. These are just a few of the many awards Lawrence has received.

Since the 1960s Lawrence has spent much of his time teaching. He was a professor of art at the University of Washington in Seattle for many years. Most recently he has dedicated his talents to book illustration. His panels from the Harriet Tubman series were published in a volume called *Harriet and the Promised Land* in 1967. And in 1970 he lent his hand to an edition of Aesop's Fables (a new edition of this work appeared in 1998). In addition to the publication of his book *The Great Migration*, the early 1990s saw his panels about abolitionist John Brown published in *John Brown: One Man against Slavery*. In all of these endeavors, Lawrence has labored to reveal the commitment to freedom and justice of people struggling for life's most basic needs and in so doing, miraculously maintaining their humanity and a sense of hope.

Sources for More Information

Books

Howard, Nancy Shroyer, *Jacob Lawrence: American Scenes, American Struggles,* Davis, 1996.

Lawrence, Jacob, *The Great Migration: An American Story,* HarperCollins, 1993.

Lawrence, Jacob, and Richard J. Powell, *Jacob Lawrence,* Rizzoli, 1992.

Wheat, Ellen, *Jacob Lawrence, American Painter,* University of Washington Press, 1986.

Led Zeppelin

Hard rock group

"Led Zeppelin defined what has become heavy metal and hard rock. . . ."

—Rolling Stone

Band formed in 1968 in England. Members include Jimmy Page (full name, James Patrick Page, born January 9, 1944) on guitar; John Paul Jones (name originally John Baldwin, born January 3, 1946) on bass and keyboards; Robert Plant (full name, Robert Anthony Plant, born August 20, 1948) on vocals; John Bonham (full name, John Henry Bonham, born May 31, 1948; died September 24, 1980) on drums.

Led Zeppelin probably will be best remembered for their magnum opus, "Stairway to Heaven," but they also epitomized the loud, long-haired, 1970s rock and roll image in general. Led Zeppelin's music was usually panned by critics during their heyday, but has survived to repeatedly win spots on all-time favorite polls and hit the charts with rereleased material and boxed sets. The band broke ground with huge arena rock smoke-and-light shows and were largely responsible for the "bad boy" stereotype as womanizers, hard drinkers, and drug users.

The group was initially formed by legendary guitarist Jimmy Page. He enjoyed moderate success with his first group, Neil Christian and the Crusaders, a Chuck Berry/Bo Diddley-styled British group. After a continuous battle with bad health problems, Page quit in 1961 to attend art school in Sutton. By then he had converted the front room of his parents' house into a makeshift studio to jam with friends. Word of the guitarist's abilities spread, and soon English producers were using Page for session work on records by the Who, the Kinks, and even Tom Jones.

Meanwhile, the Yardbirds' manager, Giorgio Gomelsky, wanted Page to replace Eric Clapton on guitar. With the money he was making on sessions, however, Page could hardly afford to leave, and instead he recommended Jeff Beck for the position. Page also began producing for Immediate Records and experimenting with his bow/guitar technique.

Page Makes the Move

In mid-1966 Yardbirds' bassist Paul Samwell-Smith quit, and Page was offered the spot. By then he was burned out from studio work and accepted. "I remember one particular occasion when I hadn't played a solo for, quite literally, a couple of months. And I was asked to play a solo on a rock & roll thing," he told Cameron Crowe. "I played it and felt that what I'd done was absolute crap. I was so disgusted with myself that I made my mind up that I had to get out of it. It was messing me right up."

On one particular night Beck was too ill to perform, so Page substituted on guitar. His flashy technique was so impressive that the band moved Chris Dreja over to bass and continued with the dual lead guitars of Page and Beck. When they were in sync with each other, the two would sound like nothing before. But, more often than not, Beck's ego would take over, and he eventually dropped out in the middle of a U.S. tour.

The group continued on with Peter Grant replacing Mickie Most as manager, but their future was very uncertain. By the spring of 1968 all remaining members except Page decided to call it quits. Two members of the Who, Keith Moon and John Entwistle, talked about forming a group with Page and Steve Winwood. "We'll call it Lead Zeppelin," joked Entwistle, "cause it'll go over like a lead balloon."

Putting It All Together

With Clapton's Cream and the Jeff Beck Group blazing new paths for the blues rock genre,

Page knew what type of band he wanted to form. His first acquisition would be bassist John Paul Jones. A veteran of early sixties sessions like Page, Jones was also an arranger—highly influenced by jazz—and equally competent on keyboards. "I jumped at the chance of getting him," Page told Stephen Davis, author of *Hammer of the Gods*.

Next in order would be a vocalist and finally, a drummer. Page was informed of a singer named Robert Plant who performed with the group Hobbstweedle. Formerly an apprentice accountant, Plant quit at age sixteen to become a bluesman, singing with Sounds of Blue, Crawling King Snakes, Tennessee Teens, Listen, and Band of Joy. Just one listen convinced Page that he had his man. "I just couldn't understand why, after he told me he'd been singing for years already, he hadn't become a big name yet," he told Davis.

Plant told Page of a drummer he had worked with previously in two other bands who would be perfect for them. John Bonham was a ham-fisted pounder who was heavily influenced by Keith Moon and Ginger Baker. With much persuasion, Page was able to pry Bonham away from the Tim Rose band, and the New Yardbirds were now complete.

Davis reported Jones's initial reaction the first time the four played together: "The room just exploded." And Plant told Cameron Crowe, "I've never been so turned on in my life." With such a unique sound, they decided they needed a different name and chose Led Zeppelin (using Led instead of Lead to prevent any mispronunciations). They first recorded in October of 1968, and Peter Grant took the tapes to Atlantic Records where reaction was so enthusiastic that the group was given a $200,000 advance and total artistic control.

Led Zeppelin in concert

Combining Blues and Rock

Unable to secure proper gigs in England, the group came to America, where they ended up touring for a year and a half. Their first album ripped into the Top 10 within five months after its release despite a poor review in *Rolling Stone.* Their reworkings of blues classics without crediting the original composers would not earn them much respect either (''Dazed and Confused'' and ''How Many More Years''). Their tour also earned the band a very well-deserved reputation of debauchery. *Zeppelin II* was written and recorded on the road and had a 400,000 copy advance order. Within two months it had bumped the Beatles' *Abbey Road* from its No. 1 American spot. This second album was also slammed by *Rolling Stone* even though it contained a new anthem for rockers, ''Whole Lotta Love.'' Once again, Zep failed to acknowledge the songwriter, this time Willie Dixon, who won a lawsuit against the band. Tour manager Richard Cole defended Zep's ''unusual'' road habits, which were becoming legendary.

"There's nothing immoral in it. It's just that most people wouldn't dream of doing it. That's the whole story of Zeppelin right there," he told Davis.

The heavy-metal rampage continued on *Zeppelin III* with "Immigrant Song," but Page and Plant were heavily influenced by the California folkies during their stay in the States. Critics said the group was going acoustic when actually they had been doing so on *I* and *II*. There was no mistaking their live shows however. "With their epic explosions of sound and light Zeppelin seemed to be a sublimation for the din of battle. A wargasm experience for its audience," wrote Davis.

"Stairway to Heaven"

In 1971 the band released an untitled album, to see if the music alone would stand up. It did, as *Led Zeppelin IV* (as it would come to be known) produced gems like "Rock & Roll," "When the Levee Breaks," and "Black Dog". But it was "Stairway to Heaven" that would come to be recognized as Zep's signature tune and one of the all-time rock classics. "It had everything there and showed the band at its best," Page said in *Hammer of the Gods*. The follow-up LP, *Houses of the Holy,* included more of Jones's keyboards and also went to No. 1 in America. The ensuing tour broke all attendance records in the States with a live show that included fog, cannons, and smoke bombs (eventual staples of hard-rock concerts).

In 1974, Zeppelin resigned with Atlantic, which gave the band their own label to work with, *Swan Song.* It proved to be a very successful venture, with bands like Bad Company, the Pretty Things, Dave Edmunds, and Detective all signed to their label. Zep's 1975 release *Physical Graffiti,* a double album tour de force, went No. 1 and, with their previous LPs and the stable of Swan Song albums, they had nine albums on the charts simultaneously.

Things were not all roses, however, as Plant was seriously injured in a car accident, and Page became addicted to heroin. Bonham became known as "The Beast," because of his monstrous temper and lack of maturity. Still, Zeppelin ruled the rock world. "It's not just that we think we're the best group in the world, it's just that we think we're so much better than whoever is Number Two," Plant told Lisa Robinson.

In 1976 they would release two albums. The first, *The Song Remains the Same,* was a double live soundtrack from their movie of 1973 concert footage. As usual, it was belittled by critics, and even die-hard fans were a little dismayed. "A few bars from one piece convince the listener he's hearing the greatest of rock & roll, then the very next few place him in a nightmarish 1970 movie about deranged hippies," Rolling Stone reported. Expectations for their studio LP, *Presence,* were high, though, due to a one million-copy advance. Although it contains some quality cuts, like "Achilles Last Stand," the record eventually wound up in the bargain bins.

Coming to An End

The band was on hold for nearly three years as Plant recovered from the mysterious death of his son Karac. Rumors were spreading that Page's dabbling in black magic had brought bad karma on the band. He was already living in the late occultist Aleister Crowley's Loch Ness mansion in Scotland, and things were looking suspicious.

In 1980 the band entered the studio to record *In Through the Out Door.* With the exception of Page's guitar on the cut "In The Evening," the LP was basically a keyboard album, composed mainly by Jones. It did give a slumping record industry a much needed boost, and the band hit the road to promote it. Tragically, on September 24, 1980, Bonham died in his sleep after an all-day drinking binge. On December 4, 1980, Zeppelin officially disbanded.

In 1990, an acclaimed four-CD box set of previously released and some unreleased Zeppelin tracks came out, and in 1993, another double-disc set was issued. Page remarked in *Rolling Stone,* "The bitter irony was getting good reviews for Zeppelin after all these years." Page also supervised the digital remastering of all nine Led Zep albums, issued as *Led Zeppelin—The Complete Studio Recordings.* Due to the success of the new CDs and the continued popularity of the long-dissolved band, some speculated there may be a reunion tour. This seems unlikely, as each of the surviving band members has pursued solo projects throughout the 1990s. Led Zeppelin's music lives on, though, and the band has proven to be one of rock's enduring legends.

Sources for More Information

Books

Davis, Stephen, *Hammer of the Gods,* Ballantine, 1985.

Periodicals

Billboard, October 16, 1993; December 13, 1997.

Guitar Player, August, 1993; February, 1998.

Rolling Stone, July 8, 1993; February 23, 1995.

On-line

The *Rolling Stone* Network, located at http://www.rollingstone.com.

Harper Lee

Novelist and essayist
(1926-)

Born Nelle Harper Lee, April 28, 1926, in Monroeville, AL; daughter of Amasa Coleman (a lawyer) and Frances Finch Lee. Education: Attended Huntingdon College in Montgomery, AL, 1944–45, and the University of Alabama, 1945–49; also attended Oxford University for one year. Religion: Methodist.

"Writing is the hardest thing in the world . . . but writing is the only thing that has made me completely happy."

As a child, Harper Lee was "a rough 'n' tough tomboy. . . . She had short, cropped hair, wore coveralls, went barefoot, and could talk mean like a boy," wrote Marianne M. Moates in *A Bridge of Childhood: Truman Capote's Southern Years.* In many ways, this description of young Lee mirrors that of her character, Scout, in the author's only completed novel, *To Kill a Mockingbird.*

The striking similarities between Lee and her fictional counterpart are also reflected in the parallels between the fictional setting of the novel and Lee's hometown. At times, Lee's use of autobiographical elements gave rise to controversy. Amid all the hoopla for Lee's winning the Pulitzer Prize was gossip that her friend, writer Truman Capote had actually written the book for her. Lee lived next door to Capote for several summers during her childhood (and he may have been the model for Dill, the "summer" friend in the novel).

According to Moates, there was also a rumor that one Monroeville family threatened to sue the author because the book's heroic, reclusive

641

Boo Radley too closely resembled someone in their family. Moates, who attended some of the hometown social events honoring Lee's early celebrity, observed: "When [Lee] had enough, she reminded people that her book was fiction, zipped her lips shut, and caught the next plane back to New York." Lee's lips stayed shut, for the most part, since the mid-1960s. A fairly reclusive author, Lee was initially surprised by reader reaction to her book. Since *To Kill a Mockingbird*'s publication, she has given few interviews.

A Timeless Classic

Whatever the reasons behind Lee's failure to publish another book, *To Kill a Mockingbird* remains very popular with young adult readers. It remains one of the most studied novels in modern American literature, in large part because its themes and characters have a timeless appeal. The *Dictionary of Literary Biography* stated that Lee's place in American letters is assured because this "novel with a universal message . . . combines popular appeal with literary excellence."

Lee spent several years writing her novel. She did not, however, begin her writing career with *To Kill a Mockingbird* in mind. In the early 1950s, Lee worked as an airline reservations clerk in New York City, writing essays and short stories during her off-hours. Encouraged by her literary agent to expand one of her stories into a novel, Lee quit her airline job. With the financial support of some friends, she spent several years revising her manuscript before submitting it to Lippincott in 1957. When editors criticized Lee's initial plot structure as being too disjointed and fragmentary, the author made some revisions, making her final—and accepted—submission in early 1960.

To Kill a Mockingbird is "quite an ambiguous title," states R. A. Dave in *Indian Studies in American Fiction,* leaving one "guessing whether it is a crime-thriller or a book on bird-hunting." In truth, the book is about a young girl's coming of age in an era of social and political upheaval. Jean Louise Finch (also known as Scout)—the novel's narrator—lives with her brother Jem and widowed father Atticus in the small fictional town of Maycomb, Alabama during the 1930s. Told from the perspective of a grown-up Scout, the novel traces the circumstances that lead Atticus to take on the case of Tom Robinson, a Black man falsely accused of raping a White woman. In the three years surrounding the trial, Scout and Jem witness the unjust consequences of prejudice and hate, while at the same time experiencing the value of courage and integrity through the example of their father. Through the course of the book, readers come to know the residents of Maycomb—good and bad—as well as the misunderstandings and long-held beliefs that lead to the book's tragic climax.

The novel's colorful characters have been a draw for young readers. Aside from independent Scout, there is stalwart Jem, and mischievous Dill Harris, whose antics and wild plans often get the trio into "worlds of trouble." Calpurnia, the Finch's Black housekeeper, helps keep the children in line; she also exposes them to Tom Robinson's world via a trip to her church for Sunday services. Arthur "Boo" Radley—perhaps the most tragic figure in the tale—is the town recluse. As the novel progresses, Scout, Jem, and Dill come to see Boo as less of a scary, shadowy figure, and more of a feeling human being. Through all the book's turmoil, Atticus Finch remains the voice of reason and restraint. While obviously disturbed and dismayed by the nature of Tom Robinson's trial, the lawyer nevertheless takes great pains to explain to his children why his participation, as well as their understanding, is necessary.

Initial critical response to Lee's story was mixed. R. A. Dave lends a supportive view, claiming that in the novel "there is a complete cohesion of art and morality. And therein lies [*To Kill a Mockingbird*'s] success. [Lee] is a remarkable storyteller. The reader just glides through the novel abounding in humor and pathos, hopes and fears, love and hatred, humanity and brutality—all affording him a memorable human experience. . . . The tale of heroic struggle lingers in our memory as an unforgettable experience."

Autobiographical Elements?

Many critics have tried to analyze the characters in *To Kill a Mockingbird* by looking at Lee's childhood. Altman notes that Lee claims the novel is not autobiographical; the author also admits, however, that a writer "should write about what [he or she] knows and write truthfully." Several researchers have found obvious similarities between fiction and Lee's history in the text. According to Moates, Lee grew up the youngest of three

children in a strictly segregated town. In her novel, she uses her mother's maiden name for her fictional family, and like her own father, makes fictional Atticus a lawyer. Moates describes Lee's father, Amasa Coleman Lee, as an attorney preoccupied by work, who, nevertheless tried to spend time with his family (much the same as Atticus).

Stories about Lee's childhood—as it meshed with writer Truman Capote—have long been part of the mystique surrounding the author's novel. Lee's real-life youthful adventures with young Capote are in many ways similar to those enjoyed by Scout and her friend Dill. According to Moates, Lee was Capote's "pal, confidante, and, at times, sparring partner." The duo—together with one of Lee's brothers—played together constantly.

Moates speculates that a reclusive neighbor may have inspired the characterization of Boo Radley. In Lee's novel, Jem describes the man/ creature he has never seen: "Boo was about six-and-a-half feet tall, judging from his tracks; he dined on raw squirrels and any cats he could catch, that's why his hands were bloodstained—if you ate an animal raw, you could never wash the blood off. There was a long jagged scar that ran across

his face; what teeth he had were yellow and rotten; his eyes popped, and he drooled most of the time."

Critical Assessment

Readers see all the people and events of *To Kill a Mockingbird* through Scout's eyes—the "structural *forte*" of the novel, asserts William T. Going in *Essays on Alabama Literature*. Going claims that many early reviewers of the novel either misunderstood or misinterpreted the way Lee tells her story. For instance, *Atlantic Monthly* reviewer Phoebe Adams refers to the narrative point of view as "frankly and completely impossible, being told in the first person by a six-year-old girl with the prose and style of a well-educated adult." Richard Sullivan of the *Chicago Tribune* is similarly puzzled by Lee's narrator: "The unaffected young narrator uses adult language to render the matter she deals with, but the point of view is cunningly restricted to that of a perceptive, independent child, who doesn't always understand fully what's happening, but who conveys completely, by implication, the weight and burden of the story." Going, however, concluded that the narrator's "evolving perception of the social milieu is handled through a "well-conceived" point of view which combines "child eyes and mature heart."

Connected to the issue of the South's racial conflict are several other themes that capture many critics' attention. For example, Edgar H. Schuster, writing in *English Journal,* points to Scout's psychological growth, the Maycomb "caste system," and education versus superstition as themes that help explain the novel's theme and structure. Scout and Jem learn a great deal from the people and events around their during the three years of the story; in particular, they learn to replace fear and ignorance with security and knowledge, asserts Schuster.

As the story progresses, Lee demonstrates how the children's contacts with the *real* Boo Radley have dispelled their gray ghosts—superstitions, prejudices, and fears. Schuster remarks, "The achievement of Harper Lee is not that she has written another novel about race prejudice, but rather that she has placed race prejudice in a perspective which allows us to see it as an aspect of a larger thing; as something that arises from phantom contacts from fear and lack of knowledge; and finally as something that disappears with the kind of knowledge or 'education' that one gains through learning what people are really like when you finally see them.'" Schuster concludes that the theme and structure unify to show the children's becoming educated to the ways of the world. He praises the novel's astute "rendering of a child's perspective through an adult's evaluation as among the most technically expert in contemporary literature."

When no second novel appeared thirty years after Lee's initial phenomenal success, many readers and critics began to question the reasons why. Associated Press writer Nancy Shulins speculated in *Item* that Lee had joined writers such as J. D. Salinger "who relinquish the spotlight at the height of fame" but "leave an indelible mark on the audiences they abandon." Except for some short pieces in popular women's magazines, Lee never published again. Like the reclusive Boo Radley, she has consistently declined to speak. Critics can only speculate as to whether this reticence was caused by Lee's disillusionment with celebrity status, or perhaps, that the ideas for writing ceased to come. Lee herself once said: "Writing is the hardest thing in the world . . . but writing is the only thing that has made me completely happy." Even without a second novel however, the author's reputation is secure.

Sources for More Information

Books

Contemporary Literary Criticism, Gale, Volume 12, 1980, Volume 60, 1990.

Dictionary of Literary Biography, Volume 6: *American Novelists since World War II,* Gale, 1980.

Marie G. Lee

**Young adult novelist
(1964–)**

Born April 25, 1964, in Hibbing, MN; daughter of William Chae-Sik (a physician) and Grace Koom-Soon (a social worker) Lee; married Karl H. Jacoby (a history professor), June 28, 1997. Education: Brown University, A.B., 1986.

In her young adult novels, *Finding My Voice, If It Hadn't Been for Yoon Jun, Saying Goodbye,* and *Necessary Roughness,* Marie G. Lee has created a blueprint for what it is like to grow up an outsider in America: the racial taunts, the feeling of otherness, the gestalt and internal disharmony that result from finally *discovering* that you are "different." Lee, an Asian American, has written out of her own deeply felt experiences growing up in America's heartland, the only Korean in her small hometown.

"I write coming-of-age stories of people who, for some reason, feel different than those around them," Lee stated. For Lee, that "reason" is most often ethnic background. "I didn't have anything like [my books] when I was growing up and wish I did," Lee continued. "I really wish there was a book describing how it felt to be called a 'chink,' to have teachers making nasty jokes about how Koreans eat dog. Asian Americans inhabit a tricky place because while our looks will always deny us from looking totally 'American,' we do not have that 'angry minority' spot to identify with. Black Panthers, A.I.M., La Raza—but Angry Asians?"

"I want readers to know . . . that behind every racial slur there's a person, and in this light, I believe books have the capacity to educate."

645

Lee's characters must contend with many of the obstacles Lee herself did growing up. "I have been asked more than once when I am going to be through with the 'race thing' and go onto more 'universal themes,'" Lee noted in an *ALAN Review* article. "I always answer that with a 'probably never.' Toni Morrison has gone so far as to say that she's never ever really felt she was an American. I don't take that extreme a view, but I do feel that growing up a person of color in this country, one that traces its history back to Anglo-European foundations, has had the effect that my perceptions of American life are inevitably filtered through a prism of race. . . . [A] writer has to know herself first, or her work won't be honest; and for me, being an American of Korean descent and being a writer are inextricably linked."

Through the Prism of Race

"I grew up in a very small town in Minnesota—Hibbing—which, perhaps not coincidentally, is where Bob Dylan also grew up," Lee remarked. "In a small town it's easy to know who's 'in' or 'out,' and not only was I a shy, bookish kid, but our family was the only family of color in town. So I spent a lot of time holed up in the library, not only because I liked to read (which is still true) but also because it was easier than dealing with the kids from school." Lee's parents immigrated from Korea in 1953; her father was a physician and her mother a social worker. Theirs was a comfortable upper-middle class life. "My parents were not the typical Korean American parents. They let me have a lot of privacy, and, besides bugging me to study, basically left me alone." It was this time on her own in her youth, "just dreaming," that Lee credits with making her a writer.

But there was always the background noise of race and difference for Lee. "Throughout my life—starting from age three or four—I heard a lot of racist insults. Mostly it was people calling me chink, yelling from cars. But it also included teachers saying things right to my face, and in high school, there were always these girls who were trying to beat me up." Lee did well at school, a motivated student whose father hoped that she and her three siblings would follow in his career. "I was basically a nerd but tried to hide it," she stated. "It was definitely not cool to be smart at my school."

Lee also recounted in *ALAN Review* her desire to fit in. She and her friends were avid readers of *Seventeen* magazine, where she first published an essay at age sixteen. She, like her friends, identified with the all-white models who posed for the magazine. Lee saw herself as one of the blond, Scandinavian types she was growing up with, though all the while she felt like someone trying to "force your feet into a pair of shoes that you love but that don't fit."

One time Lee was offered a *Seventeen*-style make over by a local department store. "At last, I thought. *Seventeen* was going to turn me into one of those All-American girls!" But when the hairdresser and beautician were finished, Lee looked in the mirror and saw that she had been given a "China chop" haircut and eyes teased into a Cleopatra look with eyeliner. "I was humiliated," Lee wrote in *ALAN Review*. "Looking back to that time, I can see that there was definitely a sort of two-way cognitive dissonance going on: I thought of myself as culturally white, or least All-American; other people—even my friends—saw me as a China doll. I was neither."

Finding Her Voice

Lee attended Brown University, and there she gave up the idea of someday becoming a doctor like her father. "I realized that would be impossible for me, someone as squeamish as I was," Lee explained. "I was still a dutiful daughter and majored in economics so I could get a 'real' job, but all this time I was still planning to be a writer." She had come to that determination when she got her first typewriter. Publication of her essay in *Seventeen* was a confirmation of this early desire, and by the time she left for college, her drawers were crammed with finished stories.

Out of college, Lee worked in a research firm and, later, at Goldman Sachs. Meanwhile, Lee was learning how to write in her free time. She had several fine teachers, including Nancy Willard, who taught her a new way to look at her work. "Nancy basically confirmed for me that what I was writing was really valuable. It wasn't until then that I really started writing with confidence," Lee explained.

What Lee was writing was her first novel, *Finding My Voice*. As Lee once described it, the inspiration for that book resulted from a ski trip.

Driving through a small Minnesota town, Lee spotted two boys in letter jackets. "I thought to myself, I want to write a story that will capture all this: what it's like to live in the snow and the cold, what it's like being in these small towns where everybody knows everybody, and having a letter jacket means you are really *something*."

That was Lee's initial inspiration; as she was writing the book the themes of fitting in, racism, and peer and parental pressure came to her work almost of their own accord. The resulting novel was autobiographical in some respects. "My high school life wasn't exactly like Ellen's [the protagonist of *Finding My Voice*], but some of the things that happened to her were similar to things that happened to me. I had people call me names because I was Asian, and I also had very strong, close friends who helped me see that these names had little to do with me as a person."

Ellen Sung, in *Finding My Voice,* is caught between two worlds. A senior at a Minnesota high school, she is prodded to succeed and become more "American" by her immigrant parents; at the same time, she feels the effects of racism from some classmates and even teachers. A gymnast and straight A student, still Ellen is made to feel an outsider, different from the other kids. Her crush on one of the most popular boys in her class, Tomper, will probably come to nothing, she knows, as she is so shy and studious. Tormented with the epithet "chink," Ellen must learn to stand up for herself.

Critical response to Lee's debut novel was very positive. Penny Blubaugh in *Voice of Youth Advocates* called the book "a sensitive coming-of-age story" and went on to note that it "should provoke anger and thought." Concluding her review in *School Library Journal,* Libby K. White noted that Lee's first novel "gives voice to a point of view that has been wanting until recently in fiction about Asian-Americans. It is a welcome addition."

Further Explorations along the Color Line

Lee returned to the story of Ellen Sung in her third novel, *Saying Goodbye.* Ellen is now a college freshman at Harvard, in premed. Her new friend and roommate at college, Leecia, assumes

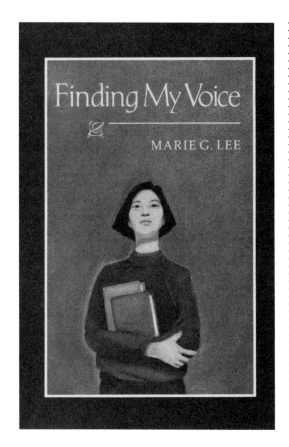

Cover of ***Finding My Voice***

that Ellen is as passionately involved in her cultural heritage as Leecia is in her own African American background. But Ellen is far more interested in studying creative writing than in multiculturalism. She begins to fall in love, however, with a Korean American named Jae whose family's shop was destroyed in the 1992 Los Angeles riots. This and a tae kwon do class she takes initiate an interest for Ellen in her Korean heritage.

Necessary Roughness was Lee's next novel for older readers, a story about finding and making a place for oneself in a new environment. The twins Chan and Young Kim are uprooted from their home in Los Angeles and move with their family to a small town in northern Minnesota. There Chan tries to fit in by turning his soccer skills to the use of high school football; his twin sister plays flute in the band. The two fight the cultural wars at home and at school. A contributor in *Kirkus Reviews* observed that football "is the central metaphor for how a Korean family confronts life, death, and assimilation in this gritty and moving novel."

In her books, Lee has created a new genre in multicultural literature for young readers—the Asian American novel, detailing more specifically the Korean American experience. Lee writes her novels not only for those, like herself, who have been the victim of racial prejudice and harassment, but also the potential harassers. Lee commented in *ALAN Review,* ''I want readers to know . . . that behind every racial slur there's a person, and in this light, I believe books have the capacity to educate.''

Sources for More Information

Books

The Asian American Almanac, Gale, 1995.

Lives of Famous Asian Americans: Literature, Chelsea House, 1995.

Oxford Companion to Women's Writing in the United States, Oxford University Press, 1995.

Rosey Grier's All-American Heroes: Multicultural Success Stories, MasterMedia, 1993.

Spike Lee

Screenwriter, actor, director, and producer (1957–)

Born Shelton Jackson Lee, March 20, 1957, in Atlanta, GA; son of William (a musician and composer) and Jacqueline (a teacher; maiden name, Shelton) Lee; married Tonya Lewis; children: Jackson, Satchel (daughter). Education: Morehouse College, B.A., 1979; New York University, M.A., 1983.

F ew Americans in the arts are able to boast the exhaustive list of achievements that Spike Lee has accomplished before his fortieth birthday. Since the mid-1980s, the Brooklyn-bred, New York University-trained filmmaker has written, directed, and acted in several successful mov- ies—creations all the more remarkable for their unique look at African American life, in settings on the streets of and in the mental landscapes of Brooklyn. Though sometimes provocative and controversial in their themes or characterizations, Lee's films transcend color lines. Almost single- handedly, he has changed the relationship between the Hollywood film industry and African Ameri- can audiences.

Not surprisingly, Lee is an iconoclastic, out- spoken, and articulate public figure. But he is also a media-savvy one with a trenchant sense of humor. Lee is particularly fluent on the subject of race in America and the many shapes and forms by which it disguises itself. After a solid childhood and a positive college experience firmly grounded in African American culture, Lee was well-equipped to enter battle when he faced serious obstacles as a

"I mean, a lot of people's attitude is, 'Look, you're successful, you have money—what do you have to be angry about?'. . . I was one of the lucky ones."

649

neophyte filmmaker. As a writer and top-notch observer of human experience, Lee was no great exception to any rule; but the combination of his talents and his vision as a filmmaker and his intense, almost enthusiastic stubbornness have helped him to usher in a new and significant era for American film.

New York Upbringing

Spike Lee was born Shelton Jackson Lee in Atlanta, the first of William and Jacqueline Lee's five children. As the family grew, they moved around; Bill Lee, a jazz musician, was drawn first to Chicago, then to the equally vibrant music scene in New York City. The Lees settled in Brooklyn about 1959, when their first son was still a two-year-old toddler—but already nicknamed "Spike" by his mother as a result of his cantankerousness.

After graduating from John Dewey High School in Brooklyn in 1975, Lee enrolled at Morehouse College in Atlanta, an historic African American college from which both his father and grandfather had graduated. At Morehouse, Lee studied mass communications, and decided to become a filmmaker halfway through. When he graduated in 1979, Lee interned at Columbia Pictures, and then won entry to the prestigious film school at New York University.

Stubborn Streak

During his first year, Lee encountered problems with his teachers and the administrators for his adamant opinions. Lee resisted "suggestions" that he pursue his education elsewhere, and after several semesters, he managed to strike a balance between his political beliefs and his artistic vision. This came to fruition with the 1982 short *Joe's Bed-Stuy Barbershop: We Cut Heads,* about a Brooklyn barber whose establishment is also an illegal numbers joint. Lee won the N.Y.U. student award for *Joe's Bed-Stuy Barbershop* that year, a peer-group honor that is not bestowed haphazardly.

Because of this success, talent agencies began courting him, but none seemed interested in expanding the themes of *Joe's Bed-Stuy* into a larger project. Undeterred, Lee wrote the script for an all-black film he called "Homecoming." The story is set at a college, not unlike Morehouse, around the festive atmosphere of its homecoming weekend. None of the talent agencies that courted him were interested in the script, and so Lee realized then that he would have to fly solo if he wanted to pursue a career as a commercial filmmaker.

Lee won a grant from a New York-area arts council and shot his first feature film, *She's Gotta Have It,* in just twelve days. It starred Tracy Camilla Johns as Nola Darling, an African American woman who enjoys three beaus—one of whom, Mars Blackmon, was played by Lee—but cannot choose between the trio, and does not want to have to choose. Lee edited the film in his studio apartment—a huge editing machine wedged next to his bed—took it to the 1986 Cannes Film Festival, and won the Prix de Jeunesse. *She's Gotta Have It* was picked up for distribution and became a massive art-house hit across the United States, grossing $8 million.

In Demand

By now, the Hollywood studios were now enthusiastically courting Lee and were more than willing to make a film about African American life after seeing how well audiences responded to *She's Gotta Have It* and its absence of poverty, misery, violence, or drugs. Island Pictures offered Lee a deal to put the "Homecoming" script into production, then changed their minds; he turned to Columbia Pictures and began shooting what would become the 1988 musical *School Daze* after receiving permission from the Atlanta University Center to film on campus. The Atlanta University Center was the administrative body that controlled Morehouse, Spelman, and three other black colleges whose campuses were almost adjacent to one another.

The cast of *School Daze* included Vanessa Williams, Tyra Banks, and Lawrence Fishburne; Lee cast himself in the role of Half Pint, a student who hopes to achieve social success by pledging the top fraternity at Mission College. In his script, Lee constructed tension around two groups of students he called "wannabes"—light-skinned students from affluent families who dressed conservatively, straightened their hair and even wore blue contact lenses—and "jigaboos," dark-skinned students who possessed a distinct street

*Movie still from **Do the Right Thing***

credibility or a rural Southern accent, and returned the sense of contempt they received from the wannabes.

Human nature's need to divide and do battle against itself was again the theme of his next film, 1989's *Do the Right Thing.* Lee let the film's theme song set viewers up in the first few minutes—Public Enemy's "Fight the Power." Lee again starred as Mookie, a pizza deliverer for a Bedford-Stuyvesant pizzeria run by Sal, an Italian-American played by Danny Aiello. Sal and his sons are the last vestiges of Bed-Stuy's once-populous Italian community, and their resentment of this changing world simmers below the surface. The action in *Do the Right Thing* takes place on the hottest day of the year, and the summer heat and sociological tensions escalate to a terrible moment when a black man becomes a casualty of police brutality in front of the pizzeria. Mookie's toss of a garbage can through the window of his employer's business is the spark that incites a riot.

With his successful track record, Lee was able to create his own production company; Forty Acres and a Mule borrowed its name from the never-realized promise to America's slaves at the end of the Civil War. *Mo' Better Blues* was the first of his films under this banner, a lushly photographed 1991 work that starred Denzel Washington as a jazz musician in Harlem in the 1940s. Lee touched upon more than one controversial theme in another film that was released in 1991: *Jungle Fever.* The screenplay, written by Lee, tracks the start-to-finish tale of an interracial romance between Wesley Snipes, in the role of architect Flipper Purify, and an Italian-American woman played by Annabella Sciorra whom he meets in the workplace.

Up until this point in his career, Lee's works had usually been met with some reproach from the film-critic community for what some viewed as their flashy camera work. *Film Comment*'s Kent Jones explained some of the technical or artistic criticisms leveled at Lee's films, citing one as his reliance on the actor-on-dolly shot (borrowed from Scorsese) which made it appear that the actors were ambling along on moving sidewalks. Lee has also been accused of keeping his actors so tightly directed that they never really seem to take on their roles, and for portraying whites in very heavy-handed terms.

Popular Works

Films

School Daze, Columbia, 1988

Do the Right Thing, Universal, 1989

Mo' Better Blues, Universal, 1991

Jungle Fever, Universal, 1991

Malcolm X, Warner Bros., 1992

Crooklyn, Universal, 1994

Clockers, Universal, 1995

4 Little Girls, HBO/Forty Acres and a Mule Filmworks, 1997

He Got Game, Touchstone, 1998

A Masterwork

Lee's 1992 opus *Malcolm X* marked a turning point in his career. He had a substantial, larger-than-life martyr as the subject, a large studio budget, and a screenplay written by James Baldwin. Lee, however, chose to make the biopic his own way, rewriting the screenplay when he found historical inaccuracies in the speeches that Baldwin had included. He hired Betty Shabazz, Malcolm's widow, as a consultant, and also worked on the screenplay with Denzel Washington, cast as the lead. Lee told Gary Crowdus and Dan Georgakas in an interview for *Cineaste* that the actor "has a good story sense. We both knew a lot was riding on this film," Lee said. "We did not want to live in another country for the rest of our lives. We could not go anywhere without being reminded by black folks, '. . . don't mess this one up.' We were under tremendous pressure on this film."

Malcolm X established Lee as a significant and respected figure in American cinema. The three-plus hour film was both a commercial success—earning more than two million dollars on the day it opened—and a critical achievement. "Spike Lee has accomplished something historic in movies: a rousing, full-sized epic about a defiantly idealistic black hero whose humanitarianism never extends to turning the other cheek," noted Peter Travers in *Rolling Stone.*

Contention and controversy were distinctly absent from Lee's next film, *Crooklyn,* bittersweet 1994 look at life in the Brooklyn of his youth. The story follows the five children of the Carmichael family, a household headed by a jazz-musician father and schoolteacher mother. One impetus Lee had with the gentleness and lack of controversy in *Crooklyn* was to show cinema-goers another side of urban youth, not one rife with the violence and gore of most contemporary films set in rough American cities. "We were able to have childhoods," Lee told *Entertainment Weekly.*

Lee did tackle the subjects of drugs, crime, and the city in his next film, *Clockers.* He adapted the screenplay from the Richard Price novel of the same name about young crack dealers. The 1995 film starred an unknown, Mekhi Phifer, as Strike, the Brooklyn crack dealer "torn between the demands of a veteran police detective (Harvey Keitel) and a local drug lord (Delroy Lindo)," wrote a contributor in *Premiere,* "and in Lee's hands it has become an epic African-American tragedy, as morally complex as it is moving and powerful."

Personal Projects

Lee also made a 1997 documentary about the bombing of a Birmingham, Alabama church during the civil rights era, *4 Little Girls.* He explored a longtime passion in his 1997 book, *The Best Seat in the House,* a basketball memoir in which he chronicles his life through the prism of his fanaticism for the New York Knicks. Lee's 1998 film, *He Got Game,* was the first of his movies to take on the theme of African Americans and the cult of professional athletics in America. The protagonist, Jesus Shuttleworth, was played by Milwaukee Bucks guard Ray Allen, and Lee's screenplay follows one week in the life of the number-one high school player in the nation as competing forces vie for his talent. Denzel Washington plays his father, a prison inmate who is paroled for a week by the state's governor on a mission to convince Shuttleworth to sign with the politician's alma mater.

Lee, who once filmed a series of hilarious commercials for Nike that starred Michael Jordan as himself and Lee as Mars Blackmon, is the head of his own agency, Spike DDB. In 1994 he married an attorney, Tonya Lee, with whom he has two children. They live in apartments in both Brooklyn and TriBeCa. "A true New Yorker, Spike Lee is learning to drive at 41," wrote Barbara Lippert in *New York* magazine. "My wife is teaching me," Lee told Lippert.

The filmmaker remains close to his siblings, and retains a strong sense of family. He knows the Lee genealogy dating back to the slave era and a couple named Mike and Phoebe. "If we all knew our history, there would be a story like that in every African-American family, and if you knew the hardships and the great heroic deeds that our ancestors did, you could be inspired to strive harder."

Sources for More Information

Books

Chapman, Kathleen Ferguson, *Spike Lee,* Creative Education, 1997.

Hardy, James Earl, *Spike Lee,* Chelsea House, 1996.

Haskins, Jim, *Spike Lee: By Any Means Necessary,* Walker and Co., 1997.

Jones, Maurice K., *Spike Lee and the African American Filmmakers; A Choice of Colors,* Millbrook Press, 1996.

Reid, Mark A., editor, *Spike Lee's Do the Right Thing,* Cambridge University Press, 1997.

Periodicals

Film Comment, January–February, 1997.

Gentleman's Quarterly, April, 1997.

Jet, October 6, 1997.

Sport, January, 1998.

On-line

Mr. Showbiz Web site, located at http://mrshowbiz.go.com/index.html.

Ursula K. Le Guin

Science fiction and fantasy novelist (1929-)

"That is what the practice of art is, you keep looking for the outside edge."

Born October 21, 1929, in Berkeley, CA; daughter of Alfred L. (an anthropologist) and Theodora Covel Brown (a writer; maiden name, Kracaw) Kroeber; married Charles Alfred Le Guin (a historian), December 22, 1953; children: Elisabeth, Caroline, Theodore. Education: Radcliffe College, A.B., 1951; Columbia University, A.M., 1952.

Considered one of the most significant authors of science fiction and fantasy to have emerged in the twentieth century, Ursula Le Guin is recognized as a gifted and original writer whose works address essential themes about the human condition in prose noted for its beauty and clarity. Le Guin is regarded as a groundbreaking writer who brought sophisticated themes and literary craftsmanship to the genre of science fiction; in addition, she is credited for being the first female writer to have made a major contribution to the genre.

In her works, Le Guin characteristically explores issues important to humanity, such as relationships, communication, the uses of power, the search for identity, and the acceptance of death. Since the 1970s, her works have incorporated a marked feminist perspective—she has addressed topics with special relevance to women, such as abortion—and have also reflected a strong environmental consciousness.

Le Guin is often credited as an exceptional maker of worlds; her books, which take place on earth, on different planets, and in settings outside of our universe, are acknowledged for the author's invention and attention to detail in her depiction of landscapes and societies. Her works also reflect Le Guin's fascination with myths, archetypes, and dreams, especially in her use of language and symbols. Most critics regard Le Guin as the creator of provocative, profound books that insightfully articulate the concerns of humanity in the context of imaginative literature.

Le Guin is perhaps best known for a series of fantasy novels called the Earthsea Quartet, which is composed of *A Wizard of Earthsea, The Tombs of Atuan, The Farthest Shore,* and *Tehanu: The Last Book of Earthsea.* The novels, which delineate the life of their main protagonist, the wizard Ged, from youth to old age, are set on various locations in Earthsea, a rural archipelago complete with its own anthropology, geology, and language. Throughout the quartet, Le Guin stresses the importance of self-knowledge through each stage of life, especially as it relates to the world. The Earthsea quartet is considered a major achievement as both fantasy literature and children's literature; in addition, the novels are often regarded as the best of Le Guin's oeuvre.

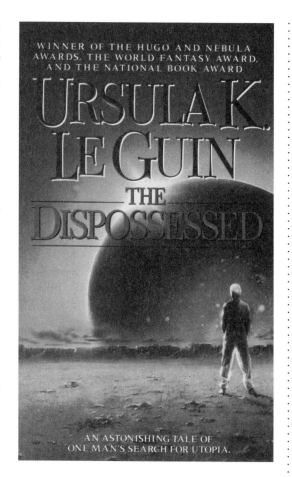

*Cover of **The Dispossessed***

Early Influences

Le Guin was born in Berkeley, California, to the noted anthropologist and educator Alfred Louis Kroeber and the writer Theodora Kroeber. Le Guin began writing poetry at five and then graduated to stories, mostly fantasy and science fiction. Le Guin was especially influenced by the Irish writer Lord Dunsany: "In spite of my familiarity with legends and myths, Dunsany came to me as a revelation," she explained. "What I hadn't realized, I guess, is that people were still making up myths. One made up stories oneself, of course; but here was a grownup doing it, for grownups, without a single apology to common sense, without an explanation, just dropping us straight into the Inner Lands. Whatever the reason, the moment was decisive. I had discovered my native country."

After graduating from high school, Le Guin attended Radcliffe College in Massachusetts. Although she claimed that she is "grateful to Harvard/Radcliffe for a splendid education," Le Guin added that she has had "to *unlearn* a great deal of

what I learned there. We were taught a sense of being *better* than other people. And yet, girls were taught to think that they were not as valuable as boys. I've had to fight against both these attitudes in myself—one is so easily influenced and malleable at eighteen." In 1951, Le Guin received her bachelor's degree in French from Radcliffe, graduating Phi Beta Kappa. "I never thought I wanted to be a writer," she noted, adding, "I always thought I was one. The big question was how could I earn a living at it?"

In 1953, Le Guin received her master's degree from Columbia University, again graduating Phi Beta Kappa. After starting on her Ph.D. in French and Italian Renaissance Literature, she received a Fulbright Fellowship to France. En route aboard the Queen Mary, she met Charles Le Guin and had a shipboard romance; the couple married six months later. After returning to the United States, Charles Le Guin finished his doctorate in history at Emory University in Atlanta while Ursula, deciding against getting her doctorate, taught French, worked at part-time jobs, and continued the serious writing she had begun two years earlier.

Develops Interest in Science Fiction

Over the next eight years, she published poetry and wrote five unpublished novels, four of them about Orsinia, an imaginary country in central Europe. Then she discovered science fiction: "When I became aware of Philip K. Dick, Cordwainer Smith and other science fiction writers," she said, "I thought to myself, 'Hey, this stuff is just as crazy as what I'm doing.' I knew where my work might fit in." After selling a short story to the pulp magazine *Fantastic,* she was on her way.

After the publication of her first science fiction novel, *Rocannon's World,* a work that blends elements from both science fiction and fantasy, Le Guin determined to, as she wrote, keep "pushing at my own limitations and at the limits of science fiction. That is what the practice of art is, you keep looking for the outside edge. When you find it you make it a whole, solid, real, and beautiful thing; anything less is incomplete." With the publication of *A Wizard of Earthsea* in 1968 and her adult novel *The Left Hand of Darkness*—a work that explores the differences between the sexes in the context of science fiction—in 1969, Le Guin claimed that she "finally got my pure fantasy vein separated from my science fiction vein . . . and the separation marked a large advance in both skill and content. Since then I have gone on writing, as it were, with both the left and right hands; and it has been a matter of keeping on pushing out towards the limits—my own and that of the medium."

The Earthsea Quartet

The first volume of the quartet, *A Wizard of Earthsea,* is considered a classic story of coming of age as well as the most popular book of the series. In it, Le Guin describes how Sparrowhawk, a richly gifted but impetuous student of magic, unleashes an evil shadow through hubris; when the boy confronts the shadow, they call each other by the same name—Ged, Sparrowhawk's true name—and he and the shadow become one. Through this act, Ged is made whole, thus beginning his preparation to become Archmage of Earthsea; in addition, he has restored balance to the world.

The next Earthsea book, *The Tombs of Atuan,* examines feminine coming of age as it describes the rite of passage of fifteen-year-old Arha, who has been hailed as the reincarnation of the Priestess of the Tombs of Atuan. *The Tombs of Atuan* is regarded as both an account of religious experience and an exploration of adolescent sexuality; in addition, reviewers have noted the lesson that Ged receives—"the necessity of mutuality," in the words of Francis J. Molson in *Twentieth Century Children's Writers.* As Le Guin explained, "The subject of *The Tombs of Atuan* is, if I had to put it in one word, sex. . . . [The] symbols can all be read as sexual. More exactly, you could call it a feminist coming of age. Birth, rebirth, destruction, freedom are the themes."

Le Guin ends *The Tombs of Atuan* with the hope that Earthsea might be united under its true king; in the third volume of the quartet, *The Farthest Shore,* Ged guides teenage Arren, the future king of Earthsea, on a quest to discover the source of the evil that is demoralizing the archipelago. The wizard and the prince journey to an island peopled by the walking, silent dead, where a former classmate of Ged's has achieved a macabre immortality. In order to restore death to its rightful place in the universe, Ged heals the crack in the fabric of the world that has been caused by the crazed wizard; however, the difficulty of the task causes Ged to lose all of his magic power.

In her *Dreams Must Explain Themselves,* Le Guin wrote, "*The Farthest Shore* is about death. That's why it is a less well-built, less sound and complete book than the others. They were about things I had already lived through and survived. . . . It seemed an absolutely suitable subject to me for young readers, since in a way one can say that the hour when a child realizes, not that death exists—children are intensely aware of death—but that he/she, personally, is mortal, will die, is the hour when childhood ends, and new life begins. Coming of age again, but in a larger sense."

Eighteen years after the publication of *The Farthest Shore,* Le Guin wrote *Tehanu: The Last Book of Earthsea,* a novel that begins twenty-five years after the end of its predecessor. In the process of raising her feminist consciousness, the author realized that she needed to tell another story about Earthsea, one about the power of womanhood; with this volume, then, Le Guin felt that she would provide a balance to the male-dominated trilogy. In an interview with Meredith Tax in the

Village Voice, the author referred to the "long, purely male tradition of heroic adventure fantasy. My Earthsea trilogy is part of this male tradition—that is why I had to write this fourth volume. Because I changed, I had to show the other side."

Works for Young Adults

Although the Earthsea books are the best known examples of Le Guin's juvenile literature, she has written several additional stories and picture books for children and novels for young adults. Her first contribution to the latter category is *Very Far Away from Anywhere Else,* published in England as *A Very Long Way from Anywhere Else.* The author's first purely realistic novel for young people, *Very Far Away* is a contemporary story about Owen Griffin and Natalie Field, talented high school seniors—Owen in science, Natalie in music—who become close friends. When Owen feels pressured to introduce sex into their relationship, Natalie gently but firmly rejects his advances; distraught, Owen flips his car over while driving recklessly. Andrew Gordon, writing in the *Dictionary of Literary Biography,* noted, "Like all of Le Guin's fiction, *Very Far Away from Anywhere Else* concerns the painful effort in becoming a whole human being."

The Beginning Place is a novel that, according to a reviewer in *Publishers Weekly,* brought Le Guin "back to the field in which she first gained fame (SF/fantasy) and simultaneously breaks new ground in her writing." The work features the adolescent characters Hugh Rogers and Irene Pannis. After running away from home to escape from his domineering mother and dead-end job, Hugh discovers a gateway to Tembreabrezi, a parallel world of eternal twilight. Irene, who has left home because of the sexual advances of her stepfather, had discovered Tembreabrezi years before and has made a home for herself there. In her review in *School Library Journal,* Amy Rolnick claimed that Le Guin's devoted fans "will recognize the artful melding of the real and the fantastic as the author at her best."

Andrew Gordon of the *Dictionary of Literary Biography* noted that the author's Earthsea books are "her finest work thus far, but as her later works indicate, she is continuing to experiment with different modes of writing and to grow in artistic range." In her entry in *Twentieth Century Children's Writers,* Jill Paton Walsh concluded, "It is hard to see how Le Guin could exceed the merit of her existing work; but also hard to put any limit on what might be expected from a writer of such variety, such force, and such psychological depth."

Don't Miss ...

A Wizard of Earthsea, Parnassus Press, 1968

The Left Hand of Darkness, Walker, 1969

The Lathe of Heaven, Scribner, 1971

The Tombs of Atuan, Atheneum, 1971

The Farthest Shore, Atheneum, 1972

The Dispossessed: An Ambiguous Utopia, Harper, 1974

Tehanu: The Last Book of Earthsea, Atheneum, 1990

Four Ways to Forgiveness, HarperPrism, 1995

Sources for More Information

Books

Bucknall, Barbara, *Ursula K. Le Guin,* Ungar, 1981.

Cummins, Elizabeth, *Understanding Ursula K. Le Guin,* University of South Carolina Press, 1990.

Olander, Joseph D., and Martin Harry Greenberg, editors, *Ursula K. Le Guin,* Taplinger, 1979.

Reid, Suzanne Elizabeth, *Presenting Ursula K. Le Guin,* Twayne, 1997.

Slusser, George Edgar, *The Farthest Shores of Ursula K. Le Guin,* Borgo, 1976.

Periodicals

Extrapolation (Ursula K. Le Guin issue), fall, 1980.

Science-Fiction Studies (Ursula K. Le Guin issue), March, 1976.

Annie Leibovitz

**Photographer
(1949-)**

"When you trust your point of view, that's when you start taking pictures."

Born Anna-Lou Leibovitz, October 2, 1949, in Westbury, CT; daughter of Sam (a U.S. Air Force colonel) and Marilyn (a modern-dance instructor) Leibovitz. Education: San Francisco Art Institute, B.F.A., 1971; studied photography with Ralph Gibson.

She is "a photographer of celebrities who has herself become a celebrity." For the past twenty-five years, no photographer has delivered more photographs of the people we most want to see than has Annie Leibovitz. Her pictures are recognizable for their bright colors, intense lighting, and above all, for unique and surprising poses. In magazine spreads and advertising campaigns, Leibovitz has demonstrated that she is a master of projecting the popular culture of our time.

Anna-Lou Leibovitz was born on October 2, 1949, in Westbury, Connecticut. Her father, Sam Leibovitz, was an Air Force lieutenant colonel and because of his career, the family moved often during Leibovitz's childhood. Her mother, Marilyn Leibovitz, was a modern-dance instructor and the chief force in raising Annie and her five siblings. Leibovitz remembers taking many dance classes from her mother and other teachers. She credits this for her later interest in photographing dancers.

During high school Leibovitz played guitar and wrote music and was the head of the school folksinging club. She also developed an interest in

658

Steve Martin in Tails
by Annie Leibovitz

painting and attended the San Francisco Art Institute, beginning in 1967. She considered a career as a painting instructor. During a vacation from school, Leibovitz visited her family, then living in the Philippines. She and her mother took a trip to Japan, where she bought a camera and began taking pictures.

When she returned to school, Leibovitz enrolled in a night class in photography. ''I was totally seduced by the wonderment of it all,'' she told a writer for *ArtNews*. ''To see something that afternoon and have it materialize before your eyes that same day. There was a real immediacy to it. I lived in the darkroom.''

Begins Long Association with *Rolling Stone*

From then on Leibovitz was hooked on photography. She worked on a kibbutz, a collectively run farm, in Israel for several months in 1969. She the most eloquent images ever made of the world of Rock and Roll.'' That project and growing acclaim for *Rolling Stone* made Leibovitz a big name among contemporary photographers. Unfortunately, she became associated with drugs as well as with rock and roll; the pressure of her career and nearness to rock's excesses led her to begin using cocaine. ''I went on that [Rolling Stones] tour to get to the heart of something, to see what it was like,'' she later told *Vanity Fair.* ''People always talk about the soul of the sitter [in a photograph], but the photographer has a soul, too. And I almost lost it.'' Leibovitz has admitted that it took her five years to ''get off the tour,'' but she did, and her career continued to climb.

took pictures while there and continued to snap away when she returned to California. In 1970 a friend suggested that she take her prints to *Rolling Stone* magazine, which was headquartered in San Francisco. *Rolling Stone* was just getting started then, a new magazine about rock music and the counterculture that had emerged in the late 1960s from the bohemia of the 1950s. Jann Wenner, the magazine's founder, was impressed by Leibovitz's photos. He began giving her assignments, paying her $47 a week before she had even graduated from college. Leibovitz recalled, ''I can never forget the sensation of being at a newsstand and seeing for the first time my photograph transformed into the *Rolling Stone* cover.''

By 1973, when she was only twenty-three years old, Leibovitz had become chief photographer for *Rolling Stone;* she stayed with the magazine for ten more years. During that time she traveled around the country and the world photographing everyone who was anyone in pop music. Her reputation was cemented by photographs of two subjects. One was former Beatle John Lennon. She snapped countless shots of Lennon between 1970 and his death in 1980. One of her most famous photographs was taken on December 8, 1980, only two hours before Lennon's murder.

The second subject that would spread Leibovitz's renown was the English group the Rolling Stones; she was hired by the band in 1975 to document their concert tour of that year. The photographs she produced as she traveled and lived with the Stones have been called ''some of

Develops Signature Style with Color

Leibovitz's early photographs were in black and white. When *Rolling Stone* began printing in color in 1974, she started using color film, staging elaborate scenes for the magazine's covers. She explained to *ArtNews,* ''When I was in school, I wasn't taught anything about lighting, I was only taught black-and-white. So I had to learn about color myself.'' Nonetheless, Leibovitz quickly developed her signature style, notable for brilliant color, partly because it printed well.

During her years with *Rolling Stone* and in her work for other magazines, Leibovitz photographed many of the biggest names in entertainment, including keyboardist-singer Stevie Wonder, rocker Bruce Springsteen, film director Woody Allen, country songbird Dolly Parton, pop singer Linda Ronstadt, actress Meryl Streep, dancer Mikhail Baryshnikov, and action film star Arnold Schwarzenegger. Initially her photographs of celebrities were like snapshots, capturing the subject in the moment. But she soon became aware of her ability to put people at ease, helping them to ''let down their guard.'' She encouraged her famous subjects to pose for her doing crazy or silly things that frequently revealed their personalities more than just a ''straight'' portrait could. Another secret of Leibovitz's success is her careful pre-shoot research of her subjects: she reads their books or poetry, sees their movies or performances, and when possible, spends time observing their daily lives.

Becomes Known for Photographing Celebrities

Her best-known photographs feature actress Whoopi Goldberg with only her face, arms, and legs peeking out of a bathtub full of milk; TV star Roseanne Arnold mud-wrestling with her husband Tom; and the artist Christo wrapped in fabric like one of his artworks. Photography writer and critic Andy Grundberg pointed out how Leibovitz "exaggerates the distinctive characteristic of [the celebrities'] public image in a way that's funny and deflating." Perhaps her most controversial photograph was for a 1992 *Vanity Fair* cover; on it appeared actress Demi Moore—nude and very pregnant.

In 1983 Leibovitz left *Rolling Stone;* shortly thereafter she became chief photographer for *Vanity Fair.* This afforded her the opportunity to photograph even more stars, including many artists, writers, poets, and dancers. That year she also mounted her first solo show, many of her portraits numbering among its sixty pictures. A reviewer for the *Christian Science Monitor* attested of Leibovitz's work: "There is humor and beauty here, as well as images that some may consider downright outrageous. . . . She goes a step beyond what is necessary to create striking images of famous people."

In 1986 Leibovitz added advertising to her list of assignments. She has contributed her photographs to the ad campaigns of numerous companies, among them Honda, Arrow shirts, Rose's Lime Juice, the Gap, and American Express. Her work on behalf of the latter earned her the coveted Clio Award, the equivalent of an Academy Award, from the advertising industry. Leibovitz says that some of the success of these photographs can be attributed to large budgets, most notably from American Express, which enabled her to fly her subjects to virtually any locale and allowed her to spend several days photographing them. "I've moved into the terrain of making pictures, composing, theatre," she told *New York* magazine.

Washington D.C. Exhibit Showcases Work

In 1991 Leibovitz was honored with a major exhibition at the National Portrait Gallery in Washington, D.C. It was only the second display of the work of a living photographer ever mounted at the site. The exhibit drew more visitors during its five weeks than ordinarily visit the National Portrait Gallery in an entire year. A book was published to accompany the show titled *Photographs: Annie Leibovitz 1970–1990.* It contains almost two hundred of her photos, dating back to her kibbutz days in 1969. In the early 1990s Leibovitz's work was shown in Arizona, Florida, Utah, Boston, and San Francisco, to name just a few of its destinations. An honor of a different sort came in 1996 when Leibovitz was chosen to be the official photographer for the U.S. Olympic team for the Summer Olympics held that year in Atlanta, Georgia.

Leibovitz herself is quite recognizable—tall, with lanky blonde hair, a prominent nose, and a broad smile. Despite the exposure she has received over the years and the stars with whom she has hobnobbed, she claims to be quite shy. An exercise enthusiast, she maintains an apartment in New York City and a home on Long Island but spends much of her time traveling on assignment. The photographer has said she sometimes regrets not having much time for her personal life, conceding, "My longest relationship has always been my work. My work has always delivered for me." But she has also claimed, "I'm happy doing exactly what I'm doing. . . . I can do this the rest of my life. It's only going to get better."

Despite its popularity, Leibovitz's work has received some criticism that it is superficial because of its emphasis on celebrities. More often, however, critics comment on how much her celebrity photographs reveal about their subject and about contemporary American culture. Leibovitz has said that it is important to her to study the work of earlier artists and photographers. Yet the unusual poses, vivid lighting, and unexpected elements in her portraiture indicate a totally modern vision. The reflection of culture and society has been the goal of many artists; Annie Leibovitz has amply achieved this aim with her camera.

Sources for More Information

Books

Leibovitz, Annie, *Dancers: Photographs,* Smithsonian Institution Press, 1992.

Leibovitz, Annie, *Photographs,* Pantheon, 1983.

Leibovitz, Annie, *Photographs-Annie Leibovitz, 1970–1990,* HarperCollins, 1991.

Madeleine L'Engle

**Fantasy novelist and memoirist
(1918-)**

*"I think that fantasy must possess
the author and simply use him."*

*Born November 29, 1918, in New York, NY; given name,
Madeleine L'Engle Camp; daughter of Charles Wadsworth
(a foreign correspondent and author) and Madeleine (a
pianist; maiden name, Barnett) Camp; married Hugh Franklin (an actor), January 26, 1946 (died September, 1986);
children: Josephine (Mrs. Alan W. Jones), Maria (Mrs.
John Rooney), Bion. Education: Smith College, A.B. (with
honors), 1941; attended New School for Social Research,
1941–42; Columbia University, graduate study, 1960–61.*

Madeleine L'Engle is a writer who resists
easy classification. She has successfully
published plays, poems, essays, autobiographies,
and novels for both children and adults. She is
probably best known for her "Time Fantasy"
series of children's books, including *A Wrinkle in
Time, A Wind in the Door,* and *A Swiftly Tilting
Planet.* These novels combine elements of science
fiction and fantasy with L'Engle's constant themes
of family love and moral responsibility.

As the daughter of a respected journalist and a
gifted pianist, L'Engle was surrounded by creative
people from birth. She wrote her first stories at the
age of five. She was an only child; in her autobiographies she writes of how much she enjoyed her
solitude and of the rich fantasy life she created
for herself.

Speaking of her childhood, L'Engle explains
in *The Summer of the Great-Grandmother:* "[My
mother] was almost forty when I was born. . . .

Once she and Father had had their long-awaited baby, I became a bone of contention between them. They disagreed completely on how I ought to be brought up. Father wanted a strict English childhood for me, and this is more or less what I got—nanny, governesses, supper on a tray in the nursery, dancing lessons, music lessons, skating lessons, art lessons."

Her father's failing health sent her parents to Switzerland and young Madeleine to a series of boarding schools, where she found herself very unpopular because of her shy, introspective ways. "I learned," L'Engle recounts in *The Summer of the Great-Grandmother,* "to put on protective coloring in order to survive in an atmosphere which was alien; and I learned to concentrate. Because I was never alone . . . I learned to shut out the sound of the school and listen to the story or poem I was writing when I should have been doing schoolwork. The result of this early lesson in concentration is that I can write anywhere."

Plays, Stories, and Novels

L'Engle became involved in theatre at Smith College, acting as well as writing plays. Soon after graduation, she was made an understudy for a Broadway production. Later she was given a few small roles and the position of assistant stage manager for Anton Chekhov's *Cherry Orchard.* The play ran for two years, and one of the performers, Hugh Franklin, eventually became L'Engle's husband. Throughout her career in the theatre, the author's writing continued, and both her theatre and boarding school experiences are evident in her first published novel, *The Small Rain.*

After publishing several books in the late 1940s, L'Engle's career as a writer was postponed in favor of raising her own family. During the 1950s, she and her husband operated a general store in rural Connecticut. L'Engle still wrote stories in her spare time, but these were invariably rejected by magazines. On her fortieth birthday, in 1958, discouraged by several years of rejections, she renounced writing completely, but found that she was unable to stop. Soon thereafter, things began to change for the author, and her writing began to sell again.

Selling *A Wrinkle in Time,* however, proved a challenge. The juvenile novel was rejected by 26 publishers in two years. Reasons given vary. The

Cover of **A Wrinkle in Time**

book was neither science fiction nor fantasy, impossible to pigeon hole. "Most objections," L'Engle recalled in an interview with *Children's Literature in Education,* "were that it would not be able to find an audience, that it was too difficult for children." Speaking to Michael J. Farrell in the *National Catholic Reporter,* L'Engle commented that *A Wrinkle in Time* "was written in the terms of a modern world in which children know about brainwashing and the corruption of evil. It's based on Einstein's theory of relativity and Planck's quantum theory. It's good, solid science, but also it's good, solid theology. My rebuttal to the German theologians [who] attack God with their intellect on the assumption that the finite can comprehend the infinite, and I don't think that's possible."

A Wrinkle in Time

In *A Wrinkle in Time,* young Meg Murry, with the help of her friend Calvin O'Keefe, must use time travel and extrasensory perception to rescue her father, a gifted scientist, from the evil forces that hold him prisoner on another planet. To release him, Meg must learn the power of love. In *A Critical History of Children's Literature,* Ruth

Hill Viguers calls *A Wrinkle in Time* a "book that combines devices of fairy tales, overtones of fantasy, the philosophy of great lives, the visions of science, and the warmth of a good family story.... It is an exuberant book, original, vital, exciting. Funny ideas, fearful images, amazing characters, and beautiful concepts sweep through it. And it is full of truth."

According to L'Engle, writing *A Wrinkle in Time* was a mysterious process. "A writer of fantasy, fairy tale, or myth," she explained in *Horn Book,* "must inevitably discover that he is not writing out of his own knowledge or experience, but out of something both deeper and wider. I think that fantasy must possess the author and simply use him. I know that this is true of *A Wrinkle in Time.* I can't possibly tell you how I came to write it. It was simply a book I had to write. I had no choice. And it was only *after* it was written that I realized what some of it meant." *A Wrinkle in Time* won the Newbery Medal in 1963, the Lewis Carroll Shelf Award in 1965, and was a runner-up for the Hans Christian Andersen Award in 1964.

L'Engle went on to write *A Wind in the Door* and *A Swiftly Tilting Planet,* which feature the characters introduced in *A Wrinkle in Time* and further develop the theme of love as a weapon against darkness. By the third book in the series, Meg and Calvin have become husband and wife and are expecting their first child, Polly. Polly has adventures of her own in novels such as *A House Like A Lotus* and *An Acceptable Time.* Although the series has been criticized as too convoluted for young readers, and some reviewers find the Murry family a trifle unbelievable and elitist, most critics praise the series for its willingness to take risks. Michele Murray, writing of *A Wind in the Door* in the *New York Times Book Review,* claimed that "L'Engle mixes classical theology, contemporary family life, and futuristic science fiction to make a completely convincing tale."

"Austin Family" Books Explore Complex Issues

L'Engle has also created a second family, the Austins, in *Meet the Austins, The Moon by Night,* *A Ring of Endless Light,* and other works. These characters, like those in the "Time Fantasy" series, explore philosophical and spiritual issues as they negotiate their relationships and the challenges that growing up entails. But the Austins' journeys—unlike Meg and Calvin's voyages across galaxies and time—involve more familiar settings and events.

In *Meet the Austins,* L'Engle's 1960 novel, the four children—John, Vicky, Suzy, and Rob—face the prospect of adopting Maggy, a spoiled and unruly foster child who initially turns their household upside-down, but slowly adjusts to her new home and becomes a member of the family. A *Times Literary Supplement* contributor noted that although the family is "much too good to be real," Maggy's "gradual improvement and acceptance by the others are the best part of the book." *The Moon by Night,* published in 1963, takes place throughout the family's cross-country camping trip. Fourteen-year-old Vicky, who narrates the story, meets Zachary Gray at a camping ground. A complex, older boy whose ideas bear little resemblance to those of Vicky's small-town family and friends, Zachary both frightens and fascinates her. The Austins continue to encounter Zachary along the way, and later Vicky meets Andy, a sunny, down-to-earth boy who competes with Zachary for her affections. In the course of their travels, Vicky learns that the world is far more complicated than she had imagined.

A Ring of Endless Light, which was named a Newbery Honor Book in 1981, finds the Austins spending the summer caring for their dying grandfather at his home near the ocean. It is sixteen-year-old Vicky's first experience with death, and the concept raises new and difficult questions. Then Commander Rodney, a Coast Guard officer and cherished family friend, is killed rescuing a drowning young man. Vicky learns that the young man was Zachary Gray, who is once again trailing Vicky, and that his near-drowning was a suicide attempt. At the funeral, Vicky meets Adam Eddington, who works with Vicky's older brother John at the marine biology station. As the summer progresses, Vicky finds four men dependent on her in different ways. She reads to her grandfather, a wise minister who, in his coherent moments, helps her sort out her confusion. Troubled Zachary takes Vicky for exciting but dangerous adventures and leans on her emotionally. Vicky also befriends Commander Rodney's grieving son Leo, who seeks more than friendship, and assists Adam with his project at the marine biology station. Although Adam thinks of Vicky as John's younger sister, thwarting her hopes for a romantic relationship, it is their work with dolphins that reveals Vicky's gift for telepathic communication and helps her find a new understanding of life and death. Carol Van Strum, writing in the *Washington Post Book World,* commented, ''The cosmic battle between light and darkness, good and evil, love and indifference, personified in the mythic fantasies of the *Wrinkle in Time* series, here is waged compellingly in its rightful place: within ourselves.''

L'Engle's practice of reviving characters from earlier novels makes all her works for young people—whether realistic or fantasy—part of an intricately connected whole. The Murry, O'Keefe, and Austin characters become increasingly real as they age and progress through their life-cycles. Similarly, new facets of Zachary Gray and Adam Eddington emerge when they are placed in diverse situations. Originally associated with Vicky Austin, Zachary meets Polly O'Keefe in Greece in *A House Like a Lotus.* In *An Acceptable Time,* Zachary visits Polly at her grandparents' house, and the two travel three thousand years into the past, to the same community that Polly's uncle, Charles Wallace, visits as a teenager in *A Swiftly Tilting Planet.* Before he meets the Austins, Adam Eddington is featured in a dangerous escapade involving Dr. Calvin O'Keefe's biological research and his twelve-year-old daughter Polly in *The Arm of the Starfish.*

Explaining her storytelling method in *Something about the Author Autobiography Series,* L'Engle stated, ''I start with what I know with all five senses, what I have experienced, and then the imagination takes over and says, 'But what if—' and the story is on.'' The author's ability to entertain is evident in her popularity with readers.

A *Publishers Weekly* survey of the nation's booksellers ranked her in the top six best-selling children's authors, while in an overview of children's book publishing, *American Bookseller* ranked L'Engle among the ten most popular children's authors in the country. But the writing process also fulfills an essential need for the author. As she stated in *Something about the Author Autobiography Series,* ''Often I am asked, 'Are you writing anything now?' Of course I'm writing something now. I'm not nice when I'm not writing.''

Sources for More Information

Books

L'Engle, Madeleine, *A Circle of Quiet,* Farrar, Straus, 1972.

L'Engle, Madeleine, *The Summer of the Great-Grandmother,* Farrar, Straus, 1974.

Something about the Author Autobiography Series, Gale, Volume 15, 1993.

On-line

Books @ Random Web site, located at http://www.dellbooks.com.

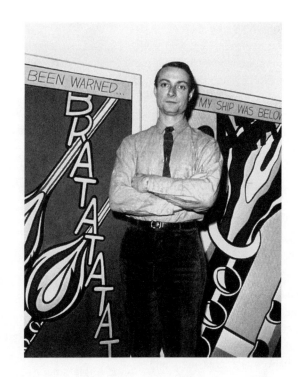

Roy Lichtenstein

Painter
(1923–1997)

"I wanted to do things you were not supposed to do. To say you were very serious about a non-serious subject inverted everything."

Born October 27, 1923, in New York, NY; died September 29, 1997, in New York, NY. Education: Studied under Reginald Marsh at the Art Students League, New York; Ohio State University, M.F.A., 1949.

Roy Lichtenstein is among a handful of artists who are virtually synonymous with pop art. Since his paintings of comic strips first caused a sensation in the early 1960s, Lichtenstein made a career of transforming images from consumer culture into gallery artifacts, challenging assumptions about "lowbrow" and "highbrow" art. Utilizing the Benday dot technique—a printing process that employs dots to create shading—he magnified the spectacle of comics and other "throwaway" art, injecting drama and irony into a supposedly disposable form and providing a crucial early model for much of the "postmodern" art that followed.

Lichtenstein was born on October 27, 1923, into a relatively prosperous New York City family. His father, Milton, owned a real estate firm. Roy graduated from Benjamin Franklin High School; though he did not study art there, he frequently painted and drew at home. Lichtenstein remembered that his father encouraged him in his artistic interests. He "thought that you should do something you like because you're going to spend your life doing it," the artist remarked in *ArtNews*.

666

Drew Maps during World War II

After high school Lichtenstein took a summer class at New York's prestigious Art Students League; he began attending Ohio State University the subsequent fall. It was one of the few colleges at the time that offered a course in studio art. Lichtenstein's studies were interrupted by the outbreak of World War II, during which he served three years drawing maps for the Allied invasion of Germany. He returned to Ohio State in 1946 and finished his bachelor's degree, going on to obtain his master's in 1949. That year he wed his first wife, Isabel Wilson; they were married twenty years and had two sons.

During the 1950s Lichtenstein held a variety of jobs to support himself and his family, working on art projects during his free time. Among other occupations, he designed window displays, worked for graphics and engineering companies, and taught art at several universities. During this period Lichtenstein's work shared some elements of abstract painting, which generally dispenses with an external subject to focus instead on the interplay of values like color and texture in order to express some emotional truth. Lichtenstein borrowed attributes of this stylistic mode, but he re-introduced a subject, often ''cowboys and Indians'' and other generic scenes from the American West. Lichtenstein was unsatisfied with this approach, however, and spent the ensuing years in search of an appropriate style. After his sons were born in the mid-1950s, he began to experiment with painting and drawing cartoons to entertain them.

In 1960 Lichtenstein began teaching at Douglass College, part of Rutgers University in New Jersey. Due in part to the influence of several artists he met at the time, he began using ideas from his cartoons. He also found inspiration in comic strips and bubble gum wrappers, sometimes blowing them up to see what they would look like in this exaggerated form. Other artists of the time, most notably Andy Warhol, were also beginning to use images from consumer culture in their work. Lichtenstein was intrigued by these subjects and developed a totally new technique to present them.

Lichtenstein's basic mode changed very little from the time he developed and perfected it in the early 1960s. It consisted of three primary elements: thick, black borders defining objects and figures in order to emphasize the flatness of the

space contained by them, brilliant—sometimes even lurid—primary colors, and the use of the Benday dot, a technique used in printing. It was named after Benjamin Day, a printer who developed this method of drafting dots of various sizes to indicate shading in printed pictures. Varying the amount of space between the points makes areas appear dark or light; the dots are printed on a printing press through screens or stencils with holes punched in them.

Used Dot Method to Make Art of ''Trash''

Lichtenstein particularly liked the mechanical look of the Benday system, though he did not use it mechanically. Instead, his dots were painted on by hand through the screen, sometimes with a toothbrush. Lichtenstein's desire was to approximate the look of commercially printed art. ''The technique,'' wrote Lichtenstein, ''since it was taken from printing, tells you that this is a picture of a picture, a reproduction.'' This was a new twist on the recurring question of what constitutes art; Lichtenstein had actually disguised the ''authentic'' medium of painting as the supposedly less valuable reproduction. He later attested that this approach ''turned out to be so interesting that eventually it became impossible for me to do any other kind of painting.''

Whaam! by Roy Lichtenstein

The first such work to gain Lichtenstein substantial attention was *Look Mickey!,* which depicts cartoon characters Mickey Mouse and Donald Duck fishing on a dock. Of course, critics objected that cartoons were not serious art and thus did not deserve a place in galleries and museums. But others realized that Lichtenstein was commenting on the widespread images of popular culture familiar to everyone, just as paintings of Greek gods would have been familiar to mainstream audiences of the past. Many found Lichtenstein's subject matter a breath of fresh air in contrast to the often somber and highly intellectual style of abstract expressionism, which had come to dominate the art world in the 1950s.

Reproduced Scenes from Comic Strips

In 1961 and 1962 Lichtenstein perfected his technique, making the dots larger and line and color crisper. He studied other subjects, such as advertising images from newspapers, the telephone directory, and even restaurant menus; rather than copy the images, he reproduced them in his own style. He also borrowed scenes from popular comic strips—especially romance comics—and painted them complete with speech bubbles. Some of his most familiar works portray worried young women wondering aloud about their love lives. Lichtenstein also painted war scenes, inspired by a mixture of his own experiences, comics, and the popular war movies of the 1940s and 1950s. One of his most famous works, *Blam!,* features a fighter plane exploding and twisting in the air. Lichtenstein commented, ''I like to make explosions into elaborate beautiful forms, which is what they

become in a comic strip.'' This was the first time a painter had used modern wartime technology as a subject.

As the 1960s progressed Lichtenstein applied his style to several other scenes, including landscapes and sunsets. In *Sinking Sun,* he painted the sun descending beneath a large cloud formation, around which its rays shine. But, according to the artist, this was not a ''real'' landscape. In Lichtenstein's words, ''It gives you the idea of landscape. But . . . it's far from reality, as artificial as it can be. It's telling you that you are looking at something beautiful, even though you know you are not. On the other hand, maybe you are.'' In fact, the unreliability of a painting, the mixed message of beauty and fakery—as opposed to the older ideal of the artwork as a window onto a beautiful world—is a staple of contemporary artistic thought.

Mocking and Paying Tribute

Lichtenstein also on occasion ''copied'' paintings by well-known artists, taking figures or scenes painted by Pablo Picasso, Henri Matisse, Piet Mondrian, and others and adapting them to his comic-strip style. One of his most famous copies is of the series of paintings of the cathedral in Rouen, France, by Claude Monet. Monet helped pioneer the nineteenth-century style called impressionism. In this manner he painted several views of the cathedral to show how the shifting sunlight changed the scene's appearance. Lichtenstein painted his five views of the church using his dot and stencil method to make ''a mechanical representation of Impressionism.'' In such efforts, he is at once mocking these old masters and paying tribute to them.

Lichtenstein also parodied abstract expressionism in his brush stroke paintings of the mid-1960s. The very act of using a brush to apply paint with a stroke was crucially important to the ideas behind abstract expressionism. Lichtenstein made fun of such grandiose theories by painting cartoon-like images of brush strokes. He wrote, ''It amused me that the brushstrokes I made were actually fake and tediously drawn out rather than being brushstrokes at all.'' Lichtenstein also applied this spirit to paintings of architectural monuments like the pyramids of Egypt and ruins of ancient Greek temples.

Combined Styles to Focus on New Themes

In the 1970s Lichtenstein again turned to new themes, among them ''mirrors''—actually round and oval canvases with areas of solid color and dots. His *Self-portrait* of 1978 presents the shoulder area of a t-shirt above which, where the head should be, is a mirror; this playful flim-flam was inspired by a painting by the surrealist painter René Magritte. Lichtenstein also painted still lifes in various modern styles during the decade.

The 1980s and 1990s brought more change to Lichtenstein's work. Several paintings of the period combine his cartoon style with the ideas of abstract expressionism. In *Two Paintings: Radiator and Folded Sheets,* he displays a pair of compositions hung side by side on a wall of which the viewer sees only a portion. One composition, the radiator, is rendered in a style resembling 1950s abstract art, while the other, the folded sheets, is represented in his recognizable comic-strip style.

This painting of two paintings hanging on a wall—the section of wall actually the canvas itself—emphasizes Lichtenstein's desire to make viewers question his medium. Which portion of this illusion is ''real?'' Yet even as he posed these challenges, Lichtenstein retained his characteristic humor and sense of the absurd. Perhaps more ironically, reproductions of his most familiar cartoon works themselves were embraced by the consumer culture, appearing on everything from greeting cards to billboards.

Lichtenstein was actively at work until he died unexpectedly, of complications from pneumonia on September 29, 1997, in New York City. Upon his death, *New York Times* art critic Michael Kimmelman called him ''the quintessential master of Pop painting.''

Sources for More Information

Books

Alloway, Lawrence, *Roy Lichtenstein,* Abbeville Press, 1983.

Walker, Lou Ann, *Roy Lichtenstein: The Artist at Work,* Lodestar Books, 1994.

Periodicals

Art in America, December, 1997.

New York Times, September 30, 1997.

Maya Lin

**Designer and sculptor
(1959-)**

"Lin's Vietnam Memorial has become a place of pilgrimage and healing, functioning as a spiritual sanctuary."

—Judith E. Stein

Born October 5, 1959, in Athens, OH; daughter of Henry Huan (dean of the Ohio University art school and a ceramic artist) and Julia Chang (an Ohio University professor of English and Asian literature and poet) Lin. Education: Yale University, B.A., 1981, M.Arch., 1986; attended Harvard University Graduate School of Design, 1983.

Sculptor and architect Maya Lin is best known as the designer of the Vietnam Veterans Memorial in Washington, D.C. Conceived as a place for personal reflection and healing, the v-shaped incision in the landscape was harshly criticized by some who favored a figurative monument. Today, the memorial is the most popular in Washington, and is visited by more than a million visitors annually. Inscribed with the names of the 58,000 servicemen killed or missing in Vietnam, the memorial has indeed become what Lin anticipated: a sanctuary for both grief and reconciliation. Although made wary of celebrity by the controversy that surrounded her throughout the construction and unveiling of the memorial, Lin regularly produces works at the public scale. In addition to her uncommon sensitivity to site and social context, critics routinely call attention to Lin's ability to erode the boundaries that have traditionally existed between architecture and sculpture.

Maya Lin was born on October 5, 1959, in the small college town of Athens, Ohio. Her parents,

Julia Chang Lin and Henry Huan Lin, immigrated to the United States from China in 1940. Both were esteemed members of the faculty at Ohio University, and they provided Maya with an environment that stimulated both her imagination and her intellectual curiosity. Maya's father was dean of the Ohio University art school and a well-known ceramic artist with his own studio, where Maya explored her creativity through the earthen materials of his craft. Julia Lin was a poet and professor of Asian and English literature, and she imbued her daughter with a love of reading.

During her school years Maya demonstrated a facility for mathematics and art. She was an above average student, and in high school took college level courses to challenge herself. It was during these studies that she was exposed to the existentialist writings of Albert Camus and Jean Paul Sartre. Existentialist philosophy, in combination with the reading of poetry encouraged by her mother, exerted a strong influence in Lin's later memorial designs. When she wasn't studying, Lin spent her free time reading, or indulging her love of nature with a walk in the woods.

Sculpture or Architecture?

After graduating from high school as co-valedictorian of her class, Lin entered Yale University in New Haven, Connecticut. There she realized her irresistible affinity for both architecture and sculpture. Despite teachers who encouraged her to pursue one discipline or the other, she found it impossible to choose between the two. Although her field of concentration was officially architecture, she was often in the art school where she took classes in sculpture.

Lin spent 1979, her junior year at Yale, abroad and made a point of visiting cemeteries throughout Europe. When she returned to Yale the following year, she enrolled in a funerary architecture design studio. As a requirement for the class, she entered the nationwide Vietnam Veterans Memorial design competition. In November of 1980, Lin visited the proposed site for the memorial, the Mall in Washington, D.C. While photographing the Mall (a grassy promenade around which many commemorative monuments are arranged), she was moved by its near emptiness. Any memorial located there, Lin concluded, must be experienced through the simultaneous acts of moving and viewing. To accomplish this, she employed two low, black granite walls, which converge at one end of the site. The walls are set into the earth, opening a space below ground. In the statement she submitted with her competition entry, Lin explained that visitors would proceed along one wall toward the narrow end of this space, and then turn and follow the other wall out. She intended this pattern of movement to be analogous to the experience of loss. Visitors see both the sky and their images mirrored in the highly polished surface of the granite, engraved with the names of roughly sixty thousand dead and missing veterans from the Vietnam War.

Vietnam Veterans Memorial

Lin's scheme was selected from 1,420 entries (the largest design competition in the history of the United States) and was revealed to the public in the spring of 1981. Public reaction was a mix of surprise and disappointment. Lin was still a twenty-one-year-old student, remarkably young to receive such a distinguished commission, and her design differed radically from heroic monuments of the past. The judges' decision invited contention. Protests against the memorial were organized by veterans groups who found the design too abstract. Coverage in the media and comments by fellow artists continued to fuel the debate over the appropriateness of the design. As emotions reached the boiling point, Lin herself was victimized by racist and sexist slurs. As she told Jim Sexton in *USA Weekend*, ''All I could think about at the time was: [All this anger] is not about the art. This is about the country coming to terms with something.''

Eventually, without Lin's input, a compromise was reached. A bronze monument composed of three servicemen supporting an American flag was to be added to the site, approximately 120 feet from the entrance to her memorial. The memorial committee never notified Lin of their decision; she heard it in a television news broadcast.

In the fall of 1982, Lin graduated cum laude from Yale and began graduate studies in architecture at Harvard University. Lin attempted to resume the inconspicuous life of a student. The opening of the Vietnam Veterans Memorial, however, was scheduled for that November. Although

Vietnam Veteran's War Memorial by Maya Lin

she was the principal designer and had overseen the construction, Lin's name was not mentioned during the dedication ceremonies. Frustrated and disillusioned, she found herself unable to focus on her classes and withdrew from Harvard's Graduate School of Design. She spent most of 1983 working in the Boston architecture office of Peter Forbes & Associates.

Despite the negative criticism associated with the memorial, both critics and visitors immediately responded to its power. "Lin's Vietnam Memorial has become a place of pilgrimage and healing, functioning as a spiritual sanctuary," asserted Judith E. Stein in *Art in America*. Lin told Sexton, "I designed it so that a child a hundred years from now will still be able to go to that piece and have a sober understanding about a high price of the war."

Beyond the Wall

In the fall of 1983, Maya returned to Yale to resume the education she had abandoned at Harvard. She studied with architect Frank Gehry, known for his sculptural approach to architecture, and sculptor Richard Serra, whose large public

works have often stirred controversy. Before completing graduate school, Lin also held an internship in Tokyo, Japan, with internationally renowned architect Fumihiko Maki. After receiving her masters degree in architecture in the spring of 1986, Lin worked in Peter Forbes's New York office, where she held the position of design associate.

In 1987 Lin founded her own studio in New York City. Projects from this early period of independent work include "Aligning Reeds," an installation of aluminum rods in a Connecticut stream bed, and "TOPO," grounds designed in collaboration with landscape architect Henry Arnold. "TOPO" occupies the median between incoming and outgoing traffic at the entrance to the Charlotte Coliseum in North Carolina. Topiary shrubs on the site are pruned to maintain precise spherical forms.

In the winter of 1987, Maya received a request from the Southern Poverty Law Center of Montgomery, Alabama, to design a memorial to those who died advancing the Civil Rights Movement. Although she was initially reluctant to design another memorial, she later embraced the opportunity. Lin researched the movement and its era for several months before visiting the site with representatives from the center. She found inspiration in a phrase from the Old Testament, which civil rights leader Dr. Martin Luther King, Jr. had quoted in his pivotal "I Have a Dream" speech of 1963. "We will not be satisfied," Dr. King proclaimed, "until 'justice rolls down like water and righteousness like a mighty stream.'"

In Lin's memorial for the Southern Poverty Law Center, those words are etched into a curving granite wall, in front of which rests a horizontal granite disk, twelve feet in diameter. A catalogue of the major events in the Civil Rights Movement, and names of activists murdered because of the roles they played, are inscribed on the upper surface of the disk. Water flows over the disk, at a barely perceptible rate, from a small hole in its center. "I realized that I wanted to create a time line," Lin told William Zinsser of *Smithsonian,* "a chronological listing of the movement's major events and its individual deaths, which together would show how people's lives influence history and made things better."

Masterworks

The Women's Table

Lin spent the early part of the 1990s designing a private residence in Williamstown, Massachusetts, and renovating a New York loft for a new Museum for African Art. Critics praised Lin's bold use of color as a backdrop for non-western art in the latter design. In 1992 Lin received a commission from Yale to design a monument commemorating women at the university. For this, Maya produced "The Women's Table," a three-foot-high elliptical table made of green granite, washed by a thin film of water. The table is engraved, in spiraling fashion, with the number of women students enrolled at Yale each year, beginning in 1701, with the college's founding, and concluding in 1993 with installation of the table. The majority of numbers are zeroes, depicting women's exclusion from the university until well into the nineteenth century.

In 1993, Lin accepted an invitation to become an artist in residence at the Wexner Center for the Visual Arts at Ohio State University. At the Wexner Center Lin produced "Ground Swell," a permanent installation within the building. "Ground Swell" occupies areas of the building that were never intended to be seen, including a rooftop. Lin

executed three versions of "Ground Swell," requiring a total of forty-three tons of shattered safety glass. Two of the installations were formed by spilling the glass, which had been lifted by a crane under Lin's direction, selectively over the chosen sites. Handled this way, the glittering glass forms small mounds, like sand poured from a pail. The third installation was raked into shape. Shortly after its completion, a vandal splashed red paint on the third "Ground Swell," requiring its removal and replacement.

Maya returned to her studio in 1994 and designed "Eclipsed Time," a fourteen-foot-long clock for the Long Island Railroad Terminal at New York City's Pennsylvania Station. Like a sundial, the piece measures time by casting a shadow across a graduated scale on the ceiling.

Wave Field

In October of 1995 Lin's "Wave Field" was dedicated at the University of Michigan's François-Xavier Bagnoud aerospace engineering building. While conducting background research for the project, Lin obtained an obscure work on fluid dynamics which contained an image of a stable, three-dimensional waveform. Excited by its beauty, Lin began a series of models exploring the form, culminating in the construction of "Wave Field." The project is composed entirely of soil and grass sculpted into the undulating waveform Lin found so compelling. In a press release issued by the Francois-Xavier Bagnoud foundation, Lin said, ''The 'Wave Field' is very special because it expresses my desire to completely integrate a work with its site. It reveals the connectedness of art to landscape, and landscape as art.''

Lin continues to accept large commissions, and has worked on installations for the Rockefeller Foundation and the new Federal Courthouse in Manhattan, New York. She frequently exhibits her smaller works in galleries in New York City. In the spring of 1996, Harvard University president presented Lin with an Honorary Doctor of Fine Arts degree. Expressing what many feel about her work, Harvard president Neil Rudenstine lauded Maya Lin as ''[a]n artist of resourcefulness and grace: poignant in remembrance of a nation's anguish, eloquent in synthesis of sculpture and design.''

Sources for More Information

Periodicals

Architectural Record, September, 1998.

Art in America, September, 1998.

Graphis, January-February, 1998.

USA Weekend, November 1–3, 1996.

Video

Maya Lin: A Strong, Clear Vision, Sanders & Mock Productions, 1997.

Robert Lipsyte

**Novelist and journalist
(1938–)**

*Born January 16, 1938, in New York, NY; son of Sidney I. (a
principal) and Fanny (a teacher; maiden name, Finston)
Lipsyte; children: Sam, Susannah. Education: Columbia
University, B.A., 1957, M.S., 1959.*

R obert Lipsyte, a journalist who covered
sports for the *New York Times* from the late
1950s to the early 1970s, has written books for
children and young adults. Lipsyte gained national
attention as a result of his sports columns. His
books feature characters who experience a transformation through a combination of hard work and
adherence to ethics. Not surprisingly, the majority
of the author's books also involve aspects of
athletics and, because of his experience as a sportswriter, Lipsyte is considered an authority in the
field of children's sports stories. In an article for
Children's Literature in Education, the author
commented, ''I don't think we have to make any
rules for sports books for children beyond asking
that they present some sense of truth about the role
of sports in our lives.''

In the article, Lipsyte also commented, ''Sports
is, or should be, just one of the things people
do—an integral part of life, but only one aspect of
it. Sports is a good experience. It's fun. It ought to
be inexpensive and accessible to everybody.'' He
added, ''In our society, sports is a negative experience for most boys and almost all girls. . . . They're
required to define themselves on the basis of
competitive physical ability.'' And, according to

*''If we write more truthfully about
sports, perhaps we can encourage
kids to relax and have fun with each
other. . . .''*

Lipsyte, sports programs are not fair because individuals with only average ability are quickly weeded out of the system.

These problems, evident in organized sports, have led Lipsyte to question the appropriateness of the nation's fixation with all levels of athletic competition. The author maintains that Americans are taught that it is good to obey a screaming coach and play even when hurt. He thinks that media coverage of sporting events promotes this myth and invites spectators to watch others play instead of participating in sports themselves. In his work *SportsWorld: An American Dreamland,* Lipsyte recounts his career as a sportswriter, using encounters with athletes in baseball, football, basketball, boxing, and tennis to give examples of and validate his philosophy.

Gets Start in Newspapers

The young Lipsyte spent hours reading and decided early on to become a writer. He received an undergraduate degree in English from Columbia University in New York and planned to continue his education by attending graduate school. Yet, unpredictably, his career as a sports reporter began. Answering an ad for a copy boy at the *Times,* he found himself working nights in the sports department, filling paste-pots, sharpening pencils, and fetching coffee for editors. Despite his decidedly unglamorous entrance into the sports department, Lipsyte opted to stay and eventually moved from his copy boy to statistician to night rewrite reporter.

Lipsyte seemed enamored with the newsroom's colorful figures and hectic pace and was eager to test his writing skills. He earned his first major assignment for the paper in 1962, covering the New York Mets in that baseball team's first year of existence. Lipsyte began covering the boxing beat for the *New York Times* in 1964 and followed Muhammad Ali's career for more than three years. In his biography of the boxer titled *Free to Be Muhammad Ali,* the author categorized Ali as ''far and away the most interesting character in that mythical kingdom I call SportsWorld.''

Debut Novel about Boxing

Lipsyte drew upon his experiences as a boxing writer to produce his first novel for young readers, *The Contender.* The protagonist, Alfred Brooks, is an orphaned seventeen-year-old boy living in Harlem. A recent high school dropout, Alfred lives with his aunt and works as a stock boy in a grocery store. The work chronicles the metamorphosis of the aimless Alfred into a disciplined young man with long-term goals.

In the fall of 1967, Lipsyte left the boxing beat to begin writing a general sports column for the *New York Times.* In *SportsWorld* he remarked, ''It was an exciting time to be writing a column, to be freed from the day-to-day responsibility for a single subject or the whims of the assignment desk. For me, after more than three years with Ali, the newly surfaced turmoil in sports seemed a natural climate.'' Responsible for three columns a week for the *New York Times,* Lipsyte had the freedom to choose his topics, but was still forced to adhere to stringent space limitations. He continued in *SportsWorld,* ''Professionally, there is a challenge, for a while at least, to creating within formalized boundaries. Over an extended period of time, however, it's a poor way to transmit information.''

Despite the acclaim his columns received, Lipsyte left the *New York Times* in the fall of 1971. In his book *Assignment: Sports* he remarked, ''I knew I'd miss the quick excitement of deadline journalism. . . . But I wanted more time to think about what I had seen during the past fourteen years, and more space to shape those thoughts into characters and stories.'' During the next eleven years he wrote books, taught journalism at college, visited schools to talk about his books, wrote jokes for a television show called *Saturday Night with Howard Cosell,* and spent nine months at the *New York Post* writing a column about the people of that city.

Lipsyte's ''Fifties'' Trilogy

In the late 1970s and early 1980s, Lipsyte wrote what he deemed a fifties trilogy consisting of the books *One Fat Summer, Summer Rules,* and *The Summerboy.* The author shares similarities with his protagonist, Bobby Marks, who also comes of age in the fifties and conquers an adolescent weight problem. Each book is set in a resort town in upstate New York called Rumson Lake where Bobby's family spends each summer. Lipsyte presents the maturation process of his protagonist from the age of fourteen to eighteen. Critics have endorsed the novels for tackling adolescent dilemmas in a realistic manner and for offering believable first-person narration.

Lipsyte was forced to battle his own problems beginning in the summer of 1978 when he was diagnosed with cancer; one year later his wife was also diagnosed with the disease. They later both suffered a recurrence. (In his 1998 work *In the Country of Illness: Comfort and Advice for the Journey,* Lipsyte chronicles their fight.) Both survived the ordeal, and eventually Lipsyte was able to return to writing.

Lipsyte's next book, *Jock and Jill,* involves themes of social responsibility and the use of pain-killing drugs in athletics. Following the publication of *Jock and Jill,* Lipsyte began another career as a television correspondent for the CBS-TV program *Sunday Morning.* He then worked as a correspondent for NBC-TV and became the host of *The Eleventh Hour* PBS program, a combination talk and interview show.

Pens Sequels

Although Lipsyte took an eight-year break from composing books, the urge to write never left him. In 1991, he published *The Brave,* a sequel to *The Contender,* his best-selling book. The idea for *The Brave*'s plot was formed while Lipsyte was on a journalism assignment at an American Indian reservation. There he met and talked with a young man who described his fear of being stuck on the reservation where high levels of disease, alcoholism, and unemployment existed. At the same time, he was also afraid of leaving the reservation and facing the ''white'' world and possible rejection and prejudice. Nonetheless, he ran away to New York City for a few days. Although he was caught and forced to return home, the action was one of personal triumph, and Lipsyte admired the boy's bravery.

In *The Brave,* Sonny Bear, a seventeen-year-old half-Indian runaway, meets Alfred Brooks in New York City. Alfred is now a forty-year-old police sergeant who seeks to curtail drug trafficking in the city. Sonny unwittingly becomes a pawn

*Cover of **The Brave***

in the drug war, yet is rescued by Alfred, who also teaches him how to box. In 1991, Lipsyte returned to the *New York Times* to write one sports column a week. In an interview with George Robinson in *Publishers Weekly* Lipsyte joked that his career is at the same place it began. ''It's 24 years later, I'm covering sports for the *Times* and writing a YA [young adult] novel about boxing!''

In 1993, Lipsyte returned to the world of young adult fiction with *The Chief.* In this book, a sequel to *The Contender* and *The Brave,* Lipsyte continues the story of Sonny Bear, now a title contender, and his relationship with his friend and publicist Marty Malcolm Witherspoon. As *School Library Journal* commented ''the major conflict is not who wins the boxing duels but how Sonny can use his hard-won fame to help his people resolve their problems.'' Lipsyte also sets up an interesting ''parallel between Sonny Bear's enthusiasm, doubt, and final recognition of strength and confidence in his boxing skills,'' suggested a *Voice of Youth Advocates* reviewer, ''and Martin's similar experiences in his writing skills.''

Also, in 1993, Lipsyte began writing sports biographies on some of the past as well as today's sports figures. In his first biography, *Jim Thorpe: 20th Century Jock,* Lipsyte not only tells Thorpe's

Don't Miss ...

The Contender, Harper, 1967

One Fat Summer, Harper, 1977

The Brave, Harper, 1991

The Chief, Harper, 1993

attempted to present athletic participation in a proper perspective for young readers. In an article for *Children's Literature in Education,* he concluded, "If we write more truthfully about sports, perhaps we can encourage kids to relax and have fun with each other—to challenge themselves for the pleasure of it, without self-doubt and without fear."

personal journey to the Olympics, but also as *Publishers Weekly* noted, "uses the story of 'perhaps the greatest all-around male athlete in American history' as a lens through which to examine the effects of racism on Native Americans." Other biographies include *Arnold Schwarzenegger: Hercules in America, Michael Jordan: A Life Above the Rim,* and *Joe Louis: A Champ for All America.*

Lipsyte continues to write his critical biographies about sports "heroes." He wishes that sports would once again be popular recreation instead of an industry that offers false hopes of stardom to millions of youngsters. As a writer, Lipsyte has

Sources for More Information

Books

Cart, Michael, *Presenting Robert Lipsyte,* Twayne, 1995.

Children's Literature Review, Volume 23, Gale, 1991.

Contemporary Literary Criticism, Volume 21, Gale, 1982.

St. James Guide to Young Adult Writers, St. James Press, 1999.

On-line

de Grummond Children's Literature Collection Web site, located at http://www.lib.usm.edu/~degrum/findaids/lipsyte.htm.

LL Cool J

**Rap singer and actor
(1968–)**

Born James Todd Smith in 1968, in Queens, NY; married, 1995; wife's name, Simone; children: one son, two daughters.

"I'm a lot more than an entertainer who wears hats and rolls up his pant's leg."

Arguably the most popular and influential member of the hip-hop nation, LL Cool J has established himself as a premiere multi-faceted entertainer and entrepreneur. His anti-violence, anti-drugs, and anti-degradation of women approach to rap and hip-hop was often times at odds with the prevailing mood of the genre. Undaunted by this, LL Cool J soldiered on, following his own vision, while the rest of the hip-hop nation tried to keep up the pace.

LL Cool J was never a proponent of the harshly violent urban imagery found in the gangsta rap genre. He explained his stance on violence in the Def Jam website: "I don't like violence. I've seen violence, seen people I love be the victims of violence and there's nothing cool about it. It plainly just doesn't interest me."

Violence in the Home

While growing up in the St. Alban's area of Queens, New York, LL Cool J was a witness to violence in his own home. He was only four years old when his mother left his father after suffering years of physical and mental abuse. His mother moved in with her parents and tried to make a new life for herself, away from her abusive husband.

679

LL Cool J's father was not so easily deterred, however, and was determined to win back his estranged wife. When she refused to return, LL Cool J's father shot her in the lower back with a 12-gauge shotgun. Rushing to see what had happened, LL Cool J also discovered that his grandfather had been shot in the stomach. Commenting on the shooting, LL Cool J related to *Jet* that "I ran to get towels from the bathroom. When I pushed them into my grandfather's stomach, I could see where his flesh had been ripped apart. . . . The way my family handled that incident—no charges pressed, that forgiveness—showed love in a way I have never seen since. From the way my family dealt with the shooting, I learned forgiveness and gained inner strength. That lesson helped me become who I am today."

Yet, LL Cool J's troubles were not over. As his mother was recovering from the wounds, she met a man who was willing to help and support her during her long period of convalescence. Unfortunately for LL Cool J, his mother's pillar of strength viewed her young son as his personal whipping boy, physically and mentally abusing him.

Seeks Relief in Music

Seeking some solace and refuge from the abuse, LL Cool J began to immerse himself in rap music. He recalled to *Jet*, "the music and rhymes helped me escape all the pain." He was rapping at nine years old, and soon afterward invented his stage name; LL Cool J was an acronym for "ladies love cool James." A gift from his grandfather was the impetus young LL Cool J needed to start his rap career. The 13-year-old had asked for a dirt bike but his grandfather, fearing for his young grandson's future, declined to honor his request and gave him some musical and recording equipment instead. Soon the high school student was strutting his stuff and flexing his vocal cords for his enraptured classmates. He began producing his own demo tapes and sending them off to the major labels with rap departments and artists. Yet the only response came from the fledgling New York-based Def Jam label.

LL Cool J signed with Def Jam, and in 1984 released his first single "I Need a Beat." The 16-year-old's song was the first single ever released by Def Jam, and his debut album, *Radio,* earned the distinction of being the first album released by Def Jam as well. The year 1985 also marked the beginning of LL Cool J's acting career as he was offered a cameo appearance in the hip-hop film *Krush Groove.* By the following year, he was on tour with some of the biggest and most notorious names in hip-hop and rap at the time, including the Beastie Boys and Run DMC.

Mama Said Knock You Out

His second album, 1987's *Bigger & Deffer,* featured the songs "I'm Bad," which became a top five R&B hit, and "I Need Love," a gentle rap ballad that became the first rap song to reach the top of the Hot Black Singles chart. *Walking with a Panther* was released in 1989 and spawned the hit song "Going Back to Cali." The following year saw the phenomenal breakthrough success of *Mama Said Knock You Out,* which tended to overshadow LL Cool J's previous accomplishments. *Mama Said Knock You Out* produced two tremendously popular hit songs. The first was "Around the Way Girl" which topped the rap and R&B charts, and became a *Billboard* top ten single. The album's title track fared even better, earning LL Cool J the 1991 Grammy Award for the best solo rap performance. This recording remained on the *Billboard* Top Pop Albums chart for over a year and lasted nearly 18 months on the Top Black Albums chart. Also in 1991, LL Cool J starred in the film *The Hard Way.*

In 1992 the rap star established the Camp Cool J Foundation, a non-profit organization that funded free camping, educational, cultural and recreational activities for young people across America. In his website, he explained his motivation behind the founding of Camp Cool J: "it's a place where kids who have achieved good grades in school and performed some community service can go to improve their academic skills and enjoy nature. Kids from around my way never had the chance to get out of the city in the summertime. I wish I had that somebody I looked up to who would scoop me up from the neighborhood and say 'Come on, we're going to put you in camp for free.'" That same year, he appeared in the film *Toys,* and in 1993 released his next album, *14 Shots to the Dome.*

Acting, Writing, Rapping

The year 1995 was another watershed for LL Cool J. That autumn, he finally wed Simone, his high school sweetheart and the mother of his three children. They were married in Long Island. LL Cool J also starred in the film *Out of Sync* and began a new career as a television actor. He had the starring role in the popular television program *In the House.*

On the music front, LL Cool J released his sixth consecutive platinum album, *Mr. Smith,* which was the showcase for a wiser and older performer. The artist claimed that *Mr. Smith* was the most honest and open album that he had created so far. He also continued to record and release the sensitive and romantic rap ballads that were becoming some of his signature songs. ''Hey Lover'' was no exception; the platinum single featured backing vocals by the R&B innovators Boyz II Men. The song shot to number three on the *Billboard* Hot 100 chart and earned LL Cool J his second Grammy

LL Cool J (right) and friends

Popular Works

Albums

Radio, Def Jam, 1985

Bigger & Deffer, Def Jam, 1987

Walking with a Panther, Def Jam, 1989

Mama Said Knock You Out, Def Jam, 1990

14 Shots to the Dome, Def Jam, 1993

Phenomenon, Def Jam, 1997

Films

Halloween H20, Dimension Films, 1998

Television

In the House, NBC, 1995–96; UPN, 1996–98

Award in 1996 for best solo rap performance. Also in 1996, Def Jam released his greatest hits album *All Change*.

The rapper released his eighth album, *Phenomenon*, in 1997. That year, he also starred in the film *Baps* and released his autobiography *I Make My Own Rules*. He commented in the Def Jam website that the release of the book was "a testimony to my growth and development as a human being. It's a way to show people how to go through negativity and come out on top if you just focus, concentrate and believe in spirituality. A lot of the songs on the album [*Phenomenon*] apply to chapters in the book, so there's an inter-relationship to the book and album."

Promoting his book in *Jet*, LL Cool J stated that "I'm a lot more than an entertainer who wears hats and rolls up his pant's leg. I'm a father with three beautiful children. I'm a husband with a wonderful wife. I'm a healing victim of abuse who has made many mistakes along the way. My real name is James Todd Smith, and in real life I am a man."

Sources for More Information

Periodicals

Billboard, January 6, 1996, pp. 12–14.

Entertainment Weekly, December 1, 1995, p. 74; July 11, 1997, p. 61.

Jet, October 9, 1995, p. 40; September 22, 1997, pp. 37–42; August 10, 1998.

National Review, October 14, 1996, p. 94.

People, October 20, 1997.

Rolling Stone, October 28, 1998; May 13, 1999.

TV Guide, October 18, 1997.

On-line

Def Jam Records Web site, located at http://www.defjam.com/artists/llcoolj/coolj03.html.

Jennifer Lopez

**Actress
(1970–)**

Born July 24, 1970, in the Bronx, New York, NY; daughter of David (a computer specialist) and Guadalupe (a teacher) Lopez; married Ojani Noa, February, 1997 (divorced, 1998).

"You know, I am ambitious and I am confident, but who isn't in this business?"

Latina actress Jennifer Lopez's wide range and her motivation to succeed has led to her breakthrough as a leading lady on the big screen. She started her Hollywood career in 1990 as one of the attractive and high-energy "fly girl" dancers on *In Living Color,* then worked her way into acting in some television pilots. Her film debut was in the multigenerational *Mi Familia (My Family),* with Jimmy Smits, and she went on to work with other giant names including Jack Nicholson and Robin Williams. After a stunning starring role in 1997 in *Selena* as the murdered Tejano singer, Lopez broke through the barrier of being typecast in ethnic roles when she starred in 1998 with George Clooney as a headstrong U.S. marshal in *Out of Sight.* Unabashedly ambitious, Lopez has worked hard and takes credit for her rise. She says that success in Hollywood, rather than being a case of luck, is "about being prepared when your opportunity comes, about being able to perform under pressure," she told Rene Rodriguez for Knight Ridder Newspapers, printed in the *Arizona Republic.* "If you're going in to audition for Oliver Stone or Francis Ford Coppola, are you gonna choke?. . . If you have a good day that day, then it's not luck. It's because you made it happen."

Lopez was born on July 24, 1970, in the Bronx, New York, the second of three daughters, including her younger sister, Lynda, and older sister, Leslie. Lopez's father, David, is a computer specialist for an insurance firm and her mother, Guadalupe ("Lupe") is a kindergarten teacher at Holy Family School in the Bronx. They are both Puerto Rican. Even as a child, Lopez wanted to be a star, despite the near-absence of Latina role models in Hollywood. David Handelman remarked in *Mirabella,* "She watched *West Side Story* over and over, dreaming of being the next Rita Moreno." As a teenager, Lopez dressed in a tomboy fashion until seeing Madonna and her ever-changing appearance. "I always admired her, liked her music, her sense of style," Lopez commented to Handelman.

Dancing Talent

Lopez graduated from Holy Family School, where her mother teaches, and went on to Baruch College in New York City. She dropped out after one semester to pursue her dancing career. While studying jazz and ballet, Lopez aspired to appear on Broadway, and in fact appeared overseas in two productions: *Golden Musicals of Broadway,* which toured Europe, and *Synchronicity,* which toured in Japan. She tried auditioning for commercials, but her heart was not in it. When hip-hop became popular, she found a niche. Lopez competed with over two thousand other hopefuls to win a spot in 1990 as one of the energetic "fly girl" dancers on the Fox comedy *In Living Color.* After staying with that for a while, the husband of one of her fellow dancers cast Lopez in a pilot that he wrote and produced called *South Central.* Though the show never made it, Lopez was getting noticed and won parts in other series pilots as well as a made-for television movie in 1993 called *Nurses on the Line: The Crash of Flight 7.*

The big-screen breakthrough for Lopez came in 1995 with a supporting part in the film *Mi Familia (My Family),* an epic story covering a number of generations of a Latino family. It also starred Jimmy Smits. Following that, Lopez landed roles in *Money Train* (1995); *Jack* (1996), starring Robin Williams; and the film noir thriller *Blood & Wine* (1997), starring Jack Nicholson. Also in 1997 Lopez made *Anaconda* and Oliver Stone's *U-Turn.* She blossomed, though, with her acclaimed starring performance in the 1997 film

Selena, about the life of the Tejano singer who was shot to death in 1995. For her portrayal, Lopez reportedly became the first Latina actress to earn $1 million.

Portrays Latina Star

Selena was revered throughout the Latino world, and for the picture, Lopez lived with Selena's family for a while to replicate the singer as closely as possible. She lip-synched to Selena's music and wore the reproductions of the singer's colorful original costumes, made from the same patterns and by Selena's own seamstress. Lopez even painted her nails with Selena's favorite color polish, L'Oreal Sangria, thanks to advice from the singer's sister Suzette, and got tips from the family on how to hold the microphone the same way as Selena did. Some Latinos protested Lopez playing the part, since Lopez is from Puerto Rican descent and not Mexican. However, the film and Lopez's portrayal were well-received; Lopez won the Imagen Foundation Lasting Image Award and the Lone Star Film & Television Award for the role, and was nominated for a Golden Globe and MTC Movie Award.

After the filming of *Selena,* Lopez's boyfriend, Ojani Noa, proposed to her at a big party and she accepted. They had met while he was waiting tables in Miami and were married about a year later, in February of 1997, but divorced sometime in 1998. Lopez did not comment on the separation, and Noa has been relatively quiet except to say that Lopez paid for their divorce and gave him some money, and that they are still friends. After their breakup, the press has speculated widely regarding her romantic affairs, linking her with musician and music company executive Sean "Puff Daddy" Combs, Sony music chief Tommy Mottola, and R&B singer Maxwell. She has denied all of the rumors, insisting that she is just friends with all of them.

Also in 1998, Lopez made a splash costarring with George Clooney in the crime story *Out of Sight.* As U.S. marshal Karen Sisco, Lopez is kidnapped by Clooney's character, Jack Foley, a bank robber, just as he is breaking out of prison. Not a violent sort, and in fact rather gentlemanly, Foley only abducts Sisco when she unwittingly messes up the breakout plan. The unlikely pair—cop

*Movie still from **Mi Familia (My Family)***

and crook—develop a romantic attraction to each other, although they know it is doomed. Philip Wuntch of the *Dallas Morning News* noted that "the film retains the wit and tempo of Elmore Leonard's novel. . . . *Out of Sight* manages to be both wry in tone and energetic in its telling." He added, "Ms. Lopez is terrific."

Critical Backlash

Despite—or perhaps because of—Lopez's newfound popularity, she went through a backlash after making some comments about fellow actresses in the magazine *Movieline*. Handelman in *Mirabella* mentioned that she made catty remarks about Gwyneth Paltrow, Winona Ryder, and Cameron Diaz, but Lopez later told Rodriguez that she was misunderstood. She sent apologies to her colleagues, but did not manage to shake her reputation as being "arrogant and temperamental," as Rodriguez put it. Lopez insisted to Handelman, "You know, I am ambitious and I am confident, but who isn't in this business?" She added, "And that [*Movieline*] article depicted me in a diva sort of way, like I'm not a nice person, and that was disturbing to me."

Whether or not she is nice, she is definitely in demand. Oliver Stone told Jeffrey Ressner in *Time*, "She's striking, strong, and has an extremely enthusiastic attitude." Lopez in the summer of 1998 worked on recording an album of pop and R&B songs for Sony and was set to star in a couple more films for 1999. Lopez told Rodriguez that being Latina is still an issue in casting for some directors, and that it is a constant battle to tend with. *Out of Sight* director Steven Soderbergh, however, claimed that he, for one, did not take into account Lopez's background. "I just thought she was the best actress for that part. Jennifer is ebullient, very positive and effervescent," Soderbergh told Rodriguez, adding, "She's really unique, because she can do just about anything, and it's not often you find someone with that kind of range."

Sources for More Information

Periodicals

Cosmopolitan, March, 1999.

In Style, May 1, 1997, p. 196.

Mirabella, July/August, 1998, p. 82.

Newsday, March 20, 1997, p. A4.

People, March 24, 1997, p. 160; May 10, 1999.

Premiere, August, 1998.

Time, March 24, 1998, p. 43.

USA Weekend, June 21, 1998, p. 18.

Vanity Fair, July, 1998, p. 114.

On-line

CelebSite Web site, located at http://www.celebsite.com.

Internet Movie Database, located at http://www.imdb.com.

Lois Lowry

**Young adult novelist
(1937-)**

Born March 20, 1937, in Honolulu, HI; daughter of Robert E. (a dentist) and Katharine (Landis) Hammersberg; married Donald Grey Lowry (an attorney), June 11, 1956 (divorced, 1977); children: Alix, Grey, Kristin, Benjamin. Education: Attended Brown University, 1954–56; University of Southern Maine, B.A., 1972, also graduate study.

"The most important things to me in my own life, as well as in my books, are human relationships of all kinds."

"The most important things to me in my own life, as well as in my books, are human relationships of all kinds," Lois Lowry once stated. "Although my books deal largely with families, I also attach a great deal of importance to friendships. Those are the things young people should pay attention to in their lives." Lowry's ability to explore young people's lives and relationships—in works both funny and serious—has made her one of today's most popular and critically acclaimed authors for young teens.

Lowry was born in 1937 in Honolulu, Hawaii. At the time of her birth, Lowry's father, a career army officer, was stationed at Schofield Barracks near Pearl Harbor. The family separated with the onset of World War II, and Lowry spent the duration of the war with her mother's family in the Amish Country of Pennsylvania. Her grandmother wasn't especially fond of children, but her grandfather adored her, and Lowry escaped the absolute trauma of war under the shelter of his affection. Much later, Lowry's wartime experience inspired her novel *Autumn Street.* As an author, Lowry has often translated her life into fiction for the purpose

*Cover of **The Giver***

couple who invite Meg to take pictures at the birth of their child.

A Summer to Die was well received by critics. The "story captures the mysteries of living and dying without manipulating the reader's emotions, providing understanding and a comforting sense of completion," observed Linda R. Silver in *School Library Journal.* Tragically, Lowry's sympathy for Meg and Molly was drawn from life. Her older sister, Helen, died of cancer when Lowry was twenty-five. "Very little of *[A Summer to Die]* was factual," she once commented, "except the emotions." The author added: "When my mother read the book she recognized the characters as my sister and me. She knew that the circumstances in the book were very different, but the characters had great veracity for her."

Following her successful debut as a novelist, Lowry continued to explore challenging adolescent topics. For example, she documented an adopted child's search for her biological mother in *Find a Stranger, Say Goodbye.* Although neither Lowry nor any of her children are adopted, she felt that the subject was important enough to be dealt with at length. She explained: "Maybe it's because of having watched my own kids go through the torture of becoming adults . . . that I think those kinds of issues are important and it's important to deal with them in a sensitive and compassionate way."

Memories of her childhood, as well as her experiences as a parent, have led Lowry to her most popular character: Anastasia Krupnik, the spunky, rebellious, and irreverent adolescent who stars in a series of books that began in 1979. The broad audience appeal of the first Anastasia book prompted Lowry to write more novels featuring her diminutive heroine. "I have the feeling she's going to go on forever—or until I get sick of her, which hasn't happened yet. I'm still very fond of her and her whole family," Lowry once remarked.

of helping others who may have suffered under similar circumstances. She once stated that she gauges her success as a writer by her ability to "help adolescents answer their own questions about life, identity and human relationships."

Courageous First Novel

Lowry's books have dealt with topics ranging from the death of a sibling and the Nazi occupation of Denmark, to the humorous antics of the rebellious Anastasia Krupnik. In her first novel, *A Summer to Die,* Lowry portrays an adolescent's struggle with her older sister's illness and eventual death. When the Chalmer's family moves to the country for the summer, 13-year-old Meg and 15-year-old Molly are forced to share a room. Already jealous of her older sister, Meg becomes increasingly argumentative and resentful when her sister's recurring nosebleeds become the focus of her parents' attention. As her sister's condition deteriorates, Meg realizes that Molly is slowly dying from leukemia. For friendship, she turns to old Will Banks, a neighbor who encourages her interest in photography, and Ben and Maria, a hippie

Focuses on Serious Issues

Lowry's fiction resumed a serious tone with the publication of *Rabble Starkey.* The twelve-year-old female protagonist Parable Ann ("Rabble") was born when her mother was fourteen. She and her mother now live with the Bigelow family while Mrs. Bigelow is hospitalized for mental illness. The care of Mrs. Bigelow's infant son, Gunther, falls primarily on the shoulders of Rabble and the Bigelow's daughter Veronica. "Their adventures meld into a warm and often surprising chronicle of small-town life," asserted a *Publishers Weekly* reviewer. "Secure in the Bigelow household, Rabble hopes for a better future." The Children's Book Committee of Bank Street College found the book equally appealing, awarding *Rabble Starkey* its Child Study Award in 1987.

In 1990 Lowry was awarded the Newbery Medal for her distinguished contribution to children's literature with *Number the Stars.* Based on a factual account, the story is set against the backdrop of Nazi-occupied Denmark. Ten-year-old Annemarie Johansen and her family are drawn into the resistance movement, shuttling Jews from Denmark into neutral Sweden. (During the Second World War this type of heroism insured the survival of nearly all of Denmark's Jews.) Newbery Committee Chair Caroline Ward was quoted by *School Library Journal:* "Lowry creates suspense and tension without wavering from the viewpoint of Annemarie, a child who shows the true meaning of courage."

A Dystopian Society

Well known for her realistic fiction as well as her comic chronicles of Anastasia, Lowry takes a very different direction in her second Newbery Award winner. *The Giver,* set in a future world, is the story of Jonas, who has been given his lifetime assignment at the age of twelve—to be the "Receiver" of his community's memories, leading him to discover terrible truths and finally to flee in desperation. In a story that is rich with allegory, "Lowry creates a chilling, tightly controlled future society where all controversy, pain, and choice have been expunged," observed a critic writing in *Kirkus Reviews.* "Lowry's development of this civilization is so deft," declared a contributor to *Publishers Weekly,* "that her readers, like the community's citizens, will be easily seduced by the chimera of this ordered, pain-free society." In

Don't Miss ...

A Summer to Die, Houghton, 1977

Find a Stranger, Say Goodbye, Houghton, 1978

Autumn Street, Houghton, 1979

Rabble Starkey, Houghton, 1987

Number the Stars, Houghton, 1989

The Giver, Houghton, 1993

a *Voice of Youth Advocates* review, Sister Mary Veronica, claimed *The Giver* "should take its place with [George] Orwell's *1984,* as a lesson written for young adults in their language."

With so many accomplishments in the field of children's literature to her credit, Lowry reflected on her career: "I remember the feeling of excitement that I had, the first time that I realized each letter had a sound and the sounds went together to make words, and the words became sentences and the sentences became stories.... Now, when I write, I draw a great deal from my own past. There is a satisfying sense of continuity, for me, in the realization that my own experiences, fictionalized, touch young readers in subtle and very personal ways."

Sources for More Information

Books

Chaston, Joel, *Lois Lowry,* Twayne, 1997.

Dictionary of Literary Biography, Volume 52: *American Writers for Children since 1960: Fiction,* Gale, 1987.

Markham, Lois, *Lois Lowry,* Learning Works, 1995.

Something About the Author Autobiography Series, Volume 3, Gale, 1986.

On-line

Dell Books Web site, located at www.dellbooks.com.

George Lucas

**Director, screenwriter, and
producer
(1944-)**

"I want Star Wars *to give people a
faraway, exotic environment for their
imagination to run free."*

*Born May 14, 1944, in Modesto, CA; son of George (a
retail merchant) and Dorothy Lucas; married Marcia
Griffin (a film editor), February 22, 1969 (divorced, 1984);
children: Amanda. Education: Modesto Junior College,
A.A., 1964; University of Southern California, B.A., 1966.*

George Lucas is one of the best-known names
in American filmmaking. His two trilogies
of films, the "Star Wars" and the "Indiana Jones"
epics, revolutionized the making of movies in
America during the 1970s and 1980s. They are
among the highest-grossing films of all time.
They also introduced a new generation of American children to unadulterated excitement, adventure, and optimism. Lucas's films typically mix
archetypal figures, familiar (but universal) themes,
and the eternal conflict between good heroes and
evil villains. In films such as *The Empire Strikes
Back* and *Indiana Jones and the Last Crusade,*
Lucas evokes mythic qualities in his characters. "I
want *Star Wars* to give people a faraway, exotic
environment for their imagination to run free,"
Lucas once told Jean Vallely in a *Rolling Stone*
interview.

Both the "Star Wars" and the "Indiana
Jones" films grew out of Lucas's own childhood
in Modesto, California. He was influenced during his 1950s childhood by trips to Disneyland,
reading comic books, and watching television.
But perhaps the greatest influence on his later
filmmaking career was television. "My favorite

things were Republic serials and things like Flash Gordon,'' he once told Kerry O'Quinn in *Starlog* magazine. "There was a television program called 'Adventure Theater' at 6:00 every night. We didn't have a TV set, so I used to go over to a friend's house and we watched it religiously.''

By the early 1960s, Lucas had moved into a different sphere. An early fascination with cars and automobile racing led to a serious accident in 1962. Lucas nearly died in the crash. His life was saved when his seat belt broke, throwing him free of the car. "You can't have that kind of experience and not feel that there must be a reason why you're here,'' he explained to Dale Pollack in the biography *Skywalking: The Life and Films of George Lucas.* "I realized that I should be spending my time trying to figure out what that reason is and trying to fulfill it.''

A Budding Filmmaker

Later that year, Lucas enrolled in Modesto Junior College, intending to study social sciences and concentrating in psychology, sociology, and anthropology. He completed the program and, following a friend's suggestion, enrolled in the film school at the University of Southern California in 1964. "I suddenly discovered how exciting films were,'' he says in an article in the *American Film Institute Report.* "I was fascinated by all the technical aspects of it. I never got over the magic of it all.''

One of the eight films Lucas made as a student was *Electronic Labyrinth: THX 1138: 4EB.* It was a science fiction film that presented a stark vision of a grim future, and traces every movement of a man on the run through the point of view of cameras and monitor screens placed along a blinding white corridor. It won the Best Film Award at the 3rd National Student Film Festival in 1967–68. It also won Lucas the attention of Hollywood powers and the esteem of his peers.

In July 1967, Lucas began an apprenticeship at Warner Brothers, working with Francis Ford Coppola. In 1967 and 1968, Lucas worked with Coppola on *Finian's Rainbow* and *The Rain People.* Later Coppola supported Lucas during the making of Lucas's first feature film, an expanded version of his student film *THX 1138. THX 1138* proved to have a rough trip to its release, and the film was released in 1971 to a lukewarm reception.

A disappointed Lucas vowed that his next work would be more upbeat and optimistic.

Captures the Early 1960s on Film

Lucas's next film won him a reputation as a major American filmmaker. It was a nostalgic look at teenage life in 1962 entitled *American Graffiti.* Lucas directed the film with the help of friends Gary Kurtz and Coppola on a shoestring budget of $780,000. Universal executives disliked the loosely-plotted movie, but nonetheless decided to release it in 1973. Two years later it had grossed $50 million and had won a Golden Globe award for best comedy, New York Film Critics and National Society of Film Critics awards for best screenplay, and five Oscar nominations. "The film is about change,'' Lucas told Stephen Farber in *Film Quarterly.* "It's about the change in rock and roll, it's about the change in a young person's life at 18 when he leaves home and goes off to college; and it's about the cultural change that took place when the fifties turned into the sixties—when we went from a country of apathy and non-involvement to a country of radical involvement. The film is saying that you have to go forward.''

American Graffiti gave Lucas the political and economic clout in Hollywood to make his next film. "I was thinking about quitting directing,'' he said to Vallely, "but I had this huge draft of a screenplay and I had sort of fallen in love with it.'' The script was very large—far larger than Lucas could use for a single film. "I wanted to make a fairy tale epic, but this was like *War and Peace.* So I took that script and cut it in half, put the first half aside and decided to write the screenplay from the second.'' The second half also expanded beyond the limits of a single film, so it in turn was cut into three parts—and they became the genesis of the *Star Wars* films: *Star Wars, The Empire Strikes Back,* and *Return of the Jedi.*

The *Star Wars* Saga

Lucas began filming *Star Wars* in 1976, on location in Tunisia and in London. So complex were the special effects that Lucas had to form his own company, Industrial Light and Magic, to handle them. Lucas insisted in a *Rolling Stone*

*Movie still from **Star Wars***

interview with Paul Scanlon that *Star Wars* is primarily "a space fantasy that was more in the genre of Edgar Rice Burroughs; that whole other end of space fantasy that was there before science took it over in the fifties. . . . I think speculative fiction is very valid but they forgot the fairy tales and the dragons and Tolkien and all the *real* heroes." Drawing on his experience in anthropology and psychology, Lucas hoped that *Star Wars* would provide a modern fairy tale for younger generations.

Despite critical misgivings about the themes and presentation of *Star Wars,* the financial returns on the movie and the sales of its tie-in merchandise gave Lucas the funds he needed to create his own production company, Lucasfilm. He also was able to build Industrial Light and Magic into a leading producer of motion picture special effects. In 1980 and 1983, he produced two more episodes in the *Star Wars* saga: *The Empire Strikes Back* and *Return of the Jedi.* He also produced several straight adventure films in conjunction with Stephen Spielberg: *Raiders of the Lost Ark* (1981), *Indiana Jones and the Temple of Doom* (1984), and *Indiana Jones and the Last Crusade* (1989). All three were based on action-adventure stories like the serials Lucas had grown up watching on television. They also drew on

Lucas's background in anthropology: the protagonist, Indiana Jones, is an itinerant archaeologist who travels around the world on his swashbuckling adventures.

The space operas and fantasy adventures of Luke Skywalker and Indiana Jones were Lucas's most popular films. However, he was also involved in the production of *Labyrinth* (1986) and the surprise fantasy hit *Willow* (1988). Several of his other efforts, however—most notably *Howard the Duck* (1986)—were financial and critical failures. Between productions, Lucas completed the building of Skywalker Ranch, his home near San Rafael, California, and expanded Lucasfilm to include separate animation, theater operations, post-production, retailing, and computer gaming facilities.

Twentieth Anniversary

Lucas's career—which had been quiet since the release of his last Indiana Jones movie in 1989—picked up again in the mid-1990s with the re-release of *Star Wars, The Empire Strikes Back,* and *Return of the Jedi.* Lucas took the opportunity to clean old prints of the films, augment the sound tracks, and add new scenes and characters using enhanced computer graphics and imaging that were not available when the movies were originally released. ''I wanted to preserve ('Star Wars' and its subsequent two sequels) so that it would continue to be a viable piece of entertainment into the 21st century,'' Lucas declared in an article published in *CNN Online.*

The three films were released at approximately three-week intervals during January, February, and March of 1997. Lucasfilm and Twentieth Century-Fox called the revamped films the *Star Wars Trilogy Special Edition* and hoped that they would prove as popular with audiences of the 1990s as they had with audiences twenty years earlier. Their hopes were more than realized. By mid-February, *Star Wars* had passed *E.T.—The Extraterrestrial* as the highest grossing film of all time.

At the same time that the twentieth-anniversary versions of the *Star Wars* trilogy were released, Lucas announced his intention of creating a series of three ''prequels'' to the films. He explained that he would produce and direct the first in the series, just as he had done with the original *Star Wars* films. Lucas has also considered taking the *Star Wars* saga beyond the conclusion of *Return of the Jedi,* but these stories are currently not organized.

The Phantom Menace

In 1999, amid much media hype, Lucas released his first prequel: *Star Wars: Episode 1—The Phantom Menace.* Set thirty years before the original *Star Wars,* the movie stars Natalie Portman as Queen Amidala, who is rescued by two Jedi knights, Qui-Gon Jinn (Liam Neeson) and Obi-Wan Kenobi (Ewan McGregor). When the evil Federation sends in killer droids, the Jedis join forces with Anakin Skywalker, a nine-year-old slave. Eventually, he will be the father of Luke Skywalker and Princess Leia, and ultimately will give in to the dark side of the force and become Darth Vader, the villain of the original *Star Wars* movie.

Even before the film was released, Lucas was being criticized for the intense media and marketing blitz surrounding the film. It's an area he's skilled at profiting from: although the first three films made $1.5 billion at the box office, the

associated toys, T-shirts, and other merchandise have made over three times that amount. Merchandise for *Phantom Menace,* ranging from bicycle helmets to Lego toys to fast-food tie-ins, could make billions more. The Hasbro Toy Company, which owns most of the rights to Star Wars toys, agreed to give Lucas 20 percent in royalties, with a guaranteed $500 million.

In addition to marketing, Lucas also controlled how and where his film would be shown. Lucasfilm also saturated the fast-food market, turning each of several major chains into a planet from the movie. Each restaurant will have toys that can't be found anywhere else, encouraging fans to visit all of them, multiple times. Even Lucas was somewhat surprised by the interest among fans, long before the film was released. He told Steve Daly in *Entertainment Weekly,* ''The whole situation that has developed around this film is pretty amazing. I mean, there's never been anything quite like this, that I've been aware of, for a movie so far before it comes out . . . it's like a game. It's fun, as long as people don't take it too seriously.''

Despite his comments, Lucas believed the hype was justified. He told Bill Moyers in *Time,* ''One of the things I like about Star Wars is that it stimulates the imagination, and that's why I don't have any qualms about the toys or about any of the things that are going on around Star Wars, because it does allow young people to use their imagination and think outside the box.'' He also said, ''I put the Force into the movie to try to awaken a certain kind of spirituality in young people—more a belief in God than a belief in any particular religious system. I wanted to make it so that young people would begin to ask questions about the mystery.''

On www.starwars.com, the official *Star Wars* site, Lucas discussed the inspiration for his stories: ''You have opinions, you are curious, you have a rich fantasy life—you are able to create stories. . . . In this one I was interested in mythology and so I set out to create a modern myth, but I also wanted it to be an action adventure serial. People ask me which of the characters is me, but I am all the characters. It all comes out of me. You have to write from a point of view, I'm not sure whether that's literal, but I definitely put a little bit of myself in everything that I do. I can't help it.''

Sources for More Information

Books

Bouzereau, Laurent, editor, *Star Wars: The Annotated Screenplays,* Del Rey, 1997.

Champlin, Charles, *George Lucas: The Creative Impulse: Lucasfilm's First Twenty Years,* Abrams, 1997.

Henderson, Mary, *Star Wars: The Magic of Myth,* Bantam Doubleday Dell, 1997.

Reynolds, David West, *Star Wars: Incredible Cross-Sections,* DK Publishing, 1998.

Reynolds, David West, *Star Wars: The Visual Dictionary,* DK Publishing, 1998.

Sansweet, Stephen J., *The Star Wars Encyclopedia,* Ballantine, 1998.

Periodicals

Entertainment Weekly, January 22, 1999; March 26, 1999; May 7, 1999.

Newsweek, February 1, 1999; May 17, 1999.

People Weekly, May 3, 1999.

Premiere, May, 1999.

Publishers Weekly, May 3, 1999.

Time, April 26, 1999; May 17, 1999.

On-line

''The Mr. Showbiz Interview: George Lucas, January 31, 1997,'' located at http:\www.mrshowbiz.com/features/ interviews/plus/lucas.html.

The official *Star Wars* Web site, located at http:// www.starwars.com.

Chris Lynch

**Young adult novelist
(1962-)**

Born July 2, 1962, in Boston, MA; son of Edward (a bus driver) and Dorothy (a receptionist; maiden name, O'Brien) Lynch; married Tina Coviello (a technical support manager), August 5, 1989; children: Sophia, Walker. Education: Suffolk University, B.A. in journalism, 1983; Emerson University, M.A. in professional writing and publishing, 1991.

"It's my job as a novelist to celebrate the oddities, or at least make them less stigmatized."

Chris Lynch writes tough and edgy streetwise fiction. Episodic and fast-paced, his stories and novels question the male stereotypes of macho identity and inarticulate violence. His youthful characters are often athletes, or wanna-be athletes, or kids who have been churned up and spit out by the system. Outsiders, Lynch's protagonists desperately want to just be themselves. "You were not born into physical greatness and all the love and worship and happiness that are guaranteed with it," the narrator muses in the short story "The Hobbyist." "But fortunately you were born American. So you can buy into it."

Using irony and a searing honesty that cuts through adolescent facades, Lynch lays out a deck of impressionistic cards of what it means to be young and urban and male in America in the 1990s, warts and all. "I was speaking at a school for disturbed kids," Lynch once commented, "and this one kid came up and said to me that everybody I write about is weird. And I thought, 'Yes. I've done my job.' Because beneath it all, we're all weird. And it's okay. It's okay to be who you are.

695

You don't have to be what others say you should be. It's my job as a novelist to celebrate the oddities, or at least make them less stigmatized."

In his novels for young adults and young readers, Lynch has used sports such as boxing and hockey as metaphors for male rites of passage, has portrayed lonely outsiders and troubled families struggling to make it, and has dealt with racism and exploitation. Violence plays a part in these books, "the hovering menace that is urban life," as Lynch described it, but his violence is never gratuitous. Lynch is part of a new generation of young adult writers who are not afraid to tackle formerly taboo subjects, who are reaching out to adolescent readers with topics relevant to them and written in an idiom they understand.

Difficult Times Growing Up

If Lynch can speak so directly to young readers, it is because he has been there. Though his youth was a much more stable one than those of many of his fictional characters, he was no stranger to the urban melange that is the backdrop for most of his work. His grammar school experience was what he calls "nurturing," but high school was a different matter for Lynch. "I hated high school—every minute. It was rigid, kind of a factory. An all-boys' football factory. Nothing like the arts was encouraged in any way."

Though Lynch had participated in street hockey, football, and baseball as a younger kid, by high school he had stopped playing. "When it was fun I played," Lynch recalled. But the football-factory ethic ruined it for him, a sentiment echoed by protagonists in many of his novels. "I'm not against all athletics," Lynch stated. "Sports has a tremendous potential for channeling energy. But instead it mostly encourages the macho ethos and schools let athletes run wild. This carries through life, and results in Mike Tysons. People who were never told what they could not do."

High school was discouraging enough for Lynch that he dropped out in his junior year and entered Boston University where he studied political science. A news-writing course at Boston University provided a stimulus for change, for discovering what he really wanted to be doing: he then transferred to Suffolk University, majoring in journalism. He also took a novel writing class

"which helped lead me closer to what I was really going for all the time. But I just wouldn't allow it. Wouldn't let myself say that I wanted to be an artist."

Becoming A Writer

After graduation, Lynch spent about six years trying to let himself admit that simple fact. He took jobs as a house painter, a driver of a moving van, and for several years proofread financial reports. In 1989 Lynch enrolled in a master's program at Boston's Emerson University in professional writing and publishing. At Emerson, Lynch found a new direction. Taking a children's writing class from Jack Gantos, he began what became his first published novel, *Shadow Boxer,* as a class assignment.

This early assignment grew until Lynch had written about sixty percent of his novel in class. With the help of Gantos, he first tried to place his manuscript with various editors, then found an agent who quickly found a willing publisher. By 1992, he was on his way, *Shadow Boxer* being readied for publication. According to Lynch, the book is about twenty percent autobiographical, a story of two brothers learning to deal with life after the death of their father, a journeyman boxer. Reviewing *Shadow Boxer* in *School Library Journal,* Tom S. Hurlburt concluded that "Lynch has written a gritty, streetwise novel that is much more than a sports story. . . ."

While *Shadow Boxer* was being prepared for publication, Lynch was already hard at work on his second novel, *Iceman,* the story of a troubled youth for whom violence on the ice is his only release. "For me, *Iceman* is the book that is closest to being autobiographical in the whole inability to express yourself. Where does that go, the frustration. It's got to go someplace. Writing it, I tapped into something very adolescent American male where anger is cool and you've got to suck it up. Acting out the whole male role thing." Stephanie Zvirin summed up the effect of the novel in *Booklist:* "This totally unpredictable novel . . . is an unsettling, complicated portrayal of growing up in a dysfunctional family. . . ."

Hope from Despair

Lynch's third book was *Gypsy Davey,* the story of a brain-damaged youth and his family who doesn't care, and of the tenement neighborhood surrounding the boy—cheap bars and drug dealers. Out of this bleak atmosphere, Lynch weaves a tale of hope, of young Davey who tries body and soul to break the cycle of parental neglect initiated by his parents and seemingly perpetuated by his older sister, Jo. Writing in *Voice of Youth Advocates,* W. Keith McCoy, noted that in spite of the dreary atmosphere of the novel, ''Lynch provokes empathy for this family and its situation, and perhaps that is the only positive outcome in the book.''

Slot Machine, Lynch's next work, was something of a departure: On the surface it is a boys-at-summer-camp comedy about an overweight youth who resists attempts at turning him into a jock. According to Stephanie Zvirin, writing in *Booklist, Slot Machine* is a ''funny, poignant coming-of-age story.'' While noting Lynch's ability to write broad, physical comedy as well as dark humor, Zvirin concluded that ''this wry, thoughtful book speaks with wisdom and heart to the victim and outsider in us all.''

''Blue-Eyed Son'' Novels

With his ''Blue-Eyed Son'' trilogy, Lynch returned to the grittier mean streets of Boston to explore latent and sometimes very overt racism. The author remarked: ''I wanted to look at racism in a microcosm. . . . I wanted to put the spotlight on us. This is what we look like. Do we know we look like this? Do we even recognize what we do as racism?''

Lynch's microcosm involves fifteen-year-old Mick, who sees his once predominately Irish neighborhood changing into a racially-mixed one as blacks, Latinos and Asians move in. Mick unwittingly becomes a neighborhood hero when he throws an egg at a Cambodian woman during a St. Patrick's Day Parade. Because of his actions, he becomes an outcast at school. Only Toy, a mysterious sort of character, remains his friend, and soon Mick begins to break off ties with his close-knit Irish family and neighborhood and hangs out with Latinos instead. His drunken, oafish older brother has Mick beaten for such treachery, ending the first book of the trilogy, *Mick.*

The story is carried forward in *Blood Relations* where Mick struggles to find himself, forming a brief liaison with beautiful Evelyn, and

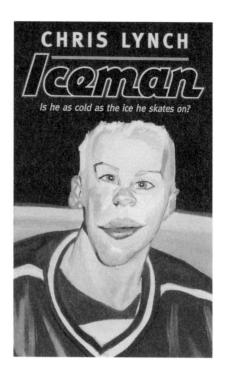

Cover of **Iceman**

finally ending up in the bed of Toy's mother. The series is concluded with *Dog Eat Dog* in which the brothers face off for a final showdown and Mick's friend Toy comes out of the closet. ''With realistic street language and an in-your-face writing style . . . Lynch immerses readers in Mick's world,'' Kelly Diller noted in *School Library Journal.*

While Lynch's inspiration for his books usually comes from his own life or from life around him in Boston, *Political Timber* was inspired by newspaper accounts of a teenager who ran for mayor of his small town. What resulted is a novel about a high school senior, Gordon Foley, who runs for mayor at the insistence of his grandfather who is an old machine politician serving time for fraud. Less bleak than much of his fiction, *Political Timber* is also unique in that it is specifically written for older teens, ''a woefully under-served constituency,'' according to Lynch. ''I wanted to portray an eighteen-year-old, someone who is on the cusp between the adult and kid world.''

A New Series Launched

In 1997, Lynch launched ''The He-Man Women Haters Club'' series. In *Johnny Chesthair,* the first book of the series, Lynch, according to *Publishers Weekly,* ''engagingly addresses questions

important to the average adolescent male, namely: what is a 'strong' man, and what to do about girls?'' In this first installment, the reader is introduced to eighth-grader Steven and his friends Jerome, Wolfbang, and Ling Ling. Their adventures are continued in *Babes in the Woods, Scratch and Sniff*, and *The Wolf Gang*. Each book, as *Horn Book* noted, relies on "humor [which] relieves this . . . [series] of adolescent angst, even in suggesting that 'he-manliness' might be nothing more than the desire to 'be bigger than just one guy alone'.''

In 1999, Lynch reintroduced readers to Elvin Bishop, the narrator of *Slot Machine*. In *Extreme Elvin*, Elvin has just begun his first year at a Catholic boys' high school. What follows, *Publishers Weekly* noted, "[is] one scatological misadventure after the next,'' but "Elvin himself grows a little more complex as the book progresses.''

"I see my books increasingly as a body of work,'' Lynch once commented. "They deal with the whole idea of identity and individuality. . . . My job is to make noise and be relevant and catch momentarily the attention of what seems to be a neglected reading group. We need to attract teenagers to the concept and let them know it is here. They've been driven away by the idea that [young adult literature] is baby food. I want to attract them again, and then deliver them to the next level of writing.''

Sources for More Information

Books

Seventh Book of Junior Authors and Illustrators, H. W. Wilson, 1996.

St. James Guide to Young Adult Writers, St. James Press, 1999.

Madonna

Singer, songwriter, record executive, and actress (1958–)

Born Madonna Louise Ciccone (pronounced "Chick-one"), August 16, 1958, in Bay City, MI; daughter of Silvio (an engineer) and Madonna (Fortin) Ciccone; married Sean Penn (an actor), August 16, 1985 (divorced, January 1989); children: (with Carlos Leon) Lourdes Maria Ciccone Leon. Education: Attended University of Michigan; studied dance in New York City with Alvin Ailey American Dance Theater and with Pearl Lang.

The career of pop music superstar Madonna has lasted longer than most of her detractors ever predicted. She has become a kind of modern-day, multimedia super-celebrity who dabbles in film, theater projects, and the occasional publishing venture in addition to her recording endeavors. But Madonna's most impressive feat may be her ability to sell millions of records around the world regardless of what the music press says about her. Rock critic Robert Christgau summed up Madonna's magic touch in *Vogue,* calling the singer-songwriter "a trailblazer in a raceless dance music with discernible roots in postpunk and Eurodisco, who is also on flirting terms with such white-bread subgenres as Vegas schlock, show tune, and house-wife ballad."

Off stage, Madonna demonstrates considerable business acumen as chief executive of her own company and record label. Her skills in guiding her career and the "Madonna" persona have, in the space of a decade, made her one of the world's wealthiest women.

"I am not going to be anybody's patsy. I am not going to be anybody's good girl."

Madonna was born Madonna Louise Ciccone in Bay City, Michigan, in 1958. The "Veronica" that is commonly cited as one of her birth names is really her confirmation name, chosen for the religious ceremony when she was in her early teens. Tragically, Mrs. Ciccone died of cancer when Madonna and her siblings were quite young. The children lived for a while with various relatives until her father settled down in Rochester Hills, a suburb of Detroit, and reunited the family.

Madonna's father, an engineer by profession, eventually married the family's housekeeper. Being the eldest daughter of a large brood meant that a greater share of household and emotional responsibilities fell on Madonna's young shoulders. Of her strict, Italian American, Roman Catholic upbringing, she recalled, "My family life at home was very repressive, very Catholic, and I was very unhappy. I was considered the sissy of the family because I relied on feminine wiles to get my way. I wasn't quiet at all. I remember always being told to shut up."

The Young Artist

Interested in dance from an early age, Madonna studied with local instructors as a teenager. She graduated early from high school and attended the University of Michigan for two years, continuing her dance training, then dropped out and moved to New York City in the late 1970s. There she attempted to get her foot in the show business door. While working in a series of low-wage jobs, she took more dance classes and eventually won a spot in the third company of Alvin Ailey's American Dance Theater.

Next, Madonna hooked up with disco performer Patrick Hernandez. She moved with him to Paris for a short time but then returned to New York City and became part of a burgeoning music scene that was combining post-punk rock shock with the quick-tempoed beats left over from the disco era. She played drums and sang for a number of New York-based ensembles, including Emmy, the Millionaires, and the Breakfast Club.

Around 1981 Madonna teamed up with boyfriend Steve Bray to form her own band, simply called Madonna. It was also around this time that she first picked up a guitar and started writing songs herself. Playing in New York City clubs, Madonna soon garnered attention with her new act. She found herself a respected manager and

began leaning toward a more funky, rhythm-and-blues-tinged sound, which went over well in the dance clubs she played. New York club disc jockey Mark Kamins, who had extensive contacts in the music business, helped win her a recording contract with Warner Bros. in 1982.

The contract with Warner Bros. led to the release of Madonna's self-titled debut album in 1983; cuts from *Madonna* slowly became underground dance club hits. When the first single, "Holiday," got extensive airplay, many listeners were surprised to find that the voice belonged to a white woman. Stardom quickly followed when the singles "Borderline" and "Lucky Star" began climbing the charts. By early 1985 Madonna had become a household name, but her second album, *Like a Virgin,* did even more for her budding career. The record quickly went platinum, buoyed by the hits "Material Girl," "Into the Groove," and the title track.

Madonna launched her first tour in the spring of 1985, initially in small venues, but as the shows began selling out in less than an hour, the dates were switched into larger arenas. That spring also saw the release of *Desperately Seeking Susan,* a movie she had made in 1984 when she was still relatively unknown. The low-budget film, directed by Susan Seidelman, became a commercial hit.

Cultural Icon

The showy "Like a Virgin" tour catapulted Madonna into a very public eye, and it was also during this period that she started to become a sort of icon for fans of her pop music. Teenaged—and even younger—girls began adopting the mid-'80s Madonna look of messy, badly-dyed hair, neon rubber bracelets, black lace bras, white lace gloves, a "Boy Toy" belt buckle, and other sartorial signifiers. The cult of Madonna even spawned the term "wannabe"—as in youngsters who "wanted to be" like the star.

Early in her career, Madonna was already becoming an accomplished songwriter—*Like a Virgin* included five cuts that she wrote herself. Her next effort, the 1986 release *True Blue,* was another success, best remembered for the "Papa Don't Preach" dilemma-of-teen-pregnancy track.

By this time, Madonna's personal life was attracting about the same amount of attention as her music and film performances. Her homes had

Madonna in concert

become bastions of high-tech security measures designed to keep an increasingly frenzied fan base and similarly persistent paparazzi out of her hair. In 1985 she had married actor Sean Penn to much media hoopla, and the ups and downs of their marriage were well-chronicled by the press. By early 1989 the marriage was on the rocks, divorce papers had been filed, and her next full-length studio album, *Like a Prayer,* was released.

Like a Prayer was especially notable for the racy videos to both the title cut and another track titled ''Express Yourself.'' Prior to its release, Madonna had inked a $5 million deal with Pepsi for some commercials and sponsorship of an upcoming tour, but the religious symbolism in the ''Like a Prayer'' video made the cola giant wary; the company canceled the deal, although the increasingly savvy businesswoman kept the money.

During the late 1980s, Madonna took intermittent breaks from her music to work in film and theater. Her role opposite Warren Beatty in 1990's *Dick Tracy* garnered major media attention as much for her performance as for her off-camera relationship with the film's star. The album that was released in conjunction with the movie featured the hit ''Vogue.'' The ''Vogue'' single was

another example of Madonna's ability to capitalize on a still-underground pop culture phenomenon. ''Vogueing'' had been a flourishing dance trend on the New York gay discotheque scene for a number of years, but Madonna's video carried it into living rooms from Iowa to Omaha. Her next album, *The Immaculate Collection,* was also released in 1990, but it was mainly an assemblage of her biggest hits to date, including ''Vogue.''

Late in 1990 Madonna became embroiled in yet another controversy, this time surrounding the video to ''Justify My Love,'' the only new track on *The Immaculate Collection.* The steamy images of slightly sado-masochistic situations and multiple partnerships, shot with Madonna's then-boyfriend Tony Ward, provoked MTV to initially ban it from airplay. The furor only boosted sales and prompted *Time* reporter Jay Cocks to point out that the flap made ''MTV look an organization of aging church elders, and [Madonna] a champion of feminism and free expression in the process.''

Madonna blended her interest in film and music in the concert documentary *Truth or Dare.* Shot during her 1990 ''Blond Ambition'' tour by video director Alex Keshishian, the work had a cinema-verite, ''you-are-there'' feel to it as it chronicled pre-show backstage prayer sessions with her dancers and followed the performer around both her L.A. abode and Manhattan apartment. *Time* reviewer Richard Corliss called it "raw, raunchy and epically entertaining . . . pure, unadulterated Madonna."

That dark well of Madonna—especially the out-there sexuality that seemed to unnerve most of her critics—was further explored in her first book, a hefty volume titled *Sex.* The 1992 tome contains racy images shot by fashion photographer Steven Meisel, along with intermittent text of Madonna's musings on sex and love written under the name of her alter ego, Dita Parlo. The $50 book was released to much fanfare, especially when some of the photographs appeared in the media prior to publication—leaked or perhaps sold by insiders.

A Head for Business

Madonna reportedly received an advance of $5.5 million for the *Sex* book from media giant Time-Warner, and the conglomerate also engineered an almost-unheard-of contract with the singer in 1991. (A year earlier, Madonna had appeared on the cover of the staid financial magazine *Forbes* under the banner "America's Smartest Business Woman?") The seven-year multimedia contract with Time-Warner, reportedly worth $60 million, gave her almost complete artistic control over her music—including her own label, Maverick—and supposedly included $5 million advances for each forthcoming album.

The *Sex* book coincided with the release of Madonna's 1992 album *Erotica.* Again, a steamy video accompanied the title track, but this time the video easily made it onto MTV playlists—albeit in the wee hours of the night. In addition to *Erotica*'s best-selling title song, the record also contains "In This Life," a track about people close to the singer who have died of AIDS, as well as "Goodbye to Innocence," a wistful look at the nature of celebrity.

Madonna showed another side of her complex persona with the late 1994 release of *Bedtime Stories.* The record featured quieter, more soul-tinged numbers, and reaction was favorable, although sales were not as brisk as for her previous records. "The eroticism she hints at on *Bedtime Stories* is actually sexier than that of her more wanton songs and videos," observed *Time* reviewer Christopher John Farley.

In 1996 Madonna starred in the much anticipated film version of *Evita,* which didn't fare well at the box office. While *Evita* was a disappointment, Madonna earned positive reviews. Richard Corliss, writing in *Time,* felt that the singer "plays Evita with a poignant weariness, as if death has shrouded her from infancy." Madonna won a Golden Globe Award for her performance.

Motherhood

During the filming of the movie, Madonna announced that she was pregnant by Carlos Leon. The news made headlines worldwide. Madonna gave birth to a girl, naming her Lourdes Maria Ciccone Leon. To prepare for her baby's arrival, the singer pared back her schedule—no concert touring or new films were planned.

But music was still part of her life. A new album, *Ray of Light,* was released in 1998. *Entertainment Weekly* called it Madonna's "best album yet, a mini-masterpiece that segues from industrial-strength electronica to bubbly disco rave-ups to honest-to-God guitar rock." In *People*, Steve Dougherty observed that Madonna "sings here in a voice grown deeper and fuller about the emptiness of fame and pleasure . . . and the rewards of mystic pursuit."

So what next for Madonna, who has shown the ability to reinvent herself time and time again? For the woman about whom *Rolling Stone* once stated: ''hers is the most scrutinized female life of the 20th century—with the possible exceptions of Diana Spencer's and Marilyn Monroe's,'' perhaps the only thing one can expect is the unexpected.

Sources for More Information

Books

Madonna: The Rolling Stone Files, Hyperion, 1997.

Rettenmund, Matthew, *Encyclopedia Madonnica,* St. Martin's Press, 1995.

Periodicals

Rolling Stone, November 13, 1997.

TV Guide, April 11, 1998.

Vanity Fair, March, 1998.

On-line

Madonna Web site from Warner Brothers Records, located at http://www.wbr.com/madonna.

Margaret Mahy

**Fantasy novelist
(1936-)**

"I began as a listener, became a teller, then a reader, and then a writer. . . ."

Born March 21, 1936, in Whakatane, New Zealand; daughter of Frances George (a builder) and May (a teacher; maiden name, Penlington) Mahy; children: Penelope Helen, Bridget Frances. Education: University of New Zealand, B.A., 1958.

Fantastical adventures that tell about how people get along in family life have made New Zealand author Margaret Mahy well-known around the world. In dozens of titles since her first book, *A Lion in the Meadow,* Mahy has written about a world full of surprising possibilities, a world familiar to children, that she insists remains real for adults. Her younger characters help each other to learn about the world of adults; through friendship tested by adventure, teens and preteens wounded by childhood experiences find healing. This healing helps them to continue their journeys into adulthood.

Critics place Mahy's work, which appeals to readers of all ages, with the best in the field of young people's literature. Mahy "has deserved her reputation as queen of the light fantastic with stories and picture-book texts which erupt with delightful visions," states *Times Literary Supplement* critic Sarah Hayes. When writing about aliens with unusual powers, intelligent adolescents, or "a primeval New Zealand of immense rain-forests and sulphurous volcanoes, . . . she writes with all the force and precision and richness of a poet,'' Elizabeth Ward observes in the *Washington Post Book World*.

Focus on Families

The family relationships of young adults is the focus of Mahy's books for that age group. In *The Haunting,* a young man finds out he is in line to inherit psychic powers that he feels are a curse more than a blessing. Barney Palmer describes a sequence of meal-time family discussions and ties them together with explanations of his own thoughts and feelings. In the end, Barney needs the help of his older sisters to ward off a series of aunts and uncles who determine to make him accept his inheritance. Hayes observes in the *Times Literary Supplement,* ''*The Haunting* manages to combine a realistic approach to family life—in which how you feel about your parents and yourself is actually important—with a strong and terrifying line in fantasy.''

Aliens in the Family combines elements of science fiction and drama. The story begins with a broken family group made up of twelve-year-old Jake's father, stepmother, and a new brother and sister who do not accept her. When an alien from outer space, a cataloguer of the universe, appeals to them for help in his escape from his pursuers the Wirdegen, the children become allies and friends through the process of problem-solving. Penny Blubaugh summarizes in *Voice of Youth Advocates,* ''Using Bond and Jake as aliens in their own situations, Mahy has written a story of families learning to accept and believe in each other in spite of, and even because of, their differences.''

The Tricksters provides an insightful look at the inner lives of people who celebrate Christmas together at a New Zealand beach house. The Hamiltons share their celebration with their British friend Anthony. During his visit, the seven family members take turns telling him the story of the house and the family who built it (the Cardinals), each giving a new twist to the story of a boy who had died by drowning. Anthony suspects the legends he hears about the boy's death and the house are not completely factual. He discovers as well that the Hamiltons are not what they appear to be. Helen J. Hinterberg remarks in the *Christian Science Monitor* that ''Mahy creates an eerie

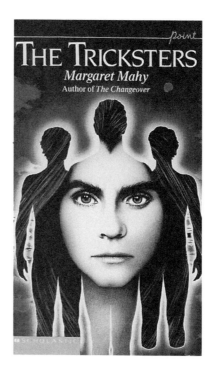

Cover of **The Tricksters**

atmosphere worthy of a classic gothic novel and suspense worthy of a first-rate thriller.''

Examines the Mystical

Family relationships and their importance to young adults is just one of the author's major themes. Hayes writes in the *Times Literary Supplement,* ''the double aspect of things—man and beast, [good] and evil, young and old—intrigues Margaret Mahy.'' *The Catalogue of the Universe* finds a balance between rational thinking and idealistic belief. The main characters are high school seniors working out the problems of identity common to that age group. The young adults discover that it takes both faith and facts to survive these experiences and achieve their goals. ''Angela and Tycho learn what they have suspected all along, that neither idealism nor rationalism [alone] is the key to coping with an existence that must be made up minute by minute,'' Colin Greenland notes in the *Times Literary Supplement.*

The Changeover: A Supernatural Romance presents a fourteen-year-old girl's collaboration with adult witches who have told her that magic is the only way to save her three-year-old brother from death. The child's health had begun to fail at about the same time that Laura's divorced mother took a growing interest in a man she does not trust. Soon after, Laura becomes convinced that an evil warlock has cast a spell on her brother, and she determines to break the spell in a ritual that turns her into a witch.

Critics believe the supernatural elements in *The Changeover* are secondary to what it teaches about growing up in a threatening environment. "The author's insights into the jagged tensions of family life in contemporary New Zealand count for much more than her world of witches," Robert Dunbar remarks in the *School Librarian*. In addition, Laura's changeover coincides with her passage through puberty. Hayes concludes, "It is rare to find a novel which captures so well the changeover from child to adult, and from what is real in the mind to what is real outside."

Memory explores how the ability to remember can be both a curse and a blessing. Main character Jonny Dart blames himself for the accidental death of his sister, and the passage of five years has not helped to ease his sense of loss. For the old woman he lives with, however, a better memory would solve problems. Because she suffers from Alzheimer's disease, Sophie forgets where she is, wakes Jonny at night thinking he is someone else, and wears a tea cozy instead of a hat. These challenges bring Jonny's attention to present realities and help him to discover that he is kind-hearted.

Mahy wrote *Memory* while thinking of her own experiences with caring for the elderly. Also, Mahy's experiences relating to the homeless gave her the idea for the book. "Driving home through an empty city at about 2 a.m., I saw an old man coming out of a supermarket car park pushing an empty trolly. The image stayed with me until I found a place for it," she says. While writing the book, she was also told of a group of derelict teens who had moved into a demented old woman's house and were taking care of her.

Characters in Nontraditional Roles

Mahy's ability to combine themes relevant to young adults with fantasy is matched by her consistently non-sexist perspective on roles and relationships. For example, though the roles of rescuer, leader, and problem-solver have been traditionally assigned to males, she gives these roles as often to females of various ages and levels of social status. Growth to sexual maturity is equally exciting and frightening to her male and female adolescents. Adults of both sexes are equally subject to weakness and failure to discern the needs of their children. All her characters face the same challenges to strike a balance between freedom and commitment, reason and emotion. And they all benefit from recognizing the power of the imagination, which they learn to celebrate as well as to contain.

Described by *Times Educational Supplement* as "sympathetic, unsentimental, effortlessly funny, . . . high quality Mahy," *Underrunners* (1993) deals with avoiding and facing difficult memories. The story centers around an abandoned boy named Tristram, who with his orphaned friend, Cecily, and his intergalactic alter ego Selsey Firebone, carry out exciting adventurers in underrunners, holes formed in the eroding soil near their New Zealand peninsula homes. The title also serves as a metaphor for the story's theme. A reviewer for *Magpies* wrote, "Cecily and Tristram are strong characters who demonstrate that trust and friendship are possible within the confusing, frustrating world of adults—especially those who will not grow up and accept that as parents they have responsibilities beyond their mid-life fantasies."

The Other Side of Darkness was chosen by the Chicago *Tribune Books* as one of 1995's Best Books for Young Readers. Twelve-year-old Hero, the youngest child in a wealthy dysfunctional family, has chosen to be mute. Hero is most fascinated by Miss Credence, a reclusive neighbor who keeps her thoughts in the past as her mansion crumbles around her. A sense of claustrophobic menace builds throughout the novel, broken by a climactic revelation at the end. A critic in *Tribune Books* stated that *The Other Side of Darkness* is "a story distinguished both for its delicately allusive language and its insight into families and adolescence.''

In her work as a librarian, Mahy is called upon to distinguish works of fact from works of fiction by shelving them separately, as if imagined stories somehow do not contain elements of truth about life. She believes the distinction is an imaginary rift. Pointing to changes in scientific theories about how the world began, she comments that what we think of as scientific fact sometimes proves to be wrong in the light of new discoveries, ''and the truest thing in science is wonder just as it is in story. And I never forget that story is as important to human beings as science, more powerful at times because it is more subversive.''

Sources for More Information

Books

Children's Literature Review, Volume 7, Gale, 1984.

St. James Guide to Young Adult Writers, St. James Press, 1999.

Marilyn Manson

Alternative rock band

"My rules and moralities are probably different from a lot of other people's."

Band formed by Marilyn Manson in 1990. Members include Ginger Fish, drums; Madonna Wayne Gacy, keyboards; Marilyn Manson (born Brian Warner in Canton, OH); Twiggy Ramirez, bass; Zim Zum (replaced Daisy Berkowitz), guitar.

Over the years, rock and roll music has witnessed several "shocking" artists, including Ziggy Stardust (David Bowie), Alice Cooper, KISS, and others who frightened parents while exciting and intriguing their fans. Marilyn Manson fit the slot of "shock" rock for the 1990s. Admittedly, singer and band founder Marilyn Manson derived his musical and performance influences from the above artists, as well as Iggy Pop, Black Sabbath, and the Beatles. Jim Farber wrote in *Entertainment Weekly:* "He sings about scabs, sodomy, and urine. He enjoys ripping his skin with broken bottles. And compares his music to an act of murder. Any authorities who don't like it, he says, 'should kill themselves.'"

Manson was born Brian Warner in Canton, Ohio, raised by his mother, a nurse, and his father, Hugh Warner, a furniture salesman. He began writing lyrics in the late 1980s with no intention of becoming a singer or forming a band. But in 1990, he did both. He invented the name Marilyn Manson, which he adopted as his own name, by watching and reflecting on American propaganda and sensationalism. After viewing talk shows and other entertainment sources, he came to the conclusion that Marilyn Monroe and Charles Manson stood out as the most popular personalities of the 1960s.

"As I got into the idea further," Manson told Jim Rose in *RIP,* "I started realizing the extreme positive and negative that I was trying to outline with these two names. There was a lot of beauty to be found in Manson. There was a lot of ugliness to be found in Monroe. The lines crossed. I resided in that gray area; that what I was doing transcended morality and sexuality."

Not long after Manson formed the group, he met Nine Inch Nails' Trent Reznor, also from Ohio. The two singer/songwriters hit it off, and when Reznor started his own record label, Nothing Records, Marilyn Manson became its first signing.

Testing Societal Limits

Marilyn Manson released its debut album in 1994. Within the year, the group was banned from playing in Salt Lake City, Utah, after Manson ripped apart a Mormon Bible onstage. "Marilyn Manson is a bit of a challenge to people's intelligence," Manson told Rose. "It's almost a little bit of a science project to see how far I can push you, and see exactly what kind of reaction I can get." Marilyn Manson also received censorship requests and disapproval from organizations such as the People for the Ethical Treatment of Animals, the Christian Coalition, and members of the British Parliament.

"My rules and moralities are probably different from a lot of other people's," Manson told Jim Farber in *Entertainment Weekly.* The band did compromise on some occasions to continue to have their music published and their live shows scheduled. "Compromise is inevitable sometimes," bassist Twiggy Ramirez told John Pecorelli in *Alternative Press.* "I mean, if you're banned in 23 states, you're not accomplishing much. No one's going to hear your message."

Marilyn Manson released their second effort, an EP called *Smells Like Children,* in 1995. The album included a cover version of the Eurythmics' hit "Sweet Dreams," which launched the EP to No. 31 on Billboard's album chart and racked up platinum sales.

"It was quite obvious to us from the beginning that the song was going to have a broader appeal than the rest of the material on the album,"

Marilyn Manson in concert

Manson told *MTV News* "From the Buzz Bin." "I felt like it was a piece of cheese on a rat trap to a lot of people who normally wouldn't listen to Marilyn Manson. They thought, 'Well, this is an innocuous little song and they ended up getting their necks snapped because they were introduced to this whole world that they weren't expecting.'" However, Tom Sinclair, a reviewer for *Entertainment Weekly,* saw the band as talentless rather than shocking: "On this artlessly assembled excuse for an album, these minor-league White Zombie wannabes throw together pointless remixes, irritating skits, and lame covers of songs by Eurythmics, Screamin' Jay Hawkins, and Patty Smith."

Second Album Climbs Charts

By the end of 1995, Manson had reorganized the band. He fired guitarist Daisy Berkowitz and hired Chicago-native Zim Zum. Manson and Zum, along with bassist Twiggy Ramirez, keyboardist Madonna Wayne Gacy, and drummer Ginger Fish, released *Antichrist Superstar* on Nothing/Interscope in 1996. The LP debuted at No. 3 on Billboard's Top 200 Albums, and included the singles "The Beautiful People" and the title track. Within the first weeks of the album's release, the American Family Association from Mississippi released a statement to warn American families against Marilyn Manson and its new album. "This should serve as a wake-up call to parents everywhere," the press release stated.

Manson claimed *Antichrist Superstar* directly attacked Christianity's "weak value system," stating that he had recorded it in an attempt to "bring on the apocalypse." He derived the idea for the album from his own experiences and the influence of concept albums such as Pink Floyd's *The Wall* and David Bowie's *Ziggy Stardust.*

The New Alice Cooper?

"Marilyn Manson would have fit just fine right alongside Ziggy Stardust and Alice Cooper, the Stooges, T. Rex—any of that back then," Manson told Pecorelli in *Alternative Press.* "And apparently, I'm gonna be the one that has to break my back to make rock music exciting again, because not too many other people are making the effort." John Pareles wrote about Manson's similarities to Alice Cooper in the *New York Times.* "Mr. Manson is the 1990's version of Alice Cooper," he wrote. "He uses a woman's name, leads a hard-rock band, and provides a stagey spectacle."

On the tour for *Antichrist Superstar,* Manson, would often lead the crowd in a chant of "We hate love! We love hate!" Adam Tepedelen wrote in a live review in *The Rocket:* "Manson is one sick little doggy; a writhing, taut body like Iggy Pop, a stage persona ('Antichrist Superstar') equal to Ziggy Stardust, Alice Cooper's flare for showbiz shock tactics, and G. G. Allin's bent for self-destruction. Love him or hate him (he'd prefer the latter), there's no denying he's a spectacle." In 1997, Marilyn Manson appeared on the Trent

Reznor-produced soundtrack for David Lynch's film *Lost Highway,* with the song "The Apple of Sodom."

Though Manson claimed the album *Antichrist Superstar* would either bring the end of the world or the end of his band, the crowds clamored for more. So what did Manson have to look forward to after the retirement of his music career? He claimed he'd like to do a stint as a Christian television evangelist . . . always pushing the limits.

But *Antichrist Superstar* caused neither the apocalypse nor Manson's retirement into evangelism. The band's third album, *Mechanical Animals,* was released in the fall of 1998, with a slightly different sound than the band's earlier work, and a slightly slicker, toned-down look for the singer. Manson admitted in a 1998 *Rolling Stone* interview with Chris Heath that he had learned a sense of empathy for people, a discovery reflected in *Mechanical Animals.* Heath commented: "When Manson began to feel emotion, he began to despair how little emotion most humans feel. They—we—are the mechanical animals of the title." But Manson's more mature vision did little to change his image. As *Time* critic David E. Thigpen stated, "Beneath the makeup, Manson is still rock's most piercing critic—blasting, among other things, youth culture, rock music and conservatives. Manson fans, fear not: his weird new look will still strike revulsion in the hearts of your parents."

Sources for More Information

Books

Manson, Marilyn, and Neil Strauss, *The Long Hard Road Out of Hell,* HarperCollins, 1998.

Periodicals

Alternative Press, February, 1997.

Rolling Stone, January 23, 1997; March 19, 1998; May 28, 1998; October 15, 1998; May 13, 1999.

Time, September 28, 1998.

On-line

The *Rolling Stone* Network, located at http://www.rollingstone.com.

Bob Marley

Singer, songwriter, and guitarist (1945–1981)

Born February 6, 1945, in Saint Ann, Jamaica; died May 11, 1981, in Miami, FL; son of Cedella Malcolm Marley; married Rita Anderson; children: Ziggy Marley.

"So it is not anger [I have] but truth, and truth have to bust out of a man like a river."

In his brief life, Bob Marley rose from poverty and obscurity to international stardom, becoming the first Third World artist to be acclaimed to that degree. It was largely through him that the world became familiar with reggae music and Rastafarianism, the religion embraced by much of Jamaica's black underclass. According to *New York Times Magazine* contributor Jon Bradshaw, Bob Marley became an influential political force in his native country by articulating "the plight of the Jamaican ghettos—urging change and preaching revolution should change not come." Because "exact and obvious" analogies to the situation in Jamaica were applicable in so many parts of the world, Marley eventually became a heroic figure to poor and oppressed people everywhere.

Robert Nesta Marley was born to Cedella Malcolm Marley when she was barely nineteen years old. The child was the result of her clandestine affair with the local overseer of crown lands in the rural parish where she lived. Captain Marley, a white man more than twice Cedella's age, married the girl to make the birth legitimate, but he left the countryside the day after his impromptu wedding in order to accept a post in the city of Kingston and had almost no contact with his wife and son for several years. As the infant grew, he became

711

the pet of his grandfather's large clan. He was known as a serious child and had a reputation for clairvoyance.

In Kingston's Ghettos

When Bob was about five years old, Cedella received a letter from her estranged husband asking that his son be sent to Kingston in order to attend school. Bob's mother reluctantly agreed and put her young son on the bus to Jamaica's largest city. Captain Marley met the child, but, for reasons unknown, he took him to the home of an elderly, invalid woman and abandoned him there. Bob was left to fend almost entirely for himself in Kingston's ghettos, which are generally considered some of the world's worst. Months passed before Cedella Marley was able to track down her child and bring him back to his country home. Before long, however, mother and child had returned to Kingston, where Cedella believed she had a greater chance of improving her lot. With them were Bob's closest friend, Bunny Livingston, and Bunny's father Thaddeus.

Jamaican society held few opportunities for blacks. Bob and Bunny grew up in an environment where violent crime was glorified by many young people as one of the few ways of getting ahead. Music was seen as another means of escape. Like most of their contemporaries, the two boys dreamed of becoming recording stars and spent their days coming up with songs and practicing them to the accompaniment of makeshift guitars they fashioned from bamboo, sardine cans, and electrical wire. By 1963, Marley's dream had come true—he'd released his first single, "Judge Not." Soon he and Bunny had teamed with another singer, Peter Tosh, to form a group known as the Wailers. Through talent shows, gigs at small clubs, and recordings, the Wailers became one of the most popular groups in Jamaica.

Rastafarianism

Their early success was based on popular dance hits in the "ska" music style, but as time passed, they added social commentary to their lyrics, and were instrumental in transforming the light, quick ska beat into the slower, bass-heavy reggae sound. The three men also came under the influence of Rastafarianism. This complex set of mystical beliefs holds that Emperor Haile Selassie I of Ethiopia (whose given name was Ras Tafari) is the living God who will lead blacks out of oppression and into an African homeland. It was once considered the religion of outcasts and lunatics in Jamaica, but in the 1960s it came to represent an alternative to violence for many ghetto dwellers. Rastafarianism lent dignity to their suffering and offered them the hope of eventual relief. Rejecting the standards of the white world that led many blacks to straighten their hair, Rastas let theirs mat up into long, ropy "dreadlocks." They follow strict dietary rules: abhor alcohol and drugs, but revere "ganja" (marijuana) as a holy herb that brings enlightenment to users. The Wailers soothed ghetto tensions with lyrical messages of peace, love, and racial reconciliation but, at the same time, they warned the ruling class of "imminent dread judgement on the downpressors."

For all their acclaim in Jamaica, the Wailers saw few profits from their early recording careers, as unscrupulous producers repeatedly cheated them out of royalties and even the rights to their own songs. In the early 1970s, Marley sought an alliance with Chris Blackwell, a wealthy white Jamaican whose record company, Island, was the label of many major rock stars. At the time, reggae was still considered unsophisticated slum music that could never be appreciated by non-Jamaican audiences. Blackwell had a deep interest in the music, however, and because he felt that the Wailers were the one group who could popularize reggae internationally, he offered them a contract and marketed their first Island album, *Catch a Fire,* just as he would any rock band. Tours of Britain and the United States helped the Wailers' sound to catch on, but perhaps the most important catalyst to their popularity at this time was Eric Clapton's cover of Marley's composition, "I Shot the Sheriff," from the Wailers' 1973 album *Burnin'.* Clapton's version became a worldwide hit and led many of his fans to discover the Wailers' music.

As their popularity increased, the original Wailers drew closer to a parting of the ways. Bunny Livingston (who had taken the name Bunny Wailer) disliked leaving Jamaica for extended tours, and Peter Tosh resented Chris Blackwell's efforts to make Bob the focus of the group. Each launched solo careers in 1975, while Marley released *Natty Dread,* hailed by *Rolling Stone* reviewer Stephen Davis as "the culmination of Marley's political art to this point." The reviewer

Bob Marley in concert

continued: "With every album he's been rocking a little harder and reaching further out to produce the stunning effect of a successful spell. Natty Dread deals with rebellion and personal liberation. . . . The artist lays his soul so bare that the careful listener is satiated and exhausted in the end." *Rastaman Vibration* was released the following year to even more enthusiastic reviews. It was full of acid commentary on the worsening political situation in Jamaica, including a denouncement of the CIA's alleged involvement in island politics that brought Marley under surveillance by that and other U.S. intelligence organizations. His prominence in Jamaica reached messianic proportions, causing one *Time* reporter to exclaim, "He rivals the government as a political force."

A Political Force

Although Marley regarded all politicians with skepticism, considering them to be part of what Rastafarians call "Babylon," or the corrupt Western world, he was known to favor Michael Manley of the People's National Party over Edward Seaga of the right-wing Jamaican Labour Party for the post of Prime Minister of Jamaica. When Manley asked Bob Marley to give a "Smile Jamaica" concert to reduce tensions between the warring gangs associated with the two parties, the singer readily agreed. On December 3, 1976, shortly before the concert was to take place, seven gunmen, suspected to be henchmen of the Jamaican Labour Party, stormed Marley's home. Marley, his wife Rita, and their manager Don Taylor were all injured in the ensuing gunfire. Despite the assassination attempt, the concert went on as scheduled. An audience of 80,000 people was electrified when Marley, bandaged and unable to strum his guitar, climbed to the stage to begin a blistering ninety-minute set. "At the close of his performance, Marley began a ritualistic dance, acting out aspects of the ambush that had almost taken his life," reported Timothy White in *Catch a Fire: The Life of Bob Marley.* "The last thing [the audience] saw before the reigning King of Reggae disappeared back into the hills was the image of the man mimicking the two-pistoled fast draw of a frontier gunslinger, his locks thrown back in triumphant laughter."

Immediately after the "Smile Jamaica" concert, Marley left the country in self-imposed exile. After a period of recuperation, he toured the native son . . . a beloved and departed friend." "He was a man with deep religious and political sentiments who rose from destitution to become one of the most influential music figures in the last twenty years," eulogized White in *Rolling Stone.* He was "an inspiration for black freedom fighters the world over. . . . When his death was announced, the degree of devastation felt beyond our borders was incalculable."

Marley has sold over 30 million records. A great testimony to his continued popularity is the $9 million campaign effort by the Jamaica Tourist Board that began in 1990. The effort incorporated an adaptation of one of Marley & the Wailers' signature songs, "One Love." "Come to Jamaica and feel all right" was utilized in television spots, magazine and newspaper ads, and direct mail in an effort to boost tourism in Jamaica.

United States, Europe, and Africa. Reviewing his 1977 release, *Exodus,* Ray Coleman wrote in *Melody Maker:* "This is a mesmerizing album . . . more accessible, melodically richer, delivered with more directness than ever. . . . After an attempt on his life, Marley has a right to celebrate his existence, and that's how the album sounds: a celebration." But *Village Voice* reviewer Roger Trilling found that *Exodus* was "underscored by deep personal melancholy, a musical echo of the rootless wanderings that followed [Marley's] self-exile from Jamaica."

In 1978, Marley injured his foot during an informal soccer game. The painful wound was slow to heal and finally forced the singer to seek medical help. Doctors informed him that he had an early form of cancer and advised amputation of his damaged toe. He refused, because such treatment was not in keeping with Rasta beliefs. Despite worsening health, Marley continued to perform until September 1980 when he collapsed while jogging in New York's Central Park during the U.S. leg of a world tour. Doctors determined that tumors were spreading throughout his lungs and brain. He underwent radiation therapy and a controversial holistic treatment in the Bavarian Alps, but to no avail. After his death on May 11, 1981, he was given a state funeral in Jamaica, which was attended by more than 100,000 people. Prime minister Edward Seaga remembered Marley as "a

Sources for More Information

Books

Davis, Stephen, *Bob Marley,* Doubleday, 1985.

Davis, Stephen, *Reggae Bloodlines: In Search of the Music and Culture of Jamaica,* Anchor Press, 1979.

Goldman, Vivian, *Bob Marley: Soul Rebel—Natural Mystic,* St. Martin's, 1981.

White, Timothy, *Catch a Fire: The Life of Bob Marley,* Holt, 1998.

Whitney, Malika Lee, *Bob Marley, Reggae King of the World,* Dutton, 1984.

Periodicals

Billboard, February 25, 1995; May 6, 1995.

Essence, February, 1995.

Guardian, October 6, 1998.

Interview, January, 1995.

Newsweek, May 25, 1981.

New York Times, May 12, 1981; May 21, 1981.

Rolling Stone, May 28, 1981; June 25, 1981.

Time, May 25, 1981.

On-line

The Rock and Roll Hall of Fame Web site, located at http://www.rockhall.com/index.html

Wynton Marsalis

**Jazz musician
(1961–)**

Born October 18, 1961, in New Orleans, LA; son of Ellis and Delores Marsalis; children (with Victoria Rowell) Jasper Armstrong Marsalis. Education: Attended Berkshire Music Center, 1978–79; Juilliard School of Music, 1979–81.

"I'm always ready to put my own neck on the line for change."

Successful jazz trumpeter Wynton Marsalis, America's top modern missionary purist of the genre, knows the essential elements that make music jazz. Influenced by the jazz artists from the early 1900s through the 1960s and annoyed with the music labeled "jazz" in the 1970s, Marsalis took on the mission of not only creating "true" jazz, but teaching its definition as well.

A jazz and classical musician and composer, Marsalis had won more than eight Grammy awards and released over 30 albums in both genres by the late 1990s. In 1997, he received the first Pulitzer Prize award ever for nonclassical music. He also co-founded and directed the ground-breaking jazz program at New York's Lincoln Center, and became an influential jazz educator for America's youth.

A Musical Family

Marsalis was born into a family of musicians on October 18, 1961, in New Orleans. His father, Ellis Marsalis, played piano and worked as a jazz improvisation instructor at the New Orleans Center for the Creative Arts. Before dedicating her life to raising her six sons, Dolores Marsalis sang in jazz bands. The second eldest child, Wynton's older brother Branford set the stage as the family's first musical prodigy. Branford Marsalis played both clarinet and piano by the time he entered the second grade, and eventually became a professional saxophonist.

Wynton Marsalis didn't follow his brother's lead quite as diligently, however. When he was six years old, his father played with Al Hirt, who gave the young Marsalis one of his old trumpets. Wynton Marsalis made his performing debut at the tender age of seven when he played "The Marine Hymn" at the Xavier Junior School of Music. As a child, Marsalis didn't take practicing the trumpet very seriously. He spent more time with his school work, playing basketball, and participating in Boy Scout activities.

When Marsalis was 12, his family moved from Kenner, Louisiana, to New Orleans. When he listened to a recording by jazz trumpeter Clifford Brown, he was moved to take his trumpet seriously. "I didn't know someone could play a trumpet like that," Marsalis later told Mitchell Seidel in *Down Beat*. "It was unbelievable." Soon after, a college student gave Marsalis an album by classical trumpet player Maurice Andre, which also sparked his interest in classical music.

Serious Student

Marsalis began taking lessons from John Longo in New Orleans, who had an interest in both genres, as well. "I hardly ever even paid him," Marsalis recalled to Howard Mandell in *Down Beat,* "and he used to give me two- and three-hour lessons, never looking at the clock."

Marsalis attended Benjamin Franklin High School in New Orleans, where he graduated with a 3.98 grade point average on a 4.0 scale. He became a National Merit Scholarship finalist and received scholarship offers from Yale University, among other prestigious schools. He also attended the New Orleans Center for the Creative Arts. At the age of 14, he won a Louisiana youth competition. This award granted him the opportunity to perform with the New Orleans Philharmonic Orchestra as a featured soloist.

During his high school years, he played a variety of music with a number of groups, including first trumpet with the New Orleans Civic Orchestra, the New Orleans Brass Quintet, an a teenage funk group called the Creators, along with his brother Branford. In 1977, Marsalis won the "Most Outstanding Musician Award" at the Eastern Music Festival in North Carolina.

He went on to study music at the Berkshire Music Center at Tanglewood in Massachusetts, where he received their Harvey Shapiro Award for the outstanding brass player. He turned down the scholarship offers from Ivy League schools to attend New York's Juilliard School of Music on full scholarship. While in school, he played with the Brooklyn Philharmonia and the Mexico City Symphony. He supported himself with a position in the pit band for Sweeney Todd on Broadway.

Gains National Attention

In 1980, Art Blakey asked Marsalis to spend the summer touring with his Jazz Messengers. His performances began to attract national attention, and he eventually became the band's musical director. While on the road with Blakey, Marsalis decided to change his image and began wearing suits to his performances. "For us, it was a statement of seriousness," Marsalis told Howard Reich in *Down Beat*. "We come out here, we try to entertain our audience and play, and we want to look good so they can feel good."

The following year, Marsalis decided to leave Juilliard to continue his education on the road. He played with Blakey and received an offer to tour with Herbie Hancock's V.S.O.P. quartet. Marsalis jumped at the chance, as the V.S.O.P. included bassist Ron Carter and drummer Tony Williams, who had both played with Miles Davis. "I knew he was only 19, just on the scene—it's a lot to put on somebody," Hancock told Steve Bloom in *Rolling Stone*. "But then I realized if we don't hand down some of this stuff that happened with Miles, it'll just die when we die."

Marsalis performed throughout the United States and Japan with the V.S.O.P. and played on the double album *Quartet*. The increased attention led to an unprecedented recording contract with Columbia Records for both jazz and classical music. He released his self-titled debut album as a leader in 1981. Later that year, he formed his own jazz band with his brother Branford, Kenny

Wynton Marsalis in concert

Kirkland, Jeff Watts, and bassists Phil Bowler and Ray Drummond.

Jazz and Classical Releases

Wynton Marsalis recorded one side of an album with his father Ellis and Branford Marsalis, called *For Fathers and Sons.* The other side was recorded by saxophonist Chico Freeman and his father Von Freeman. In 1983, Marsalis released jazz and classical LPs simultaneously. The jazz record, *Think of One,* marked the debut of his jazz quintet and sold nearly 200,000 copies, about ten times what was considered a successful jazz album. The recording and Marsalis received many comparisons to Miles Davis and other musicians of the 1960s. ''We don't reclaim music from the '60s; music is a continuous thing,'' Marsalis explained to Mandell in *Down Beat.* ''We're just trying to play what we hear as the logical extension. . . . A tree's got to have roots.''

He recorded his classical debut, *Trumpet Concertos,* in London with Raymond Leppard and the National Philharmonic Orchestra. In 1984, Marsalis set another precedent by becoming the first artist to be nominated or win two Grammy awards in two categories during the same year.

He won another Grammy award in 1987 for his album *Marsalis Standard Time Vol. 1.* During the same year, he co-founded the Jazz at Lincoln Center program in New York City. When the program began, Marsalis became the artistic director for the eleven-month season. As part of his contract, he had to compose one piece of music for each year. Despite his new position, he continued to record and tour in both jazz and classical music.

He released *Majesty of the Blues* in 1989 and *The Resolution of Romance* in 1990. He dedicated the latter to his mother, and it included contributions from his father Ellis and his brother Delfeayo. ''If you are really dealing with music, you are trying to elevate consciousness about romance,'' Marsalis explained to Dave Helland in *Down Beat.* ''Music is so closely tied up with sex and sensuality that when you are dealing with music, you are trying to enter the world of that experience, trying to address the richness of the interaction between a man and a woman, not its lowest reduction.''

Marsalis' study of New Orleans styles resulted in a trilogy called *Soul Gestures in Southern Blue* in 1990. Using history to create his present sound became Marsalis' goal, along with exploring the rich tapestry of the different eras and styles of jazz. His first commission for the jazz program at Lincoln Center, *In This House, On This Morning* was performed in 1993. In it, he used the music of the African American church as his primary inspiration.

In the fall of 1994, Marsalis announced that his septet had disbanded. However, he continued composing, recording, and performing. The following year, he produced a four-part video series called *Marsalis on Music,* which aired on PBS. In May of 1995, his first string quartet, (At the) Octoroon Balls debuted at the Lincoln Center. He continued to release classical works as well. He rerecorded the Haydn, Hummel, and Leopold Mozart concertos from *Trumpet Concertos* in 1994. Two years later, he released *In Gabriel's Garden,* which he recorded with the English Chamber Orchestra and Anthony Newman on harpsichord and organ.

Constantly Striving to Improve

"I want to keep developing myself as a complete musician," Marsalis told Ken Smith in *Stereo Review,* "so I take on projects either to teach me something new or else to document some development." Marsalis produced the Olympic Jazz Summit at the 1996 Olympics in Atlanta, and won 1996 Peabody Awards for both *Marsalis on Music* and for his National Public Radio Show "Wynton Marsalis: Making the Music." At the end of 1996, *Time* magazine named him one of America's 25 Most Influential People.

A major part of his influence went out to the country's youth. When he's not working on his own music, he traveled to schools across the country to talk about music in an effort to continue the tradition of jazz. "I'm always ready to put my own neck on the line for change," Marsalis told Lynn Norment in *Ebony.* "No school is too bad for me to go to. . . . I'll try to teach anybody. We are all striving for the same thing, to make our community stronger and richer. That's what the jazz musician has always been about."

In April of 1994, his biggest piece, *Blood on the Fields,* had its debut performance at the Lincoln Center. Marsalis composed the oratorio for three singers and a 14-piece orchestra, and it described the story of two Africans, Leona and Jesse, who found love despite the difficulties of American slavery. "I wanted to orchestrate for the larger ensemble and write for voices—something I'd never done," Marsalis said to V.R. Peterson in *People.* "I wanted to make the music combine with the words, yet make the characters seem real."

With *Blood on the Fields,* Marsalis won the first nonclassical Pulitzer Prize award in history. Because of his piece, the selection board changed the criteria from "for larger forms including chamber, orchestra, song, dance, or other forms of musical theater" to "for distinguished musical composition of significant dimension." Columbia Records released the oratorio on a three-CD set in June of 1997.

He followed the release with recordings of two other previously performed works on one album. His collaboration with New York City Ballet Director Peter Martins Jazz/Six Syncopated Movements and Jump Start written for ballet director Twyla Tharp were both included on the record. Marsalis' work in jazz and classical music combined with his often outspoken attitude toward musical integrity surrounded him with controversy throughout his career. Despite the criticism, his talent was never questioned. As Eric

Alterman described in *The Nation,* he's "a man universally acknowledged to be a master musician and perhaps the most ambitious composer alive."

Sources for More Information

Periodicals

Billboard, February 20, 1999.

Down Beat, May, 1997; December, 1997; May, 1998; November, 1998; December, 1998.

Essence, May, 1998.

Jet, April 28, 1997.

Nation, May 12, 1997.

People, May 12, 1997.

On-line

Sony Web site, located at http://www.sonyclassical.com.

John Marsden

**Young adult novelist
(1950-)**

*"I imagine I'll always be writing, all
my life, because there is something
within me that needs to tell stories."*

Born September 27, 1950, in Melbourne, Victoria, Australia; son of Eustace Cullen Hudson (a banker) and Jeanne Lawler (a homemaker; maiden name, Ray) Marsden. Education: Mitchell College, diploma in teaching, 1978; University of New England, B.A., 1981.

"I'd have to say that when I finished school I didn't have much understanding of life," John Marsden admitted in an autobiographical essay for *Something about the Author Autobiography Series* (*SAAS*). Marsden, the well-known author of books about adolescents, spent many years after finishing school drifting from job to job and seeking his true vocation. He eventually became a teacher, thereby developing a solid understanding of the language, morality, and character of his teenage students. Marsden's experience, coupled with his writing skill, has resulted in several well-received novels for young adults.

Growing up in small Australian towns during the 1950s gave Marsden experiences that were quite different from children in urban America during the same era. In Marsden's village, ice was still delivered to people for their iceboxes, cooking was mainly done on stoves powered by fuel, and no one he knew owned a television set. "I first saw television when I was ten years old. In our small Tasmanian town an electrical shop brought in a TV and put it in their window, for the wedding of Princess Margaret. On the great day the whole town gathered in front of the shop and the set was

720

switched on. All we saw was 'snow'—grey and white static, with a few figures vaguely visible through the murk,'' Marsden wrote in *SAAS*.

A Life Filled with Books

Marsden was too infatuated with literature to care if his family had a television. Marsden became such a lover of books that by the time he was in grade three, he had memorized *The Children of Cherry Tree Farm.* One teacher saw in him the seeds of a writer, letting him edit the school paper. ''This was my first taste of publication,'' he told *SAAS.* ''It was a heady experience. Seeing my name in print, having people—even adults—reacting to and commenting on what I'd written was powerful stuff.''

At the age of ten, Marsden moved with his family to the large city of Sydney. Marsden's parents enrolled him at The King's School, a prestigious private school that was run like a military establishment. There was very little Marsden liked about the place, from the stuffy uniforms to the military drills they were required to perform. Marsden spent his time in somewhat subversive activities: he wrote short books with plots that were stolen from famous mystery novels, distributed his underground newspaper about new rock bands, and read books under his desk during class.

At the time, Marsden found that there was very little literature written for adolescents. He read adult literature but was quite taken aback by his first reading of J. D. Salinger's *Catcher in the Rye,* a classic coming-of-age story that was—and still is—controversial. The book ''had me gasping for breath,'' Marsden commented in *SAAS.* ''I'd never dreamt you were allowed to write like that. . . . For the first time I was reading a genuine contemporary teenage voice. If I've had any success at capturing teenage voices on paper, it's because of what I learnt at the age of fifteen from J. D. Salinger.''

Battles Depression

After graduating, Marsden enrolled at the University of Sydney, but soon lost interest in his studies and dropped out. He drifted from job to job, yet somehow succeeded in finishing the first

Cover of So Much To Tell You

year of a law school course. However, he slipped into a deep depression and ended up in a psychiatric institution, where he met a fourteen-year-old girl who would not speak to anyone. Marsden wondered about this, and on the girl's last day at the institution he convinced her to talk. The girl's plight became the inspiration for Marsden's novel *So Much To Tell You.*

At the age of twenty-seven, bored with his latest promotion to a desk job at a delivery company, Marsden saw a newspaper advertisement about teaching classes and decided to apply. Marsden soon had a position teaching at Geelong Grammar School, a very famous Australian school. After several years of teaching, Marsden was encouraged to resume writing. Marsden told *SAAS* that during a school holiday, ''I sat down and started to write. I made two decisions that turned out to be critical. One was to use the diary format, the other was to aim it at teenage readers. These two decisions seemed to free me to write more fluently than before. I worked in an intensity of emotion, a state that I often slip into when writing.'' His efforts resulted in his debut novel, *So Much To Tell You;* with the work, Marsden established a name for himself in the field of young adult literature.

So Much To Tell You focuses on a mute girl who is sent to a special boarding school rather than a psychiatric hospital. The girl has been physically scarred in an accident. Readers get to know her through her diary entries, where her secrets are gradually revealed: her father scarred her with acid that was meant to injure her mother. One of the girl's teachers is able to break into her silent world, and at the end of the novel, there is the hope that she will begin coming out of her isolation. The book caught on quickly and soon became an Australian best-seller.

Works Stir Controversy

Marsden's *Letters from the Inside* and *Dear Miffy* have evoked controversy. *Letters from the Inside* centers around two girls, Mandy and Tracy, who have become pen pals. After a few exchanges of letters, Tracy reveals that she is actually serving time in a maximum security prison. Mandy admits that her brother is quite violent, and the end of the novel alludes to the fact that Mandy might have been attacked by him. In *Reading Time,* Ashley Freeman called *Letters from the Inside* a "compelling story, which totally involves the reader." Other critics were alarmed by the manner in which Marsden presented the subject of domestic violence. Elizabeth Gleick contended in the *New York Times Book Review* that the book "might be faulted for one reason and one reason alone: it offers not the palest glimmer of hope."

Dear Miffy, which features a jacket notice warning that "Contents may offend some readers," has engendered a similar reaction. In this novel, institutionalized teenager Tony, who comes from a broken home and a working-class environment, writes to his girlfriend Miffy, a beautiful girl from a wealthy and very troubled family. Tony's letters, which are never mailed, recount their relationship from its turbulent beginnings through its tragic conclusion.

Dear Miffy is filled with violence, sex, and profanity set against a backdrop of corruption, injustice, and dysfunctional families. Discussing the controversy surrounding the work in *Horn Book,* Karen Jameyson wrote: "In inevitable parallel with the U.S. discussion about *The Chocolate War,* [critics] point out that the shades of gray in this book are so dark as to be unrealistic. Surely no life can be so dismal; surely no group of characters can be so totally lacking in redeeming features; surely no slice of life can be so void of . . . hope." Others commentators have rallied to Marsden's support, commending his forthright treatment of difficult subjects and his capacity to endow his protagonists with an authentic teenage voice.

"Tomorrow, When the War Began"

Marsden has also written a series of adventure stories about a world ruled by children. "One of my childhood fantasies had been of a world without adults, a world in which the adults had magically disappeared and the kids were left to run the place," Marsden wrote in *SAAS.* Out of this fantasy came a series of novels that centered around an invasion of Australia. The first book in the series, *Tomorrow, When the War Began,* is about a group of teenagers who go on a camping trip in the bush. On their return they realize that everyone in their town has been captured by an unnamed enemy, and they must fend for themselves. Quickly, the group organizes to resist the invaders using the scant resources available to them, such as blowing up a lawn mower to kill an enemy soldier.

The Dead of Night and *A Killing Frost* further the story of the teenagers, narrated by Ellie, as they battle the enemy, endure physical hardships and the death of friends, and engage in romantic relationships. Even after this "trilogy" was complete, Marsden wasn't satisfied. He has also finished a fourth and fifth book in the series, *Darkness, Be*

My Friend and *Burning for Revenge,* and there are plans for more.

"I imagine I'll always be writing, all my life, because there is something within me that needs to tell stories," Marsden related to *SAAS.* Marsden returned to teaching school after taking several years off to write full-time. "The other passion of my life is the preservation of life," Marsden commented in *SAAS.* "The older I get, the more disturbed I get by the wanton destruction of other creatures by humans. . . . I hope I continue to improve in my treatment of my fellow creatures, be they animal or vegetable."

Sources for More Information

Books

Children's Literature Review, Volume 34, Gale, 1995.

Something about the Author Autobiography Series, Volume 22, Gale, 1996.

St. James Guide to Young Adult Writers, St. James Press, 1999.

On-line

MarsdenNet, located at http://www.ozemail.com.au/~andrewf/john.html.

Penny Marshall

**Actress and film director
(1943–)**

*"Some part of me must be ambitious
because I keep doing things."*

*Born October 15, 1943, in New York, NY; daughter of
Anthony W. (an industrial filmmaker) and Marjorie Irene
(a dance instructor; maiden name, Ward) Marshall; married Michael Henry (divorced); married Rob Reiner (an
actor and director), April 1971 (divorced 1979); children:
(with Henry) Tracy. Education: Attended the University of
New Mexico.*

Penny Marshall has become a major film
director with several highly acclaimed and
profitable movies to her credit. There was a time
when Hollywood seemed ready to write Penny
Marshall off as yet another one-hit wonder, an
actress-comedienne with limited skills and narrow
appeal. "Penny Marshall got into directing the
'easy' way—by becoming a television superstar
first," wrote Paula Dranov in *Cosmopolitan.* "Although a number of actors have directed movies
. . . few actresses have made a similar transition
successfully. . . . But with *Big,* starring Tom Hanks,
Bronx-born Marshall became the first woman
director of a box office bonanza."

Renowned for her modesty, Marshall calls
her success as a director "a crapshoot." Many
disagree, however. Two Marshall projects, *Big*
and *Awakenings,* have garnered Oscar nominations, proving that the former situation comedy
star can tackle both lighthearted and heavy-duty
material. "I'm used to comin' from under, so I get
a little nervous about people liking something,"
Marshall told *People* magazine. "I just basically

724

hope I don't get kicked out of this business. . . . I've just been lucky in some of the things that walked into my hands.''

Raised in the Bronx

Carole Penny Marscharelli was born in New York City on October 15, 1942. The daughter of an industrial filmmaker and a dance teacher, she was raised in the Bronx. During her early youth her family decided to shorten their surname to Marshall. Penny practically grew up in her mother's studio, studying dance from the age of three. She also managed to find her way outside, into a colorful middle-class neighborhood populated by an ethnic mix of youngsters who would achieve fame in comedy, fashion design, stage production, and publishing.

Marshall remembers her youth in the Bronx with a great deal of fondness; once she even took her daughter on a tour of the old neighborhood, where her contemporaries included future fashion designer Ralph Lauren, comedian Robert Klein, and composer Stanley Silverman. It was customary for teens in that area to hang out together on the street, joking and playing games. Although she was an accomplished dancer, Marshall was ashamed of her looks. She saw comedy as an escape from her seemingly ordinary appearance. ''I made fun of myself before anyone did,'' she told *New York,* ''because I looked like a coconut and had bucked teeth, braces, and a ponytail.''

When Marshall was 14 her mother's dance troupe, the Marshalettes, appeared on Ted Mack's Original Amateur Hour and won. The group then went on to a one-time appearance on the *Jackie Gleason Show.* This early brush with television did not make Marshall yearn for the limelight, however. Instead she enrolled at the University of New Mexico as a math and psychology major. During her sophomore year there she dropped out to marry a football player. The couple soon had both a daughter and a divorce, and Marshall found herself teaching dance in Albuquerque and barely scraping by.

By that time Marshall's brother Garry had made a name for himself as a television writer-producer. He encouraged Marshall to move to Los Angeles and take acting lessons at night while supporting herself as a secretary. He also helped Marshall get auditions and cast her in bit parts in movies he produced. In the late 1960s Marshall joined a Los Angeles repertory group known as The Committee, and there she met fellow Bronx native Rob Reiner. In 1970 both Reiner and Marshall were invited to audition for a new television comedy, *All in the Family.* Reiner was cast in one of the lead roles; Marshall narrowly missed being cast as his wife. In real life they were married in 1971.

While Reiner's career took off, Marshall struggled. A small part in an episode of *The Danny Thomas Hour* proved so traumatic that she almost quit the business. Her brother persuaded her to keep trying, however, and found her a recurring role on the popular situation comedy *The Odd Couple.* Between 1972 and 1974 Marshall appeared a number of times on *The Odd Couple* as Oscar Madison's secretary, Myrna. That part was the first in which Marshall exploited her poker-faced expressions and flat-toned voice. She also appeared on *The Bob Newhart Show,* the comedy *Friends and Lovers, The Mary Tyler Moore Show, Chico and the Man,* and *Love, American Style.* Her made-for-television movies of this period included *The Couple Takes a Wife* and *Let's Switch!*

Laverne and Shirley

A bit part on yet another popular television show became the major catalyst for Marshall's career. In the fall of 1975 she showed up on *Happy Days* as a date for Arthur ''The Fonz'' Fonzarelli. Teamed with the sprightly Cindy Williams, Marshall helped forge a promising comic chemistry. Garry Marshall, who had a hand in the production of *Happy Days,* suggested a spin-off, and a new series, *Laverne and Shirley,* was born. Set in the late 1950s, Laverne and Shirley centered around the life of two working-class roommates, one a brash Italian—Marshall's Laverne—and the other a prim but perky WASP. The show aired in 1976, following *Happy Days* in the prime time lineup; it was an immediate ratings hit. Within weeks *Laverne and Shirley* had cracked the Nielsen Top Ten; it remained in the Top Twenty for three seasons.

Laverne and Shirley made Penny Marshall famous, but not necessarily happy. By 1980 the show had sunk to near-bottom in the ratings, Marshall's marriage had ended, and she was wearing herself out on the Los Angeles party scene. ''The 1970s was a party period for most of the people I know,'' Marshall told *People.* ''We couldn't deal with being famous. We were all

Movie still from **Big**

holding onto each other. But the party's over now." After *Laverne and Shirley* was canceled Marshall found it difficult to find parts that did not echo Laverne. Worse, she found that many Hollywood insiders felt she had ridden to fame on the coattails of her brother and father, who had produced *Laverne and Shirley.* Marshall addressed herself to that charge in *People:* "This is a factory business; of course the sons and daughters of people in it are going to go in it."

Debut as Film Director

During the last few seasons of *Laverne and Shirley* Marshall had directed several episodes. She found that she enjoyed working behind the camera, but it would be years before she was offered such work in films. Her first opportunity to direct a movie came in 1986, when she became a last-minute replacement on the Whoopi Goldberg comedy *Jumpin' Jack Flash.* The film was not terribly successful, but critics did not fault Marshall for its lack of focus. Producer Jim Brooks told *People,* in fact, that Marshall was able to make the best of a difficult project. "I believed in

her," Brooks said. "She came into *Jumpin' Jack Flash* under the most insane conditions imaginable and showed a lot of imagination."

Big, Marshall's next project, held far more promise. The story follows the adventures of an adolescent boy who turns into an adult—overnight; while he looks grown up, the character remains a young teenager under his man's skin. Through a series of twists, the boy-man becomes a successful toy company executive and the love interest of a predatory businesswoman. *National Review* correspondent John Simon called *Big* "an accomplished, endearing, and by no means mindless fantasy," praising Marshall for her delicate treatment of the material. The film was one of the biggest box-office draws of 1988, earning well in excess of $85 million in theaters.

Marshall's next work bore little resemblance to *Big.* A serious drama about a rare brain condition, *Awakenings* tells the story of a young doctor, played by Robin Williams, and his treatment of a catatonic patient, played by Robert De Niro. In the course of the film the doctor revives his dormant patient and helps him to experience the world again. "If anyone in the theater has a dry eye,. . .

check them for a heartbeat,'' wrote Ralph Novak in *People*. The reviewer went on to praise Marshall for her ''beautifully staged'' sequences and her subtle control of difficult emotional territory.

Her next film, 1992's *A League of Their Own*, was a big hit both with the critics and at the box office. It was the story of the short-lived All-American Girls Professional Baseball League that was formed during World War II when male players were off fighting. Among the players were Geena Davis, Madonna, Rosie O'Donnell. Tom Hanks portrayed their team's coach, a drunken, ex-baseball star.

The Preacher's Wife

Starting with the 1995 holiday season, Marshall and O'Donnell began appearing in a series of television commercials as spokespersons for Kmart. At the same time, Marshall also worked on her next directing assignment, *The Preacher's Wife*, released in late 1996. Although based on *The Bishop's Wife*, a 1947 romantic comedy starring Cary Grant and Loretta Young, Marshall's version was not a straightforward update of the original. ''[I]t's not a remake,'' she explained in *Harper's Bazaar,* ''because the original was about greed, and mine is about loss of faith.'' The story of a preacher who has lost faith in his ability to make a difference in people's lives, *The Preacher's Wife* features singer Whitney Houston in the title role and Denzel Washington as the angel who returns to earth to help the troubled couple.

The Preacher's Wife differed from the 1947 in one other key aspect: Marshall's feel-good holiday fable featured an all-African American cast. *Time* magazine reported that the picture—with a budget in excess of $60 million—was to date the most expensive all-black picture ever produced. *The Preacher's Wife*, although successful, did not post staggering results at the box office. Nor was the saccharine holiday tale an unabashed hit with film critics. Marshall's fable, Stephen Holden wrote in *The New York Times*, produces a ''mild feel-good glow,'' although it ''squanders many opportunities to pull heart strings.''

Marshall takes such criticism in stride. ''They always say my movies are all pathos-shmathos,'' she confided to friend Carrie Fisher in *Harper's Bazaar*. ''They don't like what I do.'' Audiences, on the other hand, seem to like Marshall's penchant for pathos. ''And that's more important,'' she told Fisher. ''I'm a people person.''

With a handful of hit movies to her credit, Marshall is now in great demand in Hollywood. She divides her time between homes in Los Angeles and New York City. Marshall spends little time socializing these days—much of her spare time is spent reading screenplays for future projects. ''Some part of me must be ambitious because I keep doing things,'' she told *People*. She added: ''I won't ever act in a movie I'm directing. I could never look at myself that long.''

Sources for More Information

Periodicals

Harper's Bazaar, December, 1996.

People, December 23, 1996.

Time, December 16, 1996.

Working Woman, November–December, 1996.

On-line

E! Online Web site, located at http://www.eonline.com.

Henri Matisse

Painter
(1869-1954)

"What I dream of is an art of balance, of purity and serenity devoid of troubling or depressing subject matter."

Born December 31, 1869, in Le Cateau-Cambresis, France; died November 3, 1954, in Nice, France; married Amelie Noemie Alexandrine Parayre, 1898; children: one daughter, two sons. Education: Studied law at the Sorbonne, Paris, 1887–88; studied drawing under Bouguereau at the Academie Julian, Paris, 1892–93, and with Gustave Moreau from 1893–97, first unofficially, then, after 1895, as a student of the Ecole des Beaux-Arts; studied sculpture with Bourdelle, 1900–03.

Henri Matisse ranks among the most acclaimed and imitated of modern artists, but his innovations shocked many of his contemporaries and only gained widespread acceptance after generating substantial controversy. By the late twentieth century, however, the influence of his bold style can be observed not only in the so-called fine arts but in virtually every facet of popular culture.

Born in Le Cateau-Cambresis, France, on December 31, 1869, Matisse was raised in northern France. His parents, Emile and Gerard Matisse, ran a kind of grocery store. Unlike many artists, he did not spend time drawing or painting as a child. He was expected to take over the family business or, with luck, become a lawyer. Matisse did study law in Paris for two years; but he unwittingly doomed his legal career when, in 1890 while working as a law clerk, he began attending early morning drawing classes meant for curtain designers. While recovering from appendicitis that

728

La Danse by Henri Matisse

year, Matisse received a box of paints from his mother and soon thereafter decided to pursue a career in art. He was twenty years old.

Experiments with Various Styles

Matisse studied for several years in Paris with traditional painters. To earn money he made copies of famous works at the French national museum, the Louvre. At the time Paris was the center of a revolution in the visual arts. Besides impressionism, other new ideas were being introduced by painters like Frenchmen Paul Cézanne and Georges Seurat and Vincent van Gogh of the Netherlands. At the Louvre Matisse was attracted to the passion of Spanish artist Francisco Goya. He also admired the work of his countryman Henri Toulouse-Lautrec and, like numerous artists of the time, was fascinated by the woodblock prints of Japan. Matisse experimented with ideas from all these sources; by 1897 he was on his way to finding his own style.

The first results of his experimentation were revealed in 1898 when he painted a male nude—not in the usual flesh tones, but all in blue. This unorthodox choice reflected his conviction that color should be used to express emotion. By 1905 Matisse had become the leader of a group of artists called ''Les Fauves,'' the wild beasts, after their exhibit shocked the public. Fauvism, as their style became known, is characterized by broad strokes of very bright, often clashing color. The heightened hues and dark borders defining shapes invested their work with tremendous energy. A noteworthy example from this time is Matisse's *Woman with the Hat,* a portrait of the artist's wife, Amelie Parayre—whom he'd married in 1899—in a very large *chapeau.* Although compositionally a traditional rendering of an elegant lady, the painting's use of color—the dress, hat, and even the face are painted in patches of green, red, orange, and blue—was scandalous for the time. Matisse gained some fame when American writer Gertrude Stein and her brother Michael Stein bought the painting. Over the years, the two bought many of his works.

Except for the Steins, however, Matisse attracted few buyers of his paintings and found it difficult to support his family. He and Amelie had two sons and a daughter. Amelie Matisse set up a hat shop in Paris to earn income for the family. She continued to serve frequently as a model for her husband.

Begins Romance with Color

In 1906 Matisse traveled to Italy and North Africa, both of which strongly influenced his

Incorporates Other Styles into His Own

Around 1910 Matisse's style underwent another transformation. He delved into approaches derived from cubism and began using subtler colors, more simplified figures, and a greater number of geometric shapes. Matisse was never a cubist, but as with impressionism, he was able to incorporate many of the school's ideas and theories into his own style. This is evident in his 1911 painting *The Painter's Family,* in which the space is divided into multiple rectangular areas covered with decorative patterns of wallpaper, oriental rug designs, and upholstery prints.

After World War I Matisse began spending a substantial portion of each year in the south of France and eventually settled there permanently. Under the influence of the south's warm, sunny weather, his colors brightened again, and patterns and decorations became more prominent. He wrote that after many years of exploration, his art finally "had established a new clarity and simplicity of its own." Toward the end of the 1920s, Matisse took a trip around the world, spending six months in Tahiti, where Frenchman Paul Gauguin had done so much of his painting, and also traveling to the United States.

Soon after this visit, he received a commission from the Barnes Foundation in Pennsylvania to paint a mural in their museum, which contained many impressionist and post-impressionist works. This was the first of several interior design commissions Matisse accepted in the ensuing years. The largest project, often considered the masterpiece of his career, was the design of a chapel in the French town of Vence. Matisse created the stained-glass windows, interior decor, devotional objects, and clothing for the clergy. The chapel was dedicated in 1951.

style. In Italy he admired the frescoes of the pre-Renaissance Italian artist Giotto, with their simple, monumental style. In North Africa he was drawn to the brilliant colors and decorative patterns of Islamic art. He brought back from this trip pottery, cloths, carpets, and other items, which he often used in his paintings. His *Blue Nude (Souvenir of Biskra)* reflects these influences and his love of the human figure. Yet anatomy would ultimately take a back seat to design; in the next few years, rich colors and decorative patterns, including those of vines and flowers, seemed to overrun his paintings; in *Harmony in Red,* the pattern of the wallpaper and tablecloth leave little space in the painting for the woman standing at the table.

Matisse is also notable for repeating parts of previous paintings in newer works. For instance, in a still life from 1909, the viewer can see a section of his earlier painting *La Danse. La Danse,* along with a companion painting, *La Musique,* was commissioned by a Russian businessman named Sergei Shchukin, a great supporter of Matisse in these years. Matisse visited him in Moscow several times, and Shchukin eventually owned thirty-seven of his paintings. In 1923 Shchukin and another Russian collector opened the first museum of contemporary Western art in Moscow, including forty-eight of Matisse's works.

Matisse also used the freedom of fauvism in his early sculptures. He worked with sculpture throughout his career, adapting for the medium his many concepts of form and space.

Cuts Out

During the 1930s Matisse turned to designing and illustrating books. He began working with geometric and abstract shapes cut out of colored paper, silhouetting these against multihued backgrounds. Matisse's most famous book, *Jazz,* dates from 1947. The vivid colors, flowing shapes, and rhythmic feel evoke the qualities of that musical form. Matisse's works were exhibited often during the 1930s in major cities across Europe and the

United States. At a large exhibition in Paris in 1936, an entire room was devoted to his paintings.

In the 1940s and 1950s Matisse became increasingly handicapped due to illness. During the World War II years, he was often confined to his bed. His works from this period are smaller and include numerous book illustrations. These creations have a pronounced serenity about them, all the more remarkable since both Matisse's wife and daughter were arrested by the Nazis during this time. Amelie Matisse suffered two three-month prison sentences, and Marguerite Matisse was placed in solitary confinement, charged with resistance activities.

A Maverick to the End

War's end saw an increase in Matisse's activity. He often worked from a wheelchair or in bed, sketching designs on the wall with a piece of charcoal attached to a long pole. His last paintings recalled his favorite themes of female figures and interiors and include *Large Red Interior* from 1948. He spent many hours directing his assistants to find the perfect arrangements of his paper cutouts. Matisse passed the last years of his life designing the chapel at Vence and working on his cutouts. These free-form shapes brought together all of Matisse's ideas, from painting, sculpture, and the decorative arts. Despite his infirmities, he continued working until his death in Nice, France, on November 3, 1954, at the age of eighty-four, a maverick to the end.

Sources for More Information

Books

Essers, Volkmar, *Henri Matisse, 1869–1954: Master of Colour,* Taschen, 1987.

Girard, Xavier, *Matisse: The Wonder of Color,* translated by I. Mark Paris, Abrams, 1994.

Herrera, Hayden, *Matisse: A Portrait,* Harcourt, Brace, 1993.

Raboff, Ernest Lloyd, *Henri Matisse,* Lippincott, 1988.

Wilson, Sarah, *Matisse,* Rizzoli, 1992.

Harry Mazer

**Young adult novelist
(1925-)**

"Despite the erosion of time the child in us never dies."

Born May 31, 1925, in New York, NY; son of Sam (a dressmaker) and Rose (a dressmaker; maiden name, Lazevnick) Mazer; married Norma Fox (a novelist), February 12, 1950; children: Anne, Joseph, Susan, Gina. Education: Union College, B.A., 1948; Syracuse University, M.A., 1960.

In addition to being part of a writing family that includes wife Norma Fox Mazer and daughter Anne Mazer, novelist Harry Mazer has received critical acclaim for his many young adult novels—including *The Island Keeper, Cave under the City,* and *Who Is Eddie Leonard?*—which illustrate the values of perseverance, self-esteem, and inner fortitude. Noting that, "despite their predicaments, Mazer's protagonists usually emerge morally victorious," *Twentieth-Century Young Adult Writers* contributor Mary Lystad cited as Mazer's strength his depiction of the "emotional turmoil, the humor and pain" of adolescence. "His characters are resilient and strong," Lystad continued. "His endings emphasize compassion, understanding, resourcefulness, and honesty."

"A dream is made by real effort," Mazer once explained in an essay in *Something about the Author Autobiography Series (SAAS)*. Mazer was in his mid-thirties when he and his wife began to write every day; they wrote for the "women's true confessions" market, using the money to support the family. In 1971 Mazer published *Guy Lenny,* his first novel, and since then he has gone on to assemble an impressive body of work. Kenneth L. Donelson asserted in *Voice of Youth Advocates* that ''Mazer writes about young people caught in the midst of moral crises, often of their own making. Searching for a way out, they discover themselves, or rather they learn that the first step in extricating themselves from their physical and moral dilemmas is self-discovery.''

The son of hard-working Polish-Jewish immigrants, Mazer grew up in an apartment building in the Bronx, New York. Mazer shared the bedroom of the two-room apartment with his brother, while his parents slept in the living room, which also served as a dining room and kitchen. The halls and the stairs were Mazer's playground, and he grew up between two worlds—the park and the street—both of which he would later use in his novels.

An Uncertain Future

Changes loomed large in Mazer's life when he entered his high-school years. Questions about his future occupied his mind; jobs were scarce at the time, and many employers wouldn't hire Jews. ''My secret desire was to be a writer, but I knew nothing about how to make it happen,'' Mazer stated. ''I had the idea that if I could only write it down, if I could only put all my feelings into words, I would finally figure everything out (whatever everything was).'' Mazer attended the Bronx High School of Science, but the courses that most interested him were English and history, and the questions concerning his future still lingered.

At age eighteen Mazer joined the army. Starting out as an airplane mechanic, he volunteered for aerial gunnery school, training as a ball-turret and waist gunner. After training, Mazer was assigned to a crew on a B-17 bomber. Their last mission was flown in April 1945 when the plane was shot down over Czechoslovakia; only Mazer and one other crew member survived. ''I remember thinking afterward that there had to be a reason why I had survived,'' recalled Mazer. ''I didn't think it was God. It was chance. Luck. But why me? Chance can't be denied as a factor in life, but I clung to the thought that there was a reason for my survival.''

Mazer was discharged from the army in October of 1945, and days later began attending classes at a liberal arts college. Graduating with a liberal arts degree, Mazer took a blue-collar job while

*Cover of **Who Is Eddie Leonard?***

struggling to define himself as a writer. ''I was dramatizing myself,'' Mazer later admitted, ''imagining myself a leader of the downtrodden, pointing the way to the future. . . . I was idealistic. I was unrealistic. Most of all I was avoiding the real issues of my life. I didn't have the belief or the nerve to say I was a writer, to begin writing and let everything else take care of itself.''

Husband-and-Wife Writing Team

Politics also interested Mazer during this period; it was while working on a campaign that he met Norma Fox for the second time. He had met her two years earlier when she was fifteen and he was twenty-one, but it was the second meeting that started their on-again, off-again romance. The couple finally married and, after several moves, settled in Syracuse. Mazer worked at various jobs, doing welding, sheet metal work, and track work for the railroad.

After ten years of factory work, Mazer became a teacher. It was at this point that he and Norma talked, discovered that they both longed to be writers, and began writing every day. The insurance money from an accident finally enabled him to quit his job and begin writing full-time; the couple were soon writing two confession stories a week. "These stories demanded that I develop a character, a plot, action that rose to a climax, and a satisfying ending. And I had to do it every week, week after week. It was a demanding school," Mazer wrote in *SAAS*.

A piece in a "Dear Abby" column gave Mazer the idea for his first children's book. The column was about a boy who was concerned about an older girl he liked. She was going with someone else who was no good for her, and the boy wanted to know how he could break them up. "It was the germ that started my first book, *Guy Lenny*," Mazer revealed in his essay. *Guy Lenny* is the story of a boy whose parents are divorced, a subject that children's books of the time did not deal with. "It's a children's story because it's about a boy and is told from his point of view," explains Mazer in *SAAS;* "it's also an adult story because it's about growing up and having to live with some of the hard, intractable things of life. And that's what made it a young-adult book, a new category of fiction that was still to be named."

Focuses on Characters

Many of Mazer's novels use characters from earlier books, and father-and-son relationships appear again and again. A *Publishers Weekly* contributor maintained that Mazer "creates credible characters . . . and incorporates splashes of humor while maintaining the established mood and tone." In the novel *The Girl of His Dreams,* for example, Mazer relates the romance of Willis and Sophie, two ordinary young adults, with "a credibility apart from [the book's] fairy-tale ending," in the opinion of Marianne Gingher in the *Los Angeles Times*. Willis is a factory worker and dedicated runner who has a clear vision of exactly what the girl of his dreams should be like. Sophie does not fit this image, and their relationship develops slowly and awkwardly.

Snow Bound is another tale of two mismatched teens who are caught unprepared for a New York blizzard and must cooperate to survive. Tony is a spoiled rich kid who sets out to get revenge on his parents for not letting him keep a stray dog. He steals his mother's car and takes off in the middle of a snowstorm, picking up hitchhiker Cindy along the way. Besides getting lost, Tony wrecks the car in a desolate area, and he and Cindy must save themselves from the cold and a pack of wild dogs.

Autobiographical Novel

Highly praised by critics, *The Last Mission,* based in part on Mazer's own experiences in World War II, "represents an amazing leap in writing, far surpassing anything [the author] had written before," according to Donelson. Jewish fifteen-year-old Jack Raab is so desperate to fight against Hitler that he borrows his older brother's identification to enlist in the Army Air Forces. Jack is trained as a gunner, and he and his fellow crew members fly more than twenty missions out of England before being hit by enemy fire. Jack bails out and is the only one to survive—but ends up a German prisoner of war. While war stories are common, Donelson maintained that *The Last Mission* "conveys better than any other young adult novel, and better than most adult novels, the feeling of war and the desolation it leaves behind. . . ."

The main character in *I Love You, Stupid!* is faced with more typical adolescent problems. A senior in high school, Marcus wants to be a writer and is obsessed with sex. Marcus's erotic dreams include almost every young female he meets—everyone but Wendy, a girl he knew in grade school. Marcus even goes so far as to babysit for a young divorced woman, hoping she'll become his lover. Wendy and Marcus finally make love, but Marcus, looking for a reason to do it every day, drives Wendy away.

Teenage Protagonists

Who Is Eddie Leonard? introduces readers to the fifteen-year-old title character, who lives with an eccentric elderly woman he calls "Grandmother." When she dies, he is left alone, feeling that he must belong somewhere. A poster of a missing child named Jason Diaz changes everything for Eddie. Seeing the resemblance between himself and the missing boy, and calculating that Jason would now also be fifteen years old, Eddie hunts down the boy's family and introduces himself as their missing son.

Other novels by Mazer include *The War on Villa Street,* about a boy's attempts to find stability in a family where his father's alcoholism and his mother's passivity mean constant upheaval and relocation. Also set in an urban area, *Cave under the City* takes place during the Great Depression, as two brothers find themselves parentless after their father's departure in search of work and their mother's subsequent collapse and hospitalization. When social workers attempt to separate the boys, they flee and live among New York City's homeless population until their father returns.

Drawing on his personal concerns about modern society, Mazer served as editor of *Twelve Shots: Outstanding Short Stories about Guns,* which was released in 1997. Inviting a dozen authors to write stories concerning ''not the politics of the gun, not the heated arguments or the polemics, but the way guns are present in people's lives,'' Mazer assembles works by such well-known children's authors as Walter Dean Myers, Chris Lynch, Frederick Busch, and Rita Williams-Garcia, as well as contributing his own short story, based on his novel *The Last Mission.* While the stories included range from serious commentary on the devastation wrought by gun-related violence in modern society to humorous folk-like tales, Mazer's own anti-gun slant is made clear.

From his novels to his shorter works of fiction, Mazer's writing has been characterized by reviewers as containing a belief in the essential goodness of people, particularly young people. In his *SAAS* essay, Mazer concluded: ''I think underlying all my writing has always been the belief that beneath the surface of our differences there is a current, a dark stream that connects all of us,

Don't Miss ...

Snow Bound, Delacorte, 1973

The Solid Gold Kid (with Norma Fox Mazer), Delacorte, 1977

The War on Villa Street, Delacorte, 1978

The Last Mission, Delacorte, 1979

I Love You, Stupid!, Crowell, 1981

Hey, Kid! Does She Love Me?, Crowell, 1984

When the Phone Rang, Scholastic, 1985

The Girl of His Dreams, Crowell, 1987

City Light, Scholastic, 1988

readers and writers, parents and children, the young and the old. Despite the erosion of time the child in us never dies. The search for love never ends, the need for connection, the desire to know who we are, and the need to find someone of our own to love. How else do I keep writing for young readers?''

Sources for More Information

Books

Children's Literature Review, Volume 16, Gale, 1989.

Reed, Arthea J. S., *Presenting Harry Mazer,* Twayne, 1996.

Something about the Author Autobiography Series, Volume 11, Gale, 1991.

St. James Guide to Young Adult Writers, St. James Press, 1999.

Norma Fox Mazer

Young adult novelist and short story writer (1931-)

"I write and my readers read to find out the answers to questions, secrets, problems, to be drawn into the deepest mystery of all—someone else's life."

Born May 15, 1931, in New York, NY; daughter of Michael and Jean (Garlen) Fox; married Harry Mazer (a novelist), February 12, 1950; children: Anne, Joseph, Susan, Gina. Education: Attended Antioch College, 1949–50, and Syracuse University, 1957–59.

Norma Fox Mazer has garnered numerous awards, as well as high praise from critics, for novels like *Silver, After the Rain,* and *Saturday, the Twelfth of October* that depict teenagers in everyday situations, experiencing common problems. "At her best," observed Suzanne Freeman in the *Washington Post Book World,* "Mazer can cut right to the bone of teenage troubles and then show us how the wounds will heal." It took many years of discipline for Mazer to become such a writer, and even longer for her to consider herself one; it wasn't until she was writing her 1976 novel *Dear Bill, Remember Me? and Other Stories* that Mazer actually believed she was a real author. In an essay in *Something about the Author Autobiography Series (SAAS),* she recalled that "during the months I spent working on [*Dear Bill*], I somehow lost time, I began to believe fearlessly in the endless vitality of that mysterious source from which my imagination is constantly replenished."

Mazer grew up in Glens Falls, New York, the middle daughter in a family of three girls. Her father was a route driver, delivering such things as milk and bread, and the family lived in a succession of various apartments and houses. During

Mazer's teen years, her family started calling her the "Cold One," as she began to live more and more in her own world. Feeling like an outsider, Mazer admitted in *SAAS* that "were I to be asked to use one word to describe myself then and for years afterward, it would be—eyes. There's a picture of me around thirteen, sitting in a high-backed leather chair, looking out of the corner of my eyes, looking around, watching, a little frightened smile on my face. Along about then, it struck me, a bone-aching truth, that grown-ups—adults, these powerful mysterious people—were all play-acting; they weren't, in fact, any older, any more grown-up than I was."

A job with the school newspaper gave Mazer her first opportunity to write for publication, and writing soon became the focus of her existence at school. "But I wanted to write more than newspaper articles. There was a longing in me, vague . . . but real, almost an ache," the novelist recalled. When she was fifteen, Mazer met her future husband, Harry Mazer, for the first time. He was a friend of her older sister, and at the age of twenty-one, he seemed ancient to Mazer. Two years later, they met again, and a much more confident Mazer was determined that Harry should fall in love with her. Harry thought that Mazer was too young, though, and she had to work at making him notice her—the couple fell in and out of love and quarreled many times before finally getting married.

A Momentous Decision

During the early part of their marriage, the Mazers worked at "boring" jobs and tried to learn how to cook. Three children soon became part of the family, and Mazer took on the role of Mommy. She found, though, that she was losing her own identity, and a serious talk with her husband followed. Both Mazers revealed a desire to be a writer. They decided that if they were really serious about writing, they had to do at least a little every day. So, for three years, the Mazers spent an hour at the end of each day writing. Money from an insurance settlement finally enabled them to write full-time.

To support the family, the Mazers wrote for the "women's true confessions" market. These stories were presented as first-person confessions of women who had made serious mistakes in their

Cover of When She Was Good

lives, but were actually the work of professional writers. During the following years, the Mazers each wrote one of these 5,000–8,000 word stories every week, leaving little time to devote to the writing of novels. In 1970 Mazer managed to find the time to write the novel *I, Trissy,* and it was published the following year. *A Figure of Speech* came two years later and received a National Book Award nomination. "I remember meeting a member of the National Book Award committee some time after *A Figure of Speech* had received a . . . nomination and hearing him say to me, '. . .and you just came out of nowhere.' I laughed. My 'nowhere' had been the ten years I'd spent writing full time and learning the craft."

Young Adult Works Draw Praise

Mazer has been particularly noted for her young adult novels, some of which she has written with her husband. *Taking Terri Mueller,* for example, earned her an Edgar Award from the Mystery Writers of America, although she had not intended it as a mystery. The book follows Terri Mueller and her father as they wander from town to town, never staying in one place for more than a year.

Although Terri is happy with her father, she is old enough to wonder why he will never talk about her mother, who supposedly died ten years before; an overheard discussion leads Terri to discover that she had been kidnapped by her father after a bitter custody battle.

In the novel *Babyface,* Mazer handles another parent/daughter relationship that is threatened by secrets. Toni Chessmore believes she has perfect parents and an ideal best friend. During the summer of Toni's fourteenth year, though, her opinions begin to change when her father has a heart attack and she goes to stay with her sister in New York. Toni learns shocking secrets about her parents' past, and has a hard time dealing with them when she returns home.

Examines Family Relationships

In both *A Figure of Speech* and *After the Rain,* Mazer deals with the relationship between a young girl and her grandfather. In *After the Rain* Rachel's grandfather, Izzy, has cancer, so Rachel begins to go with him on his long afternoon walks. Izzy's crusty exterior has often prevented his family from getting close to him. Rachel is the youngest member of her family, half the age of her older brother, and her parents embarrass her and seem incredibly old. During the walks with her grandfather, Rachel comes to know and love him before he dies. When he is gone, she is able to deal with the death and loss, and even teach her parents a few things. A *Kirkus Reviews* contributor asserted that *After the*

Rain is "beautifully and sensitively written, sounding the basic chords of the pleasures and pains of family relationships."

Family relationships are also the focus of Mazer's *Missing Pieces.* Raised by her mother with help from her elderly aunt Zis after her father abandoned the family over a decade before, fourteen-year-old Jessie Wells wishes she had a "normal" family, and this wish has become almost an obsession. During the process of trying to get her mom to talk about the reasons for her dad's disappearance and then attempting to relocate him, Jessie gains a new understanding of family structure, using this new knowledge to help balance relationships among her friends.

Growing up in a single-parent family is given an unpleasant twist in *When She Was Good,* which Mazer published in 1997. Em Thurkill's mother died years ago, and her stepmother doesn't want to deal with her husband's children by his first marriage. When older sister Pamela moves out on her own, Em follows her, and becomes captive to Pamela's controlling personality, drastic mood swings, and daily outbursts of violent temper. After four years, Pamela's unexpected death leaves seventeen-year-old Em on her own, with no one to tell her what to do when. Beginning her story after Pamela's death, a newly liberated Em looks back at the unfortunate circumstances that brought her to this point and her sometimes self-destructive attempts to deal with the emotional void in her life.

Published in 1993, Mazer's *Out of Control* features a male protagonist named Rollo Wingate, whose friendship with the wrong crowd brings him into a situation bordering on the tragic. Rollo becomes a tagalong member of a group of three high-school juniors who dub themselves the Lethal Threesome. The trio corner fellow student Valerie Michon in a deserted part of the school and grope her. Eventually discovered and reprimanded, Rollo is uncertain why his actions so disgust his father and upset the school administration, and can't fathom why his attempt at an apology is rejected by a traumatized Valerie.

Publishes Short Story Collections

Along with her novels, Mazer has also written several short-story collections. The eight short stories in *Dear Bill, Remember Me? and Other Stories* deal with young girls going through a period of crisis. In "Up on Fong Mountain," Jessie strives to be accepted as something other than an extension of her boyfriend. Eighteen-year-old Louise in "Guess Whose Friendly Hands" knows she's dying of cancer, and merely wishes that her mother and sister would accept it as she has.

The stories in Mazer's second collection, *Summer Girls, Love Boys, and Other Short Stories,* are connected by the setting of Greene Street. In "Do You Really Think It's Fair?," Sarah tells about the death of her younger sister and questions the existence of justice. Another story, "Amelia Earhart, Where Are You When I Need You?," relates the short vacation a young girl spends with her eccentric Aunt Clare. "Each story has a strength and a sharpness of vision that delights and surprises in its maturity," commented Ruth I. Gordon in the *New York Times Book Review.*

Mazer pointed out in her autobiographical essay that there is "a kind of mystery" in all of her books: "I write and my readers read to find out the answers to questions, secrets, problems, to be drawn into the deepest mystery of all—someone else's life." Freeman asserted that "in its sharpest moments, Mazer's writing can etch a place in our hearts," and in her *Top of the News* essay, Mazer declared: "I love stories. I'm convinced that everyone does, and whether we recognize it or not, each of us tells stories. A day doesn't pass when we don't put our lives into story. Most often these stories are . . . of the moment. They are the recognition, the highlighting of . . . our daily lives. . . . In my own life, it seems that events are never finished until I've either told them or written them."

Sources for More Information

Books

Children's Literature Review, Volume 23, Gale, 1991.

Holtze, Sally Homes, editor, *Fifth Book of Junior Authors and Illustrators,* H. W. Wilson, 1983.

Holtze, Sally Holmes, *Presenting Norma Fox Mazer,* Twayne, 1987.

Something about the Author Autobiography Series, Volume 1, Gale, 1986.

On-line

William Morrow Books Web site, located at http://www.williammorrow.com.

Anne McCaffrey

**Science fiction novelist
(1926-)**

*"If you tell a good story, anybody will
read it."*

*Born April 1, 1926, in Cambridge, MA; daughter of George
Herbert (a city administrator and U.S. Army colonel) and
Anne D. (McElroy) McCaffrey; married H. Wright Johnson, January 14, 1950 (divorced, 1970); children: Alec
Anthony, Todd, Georgeanne. Education: Radcliffe College, B.A. (cum laude), 1947; graduate study in meteorolo-
gy, University of City of Dublin; also studied voice for
nine years.*

Anne McCaffrey, science-fiction's much-her-
alded "Dragon Lady," lives in Ireland in a
home called Dragonhold where she produces fantastic tales of the dragonriders of Pern. A planet
protected from deadly spores called "Thread" by
flying, fire-breathing dragons and their human
partners, Pern is a former colony of Earth which
has lost much of its scientific and historical knowledge. Hundreds of years after its founding, Pern is
divided into a near-feudal society of landholders
who often work against the less rigid communities
of dragonriders, called Weyrs. McCaffrey's emphasis on the conflicts between individuals, the
fight against Thread, and the unique telepathic
relationship between dragon and rider makes her
popular with readers of all ages, a reputation
confirmed by her continuing appearances on the
best-seller charts.

McCaffrey's characters are often women or
children who seek their niche in society and frequently must struggle against convention and adversity to succeed. These struggles reflect the

author's own childhood determination to make something of herself, as she once commented: "When I was a very young girl, I promised myself fervently (usually after I'd lost another battle with one of my brothers) that I would become a famous author and I'd own my own horse." McCaffrey credits her parents for raising her to believe she could do anything. She commented in her *Something about the Author Autobiography Series* (*SAAS*) essay: "Few women during my adolescence were encouraged to think of having independent careers, or careers at all: marriage was considered quite enough to occupy most women's lives. That's where I . . . lucked out: being subtly conditioned to have marriage, motherhood, AND self-fulfillment."

"Harper Hall" Series

McCaffrey's "Harper Hall" series, a popular Pern trilogy for younger readers, follows a teenage girl who comes from a very different situation. In *Dragonsong,* the first book, Menolly has been forbidden to play or sing her music solely because she is a girl and "girls aren't harpers." After her hand is accidentally injured and then deliberately mistreated to prevent proper healing that would allow her to play again, Menolly runs away. Outside of the Hold, she faces the dangers of Thread and the challenges of survival by herself—but she is not alone, as she befriends and cares for a set of young fire lizards, small cousins to Pern's mighty dragons. The book concludes as Menolly is rescued from Threadfall and her talent is discovered by the Harper Guild.

Menolly encounters a new set of problems in *Dragonsinger,* the second book in the trilogy. Although she has arrived at the Harper Hall and has started training to be a harper, she still must face the prejudice of some teachers and the resentment of students jealous of her talent and her fire lizards. With her usual determination, and the aid of new friends such as the apprentice Piemur, Menolly overcomes these troubles to achieve happiness. Piemur takes center stage in the third "Harper Hall" book, *Dragondrums,* and together the trilogy contains "strong characters" as well as "a nice balance between problems that are present

*Cover of **Dragonsong***

in any civilized society and a sense of humor that lightens both exposition and dialogue," Zena Sutherland writes in the *Bulletin of the Center for Children's Books.*

Science Grounds Fantastic Elements

Although Pern is inhabited by flying dragons and dominated by a near-feudal society—elements typical of fantasy worlds—McCaffrey's creation is based on solid scientific principles. The author frequently consults with scientific experts in order to make her ideas fully-fleshed and believable; 1988's *Dragonsdawn,* in fact, reveals the story of how the original colonists of Pern used genetic manipulation to develop Pern's dragons. The book features two of Pern's first dragonriders, young lovers Sean and Sorka, as they participate in the grand experiment and take up the battle against Threadfall.

But the emotional focus of the Dragonrider series—and other McCaffrey works such as the

"Crystal Singer" and "Raven Women" novels—puts the technology in the background, unlike many science fiction novels. This emphasis on people and feelings has led some critics to christen the Pern books "science fantasy." McCaffrey, however, believes the use of emotion is appropriate to science fiction. As she related in her *SAAS* entry, one of her first (and most popular) stories, "The Ship Who Sang," was born of her grief over her father's death: "'Ship' taught me to use emotion as a writing tool. And I do, with neither apology nor shame, even though I am writing science fiction, a *genre* not often noted, in those days, for any emotions, only intellectual exercise and scientific curiosities."

A Social Commentator

McCaffrey's approach also allows her to weave serious social commentary into her work, according to Edra C. Bogle in the *Dictionary of Literary Biography.* "Most of McCaffrey's protagonists are women or children, whom she treats with understanding and sympathy," Bogle says. The injustices these characters suffer, brought about by a sometimes-stifling social system, "are at the heart of most of McCaffrey's books." In fact, the majority of McCaffrey's novels feature strong heroines: the ruling Weyrwomen of the "Dragonrider" books; the determined young musician of *Crystal Singer* and *Killashandra;* the talented psychics of *To Ride Pegasus* and the "Raven Women" series; and Helva, the independent starship "brain" of *The Ship Who Sang.* Through these works, Bogle indicates, "McCaffrey has brought delineations of active women into prominence in science fiction."

McCaffrey's "Dragonriders" series has proved so popular, with each new volume hitting the bestseller lists, "that it has almost transcended genre categorization," Gary K. Reynolds asserts in the *Science Fiction and Fantasy Book Review.* For her efforts, McCaffrey received the 1999 Margaret A. Edwards Award for achievement in young adult literature. "Anne McCaffrey succeeds so well because she presents a colorful, ideally-traditional culture in which each person has his or her place, with corresponding duties and privileges; in which the moral choices are clear; and in which, 'if you try hard enough, and work long enough, you can achieve anything you desire.'" As a result, James and Eugene Sloan conclude in the *Chicago Tribune Book World,* McCaffrey's "Dragonriders of Pern" books "must now rank as the most enduring serial in the history of science fantasy."

Sources for More Information

Books

Dictionary of Literary Biography, Volume 8: *Twentieth-Century American Science Fiction Writers,* Gale, 1981.

Something about the Author Autobiography Series, Volume 11, Gale, 1991.

On-line

Official Anne McCaffrey Web site, located at http://members.aol.com/dragnhld/index2.html.

Del Rey Books Web site, located at http://www.villard.com/delrey/pern/index2.html.

Ewan McGregor

Actor
(1971–)

Born March 31, 1971, in Crieff, Scotland; married Eve Maurakis (a costume designer and writer), c. 1995; children: Clara. Education: Studied acting at Guildhall School of Music and Drama, late 1980s.

"I've been very lucky, always having something to go on to when I finish something else."

Scottish actor Ewan McGregor has achieved renown through his performances in several tough, but disparate independent film roles since the mid-1990s. Not yet thirty, McGregor has appeared as a heroin addict, an eighteenth-century seducer, a Seventies-era rock star, and a young Obi Wan Kenobi in the prequel to the *Star Wars* saga. Moreover, McGregor has become virtually a household name in the United States—not an easy market to crack for an entertainer with both intensity and an accent. Writing for the *New York Times,* Michael Dwyer compared McGregor to two other successful "Brit Pack" stars, Daniel Day-Lewis and Gary Oldman, and noted that many who have worked with McGregor describe him as "the most interesting actor to come out of Scotland since Sean Connery."

The son of teachers, McGregor grew up in the Scottish town of Crieff and attended Morrison's Academy until he was sixteen. He was an admittedly indifferent student, and was far more interested in following in the footsteps of his uncle, an actor who had appeared in all three *Star Wars* films. McGregor was taken to the theater to see Denis Lawson on the screen when he was just five or six years old, and the experience stuck with him. His uncle continued to be a profound influence in other ways—''he had long hair, beads, and a furry waistcoat,'' McGregor commented to Richard Corliss of *Time.* ''I aspired to be as different as he seemed to me.''

Makes Acting Debut

By the mid-1980s, still in his teens, McGregor began working behind the scenes at the Perthshire Repertory Theater. He then won entry into London's Guildhall School of Music and Drama, and remained there for three years. His first professional acting job was a plum one—he appeared in the 1992 British television series *Lipstick on Your Collar,* the work of the acclaimed writer Dennis Potter. From there, McGregor was cast in his first film role by Scottish director Bill Forsyth, but spoke only one line in *Being Human,* a movie that bombed at the box office.

McGregor found his metier, however, when director Danny Boyle cast him in a darkly comic 1994 film called *Shallow Grave.* In it, McGregor played a young journalist who is suddenly dealing with the ramifications of a mysterious, freshly deceased roommate and a large sum of cash, both of which he and his two other Edinburgh flatmates have messily co-inherited. *Shallow Grave* was a surprise hit in the United States as well as in the British Isles, and McGregor's performance led Boyle to cast him in the lead role for his next film.

Star Turn in Trainspotting

McGregor played Renton, the central character in *Trainspotting,* a tale of loser Edinburgh junkies waging a futile, halfhearted war against their heroin addiction. Released in both the U.K. and U.S. in 1996, the adaptation of a novel by English writer Irvine Welsh quickly became a cult hit on both sides of the Atlantic. It was a somewhat controversial one as well for the rather objective take on drug abuse at the hands of Welsh, Boyle, and physician-turned-screenwriter John Hodge. For the role, McGregor lost nearly thirty pounds to

play a convincingly emaciated junkie, and his comic turn as the cheeky Renton made him almost famous—or at least quite well known among the film's under-30 target audience.

In a rather abrupt departure, McGregor's next role after finishing work on Trainspotting called for horseback riding, top hats, and elegant Jane Austen prose—he was cast as Frank Churchill in the screen adaptation of *Emma,* which hit screens in 1996 as well. He admitted the switch from modern-day urban dope fiend to refined literary character was a bit precipitous in the end. ''I was terrible in [*Emma*],'' McGregor told Dwyer in the *New York Times.* ''I didn't believe a word I said.''

Takes Quirky Roles

He was next cast as a deranged kidnapper in another Boyle film, *A Life Less Ordinary,* opposite Cameron Diaz (1997). In a marked departure from *Shallow Grave* and *Trainspotting,* Boyle shot this film in Utah, a state that to McGregor quickly appeared far more ''foreign'' to him than New York or Los Angeles had been from Scotland.

Another challenging role came when McGregor was cast in acclaimed director Peter Greenaway's 1997 film *The Pillow Book.* In it, the actor played a bisexual man whose skin is the canvas for the calligraphic writings of a Hong Kong woman, played by Vivian Wu. The role called for a great deal of frontal nudity, but McGregor admitted that having to stand for hours while the makeup artists prepared his back was far more excruciating. Another McGregor film released in the United States was *Brassed Off,* the saga of an English brass band, a closing coal mine, and a town that will never recover. This script interested McGregor, he later said, more for its pro-labor, anti-Thatcherite political overtones than for the chance it allowed him to use his French horn skills from his youth.

Unique and challenging film scripts seem to find McGregor on their own. Another plum lead—this time as a master gardener—arrived for the actor in the form of *The Serpent's Kiss.* Shown at the Cannes International Film Festival in 1997, the movie was described by Dwyer of the *New York Times* as ''a story of landscape gardening,

sexual intrigue and deceit set in Gloucestershire, England, in 1699.'' From there, McGregor donned glitter makeup and platform shoes for his role in *Velvet Goldmine,* a film in which he plays a London glam-rocker in the early 1970s.

The New Obi-Wan Kenobi

In 1999, McGregor deviated from his previous dramatic roles to play a Jedi Knight in George Lucas' sci-fi fantasy prequel, *Star Wars: Episode I—The Phantom Menace.* In the film, McGregor plays the role of Obi-Wan Kenobi (portrayed in the original *Star Wars* by Sir Alec Guinness) who is apprenticed to Jedi Master Qui-Gon Jinn (Liam Neeson). *Rolling Stone* contributor Peter Travers stated, ''McGregor does a deft job of matching up with [Guinness] vocally.'' McGregor also learned acrobatic maneuvers for his light saber duel against Darth Maul, which critics and fans alike have called one of the highlights of the film.

The *Star Wars* experience was different for McGregor than his previous films. ''It was a mixture of exciting and boring,'' McGregor told *Interview*'s Graham Fuller. ''Every day there'd be a few moment where I would go 'F—, we're doing *Star Wars*.' But it was also a tedious film to make. There's not a lot of psychological stuff

going on when you're acting with things that aren't actually there.'' He said that playing Obi-Wan ''was very weird. The Jedi Knights have a sense of what's going to happen, so they don't freak out or panic.'' He added jokingly that ''after a while I noticed the only thing I was doing was frowning a lot.''

Despite landing the much-coveted role in such a huge movie, McGregor confessed that he has never wished for blockbuster-type stardom. The Hollywood action movie, he noted in an E! Online interview, does not interest him in the least, and mentioned a hit American film laden with aliens and special effects, including an exploding White House. ''I would shoot myself in the head before I was in a film like that, I really would,'' McGregor told E!'s Strauss. ''I think it's disgraceful.''

Far more challenging tasks than dodging spaceships seem to be in McGregor's future. He lives in London with his wife, a French film production designer, and their daughter Clara—who will be taken to see her father as Obi Wan Kenobi right about the same age as her father was back in 1977 when he saw his kin in the original *Star Wars*. ''I've been very lucky, always having something to go on to when I finish something else,'' McGregor reflected on his career in the *New York Times* article. ''And now I even have the opportunity to choose what I do. It can't get better.''

Sources for More Information

Periodicals

Entertainment Weekly, March 26, 1999.

Newsweek, February 1, 1999.

Premiere, May, 1999.

Publishers Weekly, May 3, 1999.

Time, July 15, 1996; November 3, 1997; April 26, 1999; May 17, 1999.

On-line

E! Online Web site, locate at http://www.eonline.com.

The official *Star Wars* Web site, located at http://www.starwars.com.

Robin McKinley

**Fantasy novelist
(1952–)**

Born November 16, 1952, in Warren, OH; daughter of William (in the U.S. Navy and Merchant Marines) and Jeanne Carolyn (a teacher; maiden name, Turrell) McKinley; married Peter Dickinson (an author), January 3, 1992. Education: Attended Dickinson College, 1970–72; Bowdoin College, B.A. (summa cum laude), 1975.

Robin McKinley has been described by her friends Terri Windling and Mark Alan Arnold in *Horn Book* as a "person who approaches every instant and event with such boisterousness, energy, and vehemence that even the most mundane aspects of her life are infused with vibrancy." According to Windling and Arnold, McKinley is "special and extraordinary," an "important writer of our generation." Yet McKinley has recalled that she was an awkward adolescent who spent her time alone, reading, riding horses, thinking about horses, and wishing she could have the kind of adventures boys seemed to be having.

"I despised myself for being a girl," she once explained, "and ipso facto being someone who stayed at home and was boring, and started trying to tell myself stories about girls who did things and had adventures." Just after graduating summa cum laude from Bowdoin College with a degree in English literature, McKinley began to have adventures of her own. She became the woman Windling and Arnold know, and a hero to young women readers in search of strong, honorable role models. McKinley's retellings of traditional fairy tales and

"I'm preoccupied with the notion of a woman's ability, or inability, to move within her society."

747

completely original, contemporary fantasies portray girls ''who do things.''

Freedom A Major Theme

Although feminism is not the sole force driving McKinley's creativity, it is a cause she consciously promotes. She once said, ''I am obsessed with the idea of freedom, especially because I'm a WASP female of limited imagination. I'm preoccupied with the notion of a woman's ability, or inability, to move within her society. I am not so purblind as to think that the only thing seriously wrong with our civilization is that men have more freedom of choice than women, but I strongly believe that that is one important thing wrong, and that it must be changed. Nor will I give up the idea that men and women can cope with each other in some relaxed and affectionate fashion—under this crabby exterior there beats the squashy heart of a romantic.... But meanwhile there are no princesses who wring their hands and stand around in ivory towers waiting for princes to return from the wars in my stories.''

McKinley's stories include short retellings of classics from Anna Sewell's *Black Beauty* to George MacDonald's *The Light Princess* and Rudyard Kipling's *The Jungle Book*. She has also published a number of short stories and edited *Imaginary Lands,* a collection of fantasies that includes her own ''The Stone Fey.'' McKinley has insisted that her work is written for those who want to read it, not just for young people. Yet she has also written some original picture books for children. *Rowan* is a story about a girl selecting and loving a pet dog. *My Father Is in the Navy* portrays a young girl whose father has been away for some time: as he is about to return, she tries to remember what her father looks like. McKinley is perhaps best known, however, for her novel-length retellings, and for the two books set in a world she created called Damar.

McKinley began writing the work that generated the Damarian cycle just after she graduated from college. She explained, ''I had begun—this would be about '76—to realize that there was more than one story to tell about Damar, that in fact it seemed to be a whole history, volumes and volumes of the stuff, and this terrified me. I had

plots and characters multiplying like mice and running in all directions.'' McKinley decided to take a break from the Damar story after she viewed an adaptation of ''Beauty and the Beast'' on television. McKinley was so disappointed with what she saw that she began to write a version of the classic fairy tale herself.

''Beauty'' Revisited

The resulting novel, *Beauty: A Retelling of the Story of Beauty and the Beast,* was immediately published and won praise from readers and critics alike. According to Michael Malone in the *New York Times Book Review,* the novel is ''much admired not only for its feminism but for the density of detail in the retelling.'' ''It's simply a filling out of the story, with a few alterations,'' wrote a *Kirkus Reviews* critic. McKinley's Beauty, or Honour, as she is named in this version, is an awkward child, not a beauty, and her ''evil sisters'' are caring and kind. Critics have also praised McKinley's handling of fantasy in the medieval setting. ''The aura of magic around the Beast and his household comes surprisingly to life,'' commented a *Choice* critic.

McKinley resumed work on her Damar stories, and a collection of stories called *The Door in the Hedge,* during the late 1980s. *The Blue Sword,* McKinley's second novel, was published in 1982. The hero in this novel is Harry Crewe, an adolescent woman who must forge her identity and battle an evil force at the same time. The plot takes off when Harry is kidnapped and learns (from her kidnappers) how to ride a horse and battle as a true warrior. While she struggles in the tradition of the legendary female hero of Damar, Aerin, Harry becomes a hero in her own right. Although the story is set in the fantastic world of Damar (which Darrell Schweitzer characterizes as ''pseudo-Victorian'' in *Science Fiction Review*), critics have noted that Harry is a heroine contemporary readers may well understand.

Like the retelling, *Beauty, The Blue Sword* earned McKinley recognition and praise. *The Blue Sword,* however, provided critics with an understanding of McKinley's ability to create entirely original plots, characters, and fantastic worlds.

Moreover, critics and readers alike enjoyed the richness and excitement of the book. *Booklist* contributor Sally Estes, for example, described *The Blue Sword* as "a zesty, romantic heroic fantasy with . . . a grounding in reality that enhances the tale's verve as a fantasy." For *The Blue Sword* McKinley was awarded a Newbery honor.

The Hero and the Crown

In *The Hero and the Crown,* the next Damar novel, readers are taken back in time to learn about the legendary warrior woman Harry so revered. McKinley explained, "I recognized that there were specific connections between Harry and Aerin, and I deliberately wrote their stories in reverse chronological order because one of the things I'm fooling around with is the idea of heroes: real heroes as opposed to the legends that are told of them afterwards. Aerin is one of her country's greatest heroes, and by the time Harry comes along, Harry is expected—or Harry thinks she is—to live up to her. When you go back and find out about Aerin in *Hero,* you discover that she wasn't this mighty invincible figure. . . . She had a very hard and solitary time of her early fate."

At first, Aerin is graceless and clumsy; it takes her a long time to turn herself into a true warrior, and she suffers many traumas. Yet she is clever and courageous, bravely battling and killing the dragons that are threatening Damar. Merri Rosenberg asserted in the *New York Times Book Review* that McKinley "created an utterly engrossing fantasy, replete with a fairly mature romantic subplot as well as adventure." In the opinion of Mary M. Burns in *Horn Book, The Hero and the Crown* is "as richly detailed and elegant as a medieval tapestry. . . . Vibrant, witty, compelling, the story is the stuff of which true dreams are made."

The Hero and the Crown earned McKinley the coveted Newbery Medal in 1985 for the best American children's book of the year. McKinley shared her mixed feelings about winning the award: "The Newbery award is supposed to be the peak of your career as a writer for children or young adults. I was rather young to receive it; and it is a

Cover of **Beauty**

little disconcerting to feel—okay, you've done it; that's it, you should retire now." Fortunately for her fans, McKinley continued to write retellings of traditional favorites and original stories and novels.

New Tales from Old Ones

The Outlaws of Sherwood provides one example of McKinley's penchant for revising and reviving a traditional tale. Instead of concentrating on Robin Hood—or glorifying him—McKinley's novel focuses on other characters in the band of outlaws and provides carefully wrought details about their daily lives: how they get dirty, and sick, and how they manage their outlaw affairs. Robin is not portrayed as the bold, handsome marksman and sword handler readers may remember from traditional versions of the "Robin Hood" story. Instead, he is nervous, a poor shot, and even reluctant to form his band of merry men. Not surprisingly, the band of merry men in *The Outlaws of Sherwood* is a band of merry men and *women.* "The young women are allowed to be angry, frankly sexual, self willed—and even to outshoot the men, who don't seem to mind,'' related *Washington Post Book World* reviewer Michele Landsberg. Maid Marian stands out as a brilliant, beautiful leader and amazingly talented archer. *The Outlaws of Sherwood* is ''romantic and absorbing . . . [and] the perfect adolescent daydream where happiness is found in being young and among friends,'' concluded Shirley Wilton of *Voice of Youth Advocates.*

McKinley's *Deerskin* also demonstrates her talent for creating new tales out of the foundations of old ones. As Betsy Hearne of *Bulletin of the Center for Children's Books* noted, *Deerskin* is an ''adult fantasy'' for mature readers; it presents a ''darker side of fairy tales.'' Based on Perrault's ''Donkeyskin,'' a story in which a king desires his own daughter after his queen dies, McKinley's novel relates how a beautiful princess is raped by her father after the death of her mother. This ''is also a dog story,'' Hearne reminded readers: Princess Lissar survives the brutal attack, and her emotional trauma afterwards, because of her relationship with her dog, Ash. ''Written with deep passion and power, *Deerskin* is an almost unbearably intense portrait of a severely damaged young woman. . . . [T]here is also romance, humor, and sheer delight,'' commented Christy Tyson in *Voice of Youth Advocates.* ''*Deerskin* is a riveting and relentless fairy tale, told in ravishing prose,''

concluded *School Library Journal* critic Cathy Chauvette.

While McKinley has asserted that ''Damar has never been a trilogy'' and doesn't want to close off her own mental access to Damar by embedding it completely in text, she has facilitated her readers' access to Damar. Some of the stories in *A Knot in the Grain and Other Stories* are set in Damar and include familiar characters. All of these stories, according to Betsy Hearne in *Bulletin of the Center for Children's Books,* bear ''McKinley's signature blend of the magical and the mundane in the shape of heroines'' who triumph and find love despite the obstacles they face. The stories demonstrate McKinley's ''remarkable ability to evoke wonder and belief,'' asserted *Horn Book* contributor Ann A. Flowers.

McKinley stated why she thought such work is important: ''As a compulsive reader myself, I believe that you are what you read. . . . My books are also about hope—I hope. Much of modern literature has given up hope and deals with anti-heroes and despair. It seems to me that human beings by their very natures need heroes, real heroes, and are happier with them. I see no point in talking about how life is over and it never mattered anyway. I don't believe it.''

Sources for More Information

Books

Dictionary of Literary Biography, Volume 52: *American Writers for Children since 1960: Fiction,* Gale, 1986.

St. James Guide to Young Adult Writers, St. James Press, 1999.

On-line

William Morrow Books Web site, located at http://www.williammorrow.com.

Sarah McLachlan

Singer, songwriter, and guitarist (1968–)

Born January 28, 1968, in Halifax, Nova Scotia, Canada; daughter of Jack (a marine biologist) and Dorice (a student) McLachlan; married Ashwin Sood (a musician), 1997.

"I'm a humanist before I'm a feminist, or anything else."

Sarah McLachlan knows where the best music comes from: "Sonically," she told *Cover* magazine's KK Kozik, "moving water is perhaps my all-time favorite sound." Water has both its aural and thematic relevance for McLachlan. "Being around any kind of water is one of the most important things in my life," she averred. "I find it soothing and it's a very female thing, too. The ocean is like the womb and I'm fascinated, drawn in." Indeed, McLachlan herself has a fluid quality; her voice is noted for its liquidity, and her lyrics and production values, for their tempest and storm.

McLachlan comes by her turbulent personality honestly. Born in Halifax, Nova Scotia, McLachlan led a relatively sequestered life while growing up. David Thigpen of *Time* reported that McLachlan was "a shy, awkward child who never fell in with the crowd." He described her as a teenager who "would kill time on long, frozen winter nights writing songs." *Billboard*'s Timothy White provided a more complex portrayal of McLachlan's youthful existence. Her mother, Dorice, sacrificed her "own academic aspirations" in order to support her husband, Jack, an

751

American marine biologist, and then acquainted "her little girl with the isolation that regret places in the path of personal fulfillment." But for White, the results were worth celebrating. "McLachlan was able to fuse her mother's depth of pathos and her father's detached analysis into a calm grasp of our culture's callous objectification of women," he concluded.

"astonishing strength and clarity"

From the start of her career at age 19, McLachlan was compared to other female songwriters such as Joni Mitchell, Kate Bush, Sinead O'Connor, and Tori Amos, comparisons one might ascribe to what Elysa Gardner of *Rolling Stone* called a voice of "astonishing strength and clarity [that] may drift at any given time from a sirenlike middle range to a ghostly soprano." She has remarkable range and tends toward lyrics which explore relationships between women and men.

During her childhood, McLachlan sought out the serenading voices and sentiments of folk-rock singers Joan Baez, Cat Stevens, and Simon and Garfunkel. She had twelve years of training on guitar, six on piano, and five years of voice lessons, all of which surely contributed to what *Billboard*'s Timothy White referred to as "the wit, literate grace, and unfussy intricacy of her material." As a teenager, McLachlan worked at restaurant counters and as a dishwasher in Halifax, riding out the calm before her musical storm.

Her first album, *Touch,* released in 1988, suggested a waif-like quality to Elysa Gardner. But her second album, *Solace,* in 1991, revealed a sturdier woman, one less "ethereal," one "trying to come down to earth a bit." McLachlan said of *Solace,* "There's a lot more of myself in my writing [there]—more the way I think, more the way I talk." Critics generally agree that with McLachlan's third album, *Fumbling Towards Ecstasy,* released in 1994, she revealed a new maturity as singer, songwriter, and woman. *Fumbling Towards Ecstasy* reveals a woman with a more broad sensibility; her self-awareness and her melancholy meet a political consciousness.

Fumbling a Mature Work

McLachlan has referred to the relevance here of her increased self-respect and gender appreciation. She told *Billboard,* "It took me six years to learn how not to edit myself, to remain open in my music so that I touched greater levels of darkness as well as some positive areas of escape." When KK Kozik noted the "femininity" of *Fumbling,* McLachlan succinctly replied, "I love women. I'm fascinated by them. . . . I'm definitely starting to realize more of my responsibility as a woman."

While the bulk of critical response to McLachlan's music has been admiring, some criticism contained a disparaging tone. Dave Jennings of *Melody Maker* was dismayed by the excess of "vulnerability" he found in *Solace,* which while couched in nature imagery did not add up to "New Age consciousness, but really . . . just old-school singer-songwriter preciousness." Similarly, *Spin*'s Joy Press found the lyrics of *Fumbling* "mature with a capital M, to the point of sophomoric pseudo-profundity." Other critics, however, found in that album both an artist and a portrait of that artist. *Time*'s Thigpen attempted to remove the debate from the gender-biased charge of confessionalism: "Far from indulging in simple emotional bloodletting," he wrote, "McLachlan creates exquisitely poised songs that resist anger or pathos."

In *Fumbling,* KK Kozik appreciated McLachlan's newfound "desire and capacity to understand more than just herself," a departure from the concerns of *Touch and Solace.* McLachlan agreed. A trip to Southeast Asia in 1993, for which she represented her Canadian peer group, afforded her both disillusionment and wisdom. She admitted that she sang less about victimization and self-pity as a result of that mission whose focus was AIDS, prostitution, and poverty. While viewing some particularly gruesome photographs, McLachlan stated, "I all of a sudden got so horrified with humanity and so disillusioned. How can people be so cruel. . . . Do we learn nothing from history? But the aftermath of that is, 'I feel so blessed.'"

Though McLachlan does not address the Cambodian situation directly in her songs, its impact can be felt. Critics imply that the garnered

*Sarah McLachlan in
concert*

knowledge enriched her lyrics and music, even while both remained devoted to interpersonal relationships. Thigpen identified McLachlan's audience as "the desperately troubled," to whom she offers the suggestion "that the answers to life's emotional earthquakes can come through perseverance and compassion." Terry McBride, the president of Nettwerk Records, remarked, "There's more soul in her singing on this album. [This] record finally makes you believe that she means what she says."

Lilith Fair

As she prepared to go on tour in 1994, McLachlan suggested that she tour with singer Paula Cole. When promoters balked at the idea of her having a female opening acting, claiming fans wouldn't pay to see two women on the same stage, McLachlan was motivated to create a festival that featured only female performers. A friend of McLachlan's came up with the name Lilith, the mythical first wife of Adam who was thrown out of Eden for not being properly subservient. In 1996, the concept was tested in a four-market tour that attracted 40,000 fans. Plans were quickly made to turn the Lilith Fair into an alternative-rock alternative to male-dominated summer music tours like Lollapalooza and H.O.R.D.E. The summer of 1997 was set for a 35-date North American tour with a rotating lineup that included Tracy Chapman, Jewel, the Indigo Girls, Suzanne Vega, Fiona Apple, Paula Cole, Sheryl Crow, Joan Osborne, The Cardigans, Mary Chapin Carpenter. McLachlan remained the only constant act.

The media often referred to the Lilith Fair as Estrofest and Girlie-palooza. The press questioned whether McLachlan's brainchild was a feminist movement. ''I'm a humanist before I'm a feminist, or anything else,'' she said in *Interview*. She said her promotion company recommended she make that clear in the fair's first press kit, to prevent the festival from becoming ''a hard-core feminist rally.''

Arista Records, McLachlan's record label, expected the release of her fourth album, *Surfacing*, to launch the singer/songwriter into superstardom. Not only because of the success of her previous album, but also because she spearheaded the Lilith Fair. The release of *Surfacing* was scheduled in conjunction with the 1997 summer music festival.

A change had overcome McLachlan since last seen by fans. She cropped the curly, shoulder-length hair that characterized her throughout most of her career. But the change wasn't limited to her physical appearance, it was seen in her music, as well. *Billboard* said of the album, ''While *Surfacing* still largely features McLachlan's pensive and confessional mode, evident in album tracks 'Building A Mystery,' 'Sweet Surrender,' and 'I Love You,' there's more confidence, more maturity in her writing than previously seen.'' *Surfacing* debuted in the No. 2 spot on Billboard's Top 200 album chart.

Creating songs for the album took longer than expected because McLachlan suffered from writer's block after the two-and-a-half-year *Fumbling Towards Ecstasy* tour. ''This has been the hardest record I've had to write,'' McLachlan admitted in *Billboard*. ''For a long time, I thought I wasn't going to write any more good songs. . . . The big challenge this time was trusting myself.'' The success of *Surfacing*, which would include an industry award for best songwriting, and the Lilith

Fairs proved she mastered trust in herself. *Harper's Bazaar* proclaimed, ''McLachlan has transformed herself from an insecure, self-doubting cult figure to the confident overseer of a small enterprise.'' *Rolling Stone* said of McLachlan: ''. . . she cast aside her waifish image in favor of a new role: Champion other women in the music industry.''

In a Position of Strength

The 1997 Lilith Fair grossed $18 million, with $700,000 raised for charitable women's groups. It became the summer's hottest music festival, outselling events like Lollapalooza. ''I love how powerful this whole thing makes me feel,'' she told *Maclean's*. ''Not a selfish power, but a strength that's coming from everyone around me.'' By 1998 the Lilith Fair had grown to 57 corporate-sponsored shows held over two and a half months. ''I don't have any grand plans for the ramifications of Lilith,'' McLachlan said in *Billboard*. ''It just shows that women are strong and have a beautiful and positive force.'' In 1999 McLachlan announced that that year's Lilith Fair would be the last, saying that she and her fellow Lilith performers needed a break.

Despite her hectic schedule, McLachlan took time out for a vacation to Jamaica in February 1997. While there, she eloped with her drummer, Ashwin Sood. She credits her husband for lending his support to her while on tour, telling *Maclean's*, ''I don't think I could do all this if he wasn't out here with me.''

McLachlan was recognized by the industry for her success and leadership. Based on the strength of her work as creator of the Lilith Fair, She was listed at No. 60 in a 1997 *Entertainment Weekly* ''Power 100'' list. In 1998 she won four Juno awards—Canada's equivalent of the Grammy—for best female vocalist, best songwriter, best album for *Surfacing*, and best single for ''Building a Mystery.''

Also in 1998, McLachlan was named *Chatelaine* magazine's Woman of the Year. In an article about their latest honoree, the magazine wrote: ''McLachlan's tour succeeded because through it, she shouted what many women, young and old, still whisper: waddya mean we can't do what the guys can? She may have not intended it, but her actions have made her a symbol beyond the music world, a symbol of confidence in taking centre stage.''

Sources for More Information

Periodicals

Chatelaine, January, 1998.

Harper's Bazaar, August, 1998.

Interview, July. 1997.

Maclean's, July 28, 1997; December 22, 1997; November 30, 1998.

People, October 20, 1997.

Rolling Stone, December 25, 1997.

Seventeen, June, 1998.

On-line

Lilith Fair Web site, located at http://www.lilithfair.com.

Sarah McLachlan Web site, located at http://www.aristarec.com/aristaweb/SarahMcLachlan/.

Metallica

Heavy metal band

''In a world of hairspray-and-mascara glam rock, Metallica sticks out like a junkyard mongrel at a poodle show.''

—Bass Player magazine

Group formed in 1981. Members include Kirk Hammett (lead guitar; raised in San Francisco, CA; studied guitar with Joe Satriani, 1983; replaced Dave Mustaine, 1983, who had replaced Lloyd Grant), James Hetfield (vocals, rhythm guitar), Jason Newsted (bass; raised in Niles, MI; replaced Cliff Burton, who died in a tour bus accident, 1986), Lars Ulrich (drums).

"In a world of hairspray-and-mascara glam rock, Metallica sticks out like a junkyard mongrel at a poodle show,'' wrote Karl Coryat of *Bass Player* magazine. The San Francisco Bay Area's Metallica, a flagship speed-metal—or ''thrash''—band has emerged as one of America's most popular heavy metal outfits, a result, no doubt, of the group's steady maturation during the dues-paying 1980s. Metallica's self-named 1991 release addressed the decidedly adult topics of nuclear holocaust, mental illness, suicide, and the dangers of drug addiction. Yet despite these grim themes, Metallica's music runs contrary to heavy metal's one-dimensional image; their sound involves more than just bone-breaking chords and fire-and-brimstone lyrics. The band has distinguished itself with a grungy sophistication well beyond the work of its predecessors. Members of Metallica are rude and cheeky, but they're proficient. *Bass Player*'s Coryat attested, ''Their famous 'Metal Up Your Ass' T-shirt ensured Metallica a notorious place in rock-and-roll history.'' Taste in merchandising notwithstanding, *Spin* magazine's Alec Foege called Metallica "a burnished black gem."

Metallica coalesced in 1981 with singer-guitarist James Hetfield, drummer Lars Ulrich, bass player Cliff Burton, and lead guitarist Dave Mustaine. Mustaine, who had taken over for early collaborator Lloyd Grant, was replaced in 1983 by Kirk Hammett. Their first album, *Kill 'Em All,* attracted droves of "head-banging" fans. The follow-up releases *Ride the Lightning* and *Master of Puppets* were greeted with even more enthusiasm by the world's heavy metal constituency, which enabled the band to strut their stuff with fellow "metalheads" on the enormous Monsters of Rock Tour. That outing featured a free concert in Moscow that was attended by 500,000 Soviet metal fans. Infamous spittoon in tow for this tour and others—band members needed a place to deposit their chewed tobacco—Metallica was increasingly credited with single-handedly revitalizing heavy metal music, paving the way for other thrash bands like Slayer and Megadeath.

Accident Changes Band

Tragedy struck Metallica on September 27, 1986, when the band's tour bus went into a ditch in Sweden, killing bassist Cliff Burton. After a brief hiatus the band reassembled and began looking for a replacement for Burton. Attempting to fill the bass player's shoes and duplicate his eccentric, unbridled style seemed impossible. Burton had never been a particularly smooth player, but other band members had not attempted to reign him in. They did try once, however, to persuade him to forego his bell-bottom jeans in favor of more traditional heavy metal garb, but quickly realized the attempt was futile; Burton was set in his ways and rarely influenced by others. In truly bizarre heavy metal fashion, one of his dreams had been to invent a gun that shot knives instead of bullets.

To refurbish their lineup, the members of Metallica decided to settle on someone completely different from Burton: Jason Newsted, then with the Phoenix band Flotsam & Jetsam. Newsted was raised in Niles, Michigan, and had decided to turn professional after playing in bands throughout high school. He told Coryat, "I heard Cliff (Burton) had died the day after the accident. . . . I was a huge Metallica fan at the time. When I was looking at the blurb in the paper, I was sad, but things

started flashing through my mind. . . . I just thought if I could play 'Four Horsemen' once with those guys, I'd be really happy."

Burton had been a remarkable soloist, but Newsted provided Metallica with a more cohesive sound. Burton's sound had not been well-defined, particularly when he played low on the guitar's neck. Newsted chose to mirror the band's guitar riffs precisely instead, producing a newly unified guitar effect. This sound dominated the new band's 1988 double album. Titled . . . *And Justice for All,* the record went platinum and earned a Grammy Award nomination, despite a dearth of radio airplay. The release of *Justice* coincided with Metallica's return to its musical roots: the groundbreaking metal stylings of 1970s rock giants Led Zeppelin and Black Sabbath. This resolve became the cornerstone for the 1991 release, *Metallica.*

Into the Limelight

Still steely, but a little slicker, *Metallica* was produced by Bob Rock, who had also worked with metal acts Motley Crue, Loverboy, and Bon Jovi. Buoyed by the dark, driving single "Enter Sandman," *Metallica* sold 2.2 million copies in its first week. Metallica's hard-won versatility is showcased on the record with guitarist Hammett's winsome wah-wah, and open-throated, more melodic vocals from Hetfield. The band earned Grammys in both 1990 and 1991 and effectively ascended to a new strata of heavy metal superstardom.

Featured on the covers of both *Rolling Stone* and *Spin,* Metallica's popularity seemed to know no bounds. With increased media coverage, it became clear that the band's appeal was not narrowly bohemian, political, or reflective of any trend—except perhaps anger. *Village Voice* contributor Erik Davis wrote that "Metallica's 'image'—dark shades, frowns, and poorly conceived facial hair—allies them with a musical culture of refusal. They haven't stopped dragging mud onto the carpet and slamming their bedroom doors without saying hello. 'Enter Sandman' has touched the brains of fry cooks and Bud guzzlers across the land."

Analysis of Metallica's lyrics reveals the band's unique penchant for conjuring up the timeless grandiosity of myth by placing the object of a line before its subject: "This fight he cannot win," and "Off the beaten path I reign" are two examples. The band's head-banging thrash metal songs are

James Hetfield of Metallica in concert

short, but not sweet; they're delivered with grim, tight expressions, and a minimum of emotion, which gives the impression that the entire band is grimacing. Metallica's albums have few tender spots; songs range from the brutal ''Sad But True'' to the sweet and gritty ''Ride the Lightning,'' from the praised pagan slant found on ''Of Wolf And Man'' to the metaphysical musings of ''Through the Never.'' Commenting on their larger musical style—''Metallica's riffs crack like glaciers''—the *Village Voice*'s Davis said of the band, ''They hew thrash to a rigorous minimalism.''

Spin's Foege waxed mathematic in his assessment of Metallica, writing, ''At turns algebraically elegant and geometrically raucous, present-day Metallica can stop and start on a dime.'' With their popularity showing no signs of flagging, their musical and lyrical virtuosity on the upswing, and their fans more crazed than ever, Metallica is a speeding bullet heading perilously close to the heads of those adults with barely tolerant, thin-lipped expressions molded onto their faces. The band's motto, after all, is ''Bang Those Heads That Don't Bang.''

Headlines
Lollapalooza

Rolling Stone did a feature in on the band June 1996 as it prepared to turn out its sixth studio album, *Load.* The band was feeling pressure on two fronts: they were pressed to finish *Load* by its release deadline, and they had been selected as the opening act for that year's alternative-rock Lollapalooza tour. ''The weight, the expectations of other people—that's all there, and that's all huge,'' Newsted admitted in *Rolling Stone.* He added, ''But it doesn't weigh on us so heavy we don't put out the music *we* want to put out.''

Load was musically different from the band's blockbuster *Metallica,* released five years before, with a reviewer in *Guitar Player* claiming that ''Metallica's modus operandi is changing.'' In a display of band democracy, Metallica eased up on the traditional Hetfield/Ulrich songwriting to draw more from guitarist Kirk Hammett and bassist Jason Newsted's riffs, ''allowing the band a surprising level of stylistic diversity,'' according to *Guitar Player.* With songs inspired by Motorhead, Black Sabbath, Soundgarden, Neil Young, and Tom Waits, *Load* was cited by many critics as a sign of the band's musical evolution.

Others, however, complained that the band had gone too mainstream by pandering more to the trendy alternative rock crowd than heavy metal fans. Hammett denied it. ''We never let mainstream music filter into our psyches too much,'' he told Joe Gore in a *Guitar Player* interview. ''We try not to let ourselves be influenced too much by what goes on around us musically.'' Instead, Hammett said, the band had grown musically, incorporating more blues techniques into their music. Hammett believed that Metallica more likely influenced alternative rock than conformed to it. ''People will argue with me until the cows come home, but I think in a small way we opened the doors for the Seattle thing,'' he said to Gore. ''Because we were a loud guitar band, it enabled people to open their ears to other bands of that sort.''

Less than two years later the band released *Reload* that contains, according to *People,* ''music that will appeal to those thinking headbangers who once flocked to Nirvana and Pearl Jam.'' Reviews were mixed—some critics saw further proof of the band's musical evolution, while others found *Reload* merely a death-and-Satan-themed tribute to

their last album. *Stereo Review* said of the band's seventh major release, ''Metallica could have just as easily called this one *Rehash* or *Redux,* since the thirteen tracks have their origins in the sessions for the band's previous album, *Load.*''

Garage Inc. was the band's last album of the decade, a double-CD of cover tunes with one disc serving as a collection of Metallica's previously released covers from the 1980s, and the second featuring eleven new covers. *Entertainment Weekly* reviewer Tom Sinclair claimed *Garage Inc.* revealed that Metallica was ''deep into a mid-life crisis.'' The album's new covers included obscure tracks by Blue Oyster Cult (''Astronomy''), Black Sabbath (''Sabbra Cadabra''), as well as some by forgotten metal bands like Diamond Head, The Anti-Nowhere League, and Discharge. Despite some disappointment with the work, Sinclair granted that ''*Garage Inc.* is an intermittently exhilarating joyride.''

Sources for More Information

Periodicals

Entertainment Weekly, December 18, 1998.

Guitar Player, October, 1996.

People, December 8, 1997.

Rolling Stone, June 27, 1996; December 10, 1998.

Stereo Review, March, 1998.

On-line

The Metallica Club, located at http://www.metclub.com/main.html.

Choice Cuts

Piet Mondrian

Painter
(1872-1944)

"Like religion, art is superhuman and cultivates the superhuman element in man, and it is consequently a means of human evolution."

Born March 7, 1872, in Maersfoort, Netherlands; died February 1, 1944, in New York, NY; son of the painter Pieter Cornelis Mondriaan. Education: Studied drawing with his father, and painting with his uncle, Frits Mondriaan; teachers training in drawing; studied with Joh-Braedr van Uberfeldt at the Rijksakademie, Amsterdam, 1892–94, and attended evening classes, 1894–97.

Until he was almost forty years old, Piet Mondrian was known primarily as a competent painter of landscapes and other traditional subjects in his native Holland. When he became aware of the ideas of modern art, however, Mondrian adopted them completely and pushed them forward as few other artists had. By the end of his life he was considered one of the world's most important abstract painters, having jettisoned representation altogether in favor of compositions comprised exclusively of geometric shapes and color. Motivated by a desire to simplify art to its very essence, Mondrian substantially influenced modern art in both its theory and practice and held significant sway over contemporary architecture and fashion as well.

Mondrian—born Pieter Mondriaan on March 7, 1872, in Maersfoort, the Netherlands—was one of five children of a middle-class family from a small Dutch town. His father, also named Pieter Mondriaan, was a schoolmaster and enjoyed drawing as a hobby. Other family members were also artists; young Pieter had his first painting lessons from an uncle. The family lived by very strict religious principles enforced by the dominating Pieter senior, who insisted that his son also become a teacher. The boy decided that he wanted to teach drawing and, after studying hard in local schools, convinced his father to let him go to the Academy of Fine Arts in the capital city of Amsterdam.

Art School

Mondrian was twenty years old when he arrived in the city. He studied diligently for three years at the academy and—unlike his peers—avoided Amsterdam's world-renowned nightlife. He then attended drawing classes at night and held a variety of jobs to support himself, including illustrating science textbooks, teaching art, and copying paintings in museums.

Mondrian was a capable, if traditional, painter; he displayed a marked preference in this phase of his artistic development for landscape scenes of rural Holland, with its windmills, churches, and wide, flat plains. He also painted flowers, often devoting an entire canvas to one meticulously observed blossom. Until about 1908 Mondrian had little exposure to the experiments percolating in the art world.

In the summer of 1908 Mondrian spent time with a group of painters on a small island in Holland. Among them were two older Dutch artists who strongly influenced Mondrian, Jan Sluyters and Jan Toorop. Both of these men had been to Paris and greatly admired the work of Henri Matisse, their countryman Vincent van Gogh, and other exponents of the style called fauvism. Through Sluyters and Toorop, Mondrian learned about radical new forms; he immediately began to expand his technical horizons. His colors became more intense and were applied more randomly, and he explored different kinds of brush strokes. His most famous painting from this time, *The Red Tree*, depicts a large, leafless tree, the trunk and branches of which he rendered in reds and purples against a bright blue background so that it would bristle with energy. One can discern the evolution of Mondrian's style during this period by comparing his many tree paintings.

Mill by the Water, 1900

The Red Tree, 1909

Still Life with Ginger Pot, 1912

Pier and Ocean, 1915

Composition in Blue B, 1917

Composition with Red, Blue, and Yellow, 1917

Broadway Boogie-Woogie, 1942

Victory Boogie-Woogie, 1943

Masterworks

Minimalist Style

In 1911 Mondrian went to Paris and quickly became caught up in the excitement created by the new artistic style known as cubism. The strong geometric lines of this mode greatly appealed to Mondrian; he appropriated a number of cubist ideas and spent his years in Paris hammering out a unique style of his own. He simplified forms, condensed shapes, and removed details, all in pursuit of composition refined to its bare bones.

Mondrian immersed himself in the various theories and philosophies of art throughout his life; one writer commented that he painted merely to illustrate such ideas. Yet Mondrian's theoretical bent hasn't prevented viewers from perceiving great beauty in his work. The pinnacle of his explorations came when he eliminated all subjects from his paintings, making them completely abstract. His most prominent works contain only vertical and horizontal lines—usually black—and are limited in hue to the primary colors—red, blue, and yellow. Mondrian's style, which he called plasticism, remains instantly recognizable.

Mondrian detailed his many artistic philosophies in a magazine called *De Stijl*, which he founded with fellow artist Theo Van Doesburg in 1917. De Stijl was also the name given to the style they developed; it stressed exactness, abstraction, and strict adherence to the formal theories Mondrian and others held. Members of the De Stijl school were not only painters but also architects, designers, and interior decorators. Most eventually broke with the group to embrace other styles, but De Stijl

Large Composition
by Piet Mondrian

remained a powerful influence on twentieth-century design.

Work Exhibited Around the World

Throughout the 1920s and 1930s, Mondrian worked to more fully delineate his ideas, and his paintings appeared in exhibitions in Paris, New York, and elsewhere. In 1938 he moved to London, anticipating that war would soon begin in Europe, but he was forced to leave the city less than two years later when German air raids there began to make life very difficult. He went to New York in October 1940.

The modern, urban environment of New York City entranced Mondrian; he loved the geometry of the buildings and their lighted windows at night, the horizontals and verticals of the streets, and the tall skyscrapers reaching for the sky. Mondrian's last compositions, painted in New York, are among his most popular. Gone are the heavy black grid lines. The arrangements of yellow, black, and red squares hum with the energy of city blocks and the pulsing rhythms of jazz, which inspired many a painter of the era. For more than twenty years, Mondrian had given no descriptive titles to his paintings; they were called simply *Composition No. 1* or *Composition with Red, Blue, and Yellow*. In New York—apparently intoxicated by city life and American music—he gave his last works titles like *Broadway Boogie-Woogie* and *Victory Boogie-Woogie*.

But Mondrian lived little more than three years in New York; he died of pneumonia on February 1, 1944, at the age of seventy-two. Although he had led a generally quiet and solitary life, he helped to pioneer a style through which he vividly expressed a shared vision of modern life. His influence has been wide indeed, from the work of kinetic artist Alexander Calder to the avant-garde fashion designers of the 1960s.

Sources for More Information

Books

Blotkamp, Carel, *Mondrian: The Art of Destruction,* Abrams, 1995.

Busignani, Alberto, *Mondrian: The Life and Work of the Artist Illustrated by 80 Colour Plates,* Thames & Hudson, 1968.

Milner, John, *Mondrian,* Abbeville Press, 1992.

Claude Monet

Painter
(1840–1926)

"Monet is only an eye, but, my God,
what an eye!"

—artist Paul Cezanne

Born November 14, 1840, in Paris, France; died December 5, 1926, in Giverny, France; son of a grocer and his wife; married Camille Doncieu, 1870 (died, 1879); married Alice Hoschede, 1892 (died, 1911); children: (first marriage) Jean, Michel (sons). Education: Attended Academie Suisse, 1859–60; studied painting under Eugene Boudin, 1856–59, and Charles Gleyre, 1862.

Associated as much with the inspiration for his art as with his many paintings, Claude Monet is considered by many to be the foremost, as well as the founding, member of the Impressionist school of painting. Concerned with the play of light on the landscape, Monet's works exhibited new uses of both color and brush technique that were considered revolutionary within the art establishment of his day. Today he is best known for the series of "Water Lilies" paintings that he completed later in his life; his gardens in the French town of Giverny have also sparked a great deal of interest among horticulturalists and garden designers due to their sophisticated use of color. As the painter Cezanne is reported to have said, "Monet is only an eye, but, my God, what an eye!"

Monet was born in Paris, France, in November of 1840. The son of a grocer and his wife, Monet moved with his family to the seaside city of Le Havre in 1845, where he would remain for the rest of his childhood. Distracted and undisciplined, the young Monet was dismissed by both his teachers and his parents as not destined to amount to much. His only interest, his art, became visible when Monet reached his teens; the young man gained a reputation for drawing caricatures of prominent persons and friends, a talent he had put to work to make money by the time he was fifteen.

Early Mentor Proves Major Influence

In 1856, when Monet was sixteen, he met the painter Eugene Boudin, who recognized the younger man's talent. Boudin took the young painter under his wing and imbued in him his own passion for painting outside, in *plein air,* where the beauty and intricacy of nature could truly be seen and captured. This love of working outside, coupled with the older painter's fascination with water, would inform all of Monet's works, and can be seen in his first major work, ''View from Rouelles,'' which he painted at seventeen. The accurate, honest depiction of nature would also become one of the main characteristics of the school of painting he would later help to establish. Monet left Le Havre in 1859; he would acknowledge his artistic debt to his friend and mentor by returning repeatedly to visit Boudin throughout the older artist's lifetime.

While Monet had found a kindred spirit in Boudin, the constrictions of Le Havre to a young artist were too much. Paris, then the artistic center of Europe, beckoned, with its creative energies and communities of like-minded people, and Monet arrived there in 1859. The nineteen-year-old painter soon became disillusioned by the conformity to traditions he had not been conditioned to follow. Rejecting many of the formalized programs of study offered to him—including the highly acclaimed l'Ecole de Beaux Arts, a bastion of traditionalism—he eventually enrolled at the Academie Suisse, known for its less-structured atmosphere.

Even in his early work, Monet showed Boudin's influence through his belief in the importance of natural light and positioning. His method of working was to examine a setting at varying times of day and to capture its subtle transition through the seasonal shifts. A pencil sketch would provide the basis for his oil painting; on it not only the objects but the position of light and shadow would be carefully noted. His actual method of painting involved a series of sessions as short as fifteen minutes at the same time each day so as to capture similar patterns of light and shadow. He used five pure colors, placing them either side by side or one atop the other, thereby allowing the eye of the viewer, rather than the artist, to create variations of tone within each picture.

Monet was drafted into service for his country and went to Algeria with the Chaussures d'Afrique. Finding himself in a totally new environment, the young artist gained an even deeper awareness of light and landscape through exposure to the African continent, despite the brevity of his service: in less than a year Monet had contracted typhoid and was shipped back to France through the intervention of an influential aunt. His aunt's only condition: that he make a committed effort to gain formal schooling in art. Still adamant in his refusal to attend the Ecole des Beaux Arts, Monet opted to join the studio of painter Charles Gleyre, a noted benefactor to struggling young artists that at that time included Pierre-August Renoir. Befriending Renoir as well as students Frederic Bazille and Alfred Sisley, Monet often escaped with the group to the forests of Fontainbleau, where the diverse landscape and the play of sunlight upon the natural vegetation inspired each of the young men.

While his artistic vision and technique broke with the classical and religious themes, dull, muted colors, and clearly defined images then in vogue in the Salon—the Paris art world's annual exhibition—Monet realized that only through the acceptance of his work by the Academie would he be a success as a painter. In conformance with the fashion of the day, he painted several indoor still-lifes. While his smaller paintings met with approval, the textured surface of Monet's larger canvasses invited criticism from artists who aspired to glass-smooth surfaces free of visible brush-strokes. Undaunted, he continued, finally producing ''The Woman in the Green Dress'' in 1866. This painting, reportedly painted in only four days and which featured the artist's girlfriend, Camille Doncieux, as its model, finally brought Monet the acclaim he had been seeking and gained him recognition in artistic circles in and around Paris. His next goal was admission to the Academie, and he worked diligently for the next year, finally producing ''Women in the Garden'' in 1866. Despite his efforts, the work was rejected for admission into the Salon.

Meanwhile, the young artist's financial circumstances were deteriorating. Because he was

Impression: Sunrise
by Claude Monet

living with his girlfriend, his family ceased providing him with an allowance; furthermore, Camille had become pregnant with the first of the couple's two sons. The pair was forced to separate, Camille remaining in Paris with family while Monet moved in with his aunt, Madame Lecadre. With the outbreak of the Franco-Prussian war in 1870, he finally left France altogether and temporarily moved to London in order to avoid another term in the military. In England, the French artist became familiar with the works of his British counterparts, among them John Constable, who focused on natural scenes of the countryside around his home and whose works were imbued with a fresh awareness of light and shadow, and landscape artist and watercolorist J. M. W. Turner.

Painting Establishes New Trend

Returning to France in 1871, Monet and Camille (whom he had married just months before) settled at La Havre, where he would paint his—indeed, one of modern art's—most significant works. A view of Le Havre harbor viewed from the artist's window, "Impression: soleil levant" ("Impression: Sunrise") was completed in 1872 and exhibited two years later in Paris at the studio of photographer Nadar, sparking the school of art that now bears its name. Impressionism, which as a trend began in the 1860s, is characterized by the painter's attempt to capture the play of sunlight on both the landscape and adults and children engaged in gentle, idyllic pastimes, in stark contrast to the deep, somber tones common in the works of painters in the major studios of the day.

By now Monet had returned to Paris, where he and his wife and children lived together at Vetheuil, in a house near the Seine. His first few years in Paris had been relatively stable; he had been able to satisfy the creditors that had hounded him during previous years and could now dedicate himself to his painting, often joined by friends Renoir and others of like mind and artistic sensibility. Unfortunately, the 1874 exhibition, which included works by Renoir, Edouard Manet, Degas, Cezanne, Pissarro, and Sisley, proved to be a financial disaster due to the controversial reception of the "impressionist" style. It was only with the help of Manet and the sale of several of his works at the Hotel Drouot that the artist could support his family. He and his family were able to remain together by taking up residency at the home of friends Ernest and Alice Hoschede, where they stayed from 1878 to 1881. After his retail stores went bankrupt, Ernest was forced to flee from France, leaving Alice and six children to fend for themselves, with Monet the sole breadwinner among the two families.

Creates Masterful Gardens at Giverny

Monet's second son, Michel, was born in 1877, and Camille died of tuberculosis two years later. In 1892, after receiving news that Ernest Hoschede had died, Monet married the now-widowed Alice, moving with her, his two sons, and Alice's six children to a cottage on a former apple orchard in the village of Giverny, located to the northwest of Paris, where he would remain until his death in 1926. The impressionist group, which had been initially unified by the criticisms levelled against its young members, gradually dissolved, each artist going on to develop his own style as acceptance toward them grew. Monet had finally established a reputation as an artist of note through adopting a serial approach to landscape paintings, and was now living in comfort.

The early 1890s found the painter at work on a series of paintings of haystacks; in 1891 he produced a series of twenty-four separate renderings of a poplar grove that lined a stretch of waterway near his home at Giverny. By the following year, the painter was hard at work on a series of oils depicting the cathedral at Rouen, each version reflecting a shift in the natural light due to the changing seasons. His last significant series of painting was ''Water Lily Pool,'' begun in 1900, which depicted a water garden the artist had constructed on his estate.

While this series would eventually become among his most admired by lovers of his art, their creation proved a constant frustration to the elderly artist, who burned several of the canvases (by some accounts, up to five hundred canvases) and remained unconvinced that the remaining pictures were of exhibition quality. Deteriorating sight would cause him further frustration, and many of

his final works reflected the distorted color sense that he himself experienced due to changes in his vision. In contrast to the artist's own appraisal of his work, the 1909 exhibit of his ''Water Landscapes'' would create a groundswell of interest in Monet's works.

Surprisingly, the gardens that the artist would become devoted to during the final decades of his life would be among his most enduringly popular works—in fact, they have drawn millions of tourists to Giverny since the house and grounds were painstakingly restored and opened to the public in September of 1980.

Sources for More Information

Books

Howard, Michael, *Monet,* Bison Books, 1989.

Russell, Vivian, *Monet's Gardens: Through the Seasons at Giverny,* Stewart, Tabori & Chang, 1995.

Spate, Virginia, *Monet: His Life and Work,* Rizzoli, 1992.

Tucker, Paul, *Monet in the '90s: The Series Paintings,* Museum of Fine Arts/Yale University Press, 1995.

Masterworks

Women in the Garden, 1866

Terrace at the Seaside, Sainte-Adresse, 1866

Impression: Sunrise, 1872

Wild Poppies, 1874

Gare Saint-Lazare, 1877

Rue Montorgueil Decked Out with Flags, 1878

The Cliff Walk, 1882

Boating on the River Epte, 1887

Haystacks, 1891

Cathedral at Rouen, 1894

Water Garden at Giverny, 1899–1900

Water Lilies, 1916–23

Alanis Morissette

Singer and songwriter
(1974-)

"When I'm onstage, it's very spiritual. I feel very close to God when I'm up there."

Born June 1, 1974, in Ottawa, Ontario, Canada; daughter of Alan (a high school principal) and Georgia (a teacher) Morissette.

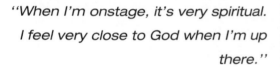lanis Morissette's 1995 release *Jagged Little Pill* sold over ten million copies and won her four Grammy Awards. Its slew of hit singles, kicked off with the vituperative "You Oughta Know," made Morissette an alternative music star overnight. Yet the singer- songwriter also endured some flak for her success, especially after word leaked out that she had suffered a rather unsuccessful earlier incarnation as a big-haired, drum-machine-backed teen singer in Canada. Nevertheless, the candid songs of *Jagged Little Pill,* penned by Morissette as she matured out of her teens, spoke to a broad cross-section of adolescents and adults alike.

Morissette was born June 1, 1974, in Ottawa, Ontario, one of a set of twins born to Alan and Georgia Morissette. Alanis and her twin Wade joined older brother Chad, and for a time the family lived in Europe when the elder Morissettes—both teachers—took jobs at a military base school. As a young teen in Ottawa again, Morissette attended Catholic schools and was a straight-A student. A self- described overachiever, she began piano at age of six and wrote her first song at age nine, and her talents eventually landed her on television. Her biggest success came with a

768

recurring role on *You Can't Do That on Television,* a kids' show on the Nickelodeon cable channel in the mid-1980s.

Begins Recording Career

With the earnings from the television show, Morissette produced her first single on her own label, Lamor Records. The 1987 release, "Fate Stay with Me," was recorded with the musical expertise from former members of the Stampeders, Canadian rockers who had a 1971 hit with "Sweet City Woman." As a single written by a thirteen-year-old, "Fate Stay with Me" was no monster hit but did attract the attention of MCA Canada, who signed Morissette. Her first full-length record, *Alanis,* debuted in 1991, followed by *Now Is the Time* a year later.

But it was not yet Morissette's time at all. Her career enjoyed some minor successes, but she remained pigeonholed; MCA even had her touring with the much-maligned Vanilla Ice. She did get a chance to hone her songwriting skills over two albums, however, and later, after her major success with *Jagged Little Pill,* refused to be embarrassed by a persona whom unkind journalists compared with Debbie Gibson or Tiffany. "I wasn't writing to communicate anything, and I was definitely not ready on the self-esteem level to indulge myself and all my personal turmoil," she told J. D. Considine of the *Chicago Sun-Times.*

Jagged Little Pill would bare some of the personal dramas that engulfed Morissette in typical coming-of-age passages, but she has spoken about certain moments in her late teens as definite turning points. In one incident, she had a breakdown in front of her parents—partly as a result of the pressures she felt as a combination teen star/overachiever/perfect daughter. Discovering the 1991 Tori Amos LP *Little Earthquakes* helped inspire Morissette to begin writing from the heart. Coincidentally, Amos had also suffered an off-target launch as an alterna-pop performer under the moniker Y Kant Tori Read, and later succeeded by writing straightforward, deeply personal songs.

Morissette came to see the necessity of leaving Canada for the more inspiring climes of Los Angeles. She underwent the usual big-city trials during her first weeks. She was held up at gunpoint. She was broke. She tried to find someone to work with, but no one seemed to click. Finally she approached Glen Ballard, an unlikely hero. Ballard was a producer with a home studio who had crafted tunes for Wilson Phillips and Paula Abdul. But he didn't try to mold her into something salable: "I felt that he wasn't judging me, and I felt that he had enough security within himself to give the ball to a 20-year-old and let her go with it," she told Considine. Within a period of two weeks, they recorded most of what would become *Jagged Little Pill,* and shopped their demo tape around. Executives at Maverick Records heard it and signed Morissette in 1994. Their ultimate boss, however, is none other than Madonna, who became CEO of the subsidiary as part of her lavish contract with Warner Brothers. Morissette was just twenty.

Amazing Success

Jagged Little Pill, released in the spring of 1995, displayed a drastic change from Morissette's former recording efforts. "The sound is more muscular; her voice is rawer, the guitar work more aggressive," wrote Christopher John Farley in *Time,* "and while the words are rarely as smart as they seem to think they are, this is straight-ahead rock, sweetened somewhat with pop melodiousness." Its initial single, "You Oughta Know," was a catchy diatribe against a former lover. Later, rumors surfaced that Morissette may have been writing about someone specific she had dated, such as television comic Dave Coulier, but the singer has said that it was merely a composite of several doomed relationships.

Success made Morissette an easy target for criticism, however, once her new American fans—who had never heard of her—discovered her previous incarnation via snipey rock critics. There were rumors that Maverick was surreptitiously buying up all unsold copies of the early-'90s releases, and worse, that Ballard had done much of the work for *Jagged Little Pill.* Yet Morissette refused to evade her former teenybopper persona, and debunked the tales of Maverick's attempts to hide it. Instead, she told Jon Beam of the *Minneapolis-St. Paul Star Tribune* that her early brush with fame helped her keep a level head

when the real fame came knocking. Her experiences, she asserted, "made me not become a heroin addict and become completely overwhelmed with how crazy this life is that I'm leading right now."

Morissette's newly out-of-control life included extensive touring in support of *Jagged Little Pill* throughout much of 1995 and 1996. In early 1996 the record won four Grammy Awards, including Album of the Year, and *Jagged Little Pill* would eventually sell a staggering ten million copies. Nor surprisingly—given the fervor of her fan base—Morissette has described singing on stage as similar to a religious experience: "When I'm onstage, it's very spiritual. I feel very close to God when I'm up there," she told *Rolling Stone*'s David Wild. Another journalist likened Morissette's stage show to "kind of like waiting for someone to have a breakdown," wrote Jae-Ha Kim in the

Chicago Sun-Times. "Flailing her arms and moving about in a pigeon-toed stance, she appears most comfortable when her face is covered by her mane of hair."

Away from the Spotlight

Still, fame did have its pressures. She began avoiding interviews with members of the Canadian media, granting access only to American journalists. For over a year and a half, Morissette made herself scarce. She traveled to Cuba and India, she trained for and competed in three triathlons, and she considered her future. She returned to the recording studio in 1998. "The challenge," she told Mim Udovitch in a *Rolling Stone* interview, "was to see if I could write a record when my whole lifestyle and situation had completely changed, and still be able to write it in a not-self-conscious way.'' The result was her sophomore album *Supposed Former Infatuation Junkie.*

Although *Supposed Former Infatuation Junkie* is, like *Jagged Little Pill,* a deeply personal work that focuses on issues such as failed relationships and self-understanding, it is more positive in tone and more spiritual in form. Udovitch wrote, ''One of the things that sets Morissette apart from the other twentysomething singer-songwriters with whom she is often and inaccurately lumped is that she writes from the point of view of someone searching for meaning in a meaningful, rather than meaningless, world.'' Morissette told *TV Guide,* referring to the meaning of the album's title, ''In the past . . . relationships . . . had negative connotations to me, but now that I understand [them] and myself a little more, I can actually enjoy being infatuated again.''

The single ''Thank U'' debuted successfully before the release of the entire album, which consists of 17 tracks and has a running time of almost 75 minutes. ''Thank U'' is a tribute to the many things that allowed Morissette to grow personally: ''Thank you, India/ Thank you terror/ Thank you disillusionment.'' Jeff Giles praised her efforts in a *Newsweek* article appearing just days before the album's release on November 3, 1998. Giles wrote, ''Morissette's new effort is a marvelous, gutsy, unconventional, pop record that makes border raids on every conceivable genre. There are acoustic guitars, piano arpeggios, heavy-metal riffs, hip-hop beats, R&B grooves, Led Zeppelin-ish exoticism and on and on.''

Morissette explored her acting talents, playing God in the film *Dogma,* a religious satire. ''I love doing things that scare me,'' she told Beam. ''It makes me feel alive and challenged. It makes me feel like I'm growing. That comfort-zone area, I hate it.'' She also stirred up controversy in the music video industry by appearing nude in the video version of ''Thank U.''

Morissette lives in Brentwood, California, with boyfriend Dash Mihok, the subject of the love song ''So Pure,'' appearing on the *Infatuation* album. Estimated to be worth more than $50 million, Morissette will not need to enter the recording studio any time soon to pay the rent. However, her appeal to an audience that consists of teens, twentysomethings, and thirtysomethings will insure that fans will be ready and waiting for her next effort.

Choice Cuts

Jagged Little Pill, Maverick, 1995

Supposed Former Infatuation Junkie, Maverick, 1998

Sources for More Information

Periodicals

Entertainment Weekly, December 25, 1998.

People, December 30, 1996.

Rolling Stone, November 26, 1998; May 13, 1999.

Time, February 26, 1996.

On-line

Alanis Morissette Web site, located at http://www.maverickrc.com/alanis/.

Toni Morrison

**Novelist
(1931–)**

*"My aim is to reach all readers who
are not fearful of being challenged
and are willing to take this human
journey with me."*

*Born Chloe Anthony Wofford, February 18, 1931, in Lorain,
OH; daughter of George (a shipyard welder) and Ramah
(Willis) Wofford; married Harold Morrison (an architect),
1958 (divorced, 1964); children: Harold Ford, Slade Kevin.
Education: Howard University, B.A., 1953; Cornell Uni-
versity, M.A., 1955.*

Prior to October 1996, Nobel laureate and
Pulitzer Prize-winning author Toni Morrison
was no stranger to notoriety. She had received
media attention for her highly regarded written
works, and events in her personal life had gained
public attention. Three of her six novels had been
best-sellers, and the others had been steady sellers
throughout their years in print. Nevertheless,
Morrison's fame increased considerably when television talk show host Oprah Winfrey announced
on her October 18, 1996, broadcast of *The Oprah
Winfrey Show* that Morrison's 1977 novel *Song
of Solomon* was the latest selection for Oprah's
Book Club. Soon after Winfrey's announcement,
Morrison's novel, became a runaway commercial
success, selling more than 500,000 and appearing
in the top five on the *New York Times* best-
seller list.

Song of Solomon, which depicts a Black man's
quest for identity and discovery of his heritage, is
"not an easy read," according to Morrison in an
interview with *People*'s Lan N. Nguyen; the narrative style is dense and poetic, and the characters

and events are multifaceted and complex. Remarkably, Winfrey's popularity and status as a public role model for many Americans has enabled her to persuade people to read *Song of Solomon* despite the novel's intimidating qualities, and Morrison's works are now being read by an entirely new audience. As Morrison once stated: "My aim is to reach all readers who are not fearful of being challenged and are willing to take this human journey with me."

Roots in Ohio

Morrison's own "human journey" began on February 18, 1931, in Lorain, Ohio, when she was born Chloe Anthony Wofford, daughter of George and Ramah Wofford. Although her novels are not explicitly autobiographical, they are grounded in her experiences as a child growing up in Ohio, where as an adolescent she read the works of English author Jane Austen, French writer Gustave Flaubert, and classic Russian novelists. In an essay in *Black Women Writers at Work,* Morrison explained the influence of her early years in Ohio on her writing: "I am from the Midwest so I have a special affection for it. My beginnings are always there. . . . No matter what I write, I begin there."

Morrison's parents were hardworking and very proud of their African American heritage, instilling in their children self-esteem and a desire to distinguish themselves by leading honorable, principled lives. Morrison's father often worked several jobs to support his family, and her mother took a series of low-paying, menial jobs in order to send Morrison money while she was attending college. After graduating with honors from Lorain High School, Morrison attended Howard University in Washington, D.C., where she studied English and earned a bachelor's degree in 1953. It was while she was a student at Howard University that Morrison changed her first name to Toni, because she had encountered difficulty with people who could not pronounce Chloe. She went on to receive a master's degree in English from Columbia University in 1955.

From 1955 to 1957 Morrison taught English at Texas Southern University in Houston; in 1957 she returned to Howard University as an English instructor. While working at the university, she met a Jamaican architect named Harold

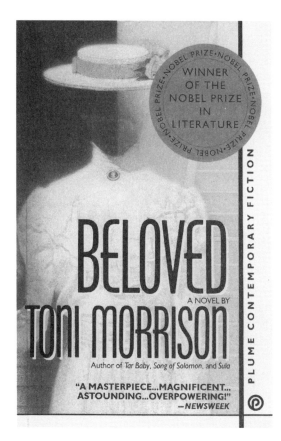

*Cover of **Beloved***

Morrison, whom she married in 1958. Ultimately the Morrisons divorced, and in 1964 Toni Morrison took the couple's two young sons, Harold Ford and Slade Kevin, to stay with her at her parents' home in Ohio. After living with her parents for more than a year, Morrison found a job as an editor with a textbook subsidiary of Random House in Syracuse, New York. Although she was a single working mother, Morrison managed to compose her first novel, *The Bluest Eye,* by writing late in the evenings after her children were asleep.

The Bluest Eye, which relates the experiences of three pre-teenaged Black girls in Lorain, Ohio, was published in 1969. The title of the novel comes from the character of Pecola Breedlove, who considers herself ugly and wishes she had blue eyes, which she believes would make her beautiful. After a series of tragedies in her life, Pecola sinks into madness and believes that she possesses the bluest eyes of anyone. *Black American Literature Forum* contributor Phyllis R. Klotman commented: "*The Bluest Eye* is an extraordinarily passionate yet gentle work, the language lyrical yet precise—it is a novel for all seasons."

Morrison's first novel was well received by critics, and in 1973 she followed it with *Sula,* which earned her a 1974 National Book Award nomination. Sula, who is regarded within her community as an evil woman, commits murder, stands by as her own mother dies in a fire, and has an affair with her best friend's husband. Nevertheless, she achieves some measure of respect for the personal freedom she demonstrates by her actions.

Critical and Popular Success

Published in 1977, Song of Solomon was awarded the National Book Critics Circle Award. The main character of the novel is Milkman Dead, a man who acquired his first name when his mother was discovered breast-feeding him when he was four years old. Milkman's search for his own identity, as well as his ancestors', is the dominant idea in the novel. In Reaching Out: Sensitivity and Order in Recent American Fiction by Women, Anne Z. Mickelson declared Morrison "deals ... with the black man who yearns to fly—to break out of the confining life into the realm of possibility—and who embarks on a series of dramatic adventures." Although Milkman figures prominently in the novel, his aunt Pilate, according to Mickelson, "emerges as the most powerful figure in the book with her calm acceptance of this world, as well as of another reality other than the fixed one of the world. She is thoroughly at home with herself, and has the kind of sensibility which is not disturbed by anything she experiences or witnesses." Critics applauded Morrison's ability to portray Milkman's journey to understanding, her blending of elements of fantasy and reality, and her use of myths and folklore in the novel. Song of Solomon was Morrison's first best-selling novel and established her as a major American writer.

Tar Baby, Morrison's 1981 novel, is set on an isolated West Indian island and focuses on the relationship between a Jadine, a Paris-educated Black model and, Son, a rebellious drifter from Florida. Jadine is attracted to Son but is torn between the young black man and a wealthy white man who has asked her to marry him. Critics interpreted the novel as an examination of what results when one attempts to deny one's heritage and praised Morrison's capacity for presenting such a cultural dilemma in an accessible manner without resolving the question for the reader.

Some commentators faulted the novel as obscure and described the characters as lacking motivation; however, many applauded Tar Baby's intricate symbolism and its insightful treatment of the themes of race, identity, love, and power.

The Masterpiece

Morrison's fifth novel, 1987's Beloved, is set in a small Ohio town shortly after the end of the Civil War and portrays the trials and tribulations of Sethe, a former slave. Sethe, who mistakenly believes that she is going to be returned to slavery, murders her baby daughter, Beloved, so that she will not have to endure the misery of life as a slave. The story of Sethe is based on an actual nineteenth-century magazine article Morrison read while conducting research for The Black Book, a history book she was editing. In Beloved, twenty years after her death, Sethe's daughter returns from the grave to seek out her mother, and Morrison uses flashbacks, fragmented dialogue, and myths to illustrate the events leading up to Beloved's death, and why Sethe refused to atone for her crime to her community.

Critics hailed Beloved as a masterpiece, lauding it as one of the finest representations of the hardships of slavery and its psychological consequences ever written. Nevertheless, despite the critical acclaim with which the novel was greeted, it failed to win either the 1987 National Book Award or the National Book Critics Circle Award. In response to what they believed was an outrageous failure to recognize Morrison's talent, forty-eight prominent black American writers and critics, including Maya Angelou, Angela Davis, Alice Walker, John Wideman, and Houston A. Baker, Jr., signed a letter to the editor that appeared in the January 24, 1988, edition of the New York Times Book Review.

The letter generated fierce debate within the New York literary community, with some critics accusing the authors of the letter of racist manipulation. Beloved was awarded the Pulitzer Prize for fiction in 1988. Morrison, who had no knowledge of the 1987 letter to the editor before it was published, responded to the news that she had won the Pulitzer by remarking in a New York Times article: "It's true that I had no doubt about the value of the book and that it was really worth serious recognition. But I had some dark thoughts about whether the book's merits would be allowed to be the only consideration of the Pulitzer committee. The book had begun to take on a responsibility, an extra-literary responsibility that it was never designed for.'' Most commentators observed that Morrison's winning of the Pulitzer Prize ended the debate sparked by the letter to the editor.

Morrison followed *Beloved* with *Jazz,* a 1992 novel that focuses on the turbulent relationship between its two main characters, a couple from Virginia who move to Harlem in 1906. The novel is set in 1926, but flashes back to events in the past, including Joe's murder of a young girl with whom he had had an affair. *Jazz* explores the themes of jealousy and forgiveness and portrays Harlem in the 1920s as symbolic of freedom and excitement for many African Americans. In a review of *Jazz* in the *Chicago Tribune,* Michael Dorris asserted that the novel is ''about change and continuity, about immigration: the belongingness you leave behind and the tied-together suitcase you carry under your arm.'' The novel was generally well received by critics, with only a few objecting to the narrative structure as confusing.

Wins Nobel Prize

In 1993 Morrison became the first African American woman to receive the Nobel Prize in literature. In awarding her the honor, the Swedish Academy called Morrison ''a literary artist of the first rank,'' and commended her ability to give ''life to an essential aspect of American reality'' in novels ''characterized by visionary force and poetic import.'' The Academy also asserted that Morrison ''delves into the language itself, a language she wants to liberate from the fetters of race. And she addresses us with the luster of poetry.''

Paradise, published in 1998, was generally warmly received by critics who found that the novel lived up to Morrison's previous works. The backdrop of the story revolves around a group of former slaves who settle in Oklahoma and found the town of Haven, where the inhabitants are haunted throughout the twentieth century by a past of bondage and rejection from light-skinned members of their own race. The novel also tackles the issues of female rebellion against a patriarchal society and the search for paradise—some sort of happiness and security—in a less than perfect world. ''With *Paradise,*'' declared Brooke Allen in the *New York Times Book Review,* Morrison has brought it all together: the poetry, the emotion, the

Masterworks

broad symbolic plan. . . . It is an ambitious, troubling, and complicated piece of work, proof that Toni Morrison continues to change and mature in surprising new directions.''

An article by the *New York Times'* Caryn James quoted a remark made by Winfrey on her program as she recalled a telephone conversation she had had with Morrison. Regarding the complex nature of her narrative style, Oprah asked Morrison, ''Do people tell you they have to keep going over the words sometimes?'' Morrison responded simply: ''That, my dear, is called reading.'' During her appearance on Winfrey's talk show, Morrison commented on the staggering growth of interest in her novel *Song of Solomon* that had been generated by the talk show host's promotion of it, asserting, ''To give it a new life that is larger than its original life is a revolution.''

Sources for More Information

Books

Morrison, Toni, *Playing in the Dark: Whiteness and the Literary Imagination,* Harvard University Press, 1992.

Harris, Trudier, *Fiction and Folklore: The Novels of Toni Morrison,* University of Tennessee Press, 1991.

Kramer, Barbara, *Toni Morrison: Nobel Prize-Winning Author,* Enslow, 1996.

Taylor-Guthries, Danille, editor, *Conversations with Toni Morrison,* University Press of Mississippi, 1994.

Eddie Murphy

**Actor and comedian
(1961–)**

"I live to make people happy."

Born April 3, 1961, in Brooklyn, NY; son of Charles (a police officer) and Lilian (a telephone operator) Murphy; married Nicole Mitchell (a model), March 18, 1993; children: (with Tamara Moore) Christian; (with Mitchell) Bria, Miles Mitchell, Shane Audra.

Eddie Murphy, who made a memorable impression with his first appearance on the comedy series *Saturday Night Live* in 1980, went on to achieve huge success as a comedian and actor. Though some of his late 1980s and early 1990s films earned poor reviews and a lackluster showing at the box office, his starring roles in such blockbusters as *48 Hours* and *Beverly Hills Cop* have made him an entertainment institution. Eddie Murphy once told his tenth grade social studies teacher, as reported in *Rolling Stone,* "I'm going to be bigger than Bob Hope." The enormously popular entertainer has turned that youthful boast into a statement of fact. He has starred on late-night television, toured before sell-out audiences, recorded a couple of best-selling comedy albums, and had leading roles in several blockbuster movies.

Born on April 3, 1961, Murphy was raised in the Bushwick section of Brooklyn, New York, and later moved to the predominantly black middle-class suburb of Roosevelt, Long Island. Growing up, Murphy spent a great deal of time watching television, practicing impressions of such cartoon characters as Bugs Bunny and Tom and Jerry.

Film director John Landis has stated that Murphy's unique point of view is rooted in his early perceptions of TV: "I grew up hooked on TV, but Eddie is TV. His world experience comes from the tube."

Before long, Murphy began working on comedy routines after school, and developing his comedy skills became his passion. Murphy made his first stage appearance in 1976, when, at the age of 15, he hosted a talent show at the Roosevelt Youth Center. He did an impersonation of soul singer Al Green, and the kids loved it. "Looking out at the audience, l knew that it was show biz for the rest of my life," the performer recalled to Richard Corliss in *Time*.

Became a *Saturday Night Live* Regular

Murphy soon started performing stand-up comedy at local clubs. Just a few months out of high school, he performed at the Comic Strip, a popular Manhattan club. One of the owners, Robert Wachs, noticed Murphy's talent, and that first appearance led to club dates throughout the East Coast. Wachs and his partner, Richard Tienken, later became Murphy's managers. Like comedian and actor Richard Pryor—one of Murphy's childhood idols—his stand-up act is raunchy, filled with four-letter words. Unlike his idol, however, Murphy has always believed in clean living: He doesn't smoke, drink, or use drugs.

When Murphy learned that the producers of NBC-TV's series *Saturday Night Live* were looking for a black cast member for the 1980-81 season, he jumped at the chance to audition. After six tries, he was finally hired as a featured player, or as he told Richard Rein of *People*, "an extra." Murphy appeared only occasionally and didn't win a spot as a regular until later in the season. Because that year's show was a flop, NBC cleaned house, and most of the cast was fired.

The only performers retained for the next season of *Saturday Night Live* were Murphy and Joe Piscopo. Murphy emerged as the show's star. As Rein explained, "He did wickedly adept—and less than worshipful—impressions of [boxer] Muhammad Ali, [actor and comedian] Bill Cosby, [musician] Stevie Wonder and Jerry Lewis." He

also created some memorable new characters, including Mister Robinson, a ghetto version of TV's Mister Rogers who spewed comments like "Can you say 'scumbucket,' boys and girls?," and a grown-up version of the Little Rascals' Buckwheat. Other hilarious characters included an irreverent version of Gumby; Velvet Jones, a pimp and huckster selling a book called "I Wanna Be a Ho," a guide for would-be prostitutes; and Tyrone Green, an illiterate convict-poet penning pieces like "Cill My Lanlord." The *New York Times* soon proclaimed that "Eddie Murphy has stolen the show."

A Budding Megastar

In 1982 Murphy recorded an album of his stand-up material. It received a Grammy nomination and eventually went gold. In that same year, he landed his first motion picture role in *48 HRS*. Director Walter Hill selected Murphy on the basis of some videotapes of *Saturday Night Live* that he had seen. Murphy played a fast-talking convict who is released from prison for two days to help a policeman, played by Nick Nolte, track down a pair of killers. The film was an instant hit, grossing more than $5 million in its first week. In mid-1983 Murphy's second movie, *Trading Places*, was released. Costarring Dan Aykroyd, this film was another hit for the budding megastar. Murphy also launched a major concert tour that year. In addition, he recorded his second comedy album, *Eddie Murphy: Comedian*. This time he won a Grammy, and the album went gold.

Murphy left *Saturday Night Live* after his fourth season. After the disastrous film *Best Defense*, Murphy came back with a blockbuster hit movie, *Beverly Hills Cop*, which had a lead role originally slated for actor Sylvester Stallone. It became Murphy's first starring role, and according to Richard Grenier, writing in the *New York Times*, it broke box-office records: "*Beverly Hills Cop* has quite stunned Hollywood. Released in early December, it . . . grossed more than its next five competitors combined."

As a result of Murphy's astounding success, Paramount Pictures signed the 23-year-old to a $25 million, six-picture contract. Added Grenier, "No black actor has ever come anywhere near the position Eddie Murphy holds today. He is quite

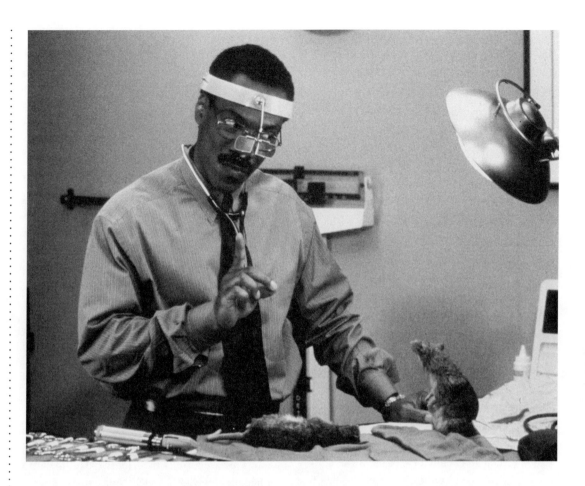

*Movie still from **Dr. Dolittle***

simply a historic figure.'' In an attempt to explain Murphy's tremendous appeal, Gene Lyons wrote, ''Murphy's most valuable gift as a performer is his saucy charm; he's not wicked, just naughty. He's a good little bad boy who can get away with murder when he smiles.''

Early in 1987, Murphy was beset by several of legal and financial problems. Misfortune with his personal finances, however, was offset by the box office success of *Beverly Hills Cop II,* released in 1987. Murphy's film *Raw,* in which he performs a stand-up comic routine, was released in December of 1987. ''This feature-length concert film,'' stated Janet Maslin in a *New York Times* review, ''is hilarious, putting Mr. Murphy on a par with Mr. [Richard] Pryor at his best.'' She continued, ''Even the ushers were laughing.'' Audiences poured in to see the movie, and it became the biggest-grossing concert film ever.

Panned by Critics, Adored by Fans

In the summer of 1988 Murphy came out with a film that was a change of pace for him. In *Coming to America,* a lighthearted romantic comedy, Murphy's character is a departure from the brash, swaggering types of his previous films. Peter Travers of *People* liked the change: ''This is Murphy's most heartfelt and hilarious performance. And his riskiest.'' Other critics knocked it. David Ansen of *Newsweek* wrote, ''*Coming to America* may be more interesting as a career move than as a movie.'' The public continued to flock to see Murphy, however, and the movie ended up as the second-biggest grossing hit of the year.

Throughout the late 1980s and early 1990s, Murphy, a superstar with unrivaled marquee value, continued to make films that critics felt were vapid star vehicles rather than thoughtful showcases for the actor's prodigious comic gifts. In 1989 Murphy made his directorial debut with *Harlem Nights,* a sprawling 1930s black gangster flick that he also wrote and produced. Although the film made $18 million in its first weekend of release, the premiere was marred by violence in theaters throughout the country, leaving one person dead and many injured. Murphy's 1990 effort, *Another 48 HRS.,* directed by Walter Hill, was generally ridiculed as a bland, stale remake of the hugely successful 1982 original.

In 1991 Murphy, who had criticized his previous contract with Paramount, secured for himself a four-movie deal with the film company, which had recently undergone a management shake-up. Hopes were rekindled that Murphy would now be surrounded by people who cared not only about money—Murphy's films had grossed more than $1 billion at that point—but also about the quality of the films featuring the star. The first movie made under that contract, *Boomerang*, confirmed those hopes. The film featured Murphy as a hot shot cosmetics executive whose woman-chasing lechery is superseded, to his dismay, by the man-hunting zeal of his new female boss, played by actress Robin Givens. In the *Boston Globe*, Jay Carr called the movie "a smart comedy that sends a few interesting messages, the big one being that Murphy has learned his lesson."

A Return to Prominence

In 1994, Murphy returned to the screen with *Beverly Hills Cop III*. The movie was faulted for relying on one-dimensional villains and formulaic car chases. Yet another box-office disappointment followed, with 1995's *Vampire in Brooklyn*. Much hope for a film comeback rested with the 1996 release of *The Nutty Professor*—a remake of the 1963 Jerry Lewis comedy classic. Released at the onset of the summer season, the movie has Murphy playing seven different roles, including an obese and buck-toothed professor. *The Nutty Professor* reaped $130 million at the box office and reaffirmed the actor's popularity with audiences as well as film critics. Murphy landed the Best Actor award from the National Society of Film Critics, and was named to *Entertainment Weekly's* list of "The 100 Greatest Movie Stars of All Time."

Following a successful stint as the voice of Mushu shrimp in the Disney animated feature, *Mulan*—Murphy again successfully revisited a classic with an update of the Hugh Lofting children's tale, *Dr. Dolittle*. "In the lowbrow yet charming update of Dr. Dolittle," Lisa Schwarzbaum wrote in *Entertainment Weekly*, " a delightful Eddie Murphy rides herd on a crass menagerie of talking animals."

The PJ's, which debuted on the Fox network in 1999, marked Murphy's return to television—this

Television
Saturday Night Live, NBC, 1981–84

Films
48 HRS., Paramount, 1982
Trading Places, Paramount, 1983
Beverly Hills Cop, Paramount, 1984
Coming to America, Paramount, 1988
The Nutty Professor, Universal, 1996
Life, Universal, 1999

time as the "foamation" series' co-creator and voice for the main character. Set in a housing project and predicated on poking fun at racial stereotypes, the series drew criticism for perpetuating negative stereotypes. *Entertainment Weekly* reported that director Spike Lee called the series "hateful towards black people," while African-American essayist Stanley Crouch referred to it as a "third-rate update of 'Amos 'n' Andy' and 'The Honeymooners.'" In spite of harsh criticism, the series drew strong ratings, outperforming other shows in its time slot—including the WB network's popular *Buffy the Vampire Slayer.*

A Family Man

While Murphy's box-office appeal has suffered some setbacks, his personal life seems to have been very rewarding. On March 18, 1993, he wed Nicole Mitchell, a successful print and runway model who had been romantically linked to Murphy since a 1988 NAACP Image Awards dinner. The couple have three children, whom Murphy credits with helping him to maintain a perspective on his career highs and lows.

"I live to make people happy," Murphy told James McBride of *People,* and his huge popularity attests that he's done exceptionally well in achieving this goal. In fact, the ability to leave his audiences happy in whatever he does may very well be the simple secret to his phenomenal success. As Richard Corliss wrote in *Time,* "More than any other entertainer in recent memory, Eddie Murphy just plain makes people feel good."

Sources for More Information

Periodicals

Entertainment Weekly, Fall 1996 Collector's Issue; July 10, 1998; March 5, 1999.

Jet, August 18, 1997.

Nation, July 27, 1998.

Newsweek, July 1, 1996.

People, July 1, 1996.

Rolling Stone, February 18, 1999.

Time, January 27, 1997.

On-line

E! Online, located at http://www.eonline.com.

Mike Myers

Actor and comedian
(1963–)

Born May 25, 1963, in Toronto, Ontario, Canada; son of Eric (an encyclopedia salesperson) and Alice (a data processor) Myers; married Robin Ruzan, May 22, 1993.

M ike Myers, the man who created his own pop culture vocabulary with jargon that included ''—Not!,'' ''Schwing!,'' and ''We're not worthy!,'' as teen metal-head Wayne Campbell in the film *Wayne's World* during the early 1990s, is a respected comedian whose live comedy performances led to a role on the long-running television program *Saturday Night Live* (*SNL*). As a regular cast member, Myers's humor was popular with the viewers, and his inspired characters, particularly Wayne, were well-received. Wayne was so popular, in fact, that several films and a television special were created around this character. In 1997, Myers starred in another film, *Austin Powers: International Man of Mystery,* which he also wrote and produced. Like Myers's other wacky alter egos, Austin Powers—a British playboy spy whose mind-set and wardrobe are trapped in the late 1960s—showcases Myers's special style of comedy.

Myers was born in 1963 in Toronto, the youngest son of British parents who had immigrated from Liverpool—home of John, Paul, George, and Ringo. ''I always thought I was related to the Beatles because my parents talked like them and nobody else in Canada did,'' Myers told Elizabeth Snead of *USA Today*. Myers credits his father's

''I always thought I was related to the Beatles because my parents talked like them and nobody else in Canada did.''

781

humor with inspiring him to do impersonations. His dad, an *Encyclopaedia Britannica* salesperson, exposed him to comedy—sometimes waking his sons at night to watch Peter Sellers movies. "I'd be dozing off while my dad was roaring at *The Mouse That Roared* or something. That was my education. I wasn't receptive to much of it the next day at school," he remarked to Gary Arnold in the *Washington Times.*

Falls for Radner and Saturday Night Live

In 1973 a 10-year-old Myers played Gilda Radner's son in a British Columbia Hydro Electric television commercial. During the four-day shoot, Myers admitted "I fell in love with her [Radner] and cried on the last day. My brothers taunted me mercilessly and called me a sucky baby for an entire year. One day they said, 'Hey, sucky baby, your girlfriend is on a TV show.' And it was *Saturday Night Live.*" The first time he saw the show, Myers dreamed of being a comedian on *Saturday Night Live,* even telling his family that one day he would be there. He was proud of Canadian cast members, such as Dan Aykroyd. For an eighth-grade assignment, Myers choose *SNL* producer Lorne Michaels as "a famous Canadian I'm proud of."

At age 20, Myers was the star of his own television series, a Canadian show called *Mullarkey & Myers* (1984–86). He also lived in England for a short time doing a comedy act. Once back in Canada, he joined the improvisational troupe Second City in Toronto in 1986; later he joined Chicago's Second City. In 1987 he was the host veejay of an all-night Canadian music video show. It was in 1989 that Myers's childhood ambition became a reality: he premiered as a cast member on *Saturday Night Live.*

Classic Characters

Myers's recurring sketch characters would become among the most memorable in *SNL*'s history. Among his classic alter egos was Simon, a little British youngster who loved to talk about his "drawrings" while he sat in the bathtub. Even more popular was Dieter, the grim, pretentious, all-black-wearing, avant-garde host of an existential German TV talk show called "Sprockets."

Linda Richman was Myers's drag impersonation of a Barbra Streisand-obsessed hostess of a call-in gossip show called "Coffee Talk." Based on Myers's mother-in-law, Richman's Yiddish refrains, "I'm a little farklempt. . . . Talk amongst yourselves," became so popular, fan clubs were developed in her honor. Barbra Streisand even made a surprise appearance during a "Coffee Talk" sketch. Linda Richman was Myers's favorite character. "[She] brings me out of my sort of shy Canadian persona."

Wayne Campbell, the teenage host of the cable community-access program "Wayne's World," was the most famous of Myers's characters. Joined by Dana Carvey as Wayne's spacey sidekick Garth, the act was based in the basement of Wayne's parents' Aurora, Illinois, home. "Wayne's World" ("Party Time! Excellent!") was littered with slacker slang ("—Not!") that became entrenched in American vernacular. Like the real Myers, Wayne loved hockey and heavy-metal music, with sketches that featured guest celebrities such as hockey great Wayne Gretzky and the band Aerosmith ("We're not worthy!"). The antithesis of political correctness, Wayne and Garth spent much time insulting authority and rating women's looks ("Schwing!").

Making Movies

In 1992 Myers developed the popular *SNL* sketch into a hit movie of the same name. Myers's wrote and starred in *Wayne's World,* which earned $122 million at the box office. The film, which was filled with many memorable scenes and lines ("if she were president she'd be Babe-raham Lincoln"), led to a sequel simply titled *Wayne's World 2.* The second movie was not nearly as big of a success, but still earned $47 million.

In 1993 Myers deviated from his *SNL* alter egos to write and star in *So I Married An Ax Murderer,* a romantic comedy about a man so afraid of commitment that he fabricates horrible traits about his girlfriend to escape the relationship. Myers also played the role of the main character's Scottish father—for which he received positive reviews. The movie did not fare that well at the box office. The comparatively lackluster turn-out for *Ax Murderer* and *Wayne's World 2* had some critics deeming Myers a has-been. The poor performance of other movies by *SNL* cast

Movie still from
Austin Powers:
International Man of
Mystery

members abandoned discussion of films based on Myers's Dieter and Linda Richman characters.

Around the same time, Myers experienced some tragic events in his personal life. In 1991 his father died of Alzheimer's disease. It deeply pained Myers's that his dad never really knew of his success. He noted in *People:* ''Dad would sometimes come to Second City shows, but he was starting to heckle the performers. He'd say things like, 'Get off the stage. Michael's the only funny one.' Dad had always had a gallows sense of humor, but this was the disease talking. By Christmas, 1989, I was on *Saturday Night Live,* but I don't think Dad ever knew it. . . . I did *Wayne's World* in August and September of 1991, and Dad died that November at age 69.'' Just prior to that, Myers's fiancee's brother was killed in a car accident.

In 1993 Myers married long-time sweetheart Robin Ruzan, whom he met in 1987 at a hockey game when she got hit by a puck. Ruzan appeared as a waitress in *Wayne's World* and helped him write *Wayne's World: Extreme Close-Up,* a book on the making of the movie. Myers wears his father's gold 1957 ''salesman of the year'' ring on his wedding finger. Myers told Steve Murray in

the *Atlanta Journal and Constitution,* ''He couldn't be at the wedding, so this was my concession to his non-presence.'' Myers noted in *People,* ''Wearing that ring keeps Dad close to me.''

It was comedian and ex-*SNL* player Bill Murray who suggested to Myers that he take time off to recover from the changes in his life. While Myers was off-screen he was hardly inactive. He toured with Barbra Streisand during her concert performances, doing a comedy act as Linda Richman from the audience. And while his next movie was still in the creation stage, Myers joined friends Matthew Sweet and Susanna Hoffs (a former member of the singing group, The Bangles) to form a retro-1960s band called Ming Tea.

Austin Powers

Myers had a sudden flash of inspiration for his next film, *Austin Powers: International Man of Mystery,* about a swinging 1960s British playboy spy thawed from a cryogenically frozen state after 30 years to prevent global devastation by Dr. Evil. He recalled to Arnold, ''I was in the car . . . on my way to hockey practice, and 'The Look of Love' came on the radio. And I realized that I would love

Popular Works

Television
Saturday Night Live, NBC, 1989–94

Films
Wayne's World, Paramount, 1992

Wayne's World 2, Paramount, 1993

So I Married an Ax Murderer, TriStar, 1994

Austin Powers: International Man of Mystery, New Line Cinema, 1997

Austin Powers: The Spy Who Shagged Me, New Line Cinema, 1999

to be in a movie that reprised [that song]. Then it grew into a movie with the flavor of everything that song implied, incorporating spies and swingers and gaudy, colorful costumes and decor and the ham-fisted horniness and obliviousness of the sexual revolution. I liked the idea of Austin as a cheerful relic of all that in our politically correct, counterrevolutionary climate.''

The movie spoofed 1960s spy flicks and TV series like James Bond, *The Avengers,* and *The Man from U.N.C.L.E.* Myers played dual roles as both Powers and Dr. Evil. Powers is a bespectacled stud with bad-teeth who dresses in psychedelic bell-bottoms, crushed velvet suits, and ruffled shirts. Like other Myers figures, Powers has his own unique vernacular, throwing around lines such as ''shag,'' and ''I'm your man, baby!'' Released in May 1997, the movie, which co-starred Elizabeth Hurley, received mixed reviews but did well at the box office.

Myers planned a serious role for his next movie. He portrayed Studio 54 co-founder Steve Rubell in a film titled *54.* Myers told *Variety,* ''I've had serious moments in some of my films, and I've done serious roles on Canadian television.'' He went on to assure his fans: ''This is not a situation where I've abandoned comedy. I love comedy.'' His return to comedy was huge, as he starred in the much anticipated Austin Powers sequel, *Austin Powers: The Spy Who Shagged Me,* which premiered in 1999. Audiences flocked to theaters, and the film enjoyed generally good reviews. Janet Maslin, writing in the *New York Times,* admitted that while the movie is ''several love beads short of its predecessor,'' it is still ''a crafty, intermittently hilarious comedy.''

With his success, Myers has become more settled in his personal life. He and his wife bought a home in Los Angeles in 1996, where they live with their three dogs. ''I said to my wife, 'I want to nest; we have to get out of our suitcase-and-futon-in-New-York phase.' I couldn't do that anymore. We would see friends with a backyard and kids and all that stuff. So now we're in our dog phase, just about to enter our kid phase. . . .'' he declared to Murray. Perhaps Myers will have the same influence on his children's sense of humor that his dad did on him. Myers told Snead that his optimistic father impressed on him two things: ''He would always say to me, 'Everything's going to be OK,' and 'Let's go have fun.'''

Sources for More Information

Periodicals

Entertainment Weekly, April 7, 1995; May 9, 1997; October 30, 1998.

Gentleman's Quarterly, June, 1999.

Maclean's, June 14, 1999.

Rolling Stone, June 10, 1999.

On-line

E! Online Web site, located at http://www.eonline.com.

Celebsite Web site, located at http://www.celebsite.com.

Walter Dean Myers

**Young adult novelist
(1937-)**

Born Walter Milton Myers, August 12, 1937, in Martinsburg, WV; son of George Ambrose and Mary (Green) Myers; raised from age three by Herbert Julius (a shipping clerk) and Florence (a factory worker) Dean; married second wife, Constance Brendel, June 19, 1973; children: (first marriage) Karen, Michael Dean; (second marriage) Christopher. Education: Attended City College of the City University of New York; Empire State College, B.A., 1984.

"There is always one more story to tell, one more person whose life needs to be held up to the sun."

Walter Dean Myers is regarded as one of the most influential African American writers of juvenile fiction. At a young age Myers perceived a lack of children's books that deal with the concerns and realities of minority children. So he took it upon himself to rectify the problem, going on to publish over sixty-five works, including children's picture books, novels for children and young adults, poetry, and nonfiction.

Frequently facing prejudice, adversity, and general ignorance during his writing career, Myers refused to compromise the subject matter and characters he used in books. His importance lies, however, in his passion and commitment to helping children in a positive way—by not only encouraging them to read, but giving minority children books to read that will speak to their realities.

Walter Milton Myers was born in Martinsburg, West Virginia. After his mother died, Myers moved to Harlem to be raised by foster parents. Most of Myers' books are set in Harlem, where he himself

785

learned the values and ideals that would later affect his writing. A severe speech disability caused Myers to act out in school. "As a result I found myself suspended from school a great deal. Although I enjoyed school, I found that I didn't always fit in." Embarrassed by the way children laughed at his speech, Myers began to withdraw in the classroom.

Discovers Love of Reading

Had it not been for his fifth grade teacher, Mrs. Conway, Myers may have never found the confidence or desire to become a writer. After she found him reading a comic book in class, she did what many other teachers would have done—she tore it up. The next day, however, she handed him the book *East of the Sun, West of the Moon,* telling him that if he was going to read in the back of the class, he might as well read something good. "Reading took on a new dimension for me" he wrote in *Something about the Author Autobiography Series (SAAS).* This, coupled with Mrs. Conway's pushing students to write their own stories to read in class, sparked a light in Myers. Intimidated by the prospect of having to read in front of the class, Myers began writing poetry to reduce the number of words he was unable to pronounce. He found that he loved writing, and he became a changed person.

Realizing that high tuition costs would keep him from attending college, Myers entered the military at age seventeen. Afterwards, he wrote articles and poetry for several magazines and newspapers. His first opportunity to really show his writing talent came when the Council on Interracial Books for Children sponsored a contest for minority writers, for which he wrote his first book, *Where Does the Day Go?,* The story depicts an African-American father who leads a group of minority children on a walk, explaining to them the difference between night and day and the uniqueness of each.

While a book editor for the Bobbs-Merrill publishing house, he wrote his second children's book, *The Dancers.* In writing it he experienced firsthand the control that publishers have over their writers' books. He recalled in *Interracial Books for Children Bulletin,* "The publisher introduced a white character for me. He's not in the story, but he appears in as many pictures as possible and seems to be in the story."

When Myers was fired from his job, he and his wife decided he should dedicate himself to full-time writing. Myers followed *The Dancers* with two more children's books, which he published under the name Walter Dean Myers, in honor of his foster parents. The book that finally brought him critical attention was a short story titled *Fast Sam, Cool Clyde, and Stuff.* An editor persuaded Myers to expand the story into a full-length book, and it became his first novel for juvenile readers.

Fast Sam is narrated by eighteen-year-old Stuff, who looks back on experiences he had when he was thirteen and living in Harlem. Hanging out with the other title characters, Fast Sam and Cool Clyde, he forms a gang called the Good People. As a close-knit group of good friends they deal with problems confronting teenagers, such as broken homes, welfare, love, drugs, street brawls, encounters with the police, and even death. Reviewers were enthusiastic about the book, especially Myers's use of "street talk" and his portrayal of the characters' tender feelings for one another. Alleen Pace Nilsen noted in *English Journal* that one of the "nicest things" was that the members of the Good People gang "try to communicate rather than to exploit each other. . . ."

Books for Minorities

After writing *Fast Sam,* Myers recognized the importance of stories minority children can relate to, stories that portray situations and settings that are truer to their realities than European-influenced juvenile fiction. The author found inspiration from the great African American writers of the past. One of the most important influences Myers found was not a work by an African American writer, however, but James Joyce, the famous Irish author. Myers had serious doubts about his own ability to become a writer, and he questioned his worth constantly. His validation came, he continued, "When I discovered *Portrait of the Artist as a Young Man* I knew that I was not alone. If Joyce had these doubts, too, and he was a writer, well—I would also become a writer" he told *SAAS.* This realization inspired Myers to write some of the most powerful children's books addressed to, but not exclusively for, minority children.

While Myers was establishing his career, he encountered many obstacles as an African American writer. First, publishers and libraries were hesitant to carry any of his books, not seeing the need or the audience for them. On the other hand, when Myers attempted to write about things other than African American life, he was faced with questions such as "With such a need for Black literature, why would you want to write about anything else?" While Myers has seen it as his goal to provide minority children with a canon of literature that speaks to them, doing so has not been an easy task.

By 1980 Myers had published picture books for children, nonfiction works, and novels for young adults. During the 1980s, Myers published "The Arrow" series of adventure tales for juvenile readers, and a host of other young adult novels. In most of the novels he portrays the lives of Harlem teenagers, touching on contemporary social problems. Myers also wrote several adventure novels, including the works in "The Arrow" series and *The Nicholas Factor* and *Tales of a Dead King*. Myers also wrote *Motown and Didi: A Love Story* and *The Outside Shot*, which are sequels to novels he wrote in the 1970s.

Examines Social Problems

One of Myers's more unusual novels is *Sweet Illusions*, a workbook about pregnancy for teenagers. Each of the fourteen chapters focuses on a fictional character who describes the experience of unexpected parenthood. Representing a social and racial cross-section of society, there are five unwed mothers, five fathers, and four family members or friends. At the end of each chapter are blank pages on which readers can write responses to what they have read. Reviewers welcomed Myers's book. Stephanie Zvirin commented in *Booklist* that "the book is an astute, realistic consideration of some of the problems associated with teenage pregnancy," providing a perspective on teenage fathers, who are "too often neglected."

In 1988 Myers published *Scorpions* and *Fallen Angels*, novels he described to Kimberly Olson Fakih in *Publishers Weekly* as "a departure" in his career—"very serious, probing work," he said. "Not that the others didn't address serious issues, too," he continued, "but the new ones

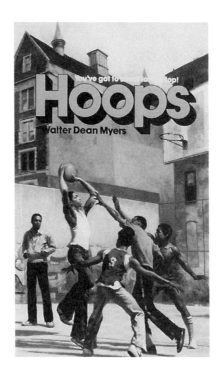

Cover of Hoops

were more difficult to write." *Scorpions* is the story of two boys who join a Harlem gang and become involved in the narcotics trade. *Scorpions* was followed by *Fallen Angels*, which Myers wrote as a tribute to his brother, who was killed in Vietnam. Featuring a seventeen-year-old boy from Harlem who joins the Army. *Fallen Angels* won several awards, among them the Coretta Scott King Award.

During the 1990s Myers continued his prolific output, writing the kind of novels that brought him recognition earlier in his career. Among his most popular books is *Darnell Rock Reporting*, published in 1994, which features the title character, a thirteen-year-old middle school student. The book tackles issues such as poverty and homelessness. But as Janice Del Negro reported in *Booklist*, "[the] story is not issue driven. It is the development of Darnell's character that moves things forward: we watch as Darnell takes his first tentative steps toward thinking and acting on his own."

Collaborates with Son

The Glory Field, also released in 1994, is an epic tale that traces the evolution of the African American experience from the slave ships to the streets of Harlem. Myers's next book, a fantasy titled *Shadow of the Red Moon,* marks his first collaborative effort with his son Christopher, who did the illustrations.

Myers has also received recognition for *Slam!,* a basketball story that features the eponymous title character as a teenager who is in control on the court, yet his personal life is rife with difficulties. Slam's grades are low, he cannot fit in with the predominately white students at his school, his grandmother is dying, and his best friend Ice is dealing crack. *Booklist* reviewer Bill Ott wrote, "... Myers does a good job of rescuing his characters from stereotype.... [He also uses] crisp details, not flowery language to achieve muscular poetry." Maeve Visser Knoth of *Horn Book* observed that "readers will appreciate *Slam!* for the honesty with which Myers portrays the dreams of one Harlem teenager."

In 1997 Myers and his son collaborated again, this time on a children's book titled *Harlem.*

Through Walter Dean Myers's poem and Christopher Myers's illustrations, the work celebrates both the promise and problems that Harlem gives to the African American community as well as its connection to Africa. *Booklist* contributor Michael Cart praised the work, calling the text "as much song as poem" while adding that "it is Harlem as a visual experience that YAs will return to again and again."

At the end of the millennium, Myers remained one of the foremost African American authors of books for children and young adults. Nearly a decade earlier he wrote in *SAAS*: "As a Black writer I want to talk about my people. The books come. They pour from me at a great rate. I can't see how any writer can ever stop. There is always one more story to tell, one more person whose life needs to be held up to the sun."

Sources for More Information

Books

Bishop, Rudine Sims, *Presenting Walter Dean Myers,* Twayne, 1991.

Children's Literature Review, Gale, Volume 4, 1982, Volume 16, 1989, Volume 35, 1995.

Patrick-Wexler, Diane, *Walter Dean Myers,* Raintree, 1996.

The Schomburg Center Guide to Black Literature, Gale, 1996.

Something about the Author Autobiography Series, Volume 2, Gale, 1986.

Willie Nelson

Singer, songwriter, and guitarist (1933–)

Born April 30, 1933, in Abbott, TX; son of Ira Nelson (a musician); married Martha Matthews, 1952 (divorced 1963); married fourth wife Annie D'Angelo, 1991; children: (with Matthews) Lana, Susie, Billy; (with D'Angelo) Lukas, Jacob.

"I don't think we're ever asked to endure anything that we can't endure."

The long and prolific career of Willie Nelson—not to mention his personal life—has been quite a roller coaster ride, slow moving at the start, then climbing straight to the stars, dipping to a heart-rending low, and finally, running straight and true once more. As Cheryl McCall of *People* wrote, "An instant success after 25 years trying, Willie didn't cut a big-selling album until he was 40." Once Nelson's career took off, however, he became "an inadvertent and unassailable national monument." In the early 1990s, though, Nelson had to overcome two crushing events—a multimillion-dollar battle with the U.S. Internal Revenue Service and the suicide of his oldest son. But, demonstrating an indomitable spirit, he managed to bounce back in the 1990s with new recordings that a number of critics have called his best in years.

Nelson was born on April 30, 1933, in Abbott, Texas. The country was mired in the Great Depression and times were rough for the little farming community. When Nelson was six months old, his mother left to find a job and never returned. Nelson and his older sister, Bobbie, were then raised by their paternal grandparents. Nelson's grandparents were strict, church-going people. They were also devoted amateur musicians who pushed the children into music and performing, teaching both Nelson and his sister how to play an instrument. Nelson's grandfather, a blacksmith by trade, gave him his first and only training on the guitar. Nelson told Teresa Taylor Von-Frederick of *McCall's* that his grandparents were "his true, and earliest, inspiration."

More Money in Music Than Cotton

Nelson worked in the cotton fields after school to help bring in some money for the family. And by the age of 10, he was an accomplished enough musician, along with his sister, to begin playing at local dances. When Nelson was in the sixth grade, he got his first professional job, with the John Raycheck Band, an Abbott polka outfit that played the bohemian clubs in the area. Needless to say, Nelson's grandmother was horrified that he was playing in beer joints. But it was undeniable that he could make much more money there than in the cotton fields.

After graduating from high school Nelson joined the U.S. Air Force but soon received a medical discharge. He returned to Abbott and formed a band and again started playing in local clubs. He attended Baylor University but quickly dropped out. He also fell in love and married Martha Matthews—he was 18 years old; she was 16. From the start, they struggled to make ends meet and soon began fighting regularly. "She was a full-blooded Cherokee," Nelson told *People,* "and every night with us was like Custer's last stand." Nelson was making as little as 50 cents a night with his band. The honky tonks and beer joints that were Nelson's second home were rough, rowdy places where the band had to be shielded from flying bottles by chicken-wire fences.

Sold First Song for $50

During the 1950s, Nelson often found work as a disk jockey. He and his wife also started a family; Nelson and Matthews eventually had three children. Nelson had been writing songs, and he now tried to sell some to help support his family.

He sold his first, "Family Bible," for $50 to pay for food and rent. It eventually became a Number One country hit. He then sold another song, "Night Life," for $150. "Night Life" went on to become one of the most-recorded songs ever. Performed by more than 70 artists, it has sold more than 30 million records, though Nelson never made a dime off the royalties. Nelson then moved to Nashville to take his shot at the big time.

In Nashville, musician and songwriter Hank Cochran helped Nelson get a job as a songwriter with Pamper Music. And by 1961, several of Nelson's songs had been recorded by country performers and had become hits. "Hello Walls" was released by Faron Young; "Crazy" was recorded by Patsy Cline (and became a classic); and Billy Walker did "Funny How Time Slips Away." Besides becoming country hits, "Hello Walls" and "Crazy" also made the pop Top 40.

Nelson next joined Ray Price's band, the Cherokee Cowboys, as a bass player. Although he was now collecting royalty checks for his songwriting, plus a salary from the band, Nelson spent his money as fast as he made it. His already stormy marriage deteriorated. (This would be the first of several broken relationships; Nelson has remarried three times). He began recording his own songs but did not meet with much success. Nelson then got together with singer Shirley Collie and recorded a couple of songs, "Willingly" and "Touch Me," that became Top 10 hits.

Throughout the 1960s, Nelson's own recordings sold few copies. He had an unusual voice—high and quavering—and he favored uncommon phrasing. His music did not fit the traditional Nashville mold, so it was considered uncommercial and as such, his records were not adequately promoted. Nelson was signed by Nashville record companies primarily for his songwriting talents. "They grudgingly allowed me to sing as long as they could cover up my voice with horns and strings," he stated in his autobiography.

Life Among the Outlaws

The night before Christmas Eve, 1969, Nelson was at a party when he was told that his house had burned to the ground. With his home

Willie Nelson in concert

devastated and his Nashville recording career going nowhere, Nelson decided to move to Texas. He settled in Austin, which was becoming the home of the "outlaws"—country singers like himself who could never quite fit in back in Nashville. These included Waylon Jennings and Kris Kristofferson. Nelson started touring the area's dance halls and county fairs and developed a growing following. In the early 1970s, he began sporting the distinctive look he wears to this day: long hair—often fashioned in two braids—and beard, bandanna headband, jeans, and running shoes.

In 1973 Nelson released the album *Shotgun Willie* for Atlantic Records; it outsold all his previous albums combined. Also in 1973, Nelson was inducted into Nashville's Songwriters Hall of Fame, and his first Fourth of July picnic—a rock-style country festival—attracted a crowd of 50,000, including rock and rollers, as well as country fans. Atlantic dropped its country division in 1974 and Nelson signed with Columbia Records, where he finally enjoyed complete creative control over his recordings. In 1975 he released the album *Red Headed Stranger,* which became a major hit; the LP rose to Number One on the country charts and

also cracked the Top 40 of the pop charts. A single from *Stranger,* "Blue Eyes Crying in the Rain," became a Top 10 hit and won Nelson his first Grammy Award. At long last, he had become a star.

By 1976 Nelson was selling records like crazy. Seven of his albums appeared on the Billboard charts that year. Gold and platinum records were rolling in. Then, in 1978, Nelson tried a new direction, releasing an album of pop standards called *Stardust.* It included such songs as the title track, by Hoagy Carmichael, and "Blue Skies," by Irving Berlin, both remade in Nelson's unique style. The set of covers became a country and pop hit.

In 1979, Nelson ventured into acting, taking a supporting role in the film *The Electric Horseman,* which starred Jane Fonda and Robert Redford. He then costarred in the 1980 movie *Honeysuckle Rose,* which was based loosely on his life. A song Nelson wrote for *Honeysuckle Rose,* "On the Road Again," reached Number One on the country charts and became a Top 20 pop hit; it also became the singer's unofficial theme song. In 1985 Nelson organized the first Farm Aid benefit concert. He had witnessed the plight of the nation's farmers and wanted to do something to assist them. Farm Aid has become a yearly event, featuring a variety of musical performers and earning millions of dollars for farm groups.

Disaster Strikes

The year 1991 began and ended with two shattering personal crises. At the end of 1990, the I.R.S. seized Nelson's properties and possessions to settle a tax debt totaled at $32 million. The agency had disallowed various tax shelters. The figure was later reduced to $16.7 million, but in January of 1991, the I.R.S. held an auction of all of Nelson's possessions. Friends and supporters stepped in and tendered bids, purchasing his property and allowing him to remain on the premises until he could buy it back. One friend bought his home, another his Pedernales Country Club and Recording Studio.

Nelson sold an album that year through an 800 number—*Who'll Buy My Memories: The I.R.S. Tapes*—to help pay off the seemingly insurmountable debt. He also toured heavily. Then, on Christmas Day of 1991, Nelson's son Billy was found dead, a suicide by hanging. "I've never experienced anything so devastating in my life," Nelson admitted to a friend. Reflecting further on his troubles, he told Alanna Nash of *TV Guide,* "I think everything we go through is a test. I don't think we're ever asked to endure anything that we can't endure." Nelson put his faith in the power of positive thinking. "I guess I'm just living in the present," he said to Nash. "So far, more good things have come along, and the more I think that

way, the more positive things happen. That's how I keep it together."

Flourishing in the 1990s

Eventually, Nelson's I.R.S. debt was negotiated down to $9 million. By 1993, he had paid off about half and had agreed to a schedule to pay off the rest. More importantly, Nelson released a daring new album in 1993, *Across the Borderline,* that was widely praised by critics. In 1996, Nelson released *Spirit,* his first album of original songs in nine years. Peter Castro wrote in *People* that with this album, "Nelson is back on the range, exploring man's painful search for love . . . an austere, mesmerizing testament to Nelson's gifts as a storyteller." *Teatro,* released in 1998, was another critical success. "A spooky flamenco hayride of a record," according to Jeff Gordinier in *Entertainment Weekly,* "*Teatro* proves that . . . over the course of four decades, Willie Nelson is hitting another moment of creative fervor."

At the turn of the century, Nelson is still going strong. Back in 1993 when he turned 60—an age he never expected to see as a performer—he told Gary Graff of the *Detroit Free Press,* "When I was 15 and thought about a 60-year-old person, I figured they were real old and had one foot in the grave. I really don't feel that way right now. I feel pretty good, in fact. Besides, I don't have anything to retire into or for. All I do is make music and play golf, and I wouldn't want to give up either one." The outlaw still rides.

Sources for More Information

Books

Nelson, Willie, and Sheldrake, Bud, *Willie: An Autobiography,* Simon & Schuster, 1988.

Periodicals

Entertainment Weekly, June 14, 1996, p. 61; September 18, 1998, p. 46.

Texas Monthly, April, 1998, p. 98.

On-line

The *Rolling Stone* Network, located at http://www.rollingstone.com.

Jack Nicholson

**Actor
(1937-)**

Born April 22, 1937, in Neptune, NJ; married Sandra Knight (divorced); children: Jennifer, Lorraine, Raymond.

One of Hollywood's biggest names, Jack Nicholson is considered not only a movie star with a slightly sinister charm, but one of the most talented actors in the business. Success eluded Jack Nicholson during his first decade as an actor and he nearly shelved his big screen ambitions. But at the age of 32, he got his big break with a small role in the 1969 film *Easy Rider.* That part, as Nicholson once told *Rolling Stone,* ''changed my life.'' Movie critics praised Nicholson for his portrayal of an attorney with an outlaw's attitude; Hollywood insiders were equally impressed, nominating Nicholson for an Academy Award.

Nicholson didn't win an Oscar then. Three decades later, however, he was a three-time Academy Award winner and had established himself as one of Hollywood's most enduring stars. ''Indeed,'' wrote Nancy Collins in a 1992 *Vanity Fair* article, ''in a business where money masquerades as art and box-office receipts constitute culture, Nicholson dominates the industry on his own terms. Not only is he one of the richest actors in Hollywood, he is also, arguably, its most revered artist. As [actor] Robin Williams so aptly put it, 'There's Jack and there's the rest of us.'''

''When you've done this as long as I have, you have to take acknowledgment with a grain of salt.''

Anatomy of an Icon

Nicholson was raised in Neptune, New Jersey. Growing up, he believed that Ethel May Nicholson (whom he called "Mud") was his mother when, in fact, she was his maternal grandmother. A small web of deception was cast shortly after his mother, June, gave birth and left home for work. When she returned two years later, she and everyone else in the family decided to keep her true relationship to Jack a secret. Once, when Jack was a teenager, Mud and June considered telling him. "But they were both so afraid of losing him," Lorraine, his aunt, told *Vanity Fair* in 1994. "They didn't trust what his reaction would be."

Nicholson was 37 when he finally learned the truth, but only when he received a 15-page letter from a man who claimed to be his father. By then, June and Mud were both dead, and only Lorraine remained to confirm the truth. While Nicholson told *Vanity Fair*'s Nancy Collins that he "wasn't upset by the deception," it's likely that the circumstances of his childhood—the abandonment by his father and to a lesser degree his mother, who also discouraged his acting career—filled him with some of the outrage and defiance he later brought to so many of his on-screen characters, from R. P. McMurphy in *One Flew Over the Cuckoo's Nest* to the Joker in *Batman.*

"Jack would never say this," says director Mike Nichols, who worked with Nicholson on the 1994 film *Wolf,* "but he works off some kind of reactor, and the little pellets of plutonium which are pain have to keep going into the reactor. So he allows pain, real pain, into his life because it goes into the reactor and keeps cooking. And he doesn't try to make his pain go away. I remember when Mama Cass died. After lunch I found him in the makeup chair weeping. I said, 'Nick, do you want to go home? Would you feel better?' And he said, 'I don't want to feel better.' And that's the key to part of him. He knows he has to go through it. He's not trying to feel better when he feels bad."

After graduating from high school (where during his senior year he was voted class pessimist and optimist), Nicholson headed to California to pursue acting. Initially he landed a job in MGM's cartoon department and studied with an acting group called The Players Ring Theater. He made his on-screen debut in Roger Corman's *The Cry Baby Killer.* For more than a decade, he played parts in low-budget films, many thrillers produced by Corman, and performed also on the stage and in television soap operas. Frustrated by his lack of success, Nicholson began to consider writing and directing.

Unexpected Big Break

Then *Easy Rider* came along. Playing an alcoholic attorney turned motorcycle outlaw, Nicholson charmed moviegoers with his sly grin and sarcasm. Ironically, Nicholson wasn't supposed to get the part, but the original actor walked off the set. "I certainly lucked in and got picked up in a period," Nicholson recalled in an interview with *Rolling Stone.* "This doesn't happen that much, contrary to what people think. The last time before me might have been James Dean."

According to Steve Erickson, a critic for *Esquire,* Nicholson did far more than establish himself as a talented actor in *Easy Rider.* "He's the movie's Trojan horse: the straight American within whom hides the voice of the counterculture, waiting for nightfall to come," Erickson wrote. "The rebellion that had characterized Nicholson's marginal movie persona throughout the previous ten years, in a string of biker and horror movies, now took on larger philosophical implications, not to mention political ones. *Easy Rider* also put him in a position to play a role no one had ever quite filled before: Counterculture Movie Star."

After *Easy Rider,* Nicholson established his talent with leading roles. He received Oscar nominations for his work in Bob Rafelson's *Five Easy Pieces,* Hal Ashby's *The Last Detail,* and Roman Polanski's *Chinatown.* Perhaps no single movie contributed to his stardom more than *One Flew Over the Cuckoo's Nest.* As R. P. McMurphy, a sane mental patient, Nicholson won an Academy Award and secured a reputation not simply as good actor, but a great one. "Jack Nicholson, like the great talents of the forties—Humphrey Bogart, Cary Grant, Edward G. Robinson—has the ability to be both evil and lovable at the same moment," Peter Guber, C.E.O. of Sony Pictures Entertainment told *Vanity Fair.* "Jack's involvement with

*Movie still from **The Shining***

film gives it a unique credibility. He makes it formidable by his presence.''

Survived a Mid-Life Slump

During the early 1980s, Nicholson struggled professionally. He directed and starred in *The Two Jakes,* an unsuccessful sequel to *Chinatown* that was 15 years in the making. But in 1985, he pulled out of his mid-career slump with his portrayal of a retired astronaut in *Terms of Endearment.* The performance won him his second Oscar and moved him gracefully into playing middle-aged characters onscreen.

Batman provided stunning proof of Nicholson's box office success. According to *People,* the actor ''inhabited the Joker's role with such fevered invention that he stole the film.'' Nicholson reportedly earned $50 million from *Batman,* a figure that clearly set him apart from his peers. ''Jack's career was based on being a puncturer of the balloons of pomposity,'' writer-producer Don Devlin told *Vanity Fair* in 1992. ''He was the anti-Establishment guy, which is why young people always loved him so much. Well, the irony now is, because of the length of his career and how successful he's become, Jack is the Establishment.''

Unfortunately for Nicholson, he didn't move with equal grace into the middle-aged period of his personal life. His 17-year romance with the actress Anjelica Huston came to a painful end when Nicholson impregnated onetime waitress Rebecca Broussard, who was 26 years his junior. Broussard and Nicholson declared their love and had two children, Lorraine and Ray. Two years later, Broussard left Nicholson for a younger man. In the meantime, Huston found herself a husband, the sculptor Robert Graham. Nicholson returned to his life as a legendary bachelor.

Beyond the Pain

Rather than withdrawing from his profession during the tumultuous years, Nicholson worked steadily. ''He's got a voracious appetite for the work,'' Meryl Streep, his costar in *Heartburn* and *Ironweed,* told *People.* ''He's never satisfied but he's always churning. It's wild. There's nobody out there that far in the movies.''

By Nicholson's standards, his 1992 performance in *Hoffa* was among his best. As *Hoffa*, Nicholson had again played the role of an outsider, a guy who skirts the edges of the system. "When you've done this as long as I have, you have to take acknowledgment with a grain of salt," he told *Gentleman's Quarterly*. "I'd be more than willing to let my body of work stand on all the work that was not as well received: *Carnal Knowledge, Batman, Hoffa, The Witches of Eastwick, The Shining*—these are movies that didn't get all that much critical support. But it's not an aspiration of mine anymore. It's an actuality to simply do the job and enjoy that as much as you can. As I say, I can't do any better work than I did in Hoffa."

In 1992 Nicholson also appeared in the blockbuster hit *A Few Good Men*, playing a gruff Marine colonel. According to Roger Ebert, writing in the Chicago *Sun-Times*, "Nicholson is always fun to watch, as he barks and snarls and improvises new obscenities." Nicholson's mid-1990s films included *The Crossing Guard* and *Mars Attacks!*, appearing on screen in 1995 and 1996, respectively. In *The Crossing Guard*, a Sean Penn film, Nicholson portrays a jewelry store owner whose daughter is killed by a drunk driver. Consumed with his need for justice and revenge, he waits for the man's release from prison so he can kill him. In a complete digression from the grim story told in *The Crossing Guard*, Nicholson appeared in the comedy spoof *Mars Attacks!* (clearly

Another Oscar

Nicholson found renewed critical acclaim and box office popularity with the 1997 film *As Good As It Gets*, costarring Helen Hunt. Nicholson takes on the role of Melvin Udall, an extremely offensive man who offers biting criticism and sarcasm to anyone who crosses his path. Udall develops a relationship with a hard-working waitress (Hunt), the only person who is able to deal with Udall's rude and eccentric behavior. In a review in *Entertainment Weekly*, Lisa Schwarzbaum says, "Nicholson digs into *As Good As It Gets* . . . with more energy than he's shown since *A Few Good Men*." For his work, Nicholson earned the Academy Award for best actor.

Looking back on his career, some critics have said that while Nicholson has played a wide range of characters—from author to astronaut to accountant—he, in fact, has a limited range. "That isn't to say that much of his work, particularly from 1970 to 1975, isn't fine. All of it has star quality," Erickson of *Esquire* wrote. "But even in first-rate performances, even as early as *Five Easy Pieces*, the persona intimidated the role. Truthfully, did you really buy him as a classical pianist?"

Even Nicholson might agree. At the close of an interview with Lynn Hirschberg of *Rolling Stone*, Nicholson was asked if he will ever write his autobiography. The actor replied, "I definitely know I won't." "Why?" Hirschberg asked. "Because," Nicholson said, "my work is autobiographical."

Sources for More Information

Periodicals

Entertainment Weekly, Fall, 1996.

Gentleman's Quarterly, January, 1996.

Rolling Stone, March 19, 1998.

On-line

E! Online Web site, located at http://www.eonline.com.

Mr. Showbiz Web site, located at http://mrshowbiz.go.com.

Nine Inch Nails

Industrial music band

Group formed in the late 1980s by Trent Reznor. Reznor was born May 17, 1965, and raised in Mercer, PA. Performs on stage with guitarist Robin Finck, keyboardist James Woolley, bass player Lohner, and drummer Vrenna.

"I think the very act of wanting to discover and uncover unpleasantries is itself positive."

—Trent Reznor

When he was 23 years old, Trent Reznor formed the electronic, machine-driven, industrial music project that would launch his career to superstardom. Nine Inch Nails, the name Reznor attached to his creative endeavor, would also completely change his life in a matter of a few short years. "It's a convenient fiction for me to work under," Reznor told Musician when asked why he decided against incorporating his own name with that of the band. Nine Inch Nails—Reznor's "convenient fiction"—would become musical fact by 1989 when it launched the previously underground industrial music genre into mainstream popularity.

Reznor grew up in Mercer, Pennsylvania, where he was raised by his grandparents after his parents divorced. His grandparents forced him to take piano lessons as a child. "I'd get into trouble because the way I played pieces was not the strict way you were meant to play them," Reznor told *RIP*. "I'd add inflections to it, play around with it, and you weren't meant to do that. . . . I realized that it was a really expressive instrument. There came that moment when I realized how I felt through a musical instrument; I was around 12 or 13 when it struck me."

797

As a teenager, Reznor joined his first band, the Innocence, where he played mostly covers of songs by Journey and the Fixx. After high school, he moved to Erie, Pennsylvania, where he played for a few months with a new wave band called Urge. He spent a year at Allegheny College studying computer engineering before moving again, this time to Cleveland, Ohio. While working a series of other odd jobs, Reznor got work as an assistant at Cleveland's Right Track recording studios, where he began to work on the foundation of Nine Inch Nails (NIN, which uses a backward second N in its graphic design) during his off hours. Reznor also played in a variety of other bands including the Exotic Birds, Slam Bamboo, Lucky Pierre, and the fictional band Problems, whose only appearance took place at the end of the 1987 movie *Light of Day*.

A Sound All His Own

Despite his other projects, Reznor continued to develop and promote his own aggressive, industrial music. Nettwerk Records first expressed interest in signing NIN, and sent Reznor and a hired live band on tour with Skinny Puppy. However, Nettwerk couldn't offer Reznor a record contract at the time because of the label's financial position. In the late 1980s, Reznor sent a demo of his music to Tee Vee Toons Records (TVT) in New York. The independent label's greatest success had come from compilations of television theme songs, but TVT owner Steve Gottlieb believed in Reznor's music—and in the NIN project—enough to sign him to the label.

In 1989, TVT released NIN's first album, *Pretty Hate Machine,* which Reznor wrote and co-produced, and on which he performed all instrumental and vocal tracks. The album's first singles, "Down in It" and "Head Like a Hole," sparked interest in the band and were huge club hits; they were followed by the release of the single "Sin." As critic Vic Garbarini of *Musician* noted of Reznor, "Though often painted as some bitter, lost soul, his music suggests deeper yearnings toward faith, hope, even charity." After the release of Pretty Hate Machine, NIN went on tour, opening for such acts as the Jesus and Mary Chain and Peter Murphy.

Recognition and press attention increased quickly for Reznor and NIN. "I lived a fairly average, anonymous, small-town life till I got the idea to do Nine Inch Nails," he told the *Los Angeles Times.* "Then, I locked myself in a studio for a year, and then got off the tour bus two years after that, and I didn't know who I'd turned into." In 1990 some misplaced footage from the video for "Down in It" landed in the hands of the FBI. The video showed a half-naked man being thrown from a building, and the FBI thought they had stumbled across a videotape of an actual murder. They quickly launched an investigation, only to discover that the half-naked man was Reznor, whom they found very much alive, on tour with the Jesus and Mary Chain. The FBI ended up with an embarrassing situation, while Reznor gained even more publicity.

Faces Legal Battle

As the success of *Pretty Hate Machine* grew, Reznor and his touring version of NIN were asked to play the first annual Lollapalooza festival tour of alternative music bands. Lollapalooza sent Reznor's debut album soaring to platinum status and he garnered heavy video rotation on MTV with "Head Like a Hole." But once the profits rolled in, Reznor and TVT saw different directions for NIN's next recording. According to Reznor, TVT and Gottlieb tried to force him toward more commercial accessibility. Reznor argued with the label over videos, singles, and tour support and insisted that TVT had not paid him the royalties he had earned. Attempting to sever his contract with the label, he ended up involved in a lawsuit. Several other record labels wanted to purchase Reznor's contract, but TVT wouldn't sell.

Reznor kept NIN touring for two years after the release of *Pretty Hate Machine* just to keep up with legal costs. Finally, he decided to return to the long-missed recording studio to work on a new NIN album. Reznor and his producer checked into recording studios using fake band names such as the Stunt Pope, because if the name NIN appeared on anything, TVT would have legally owned the sessions.

Interscope Records, determined to get NIN on their label, negotiated a joint venture with TVT. Contractually, Reznor would strictly deal with Interscope, but TVT would still get a percentage of the profits. When the ink dried, Reznor presented his next effort to Interscope, a six-song EP with two bonus tracks titled *Broken.* Most of the songs on the EP lyrically express Reznor's anger toward

Nine Inch Nails in concert

TVT and how the whole situation had affected him. ''*Broken* was a hard recording to make,'' Reznor wrote in his bio for the EP. ''*Broken* is an ugly record made during an ugly time in my life. *Broken* marks phase three of Nine Inch Nails: the becoming.''

Reznor recorded two cover versions of songs as the unlisted bonus tracks on *Broken*, industrial band Pigface's ''Suck'' and post-punker Adam Ant's ''Physical.'' Released under his own newly formed Nothing label—in conjunction with Interscope and TVT—the EP reached Number Seven on the *Billboard* charts. In 1993, it earned Reznor a Grammy Award for best metal performance with vocal. That same year, Reznor released a limited-edition CD of various remixes of tracks from *Broken*. The CD, titled *Fixed,* displays the interpretation of the material through the ears of members of bands like Foetus and Coil. Interscope/ Nothing/TVT released only 50,000 copies in the United States.

The Downward Spiral

Following the release of *Broken,* Reznor moved to Los Angeles to start work on the 1994 release *The Downward Spiral.* He recorded the album in his own Le Pig studios in the Sharon Tate mansion, where actress Tate and others had been brutally murdered by the Charles Manson family in 1969. Reznor would be the last person to live in the house before its destruction.

Reznor adopted a new musical approach on *The Downward Spiral.* As he described it to *Musician,* ''The starting point [on *Broken*] was to make a dense record. We approached the new one from the opposite point of view—a record with holes everywhere.'' *The Downward Spiral,* which debuted on the *Billboard* charts at Number Two, was written as a concept album about someone who systematically examines himself and everything around him—from comfort to delusion—to discover his own identity and purpose. ''I think the very act of wanting to discover and uncover unpleasantries is itself positive,'' Reznor told Guy Garcia of *Time.* ''The act of trying to rid yourself of these demons, to prepare yourself for the worst, is a positive thing.''

Together with bass player Lohner, guitarist Robin Finck, keyboardist James Woolley, and longtime friend and drummer Vrenna, Reznor's stage shows—like his heavily censored videos for MTV—reflect the violence and sexual imagery around which he builds his music. ''I think Nine Inch Nails are big enough and mainstream enough to gently lead people into the back room a little bit,'' he told *Rolling Stone*'s Jonathan Gold. ''I think that back room could represent anything that an individual might consider taboo yet intriguing, anything we're conditioned to abhor. Why do you watch horror films? Why do you look at an accident when you drive past, secretly hoping that you see some gore?''

Style over Substance?

Reznor defends the theatricality of his musical persona. ''I'm not trying to hide,'' he explained to Gold. ''Or make up for a lack of songs, but essentially Nine Inch Nails are theater. What we do is closer to Alice Cooper than Pearl Jam.'' Though sometimes accused of ''putting on'' the trappings of a bizarre personality for his fan's benefit, Reznor admits to honest bouts of depression. ''When I think back as far as I can remember, I've always had an element of melancholy that I should probably have therapy for,'' Reznor admitted in *Alternative Press.* ''But I'm making a career of it. I'm intensely afraid of people, and I don't like to be in social situations. I feel uncomfortable, and I think my shyness and quietness is often misinterpreted as standoffishness. . . . I'm not trying to be a rock god. I have a multitude of split personalities.''

''I'm not any more happy or content with my life than I was 10 years ago,'' Reznor told *Musician* in 1994. ''I got everything I wanted in my life . . . except I don't really have a life now. . . . I've turned myself into this music-creation-performance machine.'' Reznor plans to release a new album—his first studio effort in five years—in 1999; *The Fragile* represents ''one of the year's biggest creative leaps,'' according to *Entertainment Weekly.* As long as his melancholy and multiple personalities inspire him to continue writing music that breaks the boundaries of commercially successful hits, Reznor will continue to flood the senses of whoever will listen with his industrial brand of aggression known as Nine Inch Nails.

Sources for More Information

Periodicals

Entertainment Weekly, March 18, 1994; December 30, 1994; August 15, 1997; January 22, 1999.

Melody Maker, March 12, 1994; March 26, 1994.

Musician, March, 1994.

People, April 25, 1994; February 6, 1995.

Rolling Stone, September 8, 1994; November 2, 1995; October 17, 1996; March 6, 1997; July 8–22, 1999.

Time, April 25, 1994.

On-line

The *Rolling Stone* Network, located at http://www.rollingstone.com.

Nirvana

Alternative rock band

"Success is not what we were looking for. . . . We just want people to be able to get the records."

—Kurt Cobain

Group formed in 1987. Members include Kurt Cobain (grew up in Aberdeen, WA; committed suicide April 1994; married Courtney Love [a singer], February 24, 1992; children: Frances Bean), guitar and vocals; Dave Grohl (from Washington, DC), drums; and Chris Novoselic (from Aberdeen; wife's name, Shelli), bass.

Three Seattle musicians who play what has become known as "grunge" rock seemed an unlikely bet for acceptance into the rock and roll establishment. Decidedly punkish in their musical style—albeit at a slower pace than was the hallmark of punk rock—strident in their lyrics, and unapologetic of their calculated-to-offend offstage personalities, the group nonetheless went from the "underground" status of their initial release, *Bleach,* to mega-stardom with their first major-label effort, *Nevermind,* within the space of a few years. The latter, featuring Kurt Cobain on guitar and vocals, Chris Novoselic on bass, and David Grohl on drums, jumped to the Number One spot on the *Billboard* rock chart and was cited in many music critics' Top Ten lists just months after its release.

Cobain and Novoselic grew up near Seattle, in Aberdeen, Washington, a secluded logging town 70 miles southwest of Seattle known largely for its overcast climate. Cobain's youth was often chaotic—he lived in a trailer park with his cocktail waitress mother after the breakup of his parents' marriage. Before his parents split up, Cobain's mother recounted in *Rolling Stone,* he "got up every day with such joy that there was another day to be had. When we'd go downtown to the stores, he would sing to people." After the divorce, though, Cobain's personality underwent a transformation. "I think he was ashamed," his mother continued, "and he became very inward—he just held everything."

Pop, Metal, and Punk Influences

Until the age of nine, Cobain listened mostly to the Beatles. Then his father introduced him to heavier fare—Led Zeppelin, Kiss, and Black Sabbath. He started playing drums and hanging around with an Aberdeen group called the Melvins. Melvins leader Buzz Osborne took Cobain to a Black Flag concert, where he got his first taste of hard-core punk. Cobain was awed; he began to experiment with the guitar and tried to form a band. "I learned one Cars song and AC/DC's 'Back in Black,'" he told *Elle.* "And after that I just started writing my own. I didn't feel it was important to learn other songs because I knew I wanted to start a band." After repeatedly failing to get a group together, Osborne suggested that Cobain hook up with Chris Novoselic, a tall, shy Aberdeen kid two years older than Cobain.

Cobain and Novoselic had met at the Grays Harbor Institute of Northwest Crafts. Like Cobain, Novoselic had moved around a lot as a kid—they felt they were both misfits in a way. They further shared an appreciation for the hard-core music that was generally shunned by their heavy metal-loving peers. A tape of the San Francisco punk band Flipper cemented their commitment to the genre. "It made me realize there was something more cerebral to listen to than stupid cock rock," Novoselic told *Elle.* Exhibiting total rebellion against what they saw as the red-necked, macho establishment of their hometown, they spray painted the phrases "God is Gay," "Abort Jesus," and "Homosexual sex rules," on cars and bank buildings. For one offense Cobain was arrested and fined.

Cobain's mother kicked him out of the house after he quit high school. Homeless, he slept on friends' couches and even briefly found lodging under a bridge. By 1987, however, he and Novoselic were beginning to gain a reputation as Nirvana and were a hit at parties at Evergreen State College in Olympia.

With the help of Melvins drummer Dale Crover, the trio began to record, finishing ten songs in one afternoon taping session. The resulting demo was submitted to Sub Pop, Seattle's then-underground label, the directors of which signed them to a record contract right away. In 1988, after changing drummers, the band recorded *Bleach* in six days for $606.17. The album moved slowly at first, but eventually sold 35,000 copies between its debut and the release of the band's second effort, which caused a surge of *Bleach* sales.

After *Bleach,* Nirvana began looking for yet another drummer, this time settling, in the fall of 1990, on Dave Grohl of the Washington, D.C., band Scream. This lineup returned to the studio to find that the Nirvana sound had improved significantly. When Sub Pop sought a distributor for the upcoming second album, a bidding war ensued among record labels interested in buying Nirvana out of their Sub Pop contract. The group eventually signed to DGC, home of giants Guns 'n' Roses and Cher, for $287,000. Rumors persisted, however, that the label had shelled out up to $750,000 to obtain the trio. Cobain commented in *Spin* that those reports were "journalism through hearsay," adding that "the numbers kept getting bigger so that a lot of people believed that we were signed for a million dollars."

The group had mixed feelings about signing to a major label; they feared they would be labeled "sellouts" for trading their underground status for the promise of big money. But the opportunity to get their music heard by a larger audience—and thus spread their message to the mainstream—mitigated these concerns. Nirvana released *Nevermind* in the spring of 1991; the record took three weeks to record and earned the trio $135,000. Producer Butch Vig instinctively felt that the unintelligible, but mesmerizing, cut "Smells like Teen Spirit" would be a hit, even before it was completed in the studio. "It was awesome sounding," he told *Rolling Stone.* "I was pacing around the room, trying not to jump up and down in ecstasy."

Astounding Success

Vig's prophecy came true: The *Nevermind* single "Smells Like Teen Spirit" soared to Number One after only a few months of airplay. The accompanying video, featuring a somewhat sinister high school pep rally—Cobain has said the

song is about teenage apathy—complete with tattooed cheerleaders, a bald custodian, writhing fans, and pointedly unkempt band members, received heavy rotation on MTV. And yet the most distinguishing aspect of *Nevermind* may have been that, as *New York Times* contributor Karen Schoemer pointed out, ''Nirvana didn't cater to the mainstream; it played the game on its own terms. . . . What's unusual about [the album] is that it caters to neither a mainstream audience nor the indie rock fans who supported the group's debut album. . . .'' Calling the release ''one of the best alternative rock albums produced by an American band in recent years,'' Schoemer continued, ''*Nevermind* is accessible but not tame. It translates the energy and abandon of college rock in clear, certain terms.''

In performance, Nirvana paid homage to angry punks past—dating as far back as the mid-1960s guitar destruction of then-''mod'' Pete Townshend, leader of Britain's the Who—by smashing their equipment onstage; Cobain estimated that he probably destroyed around 300 guitars. This behavior seemed to please Nirvana's legions of fans, who thronged to their shows in anticipation of such antics.

Despite Nirvana's rapid climb to the top, Cobain and company tried to keep a balanced attitude. They rejected a limousine ride to their *Saturday Night Live* performance because they didn't want to be treated like stars. Cobain tried to refrain from drugs and the standard rock-star revelry, partially in deference to a recurring and painful stomach ailment. When questioned about the band's success, Cobain revealed in *Elle,* "Well, it's a fine thing and a flattering thing, but it doesn't matter. We could be dropped in two years and go back to putting out records ourselves and it wouldn't matter to us, because success is not what we were looking for. . . . We just want people to be able to get the records."

Kurt and Courtney

Cobain married Courtney Love, singer of the band Hole, in February 1992, and the two had a baby girl named Frances Bean. Because of reports of Love's heroin use during pregnancy, the couple was denied custody of the child and allowed to see her only under supervision. They regained custody in 1993. Cobain and Love had a contentious relationship—Cobain was once arrested for domestic assault, though the charge was later dropped—but Cobain reported that Courtney and Frances brought him more happiness than he had ever known and offset the new pressures associated with super-stardom.

The release of *In Utero*—Nirvana's much anticipated 1993 follow-up to *Nevermind*—was delayed, despite the fact that Nirvana recorded it in about a week. There were problems in production, along with rumors that producer Steve Albini was to be replaced by Scott Litt in favor of Litt's lighter, more commercial sound. Eventually Litt did remix several of the songs, but critics pointed out that the contrast between Albini and Litt's styles actually strengthened the album. There were also censorship issues. Wal-Mart refused to sell the album unless a collage by Cobain featuring fetuses was removed from the cover art and the title of the song "Rape Me" was changed to "Waif Me." While some anticipated that the group's success would compromise their music, *In Utero* solidified Nirvana's reputation as arguably the most important band of its generation.

The album reflects Cobain's ambivalence toward the band's sudden rise to fame. "This is the way Kurt Cobain spells success," wrote a *Rolling Stone* critic in a review of *In Utero,* "s-u-c-k-s-e-g-g-s." This sentiment is expressed in lyrics such as, "Teenage angst has paid off well/ Now I'm old and bored," as well as in the ferocious vocals and abrasive *Bleach*-like instrumentals of the album. *In Utero* was a popular and commercial success, hailed as an important new direction for the band—and, indeed, for alternative music as a whole. "Despite the fears of some alternative-music fans, Nirvana hasn't gone mainstream," wrote *Time*'s Christopher John Farley, "though this potent new album may once again force the mainstream to go Nirvana." *Rolling Stone* lauded *In Utero* as "a lot of things—brilliant, corrosive, enraged and thoughtful, most of them all at once."

A Tragic End

By all appearances Nirvana was at the top of its game, but tensions were high among band members and between Cobain and Love, and Cobain continued to struggle with depression, stomach pain, and drug abuse. Then tragedy struck. On April 8, 1994, several days after Cobain had escaped from a drug detox center, his body was found in his Seattle home. Cobain had died of a self-inflicted gunshot wound two days earlier. In a suicide note addressed partially to his fans, Cobain said that he no longer enjoyed performing music.

Less than six months after Cobain's death, Nirvana's last album was released, *MTV Unplugged in New York.* Recorded in 1993, the acoustic album featured songs from all three albums as well as six covers. In the wake of Cobain's suicide, Nirvana was still winning new fans, and *Unplugged* was a success. Many reviewers interpreted the album as a sign of what might have been. *Rolling*

Stone praised the album for ''displaying taste and reach and a versatility the band had newly achieved and was reveling in. . . . It's all here on Nirvana's *Unplugged*—the bile, the black-sheepishness. And all around, the aching beauty of this self-doubting, jocular smart-aleck with the honeycombed voice.''

With Cobain the central personality and creative force behind Nirvana, there was no thought of continuing the band after his death. Grohl and Novoselic went on to other projects. Cobain's influence was still being felt years after his death; in 1999, *Rolling Stone* named him ''Artist of the Decade.'' Summing up Nirvana's impact, *Rolling Stone*'s David Fricke wrote, ''Never mind all the standard issue babble about Generation X. There was nothing blank about the way Cobain wrapped up his discontent and, by extension, that of his audience, in roughshod song.''

Sources for More Information

Books

Azerrad, Michael, *Come As You Are: The Story of Nirvana*, Main Street Books, 1993.

Halperin, Ian, *Who Killed Kurt Cobain?: The Mysterious Death of an Icon*, Birch Lane Press, 1998.

Thompson, Dave, *Never Fade Away: The Kurt Cobain Story*, St. Martin's, 1994.

Woodward, Fred, *Cobain*, Little, Brown, 1997.

Periodicals

Rolling Stone, May 13, 1999.

On-line

The *Rolling Stone* Network, located at http://www.rollingstone.com.

Garth Nix

Science fiction and fantasy novelist (1963–)

Born in 1963, in Melbourne, Australia. Education: University of Canberra, B.A., 1986.

"I believe in writing stories, not didactic tracts."

Australian writer Garth Nix was weaned on fantasy novels; it is no coincidence he grew up to write such popular titles as *Sabriel* and *Shade's Children.* "My mother was reading *The Lord of the Rings* when she was pregnant with me," Nix once stated. "So I absorbed this master work of fantasy *in utero,* as it were. Later on I became a great fan of Tolkien's stories." Nix's explanation of this early influence is partly tongue-in-cheek, but it is clear from his writings that there is nothing fanciful about his dedication to his craft. A contributor in *Publishers Weekly* called *Sabriel* "excellent high fantasy."

With only a handful of novels to his credit, Nix has already made a name for himself as a fantasy and science fiction writer of note in his native Australia, and increasingly in the United States as well. Nix's lighter side can be witnessed in a trio of books in the "Very Clever Baby" series, parodies of easy readers which are intended for parents. Written for two sets of parents who had babies on the way, these books exemplify the Nix philosophy of writing: "Essentially written for me. . . . It was what I wanted to read." Nix has made a cottage industry of writing books that he himself wants to read. The serendipity to this equation is that such books please a larger audience, too.

Youth in Canberra

Though born in Melbourne in 1963, Nix was raised in Canberra, Australia's national capital. "It was (and is) an unusual city," Nix noted in his interview, "having a population then of only about 200,000 people, but all the amenities of a capital." A completely planned city, most of it was built from the 1950s on; a fitting background for the future fantasy writer to have a city growing around him as he came of age. Books formed a baseline of interest for Nix from his early youth, both inside and outside the home. "Probably the most important influence on me becoming a writer was my parents, who both read voraciously and who both write. My father is a scientist with hundreds or even thousands of publications to his name, and my mother an artist who works in paper and incorporates her writing into her work. Our house was always full of books, and there was a culture of reading."

This "culture of reading" carried over to the outside world, as well. A loyal patron of the Canberra Public Library Service, Nix visited the children's library section daily. Located between his home and school, this children's library introduced Nix to the works of Ursula Le Guin, Robert Heinlein, John Masefield, Robert Louis Stevenson, Mary Stewart, Madeleine L'Engle, Isaac Asimov, and a host of other writers.

At age seventeen, Nix joined the Australian Army Reserve, serving one weekend a month and about one month a year out in the bush. "This provided an outlet for energy that might otherwise have been misapplied," Nix commented in his interview, adding that it gave him a place to dispose of a vague sort of anger he was feeling as a teenager. "I didn't know what I was angry about, but I was definitely confused about life in general." His time in the reserves not only focussed his energies and gave him some self-discipline, but taught him an essential lesson: "removing the vague notion I had that life was supposed to be fair." Additionally, this time provided Nix with valuable information for later use when writing about anything military.

Writer in Training

After his military service, Nix traveled for six months. Most of his traveling was done out of an old Morris 1200 on the byways of England—something of a required pilgrimage for those born down under. Books were his companion, and also a typewriter, "a metal Silver-Reed which was a delight to work on. I had to sell it before I left, because I was so broke I couldn't afford the bus fare to Heathrow." But not before he had typed out his first published story on it. However, he only found out about that sale months later in Australia when he was contacted for reprint rights to his "Sam, Cars and the Cuckoo" for the magazine *Warlock*. This early sale confirmed for Nix that he could build a career as a writer.

Common sense, however, also came into play: he enrolled in a professional writing program at Canberra College of Advanced Education (now the University of Canberra) and ultimately earned his bachelor's degree in the discipline. "During my three years there I wrote half of my first published novel, *The Ragwitch*, two feature-length screenplays, and numerous articles and short stories," Nix stated. He also collaborated with other students in scriptwriting for local theater restaurants, creating audience-participation murder mysteries.

Continuing his methodical apprenticeship, Nix took a job in a bookshop upon graduation from college. "I now believe that anyone who works in publishing should spend at least three months in a bookshop, where the final product ends up meeting the customer." After six months of such work, he joined up in the other end of the book business, working as a sales representative, publicist, and then editor for Australian publishers, including HarperCollins. This work took Nix to Sydney, where he still resides. During his six years in publishing, he became a published writer, first with the "Very Clever Baby" books, and then with his novel, *Ragwitch,* begun when he was twenty-one and published six years later. *The Ragwitch* "was written from a desire to write a C. S. Lewis style book that was more gritty and real," Nix explained. "I wanted to get across more real fear, more discomfort and so on, without being disgusting or off-putting."

Nix's first novel tells the story of Paul and his sister Julia who are exploring an aboriginal midden—literally a prehistoric garbage dump. There they find a nest and inside the nest a ball of feathers containing a rag doll. From deep within himself, Paul hears an urgent warning, but too late. The rag doll transforms itself into the Ragwitch and captures Julia in its power, thus initiating "a horrific series of adventures," according to Laurie

Copping who reviewed the book in the *Canberra Times.* ''Paul enters a strange fantasy land where he searches for his sister,'' Copping continued, which involves ''strange creatures, magical animals and communication from one world to another. . . . An engrossing novel which should be enjoyed by true lovers of high fantasy.''

These early publications gave Nix encouragement to attempt something more in his life. After a long overland trip from London to Pakistan in 1992, he left publishing and went to work in public relations and marketing, forming his own company with two other partners, a position he maintained until 1998 when he left public relations to become a full-time writer.

Cover of Sabriel

Sabriel

Nix's next publication, *Sabriel,* was an important book for him. Nix's intent with this second published novel was to create ''an interesting, well-crafted fantasy that wasn't just a copy of Tolkien.'' Partly inspired by his recent journey from London to Pakistan, as well as by locations in his native Australia, *Sabriel* tells the story of a young woman trained by her necromancer-father, Abhorsen. He, unlike other necromancers, puts souls at ease rather than raising them, and Sabriel takes his lessons to heart. Attending the proper Wyverly College in Ancelstierre, Sabriel is busy learning other things than magic: music, fighting arts, English, and etiquette. Soon, however, she is involved in an attempt to save her father, protector of the magical Old Kingdom, to rescue him from the world beyond the Land of the Living. She is aided in her quest by Mogget, a powerful being in the form of a cat, and by the young prince, Touchstone, whom she has brought back from the dead. Battling her way past all forms of monsters and beasts, Sabriel finally reaches her father, only to lose him. But Sabriel learns in the process that she is truly her father's successor and that the Old Kingdom needs her protection, just as it did her father's.

Shade's Children and Beyond

''*Shade's Children* [Nix's third novel] was an example of the 'writing for me' philosophy carried to its limit,'' Nix stated. ''While my publishers and many readers wanted another *Sabriel,* I had a much grimmer book inside me that wanted to come out. So I chose to write a science fiction novel rather than fantasy (though it is really very soft SF), and much more a straight-out thriller. . . . A bleak, violent vision of a near-future world.'' Essentially another quest tale, *Shade's Children* features a young psychic, Gold-Eye, who runs away from the cruel Overlords who harvest children's brains to transplant into their evil minions. The aliens that have taken over Earth have destroyed everyone over fourteen; Shade, a computer-generated hologram, is the only nurturing adult presence. Gold-Eye, along with a band of other teenagers—Drum, Ella, and Ninde—fight the new Overlords from their sanctuary at Shade's base. Sacrifice is demanded of them, and they must learn to deal with betrayal and their own special talents.

Nix followed this work with a young adult novelization of an episode from the popular television series, *The X-Files.* Nix's contribution to the six-part series was *The Calusari.* Hard upon this, Nix began a near-sequel to *Sabriel,* entitled *Lirael: Daughter of the Clayr.* This book returns to the world of Ancelstierre and the Old Kingdom, twenty-two years after the events related in *Sabriel* but with a new cast of characters. The main characters include Lirael, one of the Clayr; Sameth, Sabriel's son; and Nicholas Sayre, an Ancelstierran and

Don't Miss ...

The Ragwitch, Pan Books, 1990

Sabriel, HarperCollins, 1995

Shade's Children, Allen & Unwin, 1997

assuming responsibility—not only for yourself, but for others or even for whole societies. Another is that even though you might get what you want, there will be a cost of some kind involved somewhere. This includes happy endings. They are possible, but generally at a cost to someone, somewhere.''

Nix is far from personal endings, happy or otherwise. Early successes in fantasy and science fiction bode well for his writing future. He is, as reviewers have noted, a writer to watch. ''My future plans for writing are to keep doing it,'' Nix concluded. ''I will probably tend to write more fantasy than science fiction, because I think I'm better at the former. I also have some plans to write a contemporary thriller or two. But who knows? Like most writers I know, my notebooks are full of ideas and concepts. It's the execution of them that's difficult.''

school chum of Sameth's. Nick's fate lies in the hands of both Prince Sameth and Lirael when he crosses into the Old Kingdom from Ancelstierre. ''In some ways *Lirael* is more complex than *Sabriel*,'' Nix related. ''It is told for a large part from two different viewpoints, and it also brings in more of the underlying story of the world. It doesn't necessarily explain anything (didactic passages in fantasy books are one of my pet hates), but it does make some things from *Sabriel* more clear, while muddying the waters about new things.''

The lack of ''didactic passages'' is another Nix hallmark. ''I never intentionally start with a theme or a message, or try to put one in,'' Nix explained. ''I believe in writing stories, not didactic tracts. However themes do seem to creep in from my subconscious, and . . . there does seem to be some basic philosophy that runs through all my books. One theme seems to be an emphasis on

Sources for More Information

Books

St. James Guide to Young Adult Writers, St. James Press, 1999.

On-line

Garth Nix Web site, located at http://www.ozemail.com/~garthnix/garthnix.html.

Joan Lowery Nixon

Historical fiction and suspense novelist (1927–)

Born February 3, 1927, in Los Angeles, CA; daughter of Joseph Michael (an accountant) and Margaret (Meyer) Lowery; married Hershell H. Nixon (a petroleum geologist), August 6, 1949; children: Kathleen Nixon Brush, Maureen Nixon Quinlan, Joseph Michael, Eileen Nixon McGowan. Education: University of Southern California, B.A., 1947; California State College, certificate in elementary education, 1949.

"Writing is hard," wrote Joan Lowery Nixon in her entry for the *Something about the Author Autobiography Series* (*SAAS*). "It's not easy. But it's such a fulfilling, enjoyable occupation that it's worth all the effort. There are days in which ideas flow and I can hardly type fast enough as I try to get every word down on paper, but there are other days during which I feel as though I'm painfully removing every word from my brain with a pair of pliers." Whether flowing freely or pried with pliers, Nixon's words have already won her the Mystery Writers of America's coveted Edgar Award for best juvenile mystery four times—the first writer to do so—and several of her other works have been nominated for that honor. "In the field of young adult mystery writers, a field crowded with authors," stated Melissa Fletcher Stoeltje in the *Houston Chronicle Magazine*, "she is by all accounts the grande dame."

Nixon was born in Los Angeles, California. Nixon recalls that at a very young age she wanted to be a writer. She created verses for every holiday

"Generation to generation, emotions don't change."

or family celebration, writing in *SAAS* that "from the time I discovered mysteries I was in love with them." Her first published work, a poem, appeared in *Children's Playmate* magazine when she was ten years old.

Teacher Inspires Career

After entering ninth grade at Le Conte Junior High in Hollywood, Nixon became interested in journalism and almost at once became editor of the school newspaper. It was at Hollywood High that Nixon met her favorite teacher, Miss Bertha Standfast. During the next three years, she enrolled in every English class taught by this lady, seeking her support in her writing. "I treasured the direction and encouragement Miss Standfast gave to me," she declared, adding, "It was she who insisted that I major in journalism when I went to college." At the age of seventeen, Nixon wrote her first article for a magazine, selling it to *Ford Times.*

One week after her high school graduation, Nixon entered the University of Southern California as a journalism student. "My training in journalism taught me discipline," she remembered. "For one thing, I learned to create at the typewriter. We took our exams on the typewriter. Journalism taught me to focus because I had to sit down and *write,* whether I felt like it or not—no waiting for inspiration. I learned the skill of finding the important facts in a story, and how to isolate them from all of the unnecessary details."

Nixon's degree in journalism did not lead to a job in that field, partly because of competition from returning war correspondents. But the Los Angeles School District was in need of teachers, so she found work as a substitute for kindergarten through third grade classes. Soon she received an assignment to teach kindergarten at Ramona Elementary School, at the same time taking night school education courses at the nearby Los Angeles City College campus.

While at USC, Nixon also met her future husband, Hershell "Nick" Nixon, who was a student majoring in naval science. Two weeks after their first date they became engaged, but their marriage was postponed until after he finished his stint in the Navy. The couple was finally united on August 6, 1949. During the three years Nixon

taught at Ramona, their first daughter, Kathleen Mary, was born.

The young family moved several time, eventually settling in Corpus Christi, Texas. The move to Texas marked an important event in Nixon's life. When she read an announcement of the upcoming Southwest Writers Conference only a little while after her arrival, she became enthusiastic about writing for children. Nixon worked every Wednesday from nine a.m to three p.m. She read the material she had completed that day to her children and often used their suggestions. Nixon even joined the Byliners, a local group of writers who read and criticized each other's manuscripts. Despite all this input, *The Mystery of Hurricane Castle* was rejected twelve times by different publishers before Criterion finally accepted it.

That first book persuaded Nixon to continue writing. Nixon soon found herself busy writing children's books, teaching creative writing classes at local children's schools, libraries, and colleges, and writing a humor column for the *Houston Post.* She eventually gave up teaching, and this decision allowed her to devote every morning to writing.

Edgar Award-Winning Mysteries

Nixon's earliest work was for young readers—it was not until later in her career that she began writing for young adults. In 1975, Nixon and her daughter Kathy attended the first International Crime Writers Congress in London, England, where a speaker's comment encouraged her to try writing a mystery for young adults. This book became *The Kidnapping of Christina Lattimore,* which was awarded the Edgar for best juvenile mystery by the Mystery Writers of America in 1980. *The Kidnapping of Christina Lattimore* tells in the title character's own words her ordeal of being kidnapped, held for ransom, and then suspected of having engineered the whole project to get money from her grandmother for a school trip.

One year after *The Kidnapping of Christina Lattimore* won the Edgar, Nixon repeated the accomplishment with *The Seance,* and in 1987 *The Other Side of Dark* made her a three-time recipient of the prize. In the latter work, seventeen-year-old Stacy wakes up to find that she has lost four years of her life in a coma after an intruder has shot her and killed her mother. Not only does she have to adapt to a new lifestyle and catch up on the missing years, but she also has to identify the killer before she becomes his next victim.

Nixon won a fourth Edgar award with her book *The Name of the Game Was Murder.* In *The Name of the Game Was Murder,* fifteen-year-old Samantha is the only person able to discover who killed her uncle. Writing in *Voice of Youth Advocates,* Suzanne Julian claimed the tale serves as "a good introductory mystery." Some of Nixon's other works include *Will You Give Me a Dream?,* a 1994 story about a mother telling her son the beginnings of a dream to put him to sleep, and *Search for the Shadowman,* a 1996 mystery featuring seventh grader Andy Bonner trying to discover which relative looted the family fortune.

In *Shadowmaker,* Katie Gillian and her mother, a well-known investigative journalist, uncover evidence that toxic wastes are being dumped nearby, and Katie finds out that what's going on at her high school may be related to the dumping. In *Murder My Sweet,* Jenny Jakes and her mystery-writing mother head to San Antonio for the reading of a distant cousin's will. The cousin, a millionaire who owns a candy company, is not yet dead, but is holding the will-reading to celebrate his birthday. The festivities are cut short when his son, Porter, is murdered. Jenny, not her mother, solves the case.

In *The Haunting,* 15-year-old Lia's parents are planning to move to Louisiana, where they will move into an old family plantation house, adopt children, and turn it into a group home. Lia, an only child, is against this plan, and is upset by the fact that she's shy and unlike the other women in her family—all brave adventurers. What's more, the house in Louisiana is haunted. In the end, though, Lia becomes strong enough to drive the evil out of the house.

That Western State of Mind

Besides her acclaimed mysteries, Nixon has won awards for her historical fiction. Two volumes of her "Orphan Train" quintet, *A Family Apart* and *In the Face of Danger,* won the Golden

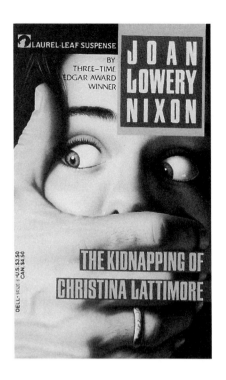

*Cover of **The Kidnapping of Christina Lattimore***

Spur Award—the Western Writers of America's equivalent of the Edgar. The idea, she said in *Artists and Authors for Young Adults (AAYA),* came from a publisher who asked her if she had ever heard of the "Orphan Train Children." The historical Children's Aid Society, an organization of social activists, operated between 1854 and 1929 to place more than 100,000 children with foster families in the West. The children—not necessarily orphans—were usually from immigrant families living in slums in New York City.

"The West to me is a state of mind," Nixon declared in *The Writer.* "While immersed in stories set west of the Mississippi in the last half of the eighteen-hundreds, modern readers are discovering concepts like *sacrifice* and *self-denial* and *unwavering commitment to an ideal*—concepts that are not too common in today's very different world." "Writing western historical novels for young adults is immensely satisfying," she concluded. "It gives me the opportunity to show that history isn't simply a collection of dates and wars and kings and presidents, but that *children* have always helped make history, that *children* are not only important to the past but are helping to shape history being made today."

Commenting on her own writing processes, Nixon noted in *SAAS* that "even imaginary characters can have wills of their own," and related that she sees her characters in her dreams and hears them talking about the story. She always has

Writer Nixon shared her secret of writing successfully for teenagers: ''Appreciating them, really liking them—this, too, I think, is an essential part of the answer.'' Her message to young people, she declares in *SAAS,* is: ''For those of you who have hopes of becoming writers, it's important to know that you'll need that determination and persistence and the courage to continue, no matter what might happen.''

Sources for More Information

Books

Something about the Author Autobiography Series, Volume 9, Gale, 1990.

St. James Guide to Young Adult Writers, St. James Press, 1999.

two levels in her mystery novels, ''a problem to solve, and a mystery to solve,'' she stated. ''Later the characters can weave them together.'' In *The*

No Doubt

Alternative rock band

Band formed in 1987 in Anaheim, CA, by Gwen Stefani, her older brother Eric, and high school classmate John Spence. Members include Tom Dumont, guitar; Tony Kanal, bass; Gwen Stefani, vocals; and Adrian Young, drums.

"Female rock stars like Gwen Stefani aren't supposed to exist anymore."
—Entertainment Weekly

After nine years melding an eclectic mix of musical styles into a dance-happy retro sound, the southern California band No Doubt attained chart-topping success and MTV fame in 1996 on the strength of the radio-ready single "Just a Girl." The song appears on the breakthrough album *Tragic Kingdom,* the band's third, which represents "a virtual Cuisinart of the last two decades of pop," David Browne wrote in *Entertainment Weekly.* He went on to describe the CD's sound as "a hefty chunk of new-wave party bounce and Chili Peppers-style white-boy funk with dashes of reggae, squealing hair-metal guitar, disco, ska-band-horns, and Pat Benatar." The band's frontwoman, Gwen Stefani, sets the tone with ferocious vocals and on-stage swagger that contrast with her glam-queen platinum blonde hair, spit curls, bare-midriff, and fire-engine red lipstick. "Female rock stars like Gwen Stefani," Browne wrote, "aren't supposed to exist anymore." For her part, Stefani is not letting her reputation as a rock goddess go to her head. "I think I've been able to fool a lot of people," she said, "because I know I'm a dork. I'm a geek."

No Doubt was founded in Anaheim, California in 1987 by Stefani, her brother Eric, and high

815

school classmate John Spence. "The first time I ever performed was at a talent show when I was 17," Stefani told *Spin* magazine. "It was me and my brother and some other people doing a cover of the Selector song "On My Radio." No Doubt kind of grew out of that. Originally it was just a bunch of people that didn't know how to play their instruments trying to imitate the music they liked, which was ska. I never wanted to be a rock girl. Basically, I have no idea what I'm doing or how I got here."

In December of 1987, Spence took his own life; he shot himself in the head. "He was a very important part of the band," Stefani said. "He was the one who said, 'Look, I want to be a singer.' He was the one who used to say 'No Doubt.' And that's where we got the name. It still haunts us in a way.... When your friend dies like that, and it's so unexpected, it's very traumatic. I think it taught us all a big lesson in how much one person can influence so many different people."

No Doubt Finds Its Voice

No Doubt persevered. Bass player and Prince aficionado Tony Kanal joined the band shortly after its inception. Guitarist Tom Dumont came aboard in 1988, bringing a heavy-metal style forged from earfuls of Kiss, Black Sabbath and Judas Priest. Drummer Adrian Young, who was raised on the 1970s sounds of Journey and Steely Dan as well as punk and new wave, joined the following year. Gwen, who took over lead vocals following Spence's death, grew up as a huge fan of *The Sound of Music* and, with her keyboardist brother, the Brit-band Madness. No Doubt played local parties and gained a reputation for shows that were

frenetic and fun. Gradually, the players merged into a band and crafted a genre-hopping sound from their varied influences. "We were labeled a ska band forever and it was always something we were trying to get away from," Gwen Stefani once said. "We wanted to become our own sound. For the first time on this record (*Tragic Kingdom*) I think we were able to do that—to mix up all the different influences without freaking people out."

Even after signing with Interscope Records, however, it took No Doubt years to hit the charts. After the band's self-titled debut was released in 1992, Interscope withdrew support for a No Doubt tour and shelved plans for a second record. In frustration, the band started recording songs in a garage and released the album *The Beacon Street Collection* on their own in 1995. Eventually, an Interscope subsidiary called Trauma showed interest in No Doubt and got *Tragic Kingdom* back on track. Meanwhile, Eric Stefani left the band to pursue his interest in cartooning (he became an animator for *The Simpsons*) and Gwen Stefani and Tony Kanal ended a seven-year relationship. "Eric was my biggest musical influence," Gwen said. "He's the one who said 'you be the singer,' when I was sitting on the couch watching the Brady Bunch and being as lazy as possible. If it wasn't for him I don't know what I'd be doing. It was really hard when he left, because I felt like this was his baby—his band."

Success Follows Hard Times

Again, No Doubt stayed the course and—finally—attained success. "We went to New York to do MTV," Kanal recalled in *Axcess* magazine, "and we were all there in the set and Gwen and I just looked at each other and said 'I can't believe we're doing this right now. I can't believe we're here.' It's really incredible." And despite Spence's death, Eric's departure, the Tony-and-Gwen break-up, and the record-company politics, there is no sense of angst or bitterness in No Doubt's music. *Rolling Stone* called it "ear candy with good beat ... a spry white-suburban take on ska and Blondie-esque pop." No Doubt is, basically, anti-grunge. "As people, we're angry," Stefani has said. "We went through some really bad times in the past couple years—personally and band-wise—and our whole way of dealing with that is humor and I think that's apparent in the record. Even though

No Doubt at the MTV Video Music Awards

things may have been bad, and some of the songs are sad if you really listen to them, there's still an element of humor to it all.''

Stefani once was asked if she worried about No Doubt being a one-hit wonder. ''I think that if everything was taken away tomorrow, if they dropped the tour and everybody hated us, I'd still be fulfilled,'' she responded. ''Because I can honestly say I never expected to get this far. For years, we were this underground cult band that sat in the garage and made fun of every other band on MTV,'' Stefani said. ''Now that we have a hit single, it's like a whole new fresh thing. It's a really amazing thing for a band that's been together nine years.''

Sources for More Information

Periodicals

Billboard, October 18, 1997.

Entertainment Weekly, February 16, 1997, p. 62; January 22, 1999.

Guitar Player, January, 1998.

Newsweek, January 13, 1997, p. 72.

People, May 12, 1997, p. 103; May 19, 1997.

Rolling Stone, December 26, 1996, p. 195.

Spin, June 1996, p. 75; November 1996, p. 52.

TV Guide, February 22, 1997, p. 32.

On-line

The *Rolling Stone* Network, located at http://www.rollingstone.com.

Andre Norton

Science fiction and fantasy novelist (1912-)

"I'm drawn to the science-fiction genre because it imposes no limits on my imagination."

Born Alice Mary Norton, February 17, 1912, in Cleveland, OH; name legally changed, 1934; daughter of Adalbert Freely and Bertha (Stemm) Norton. Education: Attended Western Reserve University (now Case Western Reserve University), 1930–32.

Although she has penned numerous books of historical fiction and mystery, among other kinds, Andre Norton is best known and admired for her science fiction and fantasy. Women writers were rare in the genre when she published *Star Man's Son, 2250 A.D.* in 1952, yet Norton quickly became a popular favorite, with some of her books selling more than a million copies each. Despite frequent critical dismissal of her work as lacking complexity, both Norton's fans and peers have recognized her contributions to science fiction: she is one of the few writers to be awarded both the Science Fiction Writers of America's Grand Master Award and science fiction fandom's equivalent, the Gandalf Award.

"Those who know Miss Norton's work well appreciate her highly," notes a *Times Literary Supplement* writer. "The background of her stories is a literary one and includes myth and legend and the high tone and seriousness of epic, the dark and brooding matters of tragedy." Indeed, many critics have observed that solid research is the foundation of a Norton novel, a product of her early career as a librarian.

While critics may debate Norton's literary significance, many agree that her work has been overlooked for a variety of reasons. For instance, her first books were marketed toward juvenile readers, thus Norton's novels were dismissed as relatively unimportant. In *Merlin's Daughters: Contemporary Women Writers of Fantasy*. Charlotte Spivack, proposes another explanation for Norton's lack of critical attention: ''Her wide reading public has simply taken Andre Norton for granted, not as the author of a single masterpiece but rather as a steadily dependent writer who is always there with a couple of entertaining new paperbacks every year.''

Donald Wollheim similarly remarks in his introduction to *The Many Worlds of Andre Norton* that while science fiction and fantasy readers ''may spend a lot of time discussing the sociology and speculations of the other writers, Andre Norton they read for pleasure. This is not to say that her works lack the depth of the others, because they do not,'' explains the critic. ''But it is that these depths form part of the natural unobtrusive background of her novels.''

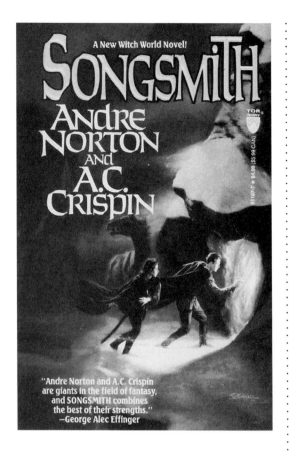

Cover of Songsmith

''Witch World''

Norton is perhaps best known for her ''Witch World'' sequence, a series of fantasy novels concerning a planet filled with creatures who travel through metaphysical gates. Interestingly, Norton has written several of the ''Witch World'' books in collaboration with other authors, including A. C. Crispin and P. M. Griffin. Before the publication of *Witch World* in 1963, Norton's editors had insisted that she omit female characters, since science fiction was considered to have a strictly masculine appeal. With the series, however, female characters became increasingly important in Norton's work, and she has written about active, intelligent heroines in many of her other novels as well. *Year of the Unicorn, Moon of Three Rings, Dread Companion,* and *Forerunner Foray* all describe the maturation of young women.

The novels of the ''Halfblood Chronicles'' fantasy series similarly describe the heroic efforts of an alienated young girl who struggles to reconcile her individuality and to end the subjugation of humans in a world where they are enslaved by a merciless race of elves. In *The Elvenbane,* the first volume of the series, a human slave gives birth to Shana, a half-elven baby who is the feared

''Elvenbane'' of prophecy. Raised by a dragon in the desert, Shana masters her unique powers and leads the Elvenbane wizards in their struggle against the elven lords in the sequel, *Elvenblood*. Reviewers cite this series as an example of how Norton creates believable, compelling, character-driven fiction.

It is the focus on the internal struggles of her characters that makes Norton's work interesting, suggests Schlobin in *The Feminine Eye: Science Fiction and the Women Who Write It.* ''Norton's reverence for the self, especially as it seeks to realize its potentials . . . is one of the major reasons why her plots are always so exciting. Her protagonists have to deal not only with dangerous external forces but also with their own maturation and personal challenges,'' stated the critic. In resolving a theme of self-fulfillment, Norton's work frequently expresses another idea of importance to her work: that to understand oneself, a person must come to understand and accept others.

An Anti-Science Approach

Critics observe that it is the mechanical, non-individualistic aspects of science that frequently provide the conflict in Norton's work; "though many of her novels are set in the future," remarks Schlobin, "she has no special affection for the technological and, in fact, science is most often the antagonist in her fiction." Rick Brooks similarly notes in *The Many Worlds of Andre Norton* that "in the battle between technology and nature, Miss Norton took a stand long before the great majority of us had any doubts. . . . Technology is a necessary evil [in her work] to get there for the adventure and to get some of the story to work. And the adventure is as much to mold her universe to her views as to entertain."

Norton revealed the reasons behind her distrust of technology to Charles Platt in *Dream Makers Volume II: The Uncommon Men and Women Who Write Science Fiction:* "I think the human race made a bad mistake at the beginning of the Industrial Revolution. We leaped for the mechanics, and threw aside things that were just as important. We made the transition too fast. And I don't like a lot of the modern ways of living. I prefer to do things with my hands; and I think everybody misses that. People need the use of their hands to feel creative." Brooks further notes: "Norton consistently views the future as one where the complexity of science and technology have reduced the value of the individual. . . . So Miss Norton is actually wrestling with the prime problem, that of human worth and purpose."

While some critics, such as Brooks, observe a higher purpose in Norton's writing, they consistently remark upon the author's ability to craft an entertaining tale. "Norton is above all committed to telling a story, and she tells it in clear, effective prose," asserts Spivack. "Not given to metaphors or lyricism, her style is focused on narrative movement, dialogue, and descriptive foreground. . . . Her scenes are moving and vivid, and both the outward action and inward growth are drawn convincingly and absorbingly."

Tackles Important Themes

Yet for all Norton's skill in creating and presenting universes to her readers, she always includes ideas of substance in her fiction. "The sheer size of [Norton's] world, which is infinitely extended in time and space, and in which nothing is outside the bounds of possibility, is matched by the size of the themes she tackles," claims John Rowe Townsend in *A Sense of Story: Essays on Contemporary Writers for Children.* In a Norton novel, he adds, "there is always something beyond the immediate action to be reached for and thought about." Because of the breadth and scope of her work, maintains Brooks, "the chief value of Andre Norton's writing may not lie in entertainment or social commentary, but in her 're-enchanting' us with her creations that renew our linkages to all life."

Another quality that makes Norton's science fiction memorable, as Wollheim stated, is her ability to evoke the "sense of wonder" that characterizes much of the genre. "Andre Norton is at home telling us wonder stories. She is telling us that people are marvelously complex and marvelously fascinating. . . . She is weaving an endless tapestry of a cosmos no man will ever fully understand, but among whose threads we are meant to wander forever to our personal fulfillment. Basically this is what science fiction has always been about."

Schlobin similarly concludes in *The Feminine Eye:* "Andre Norton, then, like all special writers, is more than just an author. She is a guide who leads us, the real human beings, to worlds and situations that we might very well expect to live in were we given extraordinary longevity. . . . The Norton future is an exciting realm alive with personal quests to be fulfilled and vital challenges to be overcome," Schlobin continued. "Is it any wonder that millions upon millions of readers . . . have chosen to go with her in her travels?"

Sources for More Information

Books

Dictionary of Literary Biography, Gale, Volume 8: *Twentieth-Century American Science Fiction Writers,* 1981, Volume 52: *American Writers for Children since 1960: Fiction,* 1986.

Elwood, Roger, editor, *The Many Worlds of Andre Norton,* introduction by Donald Wollheim, Chilton, 1974, published as *The Book of Andre Norton,* DAW Books, 1975.

Schlobin, Roger C., *Andre Norton,* Gregg, 1979.

Shwartz, Susan, editor, *Moonsinger's Friends: An Anthology in Honor of Andre Norton,* Bluejay Books, 1985.

Notorious B.I.G.

Rap artist
(1973–1997)

"There's nothing that protects you from the inevitable."

Born Christopher G. Wallace in 1973 in Brooklyn, NY; shot to death March 9, 1997, in Los Angeles, CA; son of Voletta Wallace; married, wife's name Faith Evans (a singer); children: T'yanna, (with Evans) Christopher.

Even in death, Notorious B.I.G. was bigger than life. His death at age 24—the second drive-by slaying of a gangsta rapper in a six-month span—intensified a purported deadly feud between rap music's East Coast and West Coast factions. B.I.G.'s funeral—he was buried in a white double-breasted suit and an extra-large mahogany casket—attracted rap's elite and drew hordes of fans onto Brooklyn streets. And his posthumous second album—ironically and prophetically titled *Life After Death . . . 'Til Death Do Us Part*—confirmed that the heavyweight rapper had the potential to be big, indeed, on the music charts.

At the same time, he was a hard man to pin down. A former crack dealer and convict, B.I.G. rapped his way to a better life only to lose that life to the street violence he could not leave behind. A big man, he was variously described as standing between 6-feet and 6-feet-3-inches tall and weighing between 230 and 380 pounds. Born Christopher Wallace, he used the street name Biggie Smalls and the stage name Notorious B.I.G. The product of a brutal environment, he commented on the day before his death that he wanted "to see my

kids get old." That wish, however, went unfulfilled. One some level, B.I.G., seemed to know that the odds were against him escaping his violent past. In 1994, after the release of his first album, he told the *Chicago Tribune* that he was "scared to death. . . . Scared of getting my brains blown out."

Debut Tells It Like It Is

B.I.G. shook the music world with that debut album, *Ready to Die,* an unflinching portrayal of the despair experienced daily in much of urban America—and its brutal outcomes. The album detailed drug sales, sex, violence, incarceration, and death. *Newsweek* suggested that B.I.G.'s tales of the streets and the down-and-out who populate them made him something of a modern-day Damon Runyon. The *Los Angeles Times* said the album was "jolting and uncompromising" and called B.I.G. "one of (rap) music's most talented and promising voices." He was named Rap Artist of the Year at the *Billboard* Awards in 1995 and cited as Rap Singer of the Year for the song *One More Chance.* After transporting listeners through a brutal urban landscape, the album closes with the death of its rapping narrator—who takes his own life.

B.I.G.'s music is perhaps equal parts fiction and autobiography. Before attaining fame, he was a small-time crack dealer in the tough Bedford-Stuyvesant section of Brooklyn. He never finished high school and, at age 17, was arrested on drug charges in North Carolina and spent nine months in jail. In 1995, he was arrested in New York and charged with assault after he allegedly chased two people with a baseball bat and smashed the window of their cab. He was twice arrested in New Jersey—first for allegedly robbing and assaulting a man, then on drug and weapons charges. "I can't say I'm proud of dealing drugs," B.I.G. once said. "But you do what you can to survive in the 'hood. Live in the real bad part of the 'hood for a while and you'll see how desperate it can make you." B.I.G. drew on that desperation and his law-breaking past in his songs, in which he matter-of-factly "described himself as a former drug dealer and stickup man who had turned to rapping," Jon Parales wrote in the *New York Times:* "He recalled the mundane details of bagging, transporting and selling drugs; he boasted about sexual conquests and mourned a murdered girlfriend."

Violent, Tragic End

B.I.G. was sitting in the passenger side of his GMC Suburban following a music industry party shortly after midnight on March 9, 1997. He was listening to a tape of his second album, which was to be released in two weeks. A dark-colored car—which police believe had been waiting for the rapper—pulled up beside the Suburban. Several shots from a nine-millimeter handgun were fired into B.I.G.'s upper body; he was shot in the head at least once. Then the car raced away. Notorious B.I.G. was pronounced dead when his body arrived at Los Angeles's Cedars-Sinai Medical Center. "The way it went down," said a police official, "it was a targeted hit." Police and music industry insiders quickly speculated that B.I.G.'s killing may have resulted from a volatile, vicious rift in the rap music world—conjecture that was not proven.

B.I.G. was produced by and the protege of Sean "Puffy" Combs, head of the New York City record company Bad Boy Entertainment. Combs was the rival of producer Marion "Suge" Knight, owner of Death Row Records, a leading West Coast gangsta rap label. In September 1996, six months before B.I.G.'s death, rapper Tupac Shakur—a Death Row recording artist with a promising future in films—was gunned down in a similar drive-by shooting in Las Vegas. The two rappers once shared a friendship, but it had evolved into a bitter rivalry. Shakur accused B.I.G. of copying his musical style and being involved in a 1994 incident in which Shakur was robbed and shot repeatedly. B.I.G. taunted Shakur on the song called *Who Shot Ya*, and Shakur rapped back that

he had had sex with B.I.G's wife. "The deaths of Shakur and (B.I.G.) have forced official America to peer into the world of the leading rappers, who have made millions and surrounded themselves with armed heavies," wrote a *London Times* contributor.

B.I.G. was the son of Voletta Wallace, a Brooklyn preschool teacher who named him Christopher and raised him alone. Christopher Wallace, it's been said, was a shy, overweight youngster who became a crack dealer—before morphing into Notorious B.I.G. and nearly leaving his harsh past behind by chronicling it on record. He did not make it, however. At the time of his death, B.I.G. was separated from his wife, singer Faith Evans. He and Evans had a son, also named Christopher, and B.I.G had a 4-year-old daughter, T'yanna, from a previous relationship. Two weeks before his death, according to the *Los Angeles Times,* B.I.G. was fatalistically quoted as saying: "There's nothing that protects you from the inevitable. If it's gonna happen, it's gonna happen, no matter what you do. It doesn't matter if you clean your life up and live it differently. What goes around comes around, man."

Sources for More Information

Periodicals

Interview, December, 1998.

Los Angeles Times, March 10, 1997, p. A1; March 11, 1997, p. B1; March 19, 1997, p. B1.

Newsweek, March 24, 1997, p. 74.

New York Times, March 10, 1997, p. A8.

People, March 24, 1997, p. 69; March 31, 1997, p. 108.

Rolling Stone, December 25, 1997; May 13, 1999.

On-line

"Remembering Notorious B.I.G.," located at http://www.mtv.com.

Rosie O'Donnell

Comedian, actress, and talk show host (1962–)

Born in 1962 in Long Island, NY; children: Parker Jaren, Chelsea Belle.

Rosie O'Donnell has brought her cheeky Long Island wit to stage and screen with a successful career as a stand-up comedienne and supporting actress. And with the debut of her self-titled talk show, she is being credited with classing up day-time television. Rosie O'Donnell received national recognition with film appearances in *A League of Their Own* and *Sleepless in Seattle,* as well as her own cable comedy show, *Stand-Up Spotlight.* She became a major star, however, with her 1994 send-up of Betty Rubble in the Steven Spielberg blockbuster *The Flintstones.*

It looked for a while as though O'Donnell's charms would keep her in supporting roles, however. "I'll be the best friend forever," she once told the *Los Angeles Times.* "It's fine with me. I mean, in my first movie I'm best friends with Madonna; my second movie, I'm best friends with Meg Ryan. That's not a bad career right there." Yet she did ultimately get her name in lights with the 1996 debut of her television talk show.

O'Donnell acquired her wise-cracking New York ways during a childhood spent on Long Island. She was born in 1962, the third of five children in a blue-collar Irish Catholic family. She always liked to clown and perform, but her ambition crystallized after her mother died of cancer at

"I think everybody thinks I'm the kind of girl they'd like to go have a beer with."

an early age. Unable to express her sorrow in a conventional manner, Rosie threw herself into stand-up comedy and the busy round of activities at her local high school. "I was Miss High School Everything," the comedienne told *Newsweek*. "I was the prom queen. I was the homecoming queen. I was class president. I was class clown. And something else . . . Oh, Most School-Spirited, which comes in handy in life. You never know when you might have to do a cheer."

Hooked on Stand-up

At 17, O'Donnell accepted a dare to perform stand-up comedy at an amateur night at the Round Table Restaurant on Long Island. She was quickly hooked, although she admitted in *Newsweek* that her tender years gave her little material from which to create her own jokes. After high school she attended Dickinson College and Boston University briefly, but she preferred working the comedy clubs. In 1984 her decision to pursue comedy paid off when she became a semi-finalist on the syndicated television show *Star Search*. Having won $14,000 for her appearance on that show, she moved to Los Angeles. "If you want to surf, you have to go to the water," she told *Newsweek*.

O'Donnell's progress was slow at first, but in 1986 she landed a part on the NBC situation comedy *Gimme a Break*. After two seasons with that show she moved on to the cable television channel VH-1. Initially hired as a veejay to introduce music videos, she soon moved into comedy and was rewarded with her very own show, *VH-1 Stand-Up Spotlight*. The show, with O'Donnell as host, made its debut in 1991. The exposure on VH-1 helped O'Donnell to move into feature films. In 1992 she appeared in the hit movie *A League of Their Own* as a tough-but-tender professional baseball player during World War II. According to Chris Willman in the *Los Angeles Times,* O'Donnell's character in *A League of Their Own* uttered the "most-used sound bite of 1992" when she told Madonna's character: "You think there's a man in this country who ain't seen your bosoms?" A few years later, O'Donnell and *League* director Penny Marshall would do a series of television commercials together for the K-Mart store chain.

After *A League of Their Own*, O'Donnell co-starred in another major motion picture, *Sleepless*

in Seattle, released in 1993. In that film she played a more sophisticated, college-educated editor and foil to Meg Ryan's wistful character. Asked in the *Los Angeles Times* why she always seems to be cast as someone else's best friend, O'Donnell replied: "I don't know, I think I'm just very . . . best-friend-ish. I think everybody thinks I'm the kind of girl they'd like to go have a beer with. Madonna provokes people in every way, forces them to look at who they are and what they're about and their sexuality and their feelings about interracial things. That's her essence—she's provocative. I'm really not. I'm kind of like a peanut butter and jelly sandwich and she's some wild, exotic food. It's hard to know what your own appeal is. I think it's relatability, if I was to sum it up in a word."

Continued Success in Film

That "relatability" and peanut-butter-and-jelly appeal certainly helped O'Donnell to land the role of Betty Rubble in *The Flintstones* film. The actress told the *Los Angeles Times* that she was surprised to have won the Betty role, since the cartoon character was so svelte, but that she enjoyed working on the project. "I never thought there'd be a *Flintstones* film, to tell you the truth," she said. "I was interested in playing Scooby Doo at one point, but I don't know if that's still in development."

Asked about plans for her future in *Newsweek,* the comedienne responded: "I just want to go on shows and say, 'They said, "Who can we get? Sharon Stone? No, Rosie O'Donnell."' That's generally how all [movie] scripts go." She continued to delight audiences even in films that didn't fare particularly well, such as the 1996 work *Beautiful Girls,* in which, according to Susan Stark of the *Detroit News,* "she dominates [the film's] single and most hilarious and memorable stretch, the one most likely to stay with you long after you've forgotten the rest of the movie." In the scene, Stark wrote, "O'Donnell offers an exuberantly profane guide to real women no parts excluded for the benefit of two male characters. Both are thunderstruck. Viewers would be, too, if they could quit laughing at O'Donnell's boisterous account of the truth beyond *Playboy*."

1996 also saw her co-starring in the film adaptation of the kid's classic book *Harriet the*

*Rosie O'Donnell
rehearsing for* **Grease**

Spy, but the most noteworthy development of that year for her was no doubt the chance to star in her own TV talk show. O'Donnell had taken on fewer film roles during this period because she had her hands full, having adopted a child, Parker, to raise on her own. She envisioned a daytime show as the perfect flexible job, allowing her to work shorter hours and spend her nights with her son. During the 23 days of shooting for *Harriet,* she told Robert Strauss of the *Los Angeles Times,* "I saw him an average of 40 minutes a day." Though she often described the joys of motherhood in the press, she told *People* she didn't want to raise him in public. "Fame is tough enough on me," she reasoned. "On a child, it can be impossible. If I talk about how my child was toilet-trained on TV, years later when he is a teenager people are going to remind him about it."

Yet O'Donnell's chat-show dream had as much to do with her own childhood. In the afternoons after school, she recalled to Strauss, she would watch Merv Griffin's cozy talk show. "You never saw anybody on *Merv Griffin* appearing nervous. It appeared everyone was his friend and nobody felt in dangerous territory." This was the familiar setting she wanted to create on her program. She guest hosted the *Regis and Kathie Lee* show and loved the experience; with her name attached and a format, her producers were able to set up a show for her very quickly. "I will not humiliate the guests and make them want to weep," she vowed in *Entertainment Weekly,* while also promising she would not just read off the cue cards like a zombie and do her level best to cry less than Kathie Lee. "Does she weep every day now or what?"

Her Own Show

Hosting her own show entailed a move from Los Angeles back to New York. She described the bliss of East Coast existence to Strauss: "I grew up here, so I love it here. When people recognize you on the street, it's 'How ya doin, Rosie?' and its over. In L.A., it's, 'You know, my brother was a grip on your movie and I've written a script that I got sold to Paramount [Studios]. Would you mind reading?' Yuck, it just never ends."

The program premiered in June of 1996, with actor George Clooney as O'Donnell's first guest. The show's initial ratings were higher than those

Popular Works

Television

VH-1 Stand-Up Spotlight, VH-1, 1991–94

The Rosie O'Donnell Show, Kid-Ro Productions, 1996–

Films

A League of Their Own, Columbia, 1992

The Flintstones, Universal, 1994

Now and Then, New Line Cinema, 1995

Beautiful Girls, Miramax, 1996

Harriet the Spy, Paramount, 1996

of any daytime talk show of the decade, and O'Donnell was dubbed "The Queen of Nice" by *Entertainment Weekly*. The host was concerned with providing an alternative to other talk shows in which guests were mocked or exploited. As she told Frank DeCaro in a *T.V. Guide* interview, "Johnny Carson was the king of all hosts. He understood that it was his job to make guests look good. And that when they looked good, he looked good. He would never embarrass anyone purposely or get a joke at their expense. . . . If there's a guy to emulate, he's the one."

But it was her own winning style, her unpretentious persona, her genuine and often obsessive admiration for celebrities, her love of singing and pop culture, and her clean, silly antics that made O'Donnell an instant hit with adults and children alike. DeCaro wrote that O'Donnell "single-handedly changed the face of TV talk."

The host's head writer, Randy Cohen, who formerly wrote for David Letterman, initially doubted that O'Donnell's approach would be successful. "By its nature, comedy attacks," he told *Entertainment Weekly*. "Good comedy is necessarily critical of something, and if you're busy trying to make everything 'nice,' where does that leave the comedy?" O'Donnell frequently rejects her writers' jokes, even when she finds them funny. "Because they're funny but mean, and I don't wanna do mean," she said in the same article. Janette Barber, another of her writers, remarked, "Her policy is, if she wouldn't say the joke in front of the person it's about, she won't do it."

"I've been given a great opportunity to affect so many people," O'Donnell explained to DeCaro. "It's an opportunity and a responsibility. I think that the American public is a lot more kind-hearted and looking for goodness than we give them credit for. If you give them an alternative to the mean-spirited stuff that they're fed, they will choose the alternative."

Sources for More Information

Books

Goodman, Gloria, *The Life and Humor of Rosie O'Donnell: A Biography*, Morrow, 1998.

Kallen, Stuart A., *Rosie O'Donnell*, Lucent Books, 1999.

Krohn, Katherine E., *Rosie O'Donnell*, Lerner, 1999.

Periodicals

Entertainment Weekly, May 3, 1996; June 14, 1996; June 28, 1996; July 26, 1996; December 27, 1996.

Ladies' Home Journal, February, 1999.

People, June 3, 1996.

Rolling Stone, August 22, 1996.

T.V. Guide, April 5, 1997.

On-line

The Rosie O'Donnell Show!, located at http://rosieo.warnerbros.com/wb.cgi.

Georgia O'Keeffe

**Painter
(1887-1986)**

Born November 15, 1887, in Sun Prairie, WI; died from complications of old age, March 6, 1986, in Santa Fe, NM; daughter of Francis (a farmer) and Ida (Totto) O'Keeffe; married Alfred Stieglitz (a photographer and art exhibitor), December 11, 1924 (died July 13, 1946). Education: Studied under John Vanderpoel, Art Institute of Chicago, 1905–06; William Merrit Chase, F. Luis Mora, and Kenyon Cox, Art Students League (New York City), 1907–08; Alon Bement, University of Virginia, 1912; and Bement and Arthur Dow, Columbia University, 1914–16.

"Somehow, what I painted happened to fit into the emotional life of my time."

From her roots in rural Wisconsin, painter Georgia O'Keeffe rose within an art world dominated by what she called "the men" to become the best-known female artist in the United States. A reflection of O'Keeffe's strong, independent spirit, the label of "female artist" was one that she herself disagreed with throughout her life; defiant of both social and artistic conventions, she preferred to think of herself as, simply, an "Artist," producing works that could hold their own in comparison with those of her male colleagues.

O'Keeffe was born November 15, 1887, in the rural community of Sun Prairie, Wisconsin. One of seven children born to Francis O'Keeffe, a farmer of Irish descent, and his wife, Ida, a woman of aristocratic Eastern European heritage, Georgia was raised within a large extended family that included grandparents, aunts, and uncles. O'Keeffe tended towards being a loner, preferring to go to a quiet corner of the house or yard and read or draw.

Artistic Development Is Encouraged

An amateur artist herself, Ida O'Keeffe sacrificed in order to send each of the O'Keeffe girls to an art tutor, despite the fact that the family's financial circumstances grew increasingly strained during Georgia's childhood. At the age of thirteen, O'Keeffe attended Madison, Wisconsin's Sacred Heart Convent School, where her art education included drawing still-lifes, a task that forced the young artist to develop her powers of observation. Despite the limited opportunities available to women at the turn of the twentieth century, O'Keeffe already knew she wanted more from life than the traditional—and expected—roles of wife and mother could offer.

When O'Keeffe and her family moved to Virginia in 1903, she kept up with her art studies, attending Chatham Episcopal Institute, a private school near Lynchburg. After graduating from Chatham in 1905, O'Keeffe moved to Chicago for a year in order to study at that city's Art Institute. There, under teachers like artist John Vanderpoel, she was taught the artistic traditions of the European masters, whose dark, static style was revered and copied by most artists of the period. There also she began drawing from live models and studying human anatomy. O'Keeffe became one of the top students at the Art Institute.

In 1907 the twenty-year-old artist moved to New York City, attending classes at the famous Art Students League while modeling for other art classes to help pay her way. Her instructor here was William Merritt Chase, a respected artist who taught O'Keeffe to paint rapidly using quick, short brush strokes. Through constant practice—Chase demanded a new painting from his students every day—O'Keeffe mastered the traditional European portrait painting techniques being taught. But she remained frustrated that she had not yet discovered her true "calling" as an artist.

Forced to end her studies at the Art Students League because of financial difficulties, O'Keeffe moved to her aunt's home to Chicago in 1908 and found work as a commercial illustrator, drawing lace and embroidery designs for advertising companies. She also designed the little Dutch girl, a logo that is still used on cans of Dutch Cleanser today. O'Keeffe worked in Chicago for the next two years, before leaving the Midwest altogether to teach art.

Renewed Energy

It was while attending a class at the University of Virginia in the summer of 1912 that her desire to paint and draw was reawakened. Studying art with Alon Bement, a regular faculty member at Columbia University, O'Keeffe was struck with her instructor's overriding design tenet: "to fill space in a beautiful way." During the summer of 1913, while teaching at the University of Virginia, she was introduced to the works of Russian artist Wassily Kandinsky. Inspired by Kandinsky's work, O'Keeffe resolved to begin to use her art to express her personal, non-European vision, and she returned to New York City.

Once again energized by the creative bustle of the city, O'Keeffe, like many other young avant-garde, or experimental, painters, began to frequent the 291 Gallery located on Fifth Avenue in downtown Manhattan. Co-founded by pioneering photographers Alfred Stieglitz and Edward Steichen in 1907, the gallery—with Stieglitz now at its helm—had become a mecca for artists like the radical Dadaists, who used the gallery as a meeting place and a space for holding regular exhibitions of new works.

In the fall of 1915, with money running low, O'Keeffe was forced to return to teaching. Again removed from the artistic mainstream of New York, O'Keeffe started to once again question her work as an artist. Recalling her reaction to the works of Kandinsky, she left painting with heavy oils and began to use simpler tools—charcoal and paper—as a way of more loosely shaping her inner feelings in a visual manner. The pictures that resulted were unlike anything that was being done; and the abstract direction her emotions appeared to be taking alarmed O'Keeffe, who feared she was losing her artistic ability.

During this time, O'Keeffe corresponded almost every week with longtime friend Anita Pollitzer. At the beginning of 1916, O'Keeffe rolled up some of the abstract drawings she had done in charcoal—work that she later described as a creative breakthrough, "essentially a woman's feeling"—and mailed them to her friend; Pollitzer took the drawings to Stieglitz. The gallery-owner

Georgia O'Keeffe
*standing next to **Life***
and Death

was impressed with the work, which, as Pollitzer wrote to O'Keeffe, he described as "the purest, finest, sincerest things that have entered 291 in a long while."

Begins Relationship with Stieglitz

Holding a liberal feminist viewpoint compared to most of the other leaders of the art world, Stieglitz hung O'Keeffe's drawings in his next show. Without her knowledge, the twenty-nine-year-old schoolteacher became an overnight celebrity among Manhattan's avant-garde art community. Stieglitz eventually convinced O'Keeffe to quit teaching and devote her full attention to artistic pursuits. With his financial support—and eventually as his mistress—she returned to New York City.

Joining Stieglitz in 1919, O'Keeffe gained increasing fame as, one after another, one-woman exhibits of her work were launched at his galleries 291, Intimate Gallery, and An American Place.

Interested primarily in O'Keeffe as an accomplished artist producing work as good as that of any man, Stieglitz also found himself falling in love with this aloof, independent woman. Despite an age difference of twenty-three years, the two married on December 11, 1924.

O'Keeffe's early, abstract works in charcoal astonished critics when they were first exhibited at 291 in the spring of 1916. In fact, because of their absolute originality when compared to her later work in oils, these drawings have caused some critics to think less of the many series of paintings that would follow. By abandoning this early, abstract style, it is felt, she left her artistic potential untapped.

Working in the New York apartment she shared with her husband, O'Keeffe used oils to depict the skyscrapers, clouds, and buildings that shaped the city skyline, and from their summer home she painted country vistas, gathering the shells, rocks, and flowers that later became characteristic themes in her work. Some of the more notable paintings of this period include *Lake George by Moonlight,* done in 1924, and *The Shelton with Sunspots,* a rendering of the Lexington Avenue apartment building where she and Stieglitz lived, worked in oils in 1926.

Begins Flower Paintings

After the 1920s O'Keeffe's work became increasingly objective, or realistic, in nature.

O'Keeffe especially became noted for her oversized flower paintings, which display her talent for amplifying the inner design and purpose of ordinary objects. Producing the first of her flower paintings as early as 1919, the artist arranged greatly enlarged and vibrantly colored stylized flower blossoms decoratively on the picture plane. She often did several versions of the same subject, experimenting with changes in light, position, and color. Notable among these works are *Oriental Poppies,* completed in 1928, and her famous *Jack-in-the-Pulpit* series, done during 1930.

By the end of the twenties O'Keeffe began to feel that her creativity was beginning to end; she decided to take a summer trip to Taos, New Mexico. It was during this trip in 1929 that O'Keeffe was first awakened to the austere beauty of the southwestern landscape and inspired to make it part of her creative work. In the mid-1930s O'Keeffe established a second home in Taos, away from both New York City and Stieglitz, with whom she had become semi-estranged over the years due to the marital infidelities of both.

On one hike near Taos, taken after the area had experienced a prolonged drought, O'Keeffe was unable to find the flowers that were her usual subjects. Instead, her eyes were drawn to the brilliant, sun-bleached bones that lay scattered among the cacti and low-lying brush. In the bleached desert bones of animals, where critics saw death and allusions to crucifixion, O'Keeffe saw beauty. One of her most famous paintings of this period, *Cow's Skull: Red, White, and Blue,* painted in 1931, incorporated these bones.

Moves Permanently to the Southwest

After Stieglitz died in 1946 at the age of eighty-two, O'Keeffe returned to live in the Southwest. She made her permanent home in Abiquiu, New Mexico, in 1949. From there she often travelled to visit Ghost Ranch, a remote vacation resort located several miles northwest of Espanola, New Mexico. The earthen colors—ocher, tan, and red—reflected from the New Mexico landscape to the huge canvasses she painted, both in Abiquiu and at Ghost Ranch. The simplicity of the region's landscape and its vast scale—with huge cliffs and large expanses of space—were also reflected in her work, which often utilized simple geometric shapes and large contrasts between light and shadow.

From 1947 to 1949 O'Keeffe occasionally left her home in Taos to work on retrospective exhibitions from the Stieglitz estate for display in Manhattan's Museum of Modern Art; she also directed artistic installations of her late husband's life work for the Art Institute of Chicago. Although afraid of flying at first, the elderly artist gradually became fascinated by the view above the clouds and painted several pictures, such as the *Sky above Clouds* series, painted between 1963 and 1965. As the years went by, O'Keeffe grew confident enough of the advances in air travel to attempt a world tour, which took her to Peru, Greece, and Paris among other places.

Published "Artistic" Life Story

Juan Hamilton, a young potter, entered O'Keeffe's life in 1973. Out of work and looking for a job, he started as a handyman of sorts; he remained by the otherwise reclusive artist's side until her death years later. While some biographers have hinted that a love relationship developed between the elderly painter and the young potter, it was Hamilton who encouraged O'Keeffe to write her autobiography, *Georgia O'Keeffe* (1976), which was illustrated with photographs of her paintings.

Interest in O'Keeffe's life and work rose sharply during the 1970s, a result not only of the publication of her autobiography but also of the women's movement then underway. Feminists hailed her as an icon—independent, self-sufficient, successful in a male-dominated culture; responding to the changing mood of a nation, President Gerald Ford awarded O'Keeffe the Medal of Freedom in 1977.

In the decades since this reflowering of interest in her work occurred, O'Keeffe's canvasses have been eagerly hunted by collectors willing to pay a high price for an original painting. In 1983 O'Keeffe was honored by President Ronald Reagan as the first recipient of the National Medal of the Arts. While some critics have suggested that the artist's public persona was as carefully crafted by O'Keeffe as her paintings in an effort to continue her fame as an artist even into old age, with her death in 1986, she became part of the mythos of the twentieth century. O'Keeffe died in Santa Fe; her ashes were scattered over the sunbaked hills of her beloved New Mexico.

Sources for More Information

Books

Castro, Jan Garden, *The Art and Life of Georgia O'Keeffe,* Crown, 1985.

Cowart, Jack, and Juan Hamilton, *Georgia O'Keeffe: Art and Letters,* National Gallery of Art, 1987.

Eldredge, Charles C., *Georgia O'Keeffe,* Abrams, 1991.

Hogrefe, Jeffrey, *O'Keeffe: The Life of an American Legend,* Bantam, 1992.

Lisle, Laurie, *Portrait of an Artist: A Biography of Georgia O'Keeffe,* University of New Mexico, 1986.

O'Keeffe, Georgia, *Georgia O'Keeffe,* Viking, 1976.

Robinson, Roxana, *Georgia O'Keeffe,* Harper, 1989.

George Orwell

**Novelist and essayist
(1903-1950)**

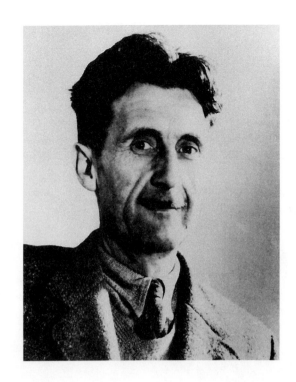

*"If you want a picture of the future,
imagine a boot stamping on a human
face—forever."*

—Nineteen Eighty-Four

*Born Eric Arthur Blair, June 25, 1903, in Motihari, India
(British citizen born abroad); died January 21, 1950, in
London, England; son of Richard Walmesley (a colonial
civil servant) and Ida Mabel (Limouzin) Blair; married
Eileen O'Shaughnessy, June 9, 1936 (died, March 29,
1945); married Sonia Brownell, October 13, 1949; children: (first marriage) Richard Horatio (adopted). Education: Graduated from Eton College, 1921.*

Writer George Orwell labored so long over
the manuscript for his novel *Nineteen
Eighty-Four* that he collapsed as he reached its end
and spent the last two years of his life bedridden.
The product of his heroic efforts is widely considered to be one of the masterworks of twentieth-
century literature. Orwell brings together several
themes in the novel—individual freedom, the influence of language, the abuse of power, and
others—which concerned him throughout his life.
Nineteen Eighty-Four, along with Orwell's satiri-
cal fable *Animal Farm,* propelled him to international fame, and the books serve as eloquent
reminders of the author's concern for his own and
future generations.

While he's best known as the creator of a
fictional future world, Orwell believed strongly in
the importance of the past. For him, this meant the
pre-1914 world of his childhood. When he was
just eight, Orwell's parents sent him on a scholarship to St. Cyprian's, an exclusive all-male pre-
paratory school. The school's strict atmosphere

and the fact Orwell was never allowed to forget that his family was poorer than those of the members of the British upper class who were his classmates, haunted Orwell ever after and influenced the themes and forms of his writings.

Becoming George Orwell

After leaving St. Cyprian's, Orwell continued his education at prestigious Eton College, also on a scholarship. He applied to the Indian Imperial Police in 1922. Upon passing the entrance examinations he was sent to Burma, then a province of British-controlled India. Orwell remained there five years, learning to speak Burmese, reading ceaselessly, and growing increasingly ill at ease with his job, which he felt furthered imperialism. He resigned his position when he returned to England in 1927, and became a writer, something he had always longed to do.

Orwell moved to Paris, hoping to live cheaply while he continued to write and learn French. Despite his enthusiasm for writing, success did not come easily or quickly for Orwell. In 1929, broke and facing a pile of rejection letters from publishers, Orwell returned to England. The one thing he had lots of was first-hand material to write about, and by October 1930 Orwell had finished a manuscript that told the story of his Parisian experiences in diary form. The work, titled *Down and Out in Paris and London,* was finally published in 1932. Although Orwell was still using his real name professionally, he requested the book be published under a pseudonym. He suggested four possible names to the publisher, but left the final choice up to Gollancz. This was how he became George Orwell.

Down and Out in Paris and London sold well, and reviews were mostly favorable. Elated by this, Orwell began working on a novel about his Burma experiences. As the summer ended, he returned to teaching, this time at a larger school. However, just after finishing the manuscript for *Burmese Days,* in December he was hospitalized with pneumonia. Under doctor's orders to recuperate for at least six months, Orwell resigned his job and moved back to the family home in Southwold on the east coast of England.

A Busy Decade

Burmese Days was published in 1934. After that, Orwell managed to publish a new book in each of the remaining years of the decade: *A Clergyman's Daughter* (1935), *Keep the Aspidistra Flying* (1936), *The Road to Wigan Pier* (1937), *Homage to Catalonia* (1938), and *Coming Up for Air* (1939). As biographer Jeffrey Meyers notes, all the books focused on ''two dominant themes—poverty and politics—or, as [Orwell] put it, 'the twin nightmares that beset nearly every modern man, the nightmare of unemployment and the nightmare of State interference.'''

The year 1936 was a watershed for Orwell. By his own reckoning this was the year that his writing became politically focused; it was also the year he officially declared himself to be a socialist. While his writing would embroil him in the political rhetoric of a world about to go to war, his personal life was happier than ever. In June, he married Eileen O'Shaughnessy, and they moved into an old house in a small village northeast of London.

Two other events of 1936 kindled Orwell's political activism: his trip to investigate unemployment in England's industrialized north, and his participation in the Spanish Civil War. From January through March, Orwell lived among the poor working class and unemployed laborers from England's coal mines. ''He came away from the mines and the North,'' note critics Peter Stansky and William Abrahams, ''in a state of guilt, anger, and compassion, and with a new, untested belief in the necessity of a political resolution.'' Much to the dismay of publisher Victor Gollancz, who had commissioned the work for his planned Left Book Club, the reportage of the first section of the book was followed by Orwell's own story of his conversion to socialism, including his railing against British socialists. Gollancz felt obliged to publish *The Road to Wigan Pier* with his own foreword, stating his inability to agree with some of Orwell's statements.

In late December 1936, Orwell traveled to Spain, beginning a six-month saga that, according to Zehr, ''provided the seminal experiences that would inform and structure *Animal Farm* and *Nineteen Eighty-Four.*'' Idealistic foreigners were also flocking to Spain, determined to defend

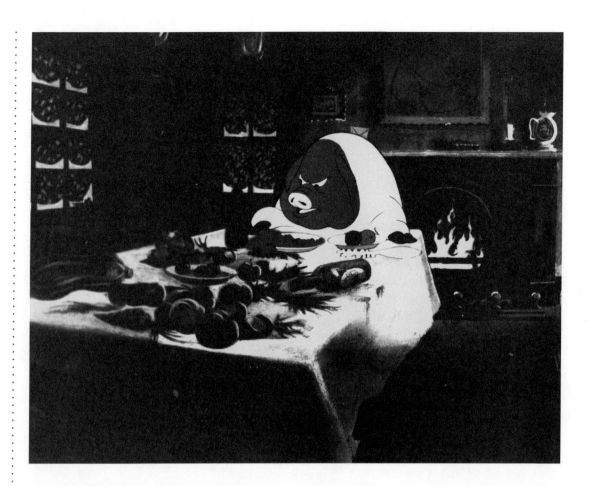

Movie still from
Animal Farm

the country's democratically elected government against a fascist takeover. While the purpose of Orwell's trip was to observe and to write about the war, he soon joined in the fighting. He was shot through the neck by a sniper, but eventually made a full recovery.

Homage to Catalonia, the book Orwell wrote about Spain, was not well received when it was published in 1938, but it eventually came to be looked upon as an essential part of the literature of the Spanish Civil War. Almost immediately upon finishing the book, Orwell began work on *Coming Up for Air,* his first novel in three years. Like *Homage to Catalonia,* the book looks back with nostalgia at a more innocent past while at the same time predicting a war-torn future.

Animals in Revolt

World War II began several months after *Coming Up for Air* was published. Eager to serve his country, Orwell and his wife moved to London. After being turned down for military duty due to poor health, he became a member of the Home Guard, Britain's civilian defense force, and worked as a radio producer for the Indian Service of the British Broadcasting Corporation (BBC). Later, Orwell became literary editor of the *Tribune,* a weekly socialist newspaper, and served as a war correspondent for the *London Observer.* He was in Germany, covering the end of the war in Europe, when he received word his wife had died during an operation. Orwell's personal loss had come just months before his biggest triumph as a writer: the publication of *Animal Farm* in August 1945. He had completed the book in early 1944, but because it was seen as an attack on Stalin—then Britain's wartime ally—its publication was delayed until the end of the war. The first edition sold out within weeks, and the book was both a critical and popular success.

Animal Farm is an allegory that can be enjoyed on two different levels. It can be read as an animal story, telling the fanciful tale of a group of barnyard animals who—after overthrowing Mr. Jones, their human master—begin their own republic based on the principles of Animalism. While pigs lead the rebellion in *Animal Farm,* other animals also figure importantly in the story, including a hard-working horse named Boxer, a

Creative and Performing Artists for Teens

skeptical donkey named Benjamin, and a raven named Moses who talks about eternal life in the Sugarcandy Mountain. On a deeper level, *Animal Farm* can also be read as a satire of Stalin's betrayal of the Russian Revolution of 1917, and other events in Soviet history.

While political satire is an integral part of the book's success, Orwell made it clear that *Animal Farm* was meant to be more than just a criticism of Russia; it was critical of all totalitarian states. Critics agree that the book will outlast the knowledge of the events it satirizes. More than one reviewer summarized the book's theme with a famous maxim of one of Orwell's fellow-countrymen, Lord Acton: "Power tends to corrupt; absolute power corrupts absolutely."

Power, and erasing memories, are themes Orwell touches on in *Animal Farm* but deals with in more detail in *Nineteen Eighty-Four,* his final novel. Most of the book was written on the island of Jura, in the Scottish Hebrides, where Orwell moved in May 1946. There, in the solitude of a rented farmhouse called Barnhill, he completed the first draft of *Nineteen Eighty-Four* by October 1947. Then, worsening tuberculosis sent him to the hospital for seven months. When he was strong enough, he returned to Jura and finished the final draft of the novel in November 1948. Unfortunately, the effort of working on the book sent him back to the hospital. On October 13, 1949, he married Sonia Brownell in London's University College Hospital. He never recovered from his illness, however, and died January 21, 1950, at 46 years of age.

"Impossible to put the book down"

Nineteen Eighty-Four was greeted with enthusiastic reviews. In a 1949 *New York Times Book Review* essay, American critic and biographer Mark Schorer wrote: "No real reader can neglect this experience with impunity. . . . He will be asked to read through pages of sustained physical and psychological pain that have seldom been equaled and never in such quiet, sober prose." The same year, eminent British novelist V. S. Pritchett's response to the first British edition of

Animal Farm, Secker & Warburg, 1945
Nineteen Eighty-Four, Harcourt, 1949

Nineteen Eighty-Four appeared in *New Statesman and Nation.* "I do not think," the critic concluded, "I have ever read a novel more frightening and depressing; and yet, such are the originality, the suspense, the speed of writing and withering indignation that it is impossible to put the book down."

A half century after *Nineteen Eighty-Four* was first published, the novel's impact is such that, according to John H. Barnsley in *Contemporary Review,* it "has become part of the common imaginative heritage of the Western world." The novel contributed a half-dozen or more words to our language, including "newspeak," "Big Brother," and "doublethink." It also gave us the term "Orwellian," used to refer to any governmental invasion of private life.

The term seems ironic, since Orwell spent most of his life exposing the truth about intrusive forms of government. To the writer, of all the intolerable acts committed in the name of totalitarianism, the most offensive was the use of lies to change the past. According to John Strachey in *The Strangled Cry and Other Parliamentary Papers,* Orwell was convinced "it was forgery, even more than violence, which could destroy human reason." The truth was of utmost importance to Orwell, whether writing about the past, the present, or the future. In *Harper's,* Irving Howe praised the author as "the greatest moral force in English letters during the last several decades: craggy, fiercely polemical, sometimes mistaken, but an utterly free man."

Sources for More Information

Books

Abrahams, William, and Peter Stansky, *The Unknown Orwell,* Constable, 1972.

Bloom, Harold, editor, *Modern Critical Views: George Orwell,* Chelsea House, 1987.

Brander, Laurence, *George Orwell,* Longmans, 1954.

Meyers, Jeffrey, *A Reader's Guide to George Orwell,* Thames & Hudson, 1975.

Crick, Bernard, *George Orwell: A Life,* Secker & Warburg, 1980.

Fyvel, T. R., *George Orwell: A Personal Memoir,* Macmillan, 1982.

Meyers, Jeffrey, *A Reader's Guide to George Orwell,* Thames & Hudson, 1975.

Al Pacino

Actor
(1940–)

Born April 25, 1940, in East Harlem, NY; children: (with Jan Tarrant) Julie Marie. Education: Studied at the Actors Studio with Lee Strasburg.

"By taking on roles of characters that were unlike me, I began to discover those characters in me."

The 1993 Academy Award for best actor in a feature film went to Al Pacino, a superstar who ranks among the best performers of his generation. Pacino has been a leading man on stage and in movies for more than 25 years. It is hard to imagine the trilogy of *Godfather* films without his chilling portrayal of Michael Corleone, or the tragic *Dog Day Afternoon* without his edgy, desperate Sonny. At home on the screen or the stage, Pacino has forged a career unique among his acting contemporaries.

Yet he has also turned down potential hit movies to do repertory theater, has taken long breaks between films, and spends a portion of each year on independent projects that may never ripen to fruition. Nevertheless, he has been nominated for six Oscars—spanning some 20 years—and his is one of the most recognizable faces in American cinema. *New York* magazine critic David Denby called Pacino "a New York acting genius," a "perfectionist who wears everyone out, a consummate New York personality and star."

Pacino loves his work. "There's no such thing as happiness, only concentration," he told *Rolling Stone.* "When you're concentrated, you're

839

happy. Also, when you're not thinking about yourself a lot, you're usually happy.'' The actor immerses himself in his craft while the cameras are rolling and talks willingly about his projects as they are released. He is intensely uncomfortable with fame, however. His reluctant sojourn in the limelight has been punctuated by periods of inactivity, his hit movies offset by a string of spectacular flops. *Vanity Fair* correspondent Ron Rosenbaum called Pacino a "fugitive movie star, clandestine prince of players, the Hamlet of Hollywood." That enigmatic pursuit of art and commerce continues as Pacino enters mid-life. He told *Gentleman's Quarterly* that he feels more at peace with his career these days. "As you do this more and more," he said, "you don't mix up your parts and yourself as much."

Boyhood Love of Acting Nurtured by Family

Alfredo James Pacino was born in 1940 in New York City. The only child of Salvatore and Rose Pacino, who separated when he was two, Al grew up in a three-room Bronx apartment with his mother and her parents. He was a sheltered child who was not allowed to venture outside without an adult, but he remembers his childhood as a happy one full of loving grandparents and aunts.

As a respite from his lonely life, Pacino would go to the movies with his mother and then act out whole scenes for his grandmother at home. His natural mimicry helped win him attention, which he craved. The spontaneous performances continued when Pacino entered public school. Naturally he found his way into school plays, and even as a youngster he dreamed of a career in theater. An indifferent student, he was talented enough to win admission to Manhattan's prestigious High School for the Performing Arts, but he dropped out at 16. For a year he held a series of odd jobs and helped to support his ailing mother, then he moved to Greenwich Village and began to audition for off-off Broadway plays.

In his early 20s Pacino met Charlie Laughton, a drama coach at the Herbert Berghof Studio. Laughton taught the young actor, helped him win auditions, and even floated him loans during periods of unemployment. Pacino told *Rolling Stone* that Laughton "introduced me to other worlds, to certain aspects of life I wouldn't have come in

contact with. He's my closest friend, and he works with me on everything." The friendship has endured to this day.

Liberated By the Actors Studio

By 1966 Pacino had appeared in enough off-off Broadway shows to qualify him for acceptance at the Actors Studio. Famous for its chief instructor, Lee Strasburg, and its school of Method acting, the Actors Studio proved fertile ground for the young Pacino. He immersed himself in serious drama. "I felt I could speak for the first time," he recalled in *Vanity Fair*. "The characters would say these things that I could never say, things I've always wanted to say, and that was very liberating for me. It freed me up, made me feel good. . . . By taking on roles of characters that were unlike me, I began to discover those characters in me."

Pacino's ethnic background and urban good looks helped him win an off-Broadway role in the one-act Israel Horovitz play *The Indian Wants the Bronx*. The show had its New York City premier in 1967 with Pacino featured as the brutal Murph, a Bronx hoodlum. The show was a hit, running for 204 performances, and Pacino won an Obie Award as the best actor in an off-Broadway production. From there Pacino moved to Broadway as the psychotic junkie Bickham in *Does a Tiger Wear a Necktie?* That play closed after a brief run, but critics singled out Pacino's chilling performance for special praise and he won a Tony Award as best supporting actor in 1969.

Other theater projects followed, including *The Local Stigmatic* in 1969, *Camino Real* in 1970, and *The Basic Training of Pavlo Hummel* in 1972. The last work, a study of the Vietnam War from the point of view of a recruit, had its premier in Boston and did not move to New York City until 1977. When it did—with Pacino in the lead—he won his second Tony Award for his performance.

Earns Landmark Role

"Movies were difficult things the first ten years of my career," Pacino told *Gentleman's Quarterly*. "I kept feeling as though this was not the medium for me." The actor did not have much of an apprenticeship in small film roles—his second feature was a starring vehicle, *Panic in Needle*

Park, in which he played a junkie desperate for heroin.

Executives at Paramount caught Pacino's performance in *Panic in Needle Park* and persuaded him to audition for *The Godfather.* At first Pacino was uncomfortable with the role of Michael Corleone, the youngest son in a brutal crime family. Likewise, the same executives urged he be dropped from the project after they viewed the early footage. Director Francis Ford Coppola insisted on retaining Pacino, however, and the actor soon grasped the difficult, coming-of-age character. *The Godfather* opened in 1972 and soon set records at the box office. *New Yorker* critic Pauline Kael praised Pacino for his ''gift for conveying the divided spirit of a man whose calculations often go against his inclinations.''

Pacino turned in classic performances in three other major motion pictures in the 1970s: *The Godfather, Part II, Dog Day Afternoon,* and *Serpico.* In *The Godfather, Part II* he reprised his role as Michael Corleone, taking over the lead as the feared crime boss. In *Dog Day Afternoon* he played a bank robber desperate to find the money to finance his male lover's sex change operation. In *Serpico* Pacino portrayed a real New York City policeman who stood up to corruption on the force and crime in the streets. Such was the actor's ability that he received Oscar nominations for all three movies.

Career Falters

Pacino's career was in full flower by the late 1970s. Then it faltered quite dramatically. The actor earned yet another Academy Award nomination in 1980 for his portrayal of a beleaguered attorney in . . . *And Justice for All,* but his subsequent films met with savage criticism. Particularly disappointing was the reception for the big-budget crime film *Scarface,* in which Pacino played drug kingpin Tony Montana. Reviewers found fault with his overly indulgent performance, his Cuban accent, and his incessant swearing throughout the movie. *Revolution* was an even bigger disaster. A *People* magazine critic called the epic based on the American Revolution "the worst movie of 1985," adding: "You are hereby advised not to walk in."

Stung by the savage reviews, Pacino dropped out of sight in 1985 and did not make another movie for three years. During his hiatus Pacino directed and produced a film version of *The Local Stigmatic* that has not yet been given a broad

release. He also starred in several stage plays, including Shakespeare's *Julius Caesar,* and gave readings at colleges and little theaters. He returned to the screen in 1989 in the romantic thriller *Sea of Love,* which was a modest hit, and then took a supporting role in *Dick Tracy* that earned him yet another Academy Award nomination.

A Return to Form

"Al Pacino's is a rise-and-fall-and-rise story," noted David Denby in *New York.* "His appearance in *Sea of Love* was something of a shock. He had aged, his right eye seemed to have a nerve sticking out of it, he was tired—but also hungry. It was a great performance, and he was powerful as Michael again in *Godfather III.*" Indeed, with *The Godfather, Part III,* Pacino announced his return to form. In 1992 he appeared in two movies, *Glengarry Glen Ross* and *Scent of a Woman,* earning Oscar nods for both.

The role that finally brought him an Academy Award was that of the blind Lieutenant Colonel Frank Slade in *Scent of a Woman.* Denby wrote of Pacino's achievement in the film: "The most famous eyes in movies now must remain dead and unfocused through long, long scenes, but the performance couldn't be more defined. It's heroic work." With the smash success of *Scent of a Woman,* Pacino's major-star status was reconfirmed.

One of the actor's most personal works is *Looking for Richard,* described by *Vogue's* John Powers as "a wildly ambitious, quasi-documentary movie" comprised of scenes from *Richard III,* interviews with such acclaimed Shakespearean actor as Kenneth Branagh, Derek Jacobi, and John Gielgud, and clips of ordinary people talking about Shakespeare. It took at least three years to make and is Pacino's "dreamchild, his labor of love," according to Powers. It was selected for screening at the prestigious Sundance Film Festival of 1996, and earned high praise from critics.

Pacino has also been involved in more mainstream, big-budget projects since winning his Oscar, including the films *Carlito's Way, Heat,* and *City Hall.* In 1997 Pacino appeared with Johnny Depp in *Donnie Brasco,* a film based on a true story. Depp played the part of Joe Pistone, an F.B.I. special agent who infiltrates the New York Mafia by gaining the confidence of the seasoned mobster Lefty, played by Pacino. In *The Devil's*

Advocate, also released in 1997, Pacino shared the screen with Keanu Reeves as a high-powered, charismatic New York attorney. Jack Knoll wrote in a *Newsweek* review of the film, "Pacino hasn't had such fun since he exposed the devilish doings among New York City cops in 'Serpico.'"

Pacino told *Gentleman's Quarterly,* somewhat in jest, that he foresees a time when he will no longer make movies. "I keep envisioning myself sitting around the duomo, sipping anisette and watching the girls and having a great life not acting," he said. Maureen Dowd, writing in *Gentleman's Quarterly,* expressed doubts that the moody Pacino will ever completely relinquish his ties to stage and screen. Dowd concluded that Pacino, with his raft of memorable roles, "is a man addicted to the high wire and the process of acting and the sound of words."

Sources for More Information

Periodicals

Entertainment Weekly, Fall, 1996.

Esquire, February, 1996.

Rolling Stone, October 17, 1996.

On-line

Mr. Showbiz Web site, located at http://mrshowbiz.go.com.

Trey Parker and Matt Stone

Writers, producers, and directors

"The challenge is to go as far out as you can but then keep it totally grounded in reality."

—Trey Parker

Trey Parker: Born in 1969, in Conifer, CO; son of a United States Geological Service geologist. Education: Attended University of Colorado, Boulder.

Matt Stone: Full name, Matthew Stone; born in 1971 in Houston, TX. Education: University of Colorado, Boulder, B.S. (mathematics).

Alien abductions, anal probes, a singing stool specimen, abundant flatulence, genetic aberrations, and some of the most foul-mouthed eight-year-olds ever imagined inhabit the bizarre, yet oddly down to earth, Colorado hamlet known as South Park. For *South Park*'s creators, Trey Parker and Matt Stone, their show is a brutal and vicious, but honest depiction of young children and their world. According to Rick Marin in *Newsweek,* the show depicts kids "who abuse each other, delight in dissing authority figures and yet possess a dumb innocence that makes their bad behavior forgivable." The caustic cruelty exhibited by the children of *South Park* has struck a responsive chord in many of the program's viewers and rabid fans.

Parker discussed the "children's lost innocence" theme with David Wild of *Rolling Stone* when he said "there's this whole thing out there [in the media and society] about how kids are so innocent and pure. That's bull. . . . Kids are malicious. . . . They totally jump on any bandwagon and rip on the weak guy at any chance. They say whatever bad word they can think of. They are total bastards, but for some reason, everyone has kids and forgets about what they were like when they have kids. It's [South Park's vicious cruelty] a total projection of what I remember. I remember making the poor kid eat the worm. I remember thinking 'What's the meanest thing I could possibly do here?'''

According to James Collins of Time, Parker's childhood refusal to flush the toilet and his father's reaction, led to the creation of South Park's infamous singing stool specimen, Mr. Hankey, the Christmas Poo. Collins added that this was ''very revealing,'' and shows that South Park's ''creators are not simply out to offend people but are exploring the surreal terrors of childhood.''

Normal Upbringing

Parker was raised in Jefferson County, Colorado, which was adjacent to the real South Park. He remarked to Wild of Rolling Stone that he ''was extremely introverted except with good friends. It was all about math and science and tae kwon do.'' When he was 13, Parker's father purchased a video camera for him and almost immediately, his young life and world began to change as he spent his weekends shooting movies.

Stone, less than two years younger than Parker, was born in Houston, Texas, although he grew up in the Denver, Colorado, suburb of Littleton. He was an honor student who was able to take trigonometry classes in the local high school when he was in the sixth grade. Despite this, Stone's excellence in academics did not save him from getting into trouble. Commenting on his academic record to Wild, Stone's mother asserted that ''I wouldn't say he was a troublemaker. I'd say he was always a good kid. He did have one teacher in elementary school who said he wasn't reading the novels she had picked out during reading time. I asked what he was doing. She said he was reading the encyclopedia.''

In Newsweek, Marin noted that Parker and Stone did not have a publicist, as ''the story of how this goofball duo made it writes itself.'' Parker and Stone met in the early 1990s when they were both attending the University of Colorado at Boulder. At the time, Parker was working on a film project entitled The Giant Beaver of Sri Lanka. According to Parker, the film focused on a young girl who wore a beaver costume and then would go out and terrorize the town. He noted that it was quite similar to the premise of the ''Godzilla'' movies.

Parker was eventually kicked out of the University of Colorado at Boulder for failing to attend a good deal of his classes. Stone, however, stayed on at the University of Colorado at Boulder and pursued studies in both mathematics and film. He earned his bachelor's degree in mathematics and hooked up with his friend Parker.

Strange, Strange Films

Undeterred by his less than perfect academic track record, Parker began work on his first feature film, which was eventually completed a few years later. The film was called Cannibal! the Musical and was envisioned by Parker as a mutant hybrid melding the musical stylings of Oklahoma! with the slasher film chic of Friday the 13th. The budget for the film was $125,000, which was a relatively small amount for a feature film. Parker managed to raise the money from donations and contributions from his family and friends. He not only wrote, produced, and directed the musical send up, but he starred in it as well. Stone also had a role in Cannibal! the Musical.

By 1995, the two roommates were struggling to survive. Parker was completing Cannibal! the Musical and as Stone related to Wild ''we were seriously starving. Down to one meal a day.'' Parker and Stone's fortunes were about to change when they were commissioned by an ardent supporter, former Fox executive Brian Graden, to create a video Christmas card for him. Graden paid the pair $1,200 for the five minute animated short film The Spirit of Christmas. The result was an obscene, rude, crude, and slightly blasphemous story about the battle for the hearts and the minds of the children of South Park. The dueling combatants were Jesus and Santa Claus. As Santa and Jesus duked it out, four of South Park Elementary School's third grade students watched in horrified excitement, anxious to learn of the outcome of the fight. The foul-mouthed little scamps who provided the blow-by-blow commentaries were: Stan Marsh, the so-called leader of the bunch; Kyle Broslofski, who was a member of one of South Park's only Jewish families; Eric Cartman, the chubby bully who was spoiled rotten and claimed to be big-boned; and Kenny McCormick, the one

Still from **South Park**

who came from a poor family, mumbles, and gets killed.

The impact of *The Spirit of Christmas* was phenomenal. According to Marin in *Newsweek,* ''the video became an underground bootleg obsession. Actor George Clooney alone duped dozens of copies.'' (Clooney later recorded the ''Grrrs'' of Sparky, Stan's gay dog.) The video immediately gained a cult status among those who saw it and the two creators of *The Spirit of Christmas* were soon inundated with offers for their services. The offers of the major film studios ranged from asking Parker to direct *Barney: The Movie* to creating a television series based on the characters from *The Spirit of Christmas.* Most of the offers, according to Parker, missed the point. Parker and Stone believed that the appeal of *The Spirit of Christmas* was due to a combination of the behaviors, situations, and encounters the children's characters found themselves in, as opposed to the prevailing view of the vast majority of the studios, who felt that the rampant profanity drove the short and without it there would be nothing.

Parker and Stone eventually managed to find an understanding and kindred soul in Comedy Central's Debbie Liebling who was willing to let them do what they wanted to do with their show within reason. Liebling recalled her reaction to first viewing *The Spirit of Christmas,* to Mike Duffy of the *Detroit Free Press,* ''I just jumped through the roof. I though this is what we have to have.''

In 1996, Parker signed up with Celluloid Studios to function as his production house. At about the same time, Universal Studios commissioned him to create a promotional video for them. The resulting product was *Your Studio and You,* a 15 minute campy send up of the instructional films from the 1950s. The mini documentary featured performances by such luminaries as directors Steven Spielberg and James Cameron, as well as Sylvester Stallone and Demi Moore.

With Liebling and Comedy Central's blessings, Parker and Stone began to develop *South Park.* According to Marin in *Newsweek,* Parker, who does the voices of Stan and Cartman ''is the one people call the 'genius' of the pair, the self-directed hustler.'' Stone, who does the voices of Kyle and Kenny, ''is more practical and business-savvy.'' Anne Garefino, a co-executive producer of the show commented to *Newsweek,* ''Trey and Matt both have a sweetness that balances out the grossness.'' Marin concluded, ''Both still come off like dorks.''

South Park a Hit

Fleshed out of the world of *The Spirit of Christmas,* Jesus was a resident of the town and had a cable access show called Jesus and Pals. Stan's gun crazy Uncle Jimbo and his buddy Ned, the Vietnam veteran with a voice box, ran the gun shop. The children's teacher, Mr. Garrison, spread misinformation and untruths via his alter ego, hand puppet Mr. Hat. Chef was the school's cook and the children's adult confidant who believed that sweet love solved all problems. In *South Park,* the children were cruel and the adults were inept and ineffectual. One critic noted that *South Park* was a crude cross between the immature hijinks of *Beavis and Butthead* and the sometimes skewed morality of *The Simpsons.* In *Time,* Collins noted that ''It [*South Park*] is the only regular series to carry a Mature or MA rating, the harshest.'' Marin added that even though parents and educators complain about the show, ''it's worth remembering that the show's core viewers are of voting age. Almost 60 percent of them are 18–34.''

No one or thing was safe from *South Park*'s scathing pop cultural analysis as Parker explained to Duffy in the *Detroit Free Press,* ''the challenge is to go as far out as you can but then keep it totally grounded in reality.'' Furthering this train of thought, Liebling told Duffy that *South Park* served as a release valve: ''[I]n an age of political correctness. It's like a release of these restrictions. There's a vicarious thrill to going to a world that's seemingly forbidden. These children make it less threatening.'' Parker later joked to Duffy, ''*South Park* is our therapy. We don't need any (shrinks).''

Not content to rest on his laurels, Parker started to work on his next feature length film, *Orgasmo.* It was a live-action send-up of the pornography industry. Parker, the writer, director, and producer starred as a Mormon who was transformed into a porn star shortly before he was about to be married. Stone also had a role in *Orgasmo* as a pornography photographer. *Orgasmo* made its American debut at the Sundance Film Festival in January of 1998. About the same time, Parker's first film, *Cannibal! the Musical* was premiering at the anti-Sundance alternative movie celebration Slamdance Festival.

Trey Parker and Matt Stone

Popular Works

Television
South Park, Comedy Central, 1997–

Films
BASEketball, Universal, 1998

South Park: Bigger, Longer and Uncut, Paramount, 1999

The over-the-top success of *South Park* went well beyond Parker, Stone, and Comedy Central's wildest expectations. The show has earned for the network its highest ratings ever. However, there was some friction between the co-creators and the network. Parker and Stone complained that they were receiving a fraction of their show's profits. Parker commented to Marin in *Newsweek,* ''I have a friend who writes for *Just Shoot Me* [a comedy airing on NBC] who makes more a week than I do. Thirty million in T-shirt sales, and I got a check for $7,000.'' After publicly airing their financial complaints, Marin noted that ''William Morris is renegotiating their deal, and Comedy Central wants to keep its star attractions happy.'' In April of 1998, a new contract was announced that will pay Parker and Stone a minimum of $15 million for new episodes of *South Park* into the year 2000, plus a feature-length film. Parker and Stone's work has been recognized in other ways, as they were honored with a nomination for a Cable Ace Award in early 1998.

Sources for More Information

Periodicals

Entertainment Weekly, January 30, 1998, p. 69; December 25, 1998.

Newsweek, March 23, 1998, pp. 56–62.

People, August 11, 1997, p. 17.

Rolling Stone, February 19, 1998, pp. 32–41.

Spin, March, 1998, pp. 66–75.

Time, August 18, 1997, p. 74; March 23, 1998, pp. 74–76.

On-Line

South Park, Comedy Central Online, located at http://www.comedycentral.com.

Gary Paulsen

**Young adult novelist
(1939-)**

"[It's] artistically fruitless to write for adults. . . . Art reaches out for newness, and adults aren't new."

Born May 17, 1939, in Minneapolis, MN; son of Oscar (an army officer) and Eunice Paulsen; married third wife, Ruth Ellen Wright (an artist), May 5, 1971; children: (third marriage) James Wright; two children from first marriage. Education: Attended Bemidji College, 1957–58, and University of Colorado, 1976.

A prolific writer in a number of genres, Gary Paulsen is acclaimed as the author of powerful young adult fiction. Usually set in wilderness areas, Paulsen's young adult books feature teenagers who arrive at self-awareness by way of experiences in nature—often through challenging tests of their own survival instincts. A former resident of northern Minnesota, Paulsen writes from his first-hand knowledge of the outdoors and from his experiences as a hunter, trapper, and even a dogsledder in the Alaska Iditarod race.

The author's work is widely praised by critics. Paulsen displays an "extraordinary ability to picture for the reader how man's comprehension of life can be transformed with the lessons of nature," writes Evie Wilson in *Voice of Youth Advocates*. "With humor and psychological genius, Paulsen develops strong adolescent characters who lend new power to youth's plea to be allowed to apply individual skills in their risk-taking." He has been awarded Newbery Medal Honor Book citations for three of his books, *Dogsong, Hatchet,* and *The Winter Room*. He is also the recipient of the American Library Association's Margaret A.

Edwards lifetime achievement award for his contribution to literature for teens. In addition to writing young adult fiction, Paulsen has also authored numerous books of children's nonfiction, as well as two plays and many works of adult fiction and nonfiction.

Paulsen was born in Minnesota in 1939, the son of first-generation Danish and Swedish parents. During his childhood, he saw little of his father, who served in the military in Europe during World War II, and little of his mother, who worked in a Chicago ammunitions factory. He states, ''I first saw my father when I was seven in the Philippines where my parents and I lived from 1946 to 1949.'' When the family returned to the United States, Paulsen suffered from being continually uprooted. In addition to problems at school, he faced many ordeals at home. ''My father drank a lot, and there would be terrible arguments,'' he says. Eventually Paulsen was sent again to live with relatives and worked to support himself with jobs as a newspaperboy and as a pin-setter in a bowling alley.

Chance Library Visit

Things began to change for the better during his teen years. He found security and support with his grandmother and aunts—''safety nets'' as he describes them in his interview. A turning point in his life came one sub-zero winter day when, as he was walking past the public library, he decided to stop in to warm himself. ''To my absolute astonishment the librarian walked up to me and asked if I wanted a library card,'' he relates. ''When she handed me the card, she handed me the world.''

For two years in the late 1950s, Paulsen attended Bemidji College in Minnesota, paying for his tuition with money he'd earned as a trapper for the state of Minnesota. He served in the U.S. Army from 1959 to 1962 and worked with missiles. He later took extension courses to become a certified field engineer, finding work in the aerospace departments of the Bendix and Lockheed corporations. After reading an article in a trade publication, it occurred to him that he might try and become a writer.

Creating a fictitious resume, Paulsen was able to obtain an associate editor position on a men's magazine in Hollywood, California. Although it soon became apparent to his employers that he had no editorial experience, he stated that ''they could

Cover of Brian's Winter

see I was serious about wanting to learn, and they were willing to teach me.'' He spent nearly a year with the magazine, finding it ''the best of all possible ways to learn about writing. It probably did more to improve my craft and ability than any other single event in my life.''

Beginning a Prolific Career

Paulsen's first book, *The Special War,* was published in 1966, and he soon proved himself to be one of the most prolific authors in the United States. In little over a decade, working mainly out of northern Minnesota—where he moved after becoming disillusioned with Hollywood—he published nearly forty books and close to two hundred articles and stories for magazines.

His prolific output was interrupted by a libel lawsuit brought against his 1977 young adult novel *Winterkill.* Paulsen eventually won the case, but, as he notes, ''the whole situation was so nasty and ugly that I stopped writing. I wanted nothing more to do with publishing and burned my bridges, so to speak.'' Unable to earn any other type of living, he went back to trapping for the state of Minnesota.

To help Paulsen in his hunting job, a friend gave him a team of sled dogs, a gift which ultimately had a profound influence on Paulsen. On one particular run, the intensity of the moment prompted an impulsive seven-day trip by Paulsen through northern Minnesota. "I didn't go home—my wife was frantic—I didn't check lines, I just ran the dogs. . . . I was initiated into this incredibly ancient and very beautiful bond, and it was as if everything that had happened to me before ceased to exist." Paulsen afterwards made a resolution to permanently give up hunting and trapping, and proceeded to pursue dogsled racing as a hobby. He went so far as to enter the grueling twelve hundred-mile Iditarod race in Alaska, an experience which later provided the basis for his award-winning novel, *Dogsong.*

Nature Provides Backdrop

Paulsen's acclaimed young adult fiction—all written since the 1980s—often centers on teenage characters who arrive at an understanding of themselves and their world through pivotal experiences with nature. His writing has been praised for its almost poetic effect, and he is also credited with creating vivid descriptions of his characters' emotional states. *Tracker* was the first of several of Paulsen's books to receive wide critical and popular recognition. *Dogsong,* a Newbery Medal Honor book, is a rite-of-passage novel about a young Eskimo boy (Russel) who wishes to abandon the increasingly modern ways of his people. Through the guidance of a tribal elder, Russel learns to bow-hunt and dogsled, and eventually leads his own pack of dogs on a trip across Alaska and back.

Paulsen's 1987 novel, *Hatchet,* also a Newbery Honor Book, is about a thoroughly modern thirteen-year-old boy (Brian) who is forced to survive alone in the Canadian woods after a plane crash. Like Russel in *Dogsong, Hatchet*'s hero is also transformed by the wilderness. "By the time he is rescued, Brian is permanently changed," notes Suzanne Rahn in *Twentieth-Century Children's Writers;* "he is far more observant and thoughtful, and knows what is really important in his life."

Hatchet was so successful that Paulsen decided to continue Brian's experiences in three more books. In *Hatchet* Brian is rescued at the end of summer, after several months in the wilderness. Paulsen followed up with a sequel, *The River,* in 1991. Then Paulsen devised an alternate-ending sequel, *Brian's Winter,* based on the premise that Brian was not rescued at the end of *Hatchet* and must instead face the cold winter months alone in the wilderness. Critics have high praise for Paulsen's mixture of adventure and craft. "That [Brian] does survive until rescue is an expectation of the genre; that he manages *credibly* is a tribute to Paulsen's outdoor savvy and focused writing," opines Roger Sutton of the *Bulletin of the Center for Children's Books.*

Paulsen completed the *Hatchet* series with *Brian's Return,* which finds Brian confronted with a very different kind of challenge. Brian has returned home from the wilderness, gone back to high school, and must readjust to life in society. The story's resolution—described in *Kirkus Reviews* as "near mystical"—revolves around Brian's realization that his true home is the wilderness.

Paulsen relates his own tale of survival in *Eastern Sun, Winter Moon,* a story several reviewers have called shocking, painful, and vividly told. The author opens his account during World War II. In 1945 mother and son travel to the Philippines to join Paulsen's father; while on board ship, both Paulsen and his mother are witnesses to brutal horror, as they watch a plane crash into the ocean, and its defenseless passengers savagely torn apart in the shark-infested waters. In the *Los Angeles Times Book Review,* Tim Winton assesses the autobiography as a "raw portrayal of a child thrown into the horrors of war and the adult world."

Chronicles Trials of Slavery

In another critically successful book, Paulsen examines the horrors and brutality of slavery. The historically based *Nightjohn* is set in the nineteenth-century South and revolves around Sarny, a young slave girl is persuaded to learn to read by Nightjohn, a runaway slave who has just been recaptured. Some time later the eager young student is caught tracing letters in the ground; her vicious master beats her, then vents his anger by torturing Sarny's adopted "mammy" and Nightjohn. "By the time the book is completed," writes Frances Bradburn in *Wilson Library Bulletin,* "the revulsion, the horror, the awe, and the triumph are complete."

Paulsen also chronicles the dramatic personal battles associated with slavery in *Sarny: A Life Remembered.* In this story, Sarny, the young protagonist from *Nightjohn,* is now a 94-year old woman, looking back on the events of her life following her emancipation at the end of the Civil War. "Just how much of the book is based on historical facts remains fuzzy," comments Bruce Anne Shook of the *School Library Journal,* "but Sarny is a wonderful, believable character."

Reaches for "newness"

Paulsen is a tireless and inventive writer with a strong social conscience. In *The Rifle* he departs from his typical wilderness survival and coming-of-age themes to tell the "life story" of a gun. A Revolutionary-War-era flintlock rifle is the closest thing to a protagonist that Paulsen provides in this unconventional novel, which traces the history of the weapon as it passes from owner to owner, until it leads inexorably to tragedy with an accidental shooting in 1993. *Publishers Weekly* calls *The Rifle* "a truly mesmerizing tale," and *Voice of Youth Advocates* reviewer Chris Crowe praises Paulsen's gun control message as "unmistakable and powerful."

Other books by Paulsen—*Sentries, The Crossing, The Island, The Voyage of the Frog,* and *The Winter Room*—have furthered his reputation as a leading writer for young adults. Paulsen prefers to write for adolescents because, as he once commented, "[it's] artistically fruitless to write for adults. Adults created the mess which we are struggling to outlive. Adults have their minds set. Art reaches out for newness, and adults aren't new. And adults aren't truthful."

In her statement naming Paulsen as the winner of the Margaret A. Edwards Award for his lifetime contribution to teen literature, committee chair Helen Vanderluis cites Paulsen's special esteem for his young readers. "With his intense love of the outdoors and crazy courage born of adversity, Paulsen has reached young adults everywhere. His writing conveys a profound respect for their intelligence and ability to overcome life's worst realities. As Paulsen himself has said, 'I know if there is any hope at all for the human race, it has to come from young people.'"

Sources for More Information

Books

Children's Literature Review, Volume 19, Gale, 1990.

Salvner, Gary M., *Presenting Gary Paulsen,* Twayne, 1996.

St. James Guide to Young Adult Writers, St. James Press, 1999.

Pearl Jam

Alternative rock band

"I mean, my upbringing was like a hurricane, and music was the tree I held onto."

—Eddie Vedder

Band formed in Seattle, WA. Members include Dave Abbruzzese (born c. 1968 in Texas), drums; Jeff Ament (born c. 1963 in Montana), bass; Stone Gossard (born c. 1966), guitar; Dave Krusen, drums (left band 1991); Mike McCready (born c. 1965), guitar; Eddie Vedder (born Edward Louis Seversen III in Evanston, IL, c. 1965; married Beth Liebling [a writer], 1994), vocals.

"Pearl Jam is much more than a popular band to the many who look to their emotion-driven music for comfort, solidarity, and a sense of connectedness," noted *Guitar Player*'s Mike Mettler. A remarkable 1990s success story, the band is also part of the fierce Seattle rock scene that stunned the music industry by turning soulful, cathartic themes, punk attitude, and metal guitar into multi-platinum sales. Though at first thrown for a loop by their success, Pearl Jam—fronted by charismatic lead vocalist Eddie Vedder—followed their multi-platinum debut album with several strong and popular releases, making their huge appeal even harder to write off as a mere trend. Their resistance to the music industry that created them as giants led to hard times for the band, but they have continued to change and mature beyond the much-hyped grunge phenomenon.

Much of the credit for Pearl Jam's sudden and solid connection with its devoted, youthful audience must go to Vedder, whose "vocalized anguish seems to strike the raw and hurting nerve of a young generation raised on divorce and dysfunction,'' according to *People*. The singer's own troubled past informs his lyrics—rife with images of violence and loneliness—and his singing balances rage, despair, yearning, and hope in a way that has struck a chord with listeners since the release of Pearl Jam's Epic debut *Ten* in 1991. "I mean, my upbringing was like a hurricane, and music was the tree I held onto," Vedder explained to *Melody Maker*. "That's how important it was, and is. It's everything."

Developing a New Sound

Pearl Jam was started by guitarist Stone Gossard and bassist Jeff Ament. The two had played together in the Seattle outfit Green River and helped to develop the "grunge" rock sound that would later be celebrated and scrutinized by the very industry pundits who originally ignored the bands developing the trend. It was with the glam-metal group Mother Love Bone, however, that Gossard and Ament fully expected to hit the big time; fronted by flamboyant singer Andy Wood, the group was signed and had recorded an album when Wood died of a heroin overdose in 1990.

Though devastated by Wood's death, Ament and Gossard decided to put together a new project. Gossard—lacking the "ego" to move from rhythm to lead guitar, as Devon Jackson of *Details* expressed it—enlisted Mike McCready, a guitarist who had played in such unheralded Seattle bands as Shadow and Love Chile. While long an idolizer of rock trailblazer Jimi Hendrix, McCready's playing had recently been energized by the work of blues guitar greats like Muddy Waters and Stevie Ray Vaughn. Gossard's compositions, which *Guitar Player* noted were often predicated on unusual guitar tunings, provided a perfect springboard for what Mettler called McCready's "raw, Hendrix-inspired lead work."

Brought together, the two guitar players "just clicked," McCready declared. All that remained, McCready recalled to Mettler, was "to find Eddie and a drummer." Drummer Jack Irons, of alternative-rock sensations the Red Hot Chili Peppers, declined the drummer spot but recommended that Gossard and company send a tape of instrumentals to Vedder, an Evanston, Illinois native who was living in San Diego. Vedder loved the tape, wrote lyrics to three of the tunes and sang them over the

music, made his own photocopied art for it, titled the whole package "Mamasan," and sent it back to Seattle. Ament listened to it and promptly phoned Gossard, according to a *Rolling Stone* profile. "Stone," he reportedly insisted, "you better get over here."

Vedder told his new bandmates that he wanted to rehearse as soon as he arrived in Seattle. With Dave Krusen on drums, the group spent a week writing and rehearsing and then played their first show. They took the name Pearl Jam, allegedly after a mysterious preserve made by Vedder's great-grandmother. Their debut album was called *Ten;* a writer for *Details* noted that the recording contained "everything you'd expect of a Seattle band: roaring guitars, rough edges, no frills or flash. And plenty of musical hooks."

An Instant Success

The initial single from *Ten,* the furious rocker "Alive," became a major hit, thanks in part to a video that showed a raucous live performance. It was the mainstream music audience's first exposure to Vedder, whose anguished yet resilient presence became an overnight sensation. The song "Evenflow" also fared well, and the band's appearance on MTV Unplugged broadened its audience considerably. But it was the first "concept video" for a Pearl Jam song—something the group had initially vowed not to do—that took them over the top. "Jeremy," a tragic story of a misunderstood boy who kills himself before his classmates, became the group's biggest hit thanks in large part to a dramatic video by Mark Pellington. *Ten* became a multi-platinum sensation.

By the time the group finished recording its second album, the sense of anticipation in the rock world was palpable. Vedder, having emerged as a rock hero, served as tabloid fodder for months; speculation abounded that he had become an alcoholic, and one briefly circulated rumor had him dead of a heroin overdose. Despite his struggle with the limelight, however, Vedder had thrown himself into the band's new batch of songs.

Between the release of *Ten* and the completion of the follow-up, of course, there had been a

*Eddie Vedder of
Pearl Jam in concert*

few changes in the cultural landscape. Most notably, "grunge" was a term bandied about by magazine publishers, talk-show pundits, and fashion designers, and the term "the next Seattle" had been hurled at every burgeoning local music scene. Vedder himself had become an unwilling spokesperson for youthful angst, not to mention the subject of considerable theorizing on the pages of teen magazine *Sassy*.

Pearl Jam's second album, originally titled *Five Against One* but changed to *Vs.* after its initial pressing, hit retail outlets in the fall of 1993. It sold 950,000 copies in its first week, reported *Variety*, and went quintuple-platinum in three months. The record displayed an expanded musical palette, most evident in Abbruzzese's diverse rhythms and a greater range of guitar tones. Cameron Crowe ventured in *Rolling Stone* that the album "is the band's turf-statement, a personal declaration of the importance of music over idolatry." The songs cover the spectrum from the scorching "Leash" and "W.M.A." to softer, more introspective compositions like "Daughter."

Handling Fame

In their *Rolling Stone* interview with Crowe—an old friend from Seattle—the band reflected on the ramifications of large-scale success. Gossard addressed claims that fame deprives musicians of their edge: "To me, the problem with getting too big is not, innately, you get too big and all of a sudden you stop playing good music. The problem is, when you get too big, you stop doing the things you used to do. Just being big doesn't mean you can't go in your basement and write a good song."

Yet despite all of their success, Pearl Jam has not forgotten about their fans. A writer for *Billboard* noted that the band has gladly accepted the "challenge of balancing their enormous success with delivering what they think loyal fans deserve: access and reasonably priced music." The band has taken particular exception to the concept of service charges; in May of 1994 they filed a brief with the U.S. Department of Justice charging Ticketmaster, a national ticket distributer, with forming a monopoly.

Pearl Jam released *Vitalogy* in 1994, surprisingly soon after the release of *Vs.* and under the pressure of that effort's huge success. *Vitalogy* met commercial expectations, selling 877,000 copies in its first week and eventually going platinum five times over. The singles "Corduroy" and "Better Man" went into heavy rotation on rock radio. The album represented no major transformations in style or attitude, but showcased the band's greatest strengths: Vedder's distinctive voice and a muscular rock sound. In the assessment of *CMJ New Music Report*'s Scott Frampton, "*Vitalogy* reveals Pearl Jam to be simply an exceptionally talented rock band, and as much as that points to the band's brilliance, it also accounts for its paroxysms of ordinariness."

Vitalogy received mostly strong reviews. Some critics found the album uneven and questioned the inclusion of several experimental pieces. But few failed to praise Vedder's intense and powerful voice, which Frampton described vividly as conveying a "feeling of having his soul cleaved open by the events around him." "Spin the Black Circle," a song honoring the 45 rpm record, won a Grammy for Best Hard Rock Performance and the album was nominated for the Grammy's 1996 Album of the Year.

Ten, Epic, 1991

Vs., Epic, 1993

Vitalogy, Epic, 1994

No Code, Epic, 1996

Yield, Epic, 1998

Choice Cuts

Speaking Only for Themselves

"With Kurt Cobain and his agonized beauty so sadly gone, down on Pearl Jam thuds the dreaded mantle: spokesmen for their generation, genre, hometown, whatever. *Vitalogy* is their refusal," wrote *Rolling Stone* critic Paul Evans. While the band fought against being pigeonholed as grunge, Vedder continued to struggle with the meaning of stardom and against the trappings of commercial success. He refused to do interviews or make videos and attempted to arrange a *Vitalogy* tour without Ticketmaster. Unable to find appropriate venues, Pearl Jam cancelled the tour, angering some fans. Vedder did further damage to his image when, during his Grammy acceptance speech, he stated that the award "doesn't mean anything."

In the words of *Rolling Stone*'s John Colapinto, Pearl Jam's "endless crusade against their own popularity" took its toll when their next album, *No Code*, debuted at number one but dropped from the Top Twenty quickly thereafter. Colapinto found the album a genuine change for Pearl Jam and called it "the band's finest, most mature work to date—a dazzlingly varied and assured collection that ranges from Buddhist inspired chants to glam-punk raves to moody ballads." *Time*'s Christopher John Farley found less to like, stating that "too few of the songs ... explore the musical possibilities they suggest in any kind of definitive or provocative manner." Following the album's release, there were rumors that Pearl Jam was on the verge of a break-up.

If *No Code* represented an identity crisis or a crossroads for the band, *Yield*, their next effort, represented a reconciliation. With the white-hot glare of fame off of them, Pearl Jam made a lighter, livelier album that captured the fevered energy of their earlier works. With the addition of ex-Chili Pepper drummer Jack Irons, the album is edgy and fast, but also leaves room for love ballads like the whimsical "Wishlist." The band followed up the album with a tour using Ticketmaster facilities.

"They want you to hear *Yield* as an album rather than as a pop-culture event, distancing themselves even further from their anthem-mongering, trauma-sharing, flannel-flaunting youth," explained Rob Sheffield of *Rolling Stone*. "If Pearl Jam's smaller place in the universe bothers them . . . you wouldn't know it from the confidently graceful craft of *Yield*," Sheffield wrote. Reflecting their new, more yielding attitude, bassist Ament commented, "When you step back and see what our place is in the grand scheme of things, you see the most we can do is communicate with each other and make the best music we can."

Sources for More Information

Books

Neely, Kim, *Five Against One: The Pearl Jam Story,* Penguin, 1998.

Periodicals

Rolling Stone, November 28, 1996; April 2, 1998; May 13, 1999.

On-line

The *Rolling Stone* Network, located at http://www.rollingstone.com.

Richard Peck

**Young adult novelist
(1934-)**

Born April 5, 1934, in Decatur, IL; son of Wayne Morris (a merchant) and Virginia (a dietician; maiden name, Gray) Peck. Education: Attended University of Exeter, 1955–56; DePauw University, B.A., 1956; Southern Illinois University, M.A., 1959; further graduate study at Washington University, 1960–61.

Richard Peck is an award-winning author of young adult novels that explore contemporary issues such as peer pressure, single parenting, rape, censorship, suicide, and death of a loved one. In his two dozen YA titles, Peck has carved out a position for himself as a realistic writer who talks to teen readers on their own terms, imbuing them with a sense of self-confidence and empowerment. Titles such as *Don't Look and It Won't Hurt, Are You in the House Alone?, Father Figure,* and *The Last Safe Place on Earth* have won awards, accolades from educators, and a large YA readership.

But Peck also has a lighter side, and has written a series of historical novels for junior high readers, his "Blossom Culp" books, that delve into the supernatural. Peck, dubbed "the Renaissance man of contemporary young adult literature" by Patrick Jones in *Children's Books and Their Creators,* additionally has written humor, mystery, and horror YA novels as well as adult novels, and his books are often used in schools. As popular a speaker as he is a writer, Peck—a one-time teacher himself—travels thousands of miles annually to schools across the nation.

"Every late adolescent should be cut out of the pack to find out who he is."

A Tranquil Upbringing

Born on April 5, 1934, in Decatur, Illinois, Peck grew up in what he described in a *Publishers Weekly* interview with Jean Mercier as "in *middle* Middle America." The tranquil life of Peck's childhood has informed much of his fiction: the local park, the kids he knew in grammar and high school, and the old-timers who stopped by his father's filling stations telling stories with a refinement brought on by years of experience. From such characters, Peck experienced his first glimmer of literary style; from his father he acquired an early love of cars and also of Mark Twain.

The extended Peck family of aunts, uncles and grandparents all later found a home and voice in Peck's fiction. An only child for part of his youth, Peck was greatly influenced by this household full of adults who took the time to read to him and tell him stories of the old days. Growing up during the Second World War, Peck was also influenced by the propaganda of war, of the posters warning against loose lips and of kamikaze and blitzkrieg attacks. A memorable teacher in high school managed to impress on him the importance of subject matter for his writing, and after winning a scholarship, he was off to DePauw University in Greencastle, Indiana.

Peck studied his junior year in England, at Exeter University, and it was an experience that helped to open the world for him. "Every late adolescent should be cut out of the pack to find out who he is," Peck noted in *SAAS*. This cutting off from the herd, opting out of peer pressure, is a major theme in Peck's books. Returning to DePauw, Peck graduated the next year and was promptly inducted into the army. In the military, Peck's educational background helped, and he found himself writing company reports as well as ghostwriting sermons for chaplains of all denominations.

After his two years in the army, Peck went on to graduate school at Southern Illinois University. He cut his teaching teeth as an assistant in college classes, and upon earning his degree he spent two years instructing at the college level. But Peck's original plan was to teach high school English, which he did, starting with a position at Glenbrook North High School in Northbrook, Illinois, a suburb of Chicago. This suburban setting found its way into several of Peck's later novels, but for the time, the idea of writing for a living still seemed impossible to the young English teacher. For a decade Peck vacillated between teaching and textbook editing, until one day in 1971 when he decided to give up both and go into writing.

From Teaching to Writing

"I wasn't being allowed to teach as I'd been taught," Peck recalled in *SAAS*. "I turned in my gradebook and my pension plan one May day in 1971 and went home to write a novel." His years of teaching came in handy for such a task, for he had identified an audience and had also learned that kids read not to be educated but "to be reassured, to be given hope," as Peck noted in *SAAS*. His first novel was based on incidents experienced by close friends of his who took in unwed mothers. Peck decided to tell the story of one such young woman, not from the point of view of the unwed mother, but from that of a younger sister. The result was *Don't Look and It Won't Hurt*. Letty Cottin Pogrebin, writing in *New York Times Book Review*, described the book as a "textured story" and that through "the insightful eyes of the middle child we come to understand the complex forces that lead to the eldest girl's pregnancy." *Children's Book Review Service* noted that "This successful first novel . . . will touch girls with its honesty and sensitivity."

With his fifth novel, Peck introduced one of his most engaging and popular characters, Blossom Culp. And with her, Peck also traveled back in time to the early twentieth century. In *The Ghost Belonged to Me,* and its sequels, *Ghosts I Have Been, The Dreadful Future of Blossom Culp,* and *Blossom Culp and the Sleep of Death,* Peck created a heroine for younger readers. In the award-winning *Ghosts I Have Been,* Blossom discovers that she has even stronger second sight than her friend Alexander, when she is transported aboard the Titanic as it is sinking. Betsy Hearne concluded in *Booklist* that the book was an "outrageous sequence of events charmed together by skillful wordwork," and Glenda Broughton in *Children's Book Review Service* called *Ghosts I Have Been* a "thoroughly engrossing story."

Looks At Difficult Issues

Perhaps the book that earned Peck the most notoriety of all his titles is *Are You in the House*

Alone?, the story of a rape and its aftermath, told from the victim's point of view. As Alix Nelson noted in the *New York Times Book Review,* Peck's purpose was "to show how rape victims are further victimized by society and the law." Though some critics found the topic too extreme for young readers, most regarded Peck's work a powerful educational tool. It is used regularly in schools and has been published with an instructor's guide for classroom use.

Though Peck eschews the label of issue writer, he has tackled other difficult teen problems, supplying always and foremost a story, and secondarily a theme. *Father Figure* deals with the loss of a loved one and the search for meaningful family relationships. When seventeen-year-old Jim Atwater's mother kills herself to avoid the ravages of cancer, he and his younger brother, Byron, are left without a family, their father having deserted them years earlier. The two are eventually reunited with their father in Florida, however, and learn important lessons about getting by and taking people as they are. *Publishers Weekly* called *Father Figure* "the best book of many that have won Peck honors, and assuredly one of the best for all ages in many a moon," and Peck himself once dubbed it "my best book" in *School Library Journal.* With *Close Enough to Touch,* Peck dealt with teen romance, from the point of view of a young boy whose girlfriend dies, and who ultimately learns to love another. *Voice of Youth Advocates* contributor Mary K. Chelton noted that the book was "highly recommended with Kleenex."

Remembering the Good Times is a novel about teen suicide which a *Publishers Weekly* critic called Peck's "best book so far," adding: "Peck says he hopes parents will read the novel. We hope everyone will." *Unfinished Portrait of Jessica* deals with divorce and both a daughter's disillusionment with the father whom she has idolized and her ultimate reconciliation with her mother. Hazel Rochman praised the novel in *Booklist,* noting that "Peck's beautifully polished sentences hold passionate yearning, and his wit turns brand names into metaphor and reveals difficult truths in the cliches of popular culture." Peck also deals with the fundamentalist Christian right, censorship, and with a community learning to pull together in *The Last Safe Place on Earth,* "a highly topical tale," according to *Publishers Weekly.*

Cover of **The Last Safe Place on Earth**

Peck's Lighter Side

Peck also has a lighter side, writing of discovery in *Those Summer Girls I Never Met,* time-travel in *Voices after Midnight,* southern California brats in *Bel-Air Bambi and the Mall Rats,* and cyberspace in the humorous companion novels, *Lost in Cyberspace* and *The Great Interactive Dream Machine.* Of the first title in the latter two-book series written for juveniles, *Publishers Weekly* commented that "Amiable characters, fleet pacing and witty, in-the-know narration will keep even the non-bookish interested." Janice Del Negro, reviewing *The Great Interactive Dream Machine,* echoed these sentiments, noting that "Peck's humor and pacing keeps the boys—and the reader—moving right along."

In all these works of various genres, Peck has featured adolescents dealing with the major issue of finding their own way in the world, of making that first awkward step toward maturity and independence. Peck's female protagonists display the same degree of independence and resiliency as their male counterparts. In the end, Peck is conservative in what he hopes his YA titles accomplish. As he told Roger Sutton in a *School Library*

Journal interview, ''I don't know what books can do, except one point is that I wish every kid knew that fiction can be truer than fact, that it isn't a frivolous pastime unless your reading taste is for the frivolous. I wish they knew that being literate is a way of being successful in any field. I wish they all wanted to pit their own experience against the experiences they see in books. And I wish they had to do a little more of that in order to pass class in school. But in books you reach an awful lot of promising kids who write back good literate letters and give you hope. So that's the hope I have.''

Sources for More Information

Books

Children's Books and Their Creators, edited by Anita Silvey, Houghton Mifflin, 1995, pp. 512–14.

Children's Literature Review, Volume 15, Gale, 1988, pp. 146–66.

Gallo, Donald R., *Presenting Richard Peck,* Twayne, 1989.

Something about the Author Autobiography Series, Volume 2, Gale, 1986.

Robert Newton Peck

**Young adult novelist
(1928-)**

Born February 17, 1928, in Vermont; son of F. Haven (a farmer) and Lucile (Dornburgh) Peck; married Dorothy Anne Houston (a librarian and painter), 1958; children: Christopher Haven, Anne Houston. Education: Rollins College, A.B., 1953; Cornell University, law student.

"I can only write about what I know and I've never been shy about telling people what I know."

The strength of Robert Newton Peck's works stems from their striking depictions of the past. Many of his books bring to life the rural Vermont of his childhood, describing the adventures and encounters with nature that helped shape his life. The six-foot-four-inch tall Peck once described himself as follows: ''I wear mule-ear boots, a ten-gallon hat, Western shirts and weigh not quite 200 pounds.'' Peck went on to observe, ''Socially, I'm about as sophisticated as a turnip. . . . I'm an expert skier, a dismal dancer, and I love horses.'' Sophisticated or not, the author has penned a long list of books for children, many of which reflect his boyhood struggle with the competitiveness of nature and its impending threat of death. Peck, who lives on a five-hundred-acre ranch in Florida, has also written poetry, adult novels, and how-to books for would-be writers.

Educators figure prominently in Peck's fiction, thanks to the influence of his first, much-admired teacher—he still respectfully refers to her as ''Miss Kelly.'' ''A lot of my characters are teachers—all of whom are strong, fair, and respected,'' Peck once explained. Although reading was a skill revered by the Peck's family and

861

neighbors when he was a boy, not everyone was privileged enough to learn how to do it. In Peck's own family no one had ever attended school before him, although he was the youngest of seven children. Luckily, he was able to convince his parents to let him join the other students.

Life in a One-Room School

Miss Kelly kindled the minds of the first through sixth grades in what he described in an essay for *Something about the Author Autobiography Series (SAAS)* as a "tumble-down, one-room, dirt-road school in rural Vermont." There she taught the children to wash up before handling any of the few, but treasured, books. *Ivanhoe, The Wind in the Willows,* and *Tom Sawyer* were some of the classics Miss Kelly read to her classes, along with biographies of outstanding personalities such as Booker T. Washington, Mark Twain, and Charles Lindbergh.

Peck not only grew up to write many books of his own, he also married a librarian, Dorrie, in 1958. The best man at their wedding was none other than Fred Rogers, the star of the popular *Mister Rogers' Neighborhood* television show for children; Peck had met him in college. Writing about his own children, Christopher Haven and Anne Houston, Peck once stated: "I hope they both grow up to have a tough gut and a gentle heart. Because I don't want to sire a world of macho men or feminist women, but rather a less strident society of ladies and gentlemen."

A Classic Work

Peck's writing career began with *A Day No Pigs Would Die.* The book was based on memories of his father, "an illiterate farmer and pig-slaughterer whose earthy wisdom continues to contribute to my understanding of the natural order and old Shaker beliefs deeply rooted in the land and its harvest," Peck once observed. In the story, a young boy comes of age when he must summon the will to kill his pet pig on the family farm in Vermont. "The hard facts of farm life are realistically described in terse, vivid prose that has no room for sentimentality," noted a writer in the *Fifth Book of Junior Authors and Illustrators.* The book was met with mixed reviews because of the graphic account of the butchering, but for the most part "Peck has been praised for his down-to-earth, life-is-tough attitude," continued the *Fifth Book of Junior Authors and Illustrators* writer.

A Day No Pigs Would Die has since gone on to become a classic young adult novel. A 1985 article in *English Journal* stated, "For a number of reasons, the novel deserves its acclaim and popularity: the sincere, evocative reminiscences; the Twain-like humor arising from a twelve-year-old narrator's naivete; the complex characterizations; the gritty depiction of farm life; the stripped-down, yet rich style. These achievements, which establish Peck as a gifted storyteller, combine with a theme of substance—a boy's carefully guided passage into manhood and his acceptance of adult responsibility."

A boy named "Soup" is featured in Peck's 1974 book by the same name, and in a number of his following works. "Rob and Soup, though abrim with rascality, respect their beloved Miss Kelly, her Vermont virtue—and her ruler," Peck once remarked. Like Miss Kelly, the character Soup is based on a real person in Peck's life: his closest friend in childhood. Describing the real Soup in his autobiographical essay, Peck expressed his view that "When a boy has a best friend, he's the richest kid on Earth." He went on to note that Soup's "real and righteous name was Luther Wesley Vinson, and he grew up too, to become a minister."

Over the years, Peck's works have been popular with both readers and critics. *Hang for Treason* looks at the American Revolution through the eyes of a young man in colonial Vermont. One of the author's personal favorites, a historical novel titled *Eagle Fur,* concerns a sixteen-year-old boy who becomes an indentured servant to a mean-spirited fur trader. The 1979 work *Clunie* examines the life of a mentally retarded teenager, and Peck later penned *Arly* and *Arly's Run,* a pair of novels that focus on a young man's struggle to survive in 1920s Florida. *The Horse Hunters* is another novel set in the Florida outback, and tells the story of a rancher's son who proves his manhood by capturing a herd of wild mustangs.

Two Decades Later: A Sequel

Twenty-two years after the publication of his first novel, Peck reprised the story of the Rob Peck in a sequel to *A Day No Pigs Would Die. A Part of the Sky,* published in 1994, finds the thirteen-year-old Vermont farm-boy struggling to maintain the family homestead after his father has died. Although included among a listing of "The Year's Best Books for Young Readers" in the *Chicago Tribune,* the work received some criticism for failing to live up to the standard of the first book. A *Publishers Weekly* contributor noted "the author has omitted much of the detail that originally brought his setting so vividly to life, leaving the book a far less satisfying read." More damning was *New York Times Book Review* contributor Hazel Rochman, who complained that Peck's follow-up borders on parody. "This sequel," she asserted, "has the disconcerting effect of making us wonder whether we were wrong about the first book."

Nine Man Tree, set in the Florida backwoods in 1931, garnered praise for its attention to detail and colorful dialogue. While acknowledging the book's predictable plot and nearly stereotypical characterizations, a *Publishers Weekly* critic wrote that "the Southern dialect is vigorous, even poetic, and the details shine sharp as a knife blade." Similarly, *Booklist* contributor Helen Rosenberg asserted that Peck's descriptive prose and ear for the vernacular of the region "transport readers smoothly to another time and place." *Cowboy Ghost,* the tale of a young man who comes of age

during a difficult cattle drive, also received notice for its rich language—in spite of a thin plot. "Mighty flavorsome language just about disguises a predictable plot," wrote a *Publishers Weekly* contributor.

Although many of his works have been well-received by children and young adults, Peck once commented that he "didn't start out to write for any particular age group. If my books turn out to be right for teenagers, as well as adults and/or kids, it just happens that way. I can only write about what I know and I've never been shy about telling people what I know. As a matter of fact, when I told my mother . . . that three of my books were about to be published by a very important publishing house, she thought for a minute, looked up at me and said, 'Son, you always did have a lot to say.'"

No matter who reads his books, though, "motivating the young to read is a task of paramount importance to Peck," noted the *Fifth Book of Junior Authors and Illustrators.* One motivator is to read a chapter out loud to children, suggested Peck, so they will be eager to find out what happens next. "My richest talent is making a kid smile. And getting him to read and write," Peck pointed out in his autobiographical essay. He even takes the time to answer up to one hundred weekly letters from fans in the United States and abroad. As he once told an audience of teachers, "*You* find the student who's a misfit. The kid who doesn't know where he's going. The one no one cares about. You get that kid to write me a letter. *Don't* do it for him. Let *him* do it or it won't work. And I promise you that I will answer that kid's letter. And maybe, just maybe, for one day he'll be somebody. He'll be able to hold his head high."

When asked why he includes so much of himself in his writing, Peck related in his *Fiction Is Folks* that it's "because I've got so much of *me* to give. Like you, I am abrim with likes, dislikes, talents, cumbersome inabilities, joys, triumphs, and failures . . . so why should I even consider wasting such a storehouse?" He went on to say in *SAAS* that "compared to the worth of so many talented authors, my novels aren't really so doggone great. Yet secretly, I truly believe that I am the best teacher of creative writing in the entire galaxy." And most importantly, he concluded, "Life is fun. It's a hoot and a holler. If you can't revel in America and enjoy all the wonderful Americans you meet, you wouldn't be happy in Heaven or even in Florida.''

Sources for More Information

Books

Children's Literature Review, Volume 45, Gale, 1998.

Something about the Author Autobiography Series, Volume 1, Gale, 1986.

St. James Guide to Young Adult Writers, St. James Press, 1999.

I. M. Pei

Architect
(1917–)

Born Ieoh Ming Pei, April 26, 1917, in Guangzhou, China; son of Tsuyee Pei (a bank executive) and Lien Kwun Chwong (a musician); immigrated to the United States, 1935; naturalized, 1954; married Eileen Loo; children: four. Education: Massachusetts Institute of Technology, B. Arch., 1940; Harvard University Graduate School of Design, M. Arch., 1946.

"It is not just a concept, but the way that concept is executed that is important."

Arguably the most celebrated of contemporary architects, I. M. Pei has designed museums, office buildings, hotels, and libraries in the United States, Europe, and Asia for more than forty years. Rather than adhering strictly to one definable style, Pei's works fit uniquely and sometimes surprisingly into their settings. The designs for many of his structures, among them glass pyramids, shoebox-shaped concert halls, and towering skyscrapers—though often praised for their elegance and beauty of detail—have occasionally proven controversial.

He was born Ieoh Ming Pei on April 26, 1917, in Guangzhou (also known as Canton), a city in the south of China; in Chinese his name means "to inscribe brightly." His father, Tsuyee Pei—who was descended from a prosperous family of landowners—met and married Lien Kwun Chwong while he was a university student. I. M. was the second of their five children; his father was an executive with the Bank of China in Guangzhou at the time of his birth. The family moved to the British-ruled colony of Hong Kong when I. M.

865

was just a year old. During their nine years there, the boy learned English. They later moved to Shanghai, China, where Tsuyee Pei became manager of the Bank of China's main office. Shanghai was a busy, growing city, and young I. M. was fascinated by the edifices of its changing skyline, especially one that was twenty-three stories high.

Pei enjoyed a unique bond with his mother, who was a musician and devout Buddhist; he was profoundly affected by the retreats he took with her to Buddhist temples. She died when he was only thirteen years old.

Chose Architecture over Medicine

Pei's father wanted him to become a doctor, but he decided instead to pursue a career in architecture, planning to study in the United States and then return to China. In 1935 Pei sailed for America, where he entered the architecture program at the University of Pennsylvania. Finding this academic environment overly conservative, and unhappy with its emphasis on drawing, he transferred to the Massachusetts Institute of Technology (MIT) and enrolled in an engineering curriculum. He excelled, and one of his professors convinced him to continue his studies in architecture. During a summer vacation, Pei drove to Wisconsin to meet one of his idols, the architect Frank Lloyd Wright. But he did not find Wright at his Wisconsin home and so continued driving across the country to Los Angeles, where he worked for a short time at an architectural firm. Pei received his degree in 1940.

Pei's original plan to return to China was thwarted by two political events. Japan had invaded China and war was raging there. Then, in 1941, Japan and the United States entered World War II. Pei's father advised him to stay in the United States, where he worked briefly for several architectural firms. He married Eileen Loo, who had been a college student in the Boston area when Pei was at MIT. Two of their four children eventually became architects and joined their father's firm. In 1942, as World War II continued, Pei volunteered to work for the National Defense Research Committee. He was charged with the task of researching ways to destroy buildings, an assignment he did not enjoy.

Communist Revolution Prevented Return to China

After the war Pei became a graduate student and assistant professor at Harvard University's Graduate School of Design. There he studied with two important designers, Walter Gropius and Marcel Breuer. They had come to the United States from Germany, where they had founded the Bauhaus, an extremely influential school of art and modern design. Pei has said that he was especially influenced by Breuer's ideas about ''light, texture, sun, and shadow.'' Indeed, these elements have been fundamental to Pei's work.

After completing his master's degree, Pei hoped to return to China, but his homeland had just undergone a Communist revolution, which, once again, dashed his plans. Pei decided to remain in the States and a few years later became an American citizen. He was hired by a prominent real estate developer in New York City and tapped to head the company's architecture division, Webb & Knapp. For several years he worked on large urban projects, including private residences, office buildings, and open plaza spaces. Rarely would such a young architect be given responsibility for such large-scale assignments, but few architects are possessed of Pei's originality and creative instincts. His work rapidly established his reputation as a promising force in his field.

In the mid-1950s Pei founded his own architecture firm with three other architects from Webb & Knapp. They continued to work on city projects, earning praise for the Mile High Center in Denver, Colorado, the Place Ville-Marie in Montreal, Quebec, and the Society Hill project in Philadelphia, Pennsylvania. By the mid-1960s Pei's work was in great demand. One of his finest achievements of the period was the National Center for Atmospheric Research; located in an isolated area of Colorado, the building fit snugly into its environment, thanks to a design Pei said was influenced by the pueblo buildings of southwestern Indians. In the 1960s and early 1970s Pei also designed several art museums, including that of Syracuse, New York, as well as those at Cornell and Indiana universities.

The glass pyramid of the Louvre Museum in Paris

Designs Not Based on Personal Style

Pei's designs have generally sprung from a project's specific demands and not from a single, signature style. Though others have scoffed at this method, he maintains that each design problem deserves a unique solution. His approach was borne out as he was hired for increasingly high-profile tasks; in 1964 Jacqueline Kennedy selected Pei as architect of the John F. Kennedy Library in Boston. The endeavor was repeatedly interrupted, however, as the site was changed three times, requiring Pei to redesign for the specifications of each location. The completed building was the object of some criticism, but it earned Pei national attention and a gold medal in 1979 from the American Institute of Architects. Another troubled project was the John Hancock Building in Boston, designed by one of Pei's partners. The skyscraper made headlines when its huge glass windows began popping out and crashing to the street below; a complicated lawsuit and tremendous publicity almost ruined Pei's firm.

But Pei's successes of the 1970s and 1980s overshadowed this debacle. His design for the East

Building of the National Gallery of Art in Washington, D.C.—with its stark geometric shapes and large glass skylights—was hailed as a triumph. In the late 1970s Pei received a commission of enormous personal significance: after the opening of political relations between the United States and China, he was invited to design a hotel in the capital city, Beijing. It was the first time he had returned to China since 1935. His design combined modern comforts with numerous inspirations from the gardens and buildings he remembered from childhood. A few years later Pei designed a huge office tower for the Bank of China in Hong Kong, another personally resonant task as Pei's father had founded the original branch of the bank in that city.

Outraged Some with Louvre Addition

But perhaps the most significant undertaking of Pei's career began in 1983 when he was chosen by French president François Mitterand to design a major renovation and expansion of France's national museum, the Louvre. When the first phase of the project was unveiled in 1989, it was viewed "aerial delicacy," deeming it "an exquisite object." A second phase of the Louvre renovation opened in 1993. Again Pei used geometric forms and glass to bring in light. *Time* magazine admired the way these changes in the display areas of the museum transformed "a dark and dowdy cavern to a bright and logical showcase."

Pei's most recent projects have been smaller and strikingly varied, including headquarters for one of Hollywood's top talent agencies, a bell tower for a Buddhist temple in Japan, and the Miho Museum in the Shigaraki Mountains, about 12 miles outside of Kyoto, Japan. He was also commissioned to design the Rock and Roll Hall of Fame in Cleveland, Ohio, perhaps an unusual project for a seventy-five-year-old architect respected for his classic, clean, and tasteful designs (the hall opened in September 1995). But the energy and inventiveness of I. M. Pei has remained a constant throughout his career, and his thoughtful, innovative work has made him a towering figure on the modern architectural landscape.

by many as a spectacle. Pei had designed a new lobby, offices, and storage areas, all of them underground. But these were topped by a large glass pyramid and three smaller ones that stood right in the middle of the main courtyard of the Louvre.

Pei had diligently studied the history of the Louvre and French art and architecture, and he came to consider the triangular shape a primary symbol. He used glass so that the structure would not hide the majestic older buildings behind it, most of which had been constructed during the reign of Louis XIV. Though the appearance of this ultramodern structure amid the revered seventeenth-century buildings at first elicited howls of outrage, within a short time the Louvre pyramid became a symbol of Paris. Critics praised its

Sources for More Information

Books

Cannell, Michael, *I. M. Pei: Mandarin of Modernism,* Carol Southern, 1995.

Dell, Pamela, *I. M. Pei: Designer of Dreams,* Children's Press, 1993.

Wiseman, Carter, *I. M. Pei: A Profile in American Architecture,* Abrams, 1990.

Rosie Perez

Actress

Born in Brooklyn, NY; daughter of Ismail Serrano and Lydia Perez.

"If I see a door comin' my way, I'm knockin' it down."

Straight out of Brooklyn and onto the big screen, actress Rosie Perez has at a young age fashioned a career out of busting stereotypes while crafting memorable characters. Rosie Perez as seen by *Vibe* writer Mim Udovich "has major-league dimples, the face of a demonic infant, the body of a petite but nonetheless solidly built brick house, and a vocal range that starts at Betty Boop and ends somewhere around car alarm." Equally talented at drama and dance—she served as choreographer for the hip-hopping Fly Girls on the Fox television network show *In Living Color*—Perez also demonstrates a shrewd business head, acting as producer and manager.

Had Right Stuff for *Right Thing*

Though she has been less than blunt about some details of her life—her age, for instance—Perez confirms several anecdotes that suggest she came up the hard way. One of 10 children, Perez spent some of her youth in a convent home, and then was raised by an aunt in the Bushwick section of Brooklyn. A good student, she never thought of

869

herself as a performer. In fact, Perez took remedial speech courses to cure herself of an impediment that caused her to pronounce her first name "Wosie."

Perez "was studying marine biology at a college in Los Angeles—and doing the Roger Rabbit and other assorted steps at the Funky Reggae club—when [director] Spike Lee saw her and had someone slip her his business card," reported *Newsweek*'s Charles Leerhsen. Though at first Perez interpreted this gesture as just another pickup attempt, Lee proved sincere in his interest, offering Perez a small but juicy role as his girlfriend in *Do the Right Thing*. (It is also Perez who dances defiantly in the film's opening credits.)

Wide Range in Film Work

Perez had also done some television work and appeared in Jim Jarmusch's film *Night on Earth* before winning a breakthrough role—that of Gloria in the basketball comedy *White Men Can't Jump*. The character was originally written as a white, Ivy-league type, but Rosie so impressed writer/director Ron Shelton that he recrafted the part just for her. As Woody Harrelson's love interest, Perez's character also stands out with her one true obsession—*Jeopardy!* In a high point of the film, Gloria appears on the game show and beats out her rocket-scientist opponents with her encyclopedic knowledge of "Foods beginning with Q."

A semidramatic part as a waitress in *Untamed Heart* followed, showing Hollywood another side of Perez. And in 1993, in what Udovich called "her first non-big-earring role," Perez beat out the likes of Jodie Foster and Winona Ryder for the part of a deeply religious young mother who grieves for the child she lost in a plane crash that spared her in Peter Weir's *Fearless*. In this quiet, introspective character, Perez "shows she can not only perform, she can act," according to Udovich. That notion was confirmed with Perez's Oscar and Golden Globe nominations for best supporting actress in 1994.

Adds "Buzz"

Perez took a less sympathetic role in the 1994 comedy *It Could Happen to You,* as the wife of a cop (Nicolas Cage) who shares his lottery winnings, as promised with a local waitress. Despite playing the part like a gold-digging chatterbox, wrote *Los Angeles Times* critic Peter Rainer, her life-of-the-party spiritedness and rat-a-tat locutions give the film a buzz. 1995 saw her appearing on comic-actor John Leguizamo's short-lived TV variety show *House of Buggin,* and the following year saw her co-starring with Harvey Keitel in *Somebody to Love.*

While she was becoming known as Hollywood's favorite "feisty Puerto Rican" ingenue, Perez had no qualms about speaking out against a system that she says feeds on stereotype. "I hate being the novelty act," she told Udovich. "There's times when I go to like an all-white event and they get a kick out of me. I hate that sh—. And sometimes, to be quite honest with you, I'll go to an all-black event and they'll get a kick out of me. I hate that sh—, too."

Perez counters by developing her own management skills. While maintaining her acting career, she created and produced a short-lived HBO series, *Rosie Perez Presents Society's Ride,* served as executive producer for an HBO movie, *Subway Stories,* directed and managed an R&B group called 5 A.M., and directed a music video. She has also been active in raising money for AIDS research and prevention. And she has made it abundantly clear that the obstacles she rails against won't slow her down. "The racism, the sexism, I never let it be my problem," Perez told Kate Myers in an *Entertainment Weekly* interview. "It's their problem. If I see a door comin' my way, I'm

knockin' it down. And if I can't knock down the door, I'm sliding through the window. I'll never let it stop me from what I wanna do."

Films

Do the Right Thing, Universal, 1989

White Men Can't Jump, 20th Century Fox, 1992

Untamed Heart, MGM, 1993

Fearless, Warner Bros., 1993

It Could Happen to You, TriStar, 1994

Sources for More Information

Periodicals

TV Guide, August 16, 1997.

Us, July, 1994; July, 1996.

On-line

E! Online, located at http://www.eonline.com.

Mr. Showbiz Web site, located at http://mrshowbiz.go.com.

Matthew Perry

**Actor
(1969–)**

*"When I got my first laugh on-stage,
I said, 'Whoa! I really like this.'"*

*Born August 19, 1969, in Williamstown, MA; son of John
Bennett (an actor) and Suzanne (a writer and TV anchor)
Perry. Education: Attended Buckley School, 1987.*

Matthew Perry began acting at a young age,
receiving his first television role a week
after he graduated from high school. Yet he didn't
make it to stardom until he joined the cast of the hit
television series *Friends* in 1994. The soaring
success of the show put Perry and his co-stars on
the covers of magazines and caused him to become one of Hollywood's most prized eligible
bachelors. In 1997, Perry landed his first starring
role in the film with *Fools Rush In,* followed by
another lead role in *Edwards and Hunt.*

Perry was born in Williamstown, Massachusetts, but spent the majority of his youth in Ottawa,
Ontario, Canada. Before his first birthday, his
parents, John Bennett Perry and Suzanne Perry,
had divorced. Perry moved to Canada with his
mother but kept in touch with his father, often over
the phone. John Bennett Perry, an actor, became
well-known for his Old Spice cologne commercials in the 1960s. His son learned about him
through his roles on television. "He would call
once a week, and say something like, 'Watch
Mannix on Saturday; I get killed on the show,'"
Perry told Barry Koltnow in the *Orange County
Register.* "That's how I got to know my dad,
through his TV work, and I grew to respect the
business."

By 1978, Suzanne Perry had secured a job as the press secretary for Canadian Prime Minister Trudeau. Two years later, as a television anchor, she married Keith Morrison, when Perry was ten years old. The couple later had four more children. During this time, Perry spent most of his childhood on the tennis court. "When everybody else was hanging out," Perry told Joe Chidley in *Maclean's*, "I was going down to the Rockcliffe Lawn Tennis Club, which was frequented primarily by 60-year-old men, and hoping that one of them wouldn't show up, and I could be the fourth in a doubles match." At the age of 13, Perry became the number-two ranked junior tennis player in Ottawa. Around the same time, he and his tennis partner took third place at the Canadian National Championships for their age group. Perry loved to play tennis as a youth, and he loved to act. In the seventh grade at Ashbury College, he played Arriba Arriba Geneva, a gunslinger in his school production of *The Life and Death of Sneaky Fitch.* "When I got my first laugh on-stage, I said, 'Whoa! I really like this,'" Perry recalled to Karen S. Schneider in *People.*

Tennis before Acting

At the time, Perry's acting ambition came second to his desire to become a professional tennis player. He decided to move to Los Angeles to live with his father when he was 15 years old. He wanted to get to know his father better and to further pursue tennis with better opponents. His mother moved to Southern California within two years. However, once he arrived and began to play, Perry reconsidered a career in tennis. "Everybody was better trained than me in Los Angeles," he told Koltnow in the *Orange County Register.* "I was losing to guys who didn't even own tennis rackets. I decided right away to make a vocational change."

Perry's father watched his son play George Gibbs in the Buckley School production of *Our Town* with both pride and fear. "I thought, 'We've got a problem here. He's good. There's another generation shot to hell!'" he told Schneider in *People.* After that experience, Perry decided to pursue a career as an actor. He received his first break one day, when he decided to skip school. He sat in a restaurant attempting to impress three girls with his quick wit, when the waitress handed him a message written on a napkin. Director William Richert happened to have overheard the young Perry from across the room and wanted to cast him in the 1988 movie *A Night in the Life of Jimmy Reardon* starring River Phoenix.

When Perry graduated from high school, he hadn't received very good grades. His concerned father made him a deal: if he didn't find work as an actor within a year, he would go to college. He had already appeared as a guest on a few television shows, including a short run as Tracey Gold's boyfriend on *Growing Pains.* A week after he graduated, Perry landed a starring role in a Fox television sitcom called *Second Chance.* The job started a streak of bad luck with television roles, with *Second Chance* canceled after 13 weeks. After canceling the show, Fox gave Perry his own show, *Boys Will Be Boys.* Again, the show only lasted 13 weeks.

Always the Guest Star

In subsequent years, Perry became what he termed the "Guest Star Guy," appearing as a guest on several television shows. In 1988, he played a small role as Roger, Christina Applegate's prom date, in the television movie *Dance 'Til Dawn.* The following year, he landed another part in the movie *She's Out of Control.*

The 1990s looked more promising for Perry. He played the role of Desi Arnaz, Jr. in the television movie *Call Me Anna.* He appeared as a guest on the television shows *Dream On* and *Beverly Hills 90210,* and received a continuing role on *Sydney,* a series starring Valerie Bertinelli. Perry played Billy Kells, a policeman and Bertinelli's brother on the show. Again, the series was canceled after 13 episodes. Two years later, Perry landed a starring role in an ABC sitcom called *Home Free.* The streak continued, and once again it was cut after 13 episodes.

Perry had reached a conclusion: the problem stemmed from a lack of good shows. He teamed up with his friend Andrew Hill Newman and decided to write a new sitcom. They invented a series called *Maxwell's House,* which focused on the struggles of a group of friends in their twenties. The idea sparked the interest of NBC, but the network had already chosen a similar sitcom,

Movie still from
Fools Rush In

which eventually became *Friends.* At the beginning of 1994, Perry received the lead role in a television series pilot called *LAX 2194.* The show was about the lives of airport baggage handlers in the year 2194, and Perry played the "head baggage handler." Though Perry was desperate for money, the pilot never aired. While helping some friends prepare for an audition for *Friends,* Perry read the script and found his destiny. "The part of Chandler leapt off the page, shook my hand, and said, 'This is you, man!'" Perry later told David Hochman and Dave Karger in *Entertainment Weekly.*

Friends

Perry received an opportunity to audition for the part with the show's producers on a Wednesday. Thursday, he read the part for the *Friends* production company. Friday, he did it again for the executives at NBC, and the following Monday morning, he started working on the set. Unlike any other show on television, *Friends* was a sitcom about the lives and travails of three young men and three young women living in Manhattan. It was a

hit from the very first season, consistently ranking in the top, and for many weeks the show rated number three. During the summer of 1995, *Friends* often became the number-one show in rerun ratings and Perry was able to move into a three-bedroom house in the Hollywood Hills. Instead of becoming a struggling tennis player, Perry played tennis with champion John McEnroe at celebrity charity events. Success and stardom had arrived.

In 1996, the six-member cast of *Friends* made a decision to change the business of television. The co-stars had signed contracts agreeing to receive $30,000 to $35,000 per episode for five years. However, all six actors decided to make the move to renegotiate their contracts. After a stressful negotiation, they reached an agreement. Perry and his co-stars extended their contract to six years. The deal gave them $75,000 per episode for the third season, $85,000 in the fourth, $100,000 in the fifth, and $120,000 in the 1999-2000 season. Though controversial, the six actors had made their mark.

Although Perry's newfound stardom brought him more money and a new lifestyle, it predictably detracted from his personal privacy. The media jumped on the story when he dated actress Julia

Roberts for a few months. "They were just dinner [dates] and nothing happened," Perry later told Hochman and Karger in *Entertainment Weekly.* "If you have dinner with someone and the next day the country thinks you're in a relationship, it gets a little weird. I was confused about dating before *Friends.* This just makes it more confusing."

With the success of *Friends,* Perry began to receive offers for movie roles. He was initially asked to play the role of Will Smith's flying partner in *Independence Day,* but had to pass since the filming schedule conflicted with that of *Friends.* However, he accepted his first big-screen starring role in the Columbia Pictures film *Fools Rush In,* released in February of 1997. In the film Perry plays a real estate developer from Manhattan who goes to Las Vegas on business and meets a woman in a bar with whom he has a one-night stand. When she informs him that she is pregnant, the couple decide to get married and are challenged by their unfamiliarity with one another. Perry reportedly received one million dollars to play the role.

Perry's film career continued between shooting episodes of *Friends.* He starred in the 1997 film *Edwards & Hunt* with Chris Farley. In the summer of the same year, he began shooting *Imagining Emily,* a comedy he wrote with his friend Andrew Hill Newman. The movie tells the story of a man who falls in love with the adult version of his imaginary childhood playmate.

Despite the challenges of life in the spotlight, Perry enjoys acting and the attendant benefits. "I enjoy 88 percent of my life," he told Barry Koltnow in the *Orange County Register.* "The other 12 percent is a drag. But I am more than willing to accept the trade-off. It's an easy trade-off to deal

Television
Friends, NBC, 1994–

Films
Fools Rush In, Columbia, 1997

Popular Works

with, to exchange 12 percent of my life for the chance to make movies, be a part of good TV shows, and to work with great people. If it was 60 percent or even 51 percent, it might not be worth it. But I can live with this; I love my life."

Sources for More Information

Periodicals

Entertainment Weekly, February 23, 1996, p. 34; January 24, 1997, p. 18; February 14, 1997, p. 42.

Maclean's, February 24, 1997, p. 11.

New York Times, February 14, 1997, p. B14.

People, August 12, 1996, p. 39; February 17, 1997, p. 130; February 24, 1997, p. 19; May 10, 1999.

TV Guide, October 19, 1996, p. 61; May 2, 1998.

On-line

Friends Web site, located at http://www.nbc.com/tvcentral/ shows/friends/new_index.html.

Michelle Pfeiffer

**Actress
(1957-)**

"I'm always amazed at how consistent people find me and my behavior when in fact I do feel different all the time."

Born April 27, 1957, in Santa Ana, CA; married Peter Horton (divorced); married David Kelley; children: Claudia Rose, John Henry.

It takes only one glimpse of Michelle Pfeiffer to realize that she is no ordinary Hollywood beauty. Called "drop-dead gorgeous" by *Time* and chosen one of the ten most beautiful women in the world by *Harper's Bazaar,* the actress has left an indelible impression on the acting world and movie audiences alike since her career soared in the mid-1980s. Blonde, with huge almond-shaped blue eyes, the sultry Michelle Pfeiffer has been likened to such icons of the silver screen as Greta Garbo and Carole Lombard.

But while her beauty cannot be questioned, Pfeiffer's more subtle and perhaps enduring appeal comes from what director Jonathan Demme in *Vanity Fair* termed her "strength of character" and "decency of spirit." It has been these qualities that have allowed Pfeiffer, a blend of sweetness and steel, to explore a wide range of roles, maintain her integrity, and achieve a hard-won celebrity status in recent years.

Grew up as "California Girl"

Deemed a "rarefied version of a West Coast prom queen, sandblasted to a razor-cheeked fineness" by *Vanity Fair,* Pfeiffer grew up as a typical

Southern California girl—surfing at Huntington Beach, hanging out at Life Guard Station 17, and attending boarding school. Having studied stenotyping and working as a cashier in a local supermarket, Pfeiffer won recognition—and an agent—when she was chosen Miss Orange County at age 19. Her first agent and appearances in a few commercials were the upshot of this victory, and from there Pfeiffer was cast in two short-lived TV series, *Delta House* and *B.A.D. Cats.* She landed minor roles in a few films before being offered the lead in the 1982 musical *Grease 2.*

Despite the massive promotional hype surrounding the movie, *Grease 2* proved unsuccessful and Pfeiffer's career remained stagnant. According to *Newsweek,* her keen portrayal of Stephanie, head punkette of the Pink Ladies gang, might have worked against her: "Pfeiffer's uncanny ability to make people believe she's the character she's playing boomeranged. As a bubble-gum popping high-school vixen, she gave a sly, delectably sluttish performance." While this stereotype of just another blonde beauty, as limited as the character she portrayed, put Pfeiffer in jeopardy of being doomed to what one headline writer has called "bimbo limbo," the actress was convinced all along that she would transcend this stigma. "Even from the beginning, when I was doing like junk television, I still had this focus," she told *Vanity Fair.* "I knew I wasn't going to be doing that forever."

Pfeiffer waited a full year before taking on her next role, as Elvira, the haughty cocaine-addicted gangster moll in Brian De Palma's typically gripping 1983 film *Scarface.* Next was the lead in *Ladyhawke* (1985), a medieval flight of fancy costarring Matthew Broderick and directed by Richard Donner. It was during Pfeiffer's next film, *Into the Night,* in which she played a fast-lane party girl pursued by Iranians through the streets of Los Angeles, that, according to *Newsweek,* "her sense of comedy emerged, along with something both haunting and heartbreaking."

Made Career with Witches of Eastwick

The career-launching break came in 1987, when Pfeiffer landed a lead role in *The Witches of Eastwick,* based on John Updike's novel of the same name. As a small-town single mother with supernatural powers, Pfeiffer teams up with fellow witches Cher and Susan Sarandon to will an eligible bachelor into their lives. Their collective efforts are enough to lure the lecherous Darryl, played by Jack Nicholson, from New York City, and from there the story begins. Pfeiffer not only held her own against these cinematic big-leaguers, but came through with what the *New Yorker* called "a soft and fluid" comedy style "that blends right in with the others." While the movie received mixed reviews and contained one of Pfeiffer's more forgettable roles, it became a commercial hit and succeeded in transforming her career.

Doesn't See What Others See

Most who have worked with Pfeiffer have praised her technical facility—a seemingly innate awareness of the camera—but what really propels her is a sense of perfectionism and a genuine enthusiasm for her work. A Hollywood rarity, Pfeiffer has won the respect of colleagues, critics, and moviegoers alike. Yet least impressed by all the kudos is Pfeiffer herself. She enjoyed her character's bedraggled appearance in *The Witches of Eastwick* and scoffs at the appraisals of her beauty. "Meryl Streep, Dianne Wiest, they're beautiful," the actress said in an interview with *Time.* "I think I look like a duck. . . . I should have played Howard the Duck."

Another point of contention between Pfeiffer and her supporters regards her personality. "I'm always amazed at how consistent people find me and my behavior," she told *Interview*'s Peter Stone, "when in fact I do feel different all the time." Pfeiffer attributes this to the intensity of her personality, which, she confided to Stone, "gets me into trouble . . . I don't know the word balance." Pfeiffer is shy and modest, an avoider of Hollywood social scenes. For her, celebrity is a mixed blessing, an invasion of her habitually private nature. "I didn't become an actress so that my life could be exposed," she told *Vanity Fair.* "It's really the only thing that makes me contemplate [not] acting. I would give it up because I hate it that much."

In High Demand

Professionally Pfeiffer seems very much in control, achieved in part through her rigorous selection of roles and ability to milk them for all

Movie still from
Dangerous Minds

their subtleties. As the lead in Jonathan Demme's *Married to the Mob,* she played Angela DeMarco, a suburban mobster's wife who is tired of living the nightmarish parody of middle-class existence. Pfeiffer received rave reviews for her portrayal of the tender-hearted heroine. ''She gives an extraordinary performance . . . [making] Angela's toughness and her goodness believable, funny, and touching,'' remarked the *New Yorker,* and *Newsweek* commented on Pfeiffer's ''stunning mix of comic agitation and haunted vulnerability.''

Pfeiffer closed 1988 starring opposite Mel Gibson and Kurt Russell in Robert Towne's *Tequila Sunrise* and opened 1989 with Stephen Frears's *Dangerous Liaisons*. Costarring with Glenn Close and John Malkovich, she played Mme. Tourvel, an alluring and notoriously pious woman trapped in a tragic web of sexual intrigue. While *Vanity Fair* claimed that her performance "unravels with an intensity that is almost too painful to watch," *Interview* hailed Pfeiffer for possessing "a wild and rare combination of attributes: the varied skills of a character played with the demeanor of a real star." Her director, Frears, according to *Vanity Fair,* found her "extremely centered," adding that "you can't get [Michelle] to do a false thing."

Oscar Nomination

Her next series of accomplishments included Pfeiffer's first foray into the theater in a performance of Shakespeare's *Twelfth Night* and the portrayal of lounge singer Susie Diamond in Steve Kloves's film *The Fabulous Baker Boys* (1989), for which she received an Oscar nomination and won critical acclaim for her singing. In 1990 Pfeiffer was paired with Sean Connery in *Russia House*—a movie based on John LeCarré's bestselling spy novel of the same name. And in *Frankie and Johnny* (1991) she downplayed her extraordinary looks in order to play the ordinary-looking waitress Frankie to Al Pacino's Johnny. But it was her performance as Catwoman in *Batman Returns,* the 1992 sequel to *Batman,* that guaranteed her superstardom. In a role that many had sought, Pfeiffer purred, hissed, and clawed her way into the hearts of critics and fans alike. With her help, *Batman Returns* became a blockbuster that grossed over $100 million.

Pfeiffer's work also includes *The Age of Innocence* (1993) and *Wolf* (1994). The former is director Martin Scorsese's adaptation of Edith Wharton's novel of the same name. Set in the New York society of the 1870s, the movie sets up a conflict between duty and passion when the noble Newland Archer (Daniel Day-Lewis) must choose between his commitment to his fiancée and his love for the scandalous Countess Olenska (Pfeiffer). Critics were enamored, with Richard Corliss of *Time* declaring: "[Scorsese's] faithful adaptation of *The Age of Innocence* is a gravely beautiful fairy tale of longing and loss." At the other end of

the extreme was *Wolf,* a modern-day werewolf tale with Jack Nicholson as the man who turns into a wolf and Pfeiffer as the romantic interest. While the reviews were primarily positive, attendance was somewhat disappointing.

On November 13, 1993, Pfeiffer surprised friends and family by turning what they thought was a christening into a wedding ceremony. She married David Kelley, a producer and the creator of such popular television shows as *Chicago Hope, The Practice,* and *Ally McBeal.* The couple currently has two children.

Busy Career

Pfeiffer has continued to work extensively, appearing in numerous films in the late 1990s. They included *Dangerous Minds, One Fine Day,* and *The Deep End of the Ocean.* In *Dangerous Minds,* Pfeiffer played down her beauty and eloquence in a part based on the true story of LouAnne Johnson, a former U.S. Navy and Marine officer who teaches a group of tough kids in an inner-city high school. The plot centers on her attempts to save Emilio, a hot-headed student, from a doomed future in the streets. In *One Fine Day,* a modern-day romance, Pfeiffer played Melanie, an overworked architect and overcommitted single mother of a five-year-old son who begins a relationship with Jack (played by George Clooney), a single father with a five-year-old daughter.

Pfeiffer both produced and starred in *The Deep End of the Ocean,* a film based on Jacquelyn Mitchard's novel. She took on the role of Beth Cappadora, whose three-year-old son is kidnapped from a crowded hotel lobby, Cappadora succumbs to her grief and guilt, and life for her family falls into disarray—until the missing son returns at age twelve. In a review in *Time* Richard Corliss wrote, "The entire cast does fine work, but Pfeiffer is a treasure. She calibrates each nuance of loss without seeming calculating."

Pfeiffer shows no signs of slowing down in her career and continues to be one of the most high-profile actresses in Hollywood. In an *Entertainment Weekly* movie review, Lisa Schwarzbaum describes Pfeiffer as "a grade-A movie queen, sexy, beautiful, possessed of the rare Hollywood quality of mystery. And to her extra credit, she is also possessed of acting talent that, in some of her best work . . . can take your breath away."

Sources for More Information

Periodicals

Entertainment Weekly, Fall, 1996; February 12, 1999.

Los Angeles Magazine, September, 1997.

Vogue, October, 1997.

On-line

E! Online Web site, located at http://www.eonline.com.

Pablo Picasso

**Painter and sculptor
(1881-1973)**

Born Pablo Diego Jose Francisco de Paula Juan Nepomuceno Cipriano de la Santissima Trinidad Ruiz, October 25, 1881, in Malaga, Andalusia, Spain; died of pulmonary edema, April 8, 1973, in Mougins, France; son of Jose Ruiz Blasco (a painter and art teacher) and Maria (Picasso Lopez) Ruiz; lived with Fernande Olivier, 1905–12; lived with Marcelle Humbert, 1912–15; married Olga Koklova (a ballet dancer), July 12, 1918 (separated, 1935; died, 1955); lived with Francoise Gilot (a painter), 1944–53; married Jacqueline Roque, March 2, 1961; children: Paulo (died, 1975), Maya (born Maria Concepcion), Claude, Paloma. Education: Attended Provincial Fine Arts School of La Coruna, 1892–95, Academy of Fine Arts of Barcelona, 1895–96, and Royal Academy of San Fernando, Madrid, 1897.

"Not a single day without painting."

Pablo Picasso was inspired to create art from his earliest childhood and continued to nurture and realize that inspiration until his death at the age of ninety-three. Although he is best known for his paintings and drawings, he also produced sculpture, ceramic pieces, and book illustrations and designed costumes and scenery for the theater and ballet. Picasso's style went through a series of transformations during his long career, resulting in what art historians have come to call a variety of "periods." Most all of these were notable for the challenge they posed to traditional artistic boundaries. Picasso is considered by many to be the most influential artist of the twentieth century.

881

Pablo Ruiz Picasso was born on October 25, 1881, in Malaga, Spain. Picasso's natural artistic abilities were encouraged by his father, Jose Ruiz, a painter and art teacher. Also an influence on his art, Picasso's mother, Maria Picasso, loomed as a great presence in the young artist's emotional development as well. From about the age of twenty, Picasso used only the family name of his mother, a common custom in Spain. He revealed remarkable drawing skills early on and worked often in his father's studio. Though Picasso was passionate about literature and history, he disliked formal schooling and avoided it. Nonetheless, in 1896, when he was fourteen, he required just one day to complete the entrance examination of the Academy of Fine Arts in Barcelona, Spain. The rules of the academy allowed one month for completion of the test.

Influenced by Spanish Heritage

Picasso's work was influenced significantly by his Spanish heritage. He studied the Spanish master painters Diego Velázquez and El Greco and remained current on social and political issues in Spain throughout his life. But perhaps the most apparent clue to the artist's powerful bond to his homeland is the appearance of Spanish cultural symbols, such as bulls and bullfighting, in much of his work.

After attending several art schools, Picasso left Spain for France in 1900. He was nineteen years old. In Paris he became close to several artists who, like him, were destined to change the face of contemporary art. Among them were Henri Matisse, Georges Braque, Juan Gris, and Fernand Leger. He also came under the influence of many of the great artists of the late nineteenth century, including Henri Toulouse-Lautrec, Vincent van Gogh, Claude Monet, and Paul Gauguin. Some of Picasso's paintings from this early period look very much like the art of these painters, though they clearly demonstrate a distinctive style that was quickly associated with the younger artist, one that amply displayed both his talent and character.

Picasso's life in Paris was difficult, and his paintings of that era reflect this. His work from the years 1901 to 1904 are grouped into what is called his "Blue Period." The Blue Period produced paintings notable for creating a feeling of sadness in the viewer. These canvases displayed a limited range of hues and were generally bathed in blues and some greens. Many are portraits, the subjects therein thin, ghostly, and seemingly despondent.

From Blue to Rose

The work of the following three years, roughly 1904 to 1907, demonstrates another style shift, to what has been dubbed the "Rose Period." Many of the paintings from these years portray acrobats and circus performers. The change from dark, shadowy blues to warmer, brighter colors reflects an improvement in Picasso's fortunes; he was becoming more successful financially and was supported creatively by a stimulating circle of artistic and literary acquaintances. The friendship and patronage of writer Gertrude Stein—a portrait of whom would become one of the young painter's most famous—and her brother Leo were important factors in Picasso's growing renown.

Around 1906 Picasso's style underwent yet another metamorphosis; this time his unbridled inventiveness and innovation would make him the leader of a new school that was to change the world of art. Several elements were important to this development: first, Picasso became interested in the formal and technical aspects of drawing—how a subject is given structure on a flat page. He also was greatly moved by the popularity of Paul Cézanne, particularly by that painter's work of 1906 and 1907. At the same time, Matisse and others had begun studying African sculpture and ceremonial masks. These appealed to Picasso because the pieces were so different from those comprising traditional European art. Working with his friend Georges Braque, Picasso introduced a method of breaking down a subject into geometric shapes. This revolutionary approach to form became known as cubism.

Shocks World with Cubism

One of Picasso's earliest and most famous cubist paintings, *Les Demoiselles d'Avignon*, depicts a group of five women—but in an arresting new way, one unlike any before seen in Western art. The women's bodies and faces are represented

Guernica by Pablo
Picasso

as multiple shapes. Even more astounding, Picasso had painted them from several points of view, all appearing at once spread out across the space of the canvas; somehow he had learned to present the human form in profile, three-quarters view, and full face simultaneously. As his cubist ideas flowered, Picasso used vivid designs and colors to help viewers ''decipher'' the objects he had ''cubed.'' These radical steps sent a shock wave throughout the art world. Soon other artists, such as Gris, Leger, and Diego Rivera began to experiment with the new style in order to express themselves in a manner that the time-honored methods could not afford them.

Picasso continued to explore cubism and other schools of painting for many years, including surrealism, a new classicism, and symbolism. He also developed the art of collage, using a variety of materials—wood, paper, cloth, yarn—for three-dimensional works. Moreover, he made constructions of cardboard and metal. As a result of this unprecedented diversity, Picasso came to be regarded as the undisputed leader among the world's artists, his technical skills and creative abilities almost universally revered.

During World War I, Serge Diaghilev, an acclaimed Russian art critic and impresario, asked Picasso to create stage designs for his ballet troupe. The 1920s saw the artist mount several other theatrical designs. In many paintings of this period he returned to a ''classical'' style in which he presented the human form as massive sculpture, as if it were carved from marble. Most likely he was influenced by the many sculptures he saw during the time he spent in Italy during the war. This new style was a great contrast to the flatness of his

cubist art. In the late 1920s Picasso worked with sculptor Julio Gonzales making wire sculptures.

Lashes Out at War with *Guernica*

In 1937 Picasso painted what is perhaps his most famous work. During the Spanish Civil War, a small town named Guernica was destroyed by bombardment, with many people killed and injured. Picasso used his art to express his anger and grief: he painted the giant *Guernica.* He used somber colors, cubist forms, and a deep reserve of emotion to express the horror of the war. The painting, which features screaming people, mutilated corpses, flames, and injured animals, has endured as a model of antiwar sentiment.

Picasso was known for his forceful personality and colorful love life almost as much as for his work. He was also admired for letting his prodigious talents liberate his imagination; he was bound by few barriers—personal or artistic. Once he even fashioned a bull's head out of a bicycle seat and handlebars. Picasso's energy was also boundless, enabling him to work on several projects at once. ''Painting is my hobby,'' he once said. ''When I'm finished painting I paint again for relaxation.''

Unlike some artists, Picasso was very shrewd in financial matters, never settling for less than he felt his work deserved. During his lifetime his work commanded the highest prices ever earned by an artist. Picasso was also a great collector; his several homes were crammed full of all sorts of six stories high that resembled some of his cubist figures. It was larger than anything he'd made before. Picasso died on April 8, 1973, in Mougins, France.

Picasso's genius is beyond debate. He has influenced legions of artists—sculptors, architects, writers, filmmakers, poets, and musicians, as well as painters. His numerous works can be seen in museums around the world, including the Picasso Museum in Paris, where visitors can view the work that Picasso did not share with the world during his long and fruitful life.

objects he either bought or found—rocks, birdcages, African drums, pottery, posters, hats. He reportedly never threw anything away and allowed no one to move his things.

Life Marked by Creativity and Experimentation

Even in old age, Picasso never stopped experimenting. In the 1960s, when he was in his eighties, he was commissioned by the city of Chicago to create a monument for the Civic Center Plaza. He produced a metal sculpture over

Sources for More Information

Books

Heslewood, Juliet, *Introducing Picasso: Painter, Sculptor,* Little, Brown, 1993.

Lyttle, Richard B., *Pablo Picasso: The Man and the Image,* Atheneum, 1989.

MacDonald, Patricia A., *Pablo Picasso,* Silver Burdett Press, 1990.

Muhlberger, Richard, *What Makes a Picasso a Picasso?,* Viking, 1994.

Selfridge, John W., *Pablo Picasso,* Chelsea House, 1994.

Swisher, Clarice, *Pablo Picasso,* Lucent, 1995.

Venezia, Mike, *Picasso,* Children's Press, 1988.

Meredith Ann Pierce

**Fantasy novelist
(1958–)**

Born July 5, 1958, in Seattle, WA; daughter of Frank N. (a professor of advertising) and Jo Ann (an editor and professor of agriculture; maiden name, Bell) Pierce. Education: University of Florida, B.A., 1978, M.A., 1980.

"To write a novel is to be in love."

"**L**ike good baklava, a work of fiction should be multilayered. If it doesn't have its components properly situated in correct proportion, the taste and texture will be off. Plot is like the pastry: The body and support. Theme is the nut: The kernel and the heart. Style is the savor, blending honey and spice. Nothing is more delicious either to fashion or to devour," Meredith Ann Pierce once commented. Certainly, from her first novel, *The Darkangel,* to *The Son of Summer Stars,* Pierce has presented her readers with fantasies that have as many levels as a delicate pastry. She has established herself as "one of the foremost young authors of fantasy today. Her work combines a mythic inventiveness with such elemental themes as love, conflict and quest," according to Joan Nist in the *ALAN Review. Fantasy Review* contributor Walter Albert thinks Pierce's "Darkangel" trilogy "will surely be ranked with the small number of enduring fantasy classics." Such words of praise have been heaped on Pierce since the publication of *The Darkangel* and have continued with each succeeding novel.

Describing fantasy worlds full of strange beings, creatures, and places, Pierce works hard on creating the details behind the history, structure, and motivation for her characters. Sometimes the explanations and discussions the author has provided have led critics to call her prose style awkward. For example, in her review of *Birth of the Firebringer*, Hazel Rochman notes in *Booklist* that the "language is poetic, with a wonderful rhythm and sweeping images of sky and plain, but it is sometimes overheightened and awkwardly archaic." Pierce answers her critics by refusing to simplify her complex language. The author, however, defends her writing: "I can't change the way I think and I can't change my vocabulary and pretend that I don't know words that I know. . . . There are lots of word games in my stories, coined words and made up words, compound words, because I like doing that, it's very enjoyable."

Develops Love of Language

Born in Seattle, Washington, Pierce says that as a child she would spend hours talking and playing with imaginary companions. A precocious child who began to read at the age of three, Pierce started to read so young that she did not have to depend on her parents or any other adults for information. The advantage of this, she says, was "that I could feed myself information." One book that had a decided influence on Pierce was Lewis Carroll's *Alice in Wonderland;* the movie *The Wizard of Oz*—based on the Frank L. Baum book—also had a strong effect on her.

Pierce first realized writing could be a serious career when she took a class taught by children's author Joy Anderson at the University of Florida. "Through her I got a much better idea of what writing is all about," says Pierce. Anderson gave constructive criticism and encouragement as Pierce wrote her first novel, *The Darkangel,* a fantasy that takes place on the moon. The basic idea for the book, according to Nancy Willard in her review for the *New York Times Book Review,* "came to the writer 'all of a piece' during a long bus ride."

Pierce was inspired by a real-life case she read about in the autobiography by famous psychiatrist Carl Jung. A woman who was one of Jung's patients told him how she had once lived on the moon, where she met a handsome vampire who took her captive. "Jung's account of his patient and her fascinating delusion," Pierce relates in a *Horn Book* article, "served as the germinal model for [the main character] Aeriel and the first two

chapters of *Darkangel.*" Later parts of the tale borrow from the fairy tale "Beauty and the Beast" and the Greek myth "Psyche and Eros." Critics have also noticed how Pierce has—either consciously or unconsciously—borrowed from other stories.

In *The Darkangel,* readers are introduced to the young servant girl Aeriel, who must struggle to destroy the vampire who has kidnapped her mistress and thus helped to prevent evil from taking over her world. Aeriel marries the vampire Irrylath and makes him human by exchanging her heart for his. *A Gathering of Gargoyles* is the second novel in the trilogy, followed by *The Pearl of the Soul of the World.*

Good vs. Evil

Showdowns between good and evil have fascinated Pierce ever since she discovered the "Prince Valiant" comic series. "I just love the whole medieval ethos," the author reveals. "Good and evil has influenced my writing even though I'm not a Christian and don't belong to an organized religion. This sort of spirituality pervades the books whether I want it to or not."

The strength and courage that Aeriel shows in confronting evil has been noted by several reviewers. *Signal Review* contributor Elizabeth Hammill, for one, sees Aeriel as "a brave and resourceful heroine—fascinating because she possesses that fairy-tale compassion for apparently base creatures which enables her to recognize their true nature and, hence, to redeem them." Hammill goes on to say that the book effectively shows an adolescent developing a meaningful adult identity, in terms of her relationships with and effect upon others. Aeriel's courage and persistence, her determination to stand her ground in the face of danger, are a reflection of Pierce's own childhood experiences, as the author writes in a *Horn Book* article. Pierce once had to cope with an alcoholic and abusive relative who one day "had made up his mind to do me violence." But the author refused to be bullied by the relative who, faced with such determination, backed off. It was "a little bit of a revelation—that a lot of human relationships are bluff, and that's an important thing to know," she concludes.

A feature of the "Darkangel" books that critics have particularly noticed is Pierce's use of language. Cameron describes the author's style as "intensely visual, even poetic, in her descriptions and imaginative in her surprising plot turns." Walter Albert also comments in *Fantasy Review* on Pierce's poetic language in *A Gathering of Gargoyles.* Ann A. Flowers notes in her *Horn Book* review of *The Pearl of the Soul of the World,* "The great strength of the story, besides the wraithlike, haunting heroine, is the style, with shimmering, fragile textures and delicate, shadowy descriptions." Some critics have pointed out that Pierce's writing helps make her imaginary world more believable."

"As with *Darkangel,*" Pierce reveals in her *Horn Book* article, "the inception of [*The Woman Who Loved Reindeer*] was sudden, taking place on the last day of either my first or second year of high school. As I stood looking out over the flat, barren, empty playing field, a vivid image came to mind of a woman dressed in doeskin standing stock still, her mouth open, her hands reaching out after a great stag that is carrying away her child. . . . The woman is speechless, but the child is screaming . . . with delight." Pierce later developed this vision into a story by building on the Native American husk-myth in which an animal can cast off its skin to take human form; then she set her tale on an imaginary world.

The Woman Who Loved Reindeer begins by telling how young Caribou, who lives alone after her father's death, is given her sister-in-law's baby. Caribou cares for the newborn—whom she calls Reindeer—taking herbs to cause her milk to flow, even though she feels he is not quite human. She finally realizes he is a trangl—one who can take on the form of an animal or a human. When he grows old enough, Reindeer runs off to join his people—the other reindeer—but occasionally returns as a golden young man and becomes Caribou's lover. He changes from man to deer several times as he helps Caribou lead her people from their homes, which have been rent by earthquakes and eruptions, to a place on the other side of the world beyond the Land of the Broken Snow. Pregnant with Reindeer's child, Caribou now must decide whether or not to follow Reindeer by becoming a trangl herself. "The author," Ruth M. McConnell concludes in her *School Library Journal* review of *The Woman Who Loved Reindeer,* "convincingly and poetically portrays [the characters'] lives and adventures. . . . Her dealings with troll hedgewives and her visit to the Fireking's underground world are wonderfully realized."

"Easily the year's best fantasy."
—*The New York Times*

Cover of **The Darkangel**

Unicorn Trilogy

With *The Birth of the Firebringer* Pierce began a second trilogy that paints an elaborate picture of a world inhabited by unicorns. Jan, a young unicorn, proves his worth to his father, Prince of the Unicorns, and is allowed to accompany the initiates on their pilgrimage to the ancient homeland now inhabited by evil wyverns. Jan sees no vision as the others do in the sacred well and runs away, but as he flees he runs into a wyvern who tries to get him to betray his people. When Jan kills the wyvern, his noble deed results in his being able to see visions concerning his destiny as firebringer of the unicorns.

Pierce's use of language is again praised in reviews of *The Birth of the Firebringer.* For example, one *Kirkus Reviews* contributor writes, "The language here is as elegant as the unicorn people it chronicles. Unicorn rituals and mythology are woven skillfully into the story, strengthening characterization and making the fantasy believable." *School Library Journal* contributor Holly Sanhuber also comments on Pierce's use of language in her review: "The untangling of the satisfying plot and Pierce's ability to foster belief in her unicorns . . .

she has ''a reasonably good time telling little children to quit running on the stairs and helping them look for the shark books.'' But although she enjoys working in the library, she prefers writing, comparing it to ''going to sleep and dreaming a wonderful dream.'' ''To write a novel,'' she concludes in *Horn Book,* ''is to be in love.''

are enhanced by her stately use of language and the sense of their history and culture which she creates and sustains.'' *Dark Moon* is the second work in the trilogy, and *The Son of Summer Stars* concludes the series.

In addition to her writing, Pierce works full-time at her local county library. As she remarks,

Sources for More Information

Books

Children's Literature Review, Volume 20, Gale, 1990.

Sixth Book of Junior Authors and Illustrators, H. W. Wilson, 1989.

St. James Guide to Young Adult Writers, St. James Press, 1999.

Tamora Pierce

**Fantasy novelist
(1954–)**

Born December 13, 1954, in Connellsville, PA; daughter of Wayne Franklin and Jacqueline S. Pierce; married to Tim Liebe. Education: University of Pennsylvania, B.A., 1977.

"When a kid tells you that your books have made a difference in her or his life, you truly have something to be proud of."

As a youngster, Tamora Pierce often turned to books for comfort. She now hopes that young readers will do the same with her works—fantasy novels featuring strong female protagonists. "I enjoy writing for teenagers," Pierce once explained, "because I feel I help to make life easier for kids who are like I was." Pierce told *Twentieth-Century Young Adult Writers* that readers sometimes send her the kind of letters that she might have written as a teenager to the writers who inspired her and helped her to get through rough times; the author said that she finds this particularly rewarding.

Pierce was born December 13, 1954, to Wayne and Jacqueline Pierce, who divorced when she was twelve. Pierce had attended eleven schools by the time she graduated from high school. She sought solace and friendship in books. "Books were my constant friends," she recalled in the *Seventh Book of Junior Authors and Illustrators.* Her father had inspired her to start writing when she was in the sixth grade, but Pierce stopped after four years. She attended the University of Pennsylvania to study psychology, and didn't return to writing until her junior year in college, when she penned a five-page short story.

After selling another story a year later, she enrolled in a fiction writing course. "I owe my career as a writer and my approach to writing to people like my writing mentor, David Bradley (a college fiction writing teacher), who taught me that writing is not an arcane and mystical process, administered by the initiate and fraught with obstacles, but an enjoyable pastime that gives other people as much pleasure as it does me," Pierce said. "I enjoy telling stories, and, although some of my topics are grim, people get caught up in them."

On the advice of Bradley, Pierce began writing a novel. Putting her psychology degree on hold, she tried to get the 732-page work published: *The Song of the Lioness,* about an adventurous young woman named Alanna. During this time, Pierce took a number of "rent-paying" jobs, which included measuring and drawing scales of houses, reviewing martial arts movies for a magazine, reading manuscripts for Silhouette romances, tutoring high school students, and working as a tobacco farm laborer. She eventually moved in with her father and stepmother in Idaho and landed a job as a housemother in a group home for teen girls. In pursuit of her literary career, Pierce then moved to Manhattan, and on the advice of her agent she turned her novel into four books for teenagers.

A turning point in her life came when she worked as a secretary and helped to start a radio comedy and production company while she was rewriting Alanna's story. It was there that she met her husband, Tim Liebe, an actor, video maker, and writer. Working at the radio company also exposed her to an array of talent among the actors, writers, singers, dancers, and artists. It taught her that all creativity "springs from the same place, and that, to keep the mind limber, a wide variety of input, from as many sources as possible, is necessary," as Pierce explained in the *Seventh Book of Junior Authors and Illustrators.*

Secret Identity Revealed

Before Pierce began writing her fantasy works, she studied the ancient cultures and arts that often wind themselves through her imaginative plots for young readers. The first novel in Pierce's "Song of the Lioness" quartet, the 1983 work *Alanna: The First Adventure,* features Alanna, a young woman who disguises herself as a man in order to train as a knight. She then uses her physical strength and her capabilities as a healer to serve Prince Jonathan and engage in numerous medieval adventures.

The book focuses on the character's determination to avoid the traditional fate of young women her age: life in a secluded convent. Instead, she cuts her hair, binds her breasts, and, as "Alan," changes identities with her brother and begins training to become a knight in the service of her country's king. During her grueling education, she becomes close friends with Prince Jonathan, who does not know that his favorite knight-in-training is, in fact, a young woman. Only during a battle in the forbidding Black City does the prince discover Alanna's true gender; on the pair's return to the palace he makes her his squire regardless.

In Pierce's second novel, the highly praised *In the Hand of the Goddess,* Alanna, now a squire, struggles to master the skills she will need to survive her test for knighthood in the Chamber of the Ordeal. She goes to war against a neighboring country and clashes repeatedly with Duke Roger, an urbane and devious man who is determined to usurp the throne from his cousin, Prince Jonathan. Successful in her efforts to protect Jonathan despite the duke's attempts to get rid of her, she eventually decides to leave royal service and journey out into the world in search of further adventures. Barbara Evans, in *Voice of Youth Advocates,* stated that the book "will appeal to a wide range of readers because of the combination of mystical fantasy and science fiction."

In *The Woman Who Rides like a Man,* the third installment of "Song of the Lioness," Alanna is on her own. With her servant Coram Smythesson and Faithful, her cat, she encounters a tribe of desert warriors called the Bazhir. Proving her worth in physical combat, she is accepted by the Bazhir and ultimately becomes their shaman, or wizard. Alanna broadens the outlook of these desert people, raising a few women of the tribe to an equal level with the men before moving on to other adventures. And in the final volume of the quartet, *Lioness Rampant,* the stubborn heroine has become legendary for her skills in battle and for her magical powers; now she goes on a quest for the King of Tortall. Ascending to the Roof of the World after encountering numerous trials and challenges, she attempts to claim the Dominion Jewel, a precious stone said to give its bearer the power to do good. In addition to adventure, she also encounters love in the person of Liam, a warrior known far and wide as the Shang Dragon; however, his dislike of her magical powers makes their relationship a fragile one.

Magic Abounds

Magic and mystics always interested Pierce, who once worked as an instructor in the history of witchcraft at the University of Pennsylvania's Free Woman's University. Pierce's second series, "The Immortals," began in 1992 with the novel *Wild Magic.* Although Alanna makes an appearance in the novel, the new protagonist is a thirteen-year-old orphan named Daine, who has an unexplained empathy with wild creatures and a second sense that allows her to foresee danger. In fact, she is in danger of reverting to a wild creature herself until the wizard Numair teaches her to control and channel her "wild magic." Daine then uses her magical powers to stop evil humans from coercing the newly arrived Immortals—dragons, griffins, spidrens, and Stormwings—to help them accomplish destructive purposes. Called "a dynamic story sure to engross fantasy fans" by Sally Estes in *Booklist, Wild Magic* was praised by Anne A. Flowers, who maintained in her *Horn Book* review that readers will "find in Daine a strong heroine whose humble beginning makes her well-deserved rewards even more gratifying."

Wolf-Speaker continues the adventures of Daine as the fourteen year old and her mentor, the mage Numair, join a wolf pack that is at odds with humans. Men, working for an evil wizard named Tristan, have discovered opals in the wolves' hunting lands in Dunlath Valley. They scramble for the precious gems, polluting the mine and destroying the ecosystem. Hunted by Stormwings controlled by Tristan, Daine and her companions must use all their powers, including shape changing, to stop the impending ecological catastrophe. Bonnie Kunzel stated in her *School Library Journal* review that *Wolf-Speaker* "is a compulsively readable novel that YAs won't be able to put down until the final battle is over and good triumphs. Pierce's faithful readers as well as any action-adventure or animal fantasy fans will be delighted with this new series."

Daine's adventures continue in other "Immortals" novels, which include *The Emperor Mage.* Patricia A. Dollisch in *School Library Journal*

*Cover of **Sandry's Book***

said Pierce "skillfully creates a sense of time and place that enhances the plot and transforms a good read into a page turner." That book was followed by *The Realms of the Gods,* the concluding novel of the series in which Pierce's young female protagonist convinces dragons and other Immortal creatures to fight on her side against the powers of evil. Mary Jo Drungil in *School Library Journal* concluded that fans of Pierce's earlier titles "will appreciate this satisfying conclusion."

Magic also plays an important role in Pierce's fantasy series, "Circle of Magic." In *Sandry's Book,* "a rich and satisfying read," according to a *Kirkus Reviews* critic, Sandry, Daja, Briar, and Trisana—four young people from various walks of life—meet and become friends while living in a temple community. As the four protagonists overcome the negative aspects of their lives, they learn a variety of crafts as well as the use of their unique powers, including magic. The "Circle of Magic" series also includes *Tris's Book, Daja's Book,* and *Briar's Book.*

Pierce has strong feelings about series books. She wrote in an autobiographical sketch that appears on her Web site, "In life we know people over years or even decades. Series books enable writers to get some of that feel to the reader's acquaintance with characters: as in life, we follow their doings over time and through periods where they behave better than during others. Some critics argue that sticking to the same characters over several books is 'safe': it is just about as safe as real life, when people you know change, growing away from you or closer.''

A Tamer Existence

Pierce's personal life is somewhat more mundane than those of the characters she writes about. ''Occasionally I rescue hurt or homeless animals in a local park . . . [I] visit schools as often as I can, and read, read, read,'' Pierce stated. A woman with wide-ranging interests, she focuses her research in specific areas, many of which eventually become incorporated into her fantasy novels for teens. ''I am interested in medieval customs, life, and chivalry,'' she acknowledged. Pierce also studies such diverse topics as Japanese, Central Asian, and Arabic history and culture, wildlife and nature, crime, the American Civil War, the conflicts between Islam and Christianity in the Middle Ages, the Renaissance, martial arts cinema, film writing and production, history of the 1960s and 1970s, and the history of Hungary, Wallachia, and the Ottoman Empire in the 1400s and 1500s.

Pierce lives in Manhattan with her husband, Liebe, their cats and budgies, and ''a floating population of rescued wildlife,'' Pierce said in her Web site. (She also has an online fan club.) ''Having stumbled into writing for teenagers, I've learned that I love it, and I plan to keep doing it. When a kid tells you that your books have made a difference in her or his life, you truly have something to be proud of.''

Sources for More Information

Books

The Encyclopedia of Fantasy, St. Martin's Press, 1997.

Seventh Book of Junior Authors and Illustrators, edited by Sally Holmes Holtze, H. W. Wilson, 1996.

On-line

Tamora Pierce Web site, located at http://www.sff.net/people/Tamora.pierce/.

Christopher Pike

Horror novelist

Young adult novelist Christopher Pike has made a name for himself as a master of mystery and suspense. With over half a million books in print, Pike (who took his name from a character in the *Star Trek* television series) reaches his audience through stories that offer a grisly scare coupled with interesting teen protagonists and themes.

Pike did not set out to write horror novels for young adults; he originally wanted to write adult mystery and science fiction, but had little luck getting his book proposals accepted. By chance, an editor at Avon Books saw some of Pike's work and was impressed enough to suggest that he try his hand at writing a teen thriller. The result was the popular novel *Slumber Party*. Pike wrote two follow-ups to *Slumber Party—Weekend* and *Chain Letter*. By the time *Chain Letter* appeared, word-of-mouth had made all three books best-sellers. In the years since his first thrillers were published, Pike has produced an impressive number of titles whose thrills and chills delight young readers (much to the dismay of conservative parents, who recoil from the graphically violent themes in the books).

Teenagers play a big role in most of Pike's novels. His early books were especially noted for the presence of young female narrators whose observations about people and events were important to each novel's plot line. Pike explained his

"I romanticize a lot about females because they seem more complex, and because in horror novels, it's easier for the girl to seem scared."

893

Cover of **Spellbound**

out of love, and sometimes have difficulty talking to their parents and teachers.

The difference between these young people and most teens lies in how some of the fictional characters choose to solve their more difficult problems. In *Gimme A Kiss,* Jane tries to recover her stolen diary through a complicated plan of revenge that ultimately involves her in a killing. Melanie wins the lead role in a school play only to find herself playing detective after real bullets are placed in a prop gun in *Last Act.* In the *Final Friends* trilogy, the merging of two high schools results in new friendships, rivalries, and the violent death of a shy girl.

In *Monster,* "a brilliant horror story," according to Jonathan Weir in *Books for Keeps,* Mary shoots three teens at a party, claiming they were monsters. Mary's best friend Angela doesn't believe her until the evidence becomes overwhelming, and then Angela decides to take over where Mary left off. Pike has also written adult novels which may appeal to teen readers, such as 1995's *The Cold One.* In this "briskly paced new sci-fi/fantasy/horror endeavor," as a *Kirkus Reviews* critic describes it, a graduate student specializing in near-death experiences comes into contact with an ancient being who sucks the souls out of its victims. Incorporating elements of Eastern philosophy, the work is "visceral and intellectually stimulating at the same time," Tim Sullivan notes in the *Los Angeles Times Book Review.* He adds that "Pike is a modern Lovecraft, a master of creeping dread relentlessly disturbing the reader."

use of female narrators to Kit Alderdice of *Publishers Weekly:* "I romanticize a lot about females because they seem more complex, and because in horror novels, it's easier for the girl to seem scared."

Likes to Frighten

Scaring his audience is a prime motivation for Pike. He grabs his readers with plots that often involve such disparate elements as murder, ghosts, aliens, and the occult. Above all, Pike is savvy about what interests teens, to the point of including current youth trends and concerns in his books. "Pike doesn't talk down to kids; he treats them as individuals," notes Pat MacDonald in *Publishers Weekly.* She adds: "He writes commercial stories that teens really want to read."

Even though the emphasis in his novels is on murder and other ghastly deeds, Pike also presents well-defined characters whose motivations, good and bad, are examined in detail. Most of his characters are high school students whose experiences mirror those of contemporary teens. Pike's characters go to dances, throw parties, fall in and

Graphic Violence

Pike differs from other writers of young adult suspense novels in that the violence in his books is graphically detailed. For some critics, such brutality does more harm than good. Amy Gamerman of the *Wall Street Journal* describes Pike's mysteries as "gorier than most," noting that they are guaranteed to make "Nancy Drew's pageboy flip stand on end." In an article in *Harper's* on the current state of children's literature, Tom Engelhardt claims that Pike's books "might be described as novelizations of horror films that haven't yet been made. In these books of muted torture, adults exist only as distant figures of desertion . . . and junior high psychos reign supreme. . . . No mutilation is too terrible for the human face.''

Pike has also been criticized for his treatment of certain themes, including teen sexuality and life after death. In his defense, Pike offers books such as *Remember Me,* in which a young murder victim tries to prove her death was not a suicide with the help of another teen ''ghost.'' Pike told Gamerman: ''Teenagers are very fascinated by the subject of life after death. I got very beautiful letters from kids who said they were going to kill themselves before they read that book.'' James Hirsch of the *New York Times* sees the popularity of young adult mysteries with more realistic, action-filled plots as reflecting a teen audience that has ''revealed more sophisticated—some say coarse—reading tastes.'' Hirsch comments: ''Topics that were once ignored in . . . mystery books, like adolescent suicide and mental illness, are now fair game. Graphic violence raises few eyebrows, and ghosts have become, well, ghosts.''

Ultimately, Pike writes mysteries because he enjoys the work. His attraction to the young adult genre is partially due to the fact that he finds teenage characters ''extreme,'' more prone to exaggerated actions and reactions. At times, Pike is surprised by the celebrity status his readers have given him. ''A bunch of kids found out where I lived and I had to move,'' he told Gamerman. ''It spread like a rumor where I was. . . . It got weird. I have very intense fans.''

Despite his misgivings about being the object of such attention, Pike continues to turn out new thrillers. ''Pike is probably one of the most original and exciting authors of teenage fiction this decade,'' Weir asserts. ''His writing is flawless, his ideas breathtaking, and there's a mystique about him that's hard to pinpoint. He knows what his readers want and never fails to deliver.'' Pike is ''a terrific read,'' concludes MacDonald, who adds that ''there's not much out there that is. . . . Every book he does has its own identity.''

Sources for More Information

Books

Children's Literature Review, Volume 29, Gale, 1993.

Brad Pitt

**Actor
(1963–)**

"Movies are very complicated. You don't realize what it takes to get a good movie."

Born December 18, 1963, in Shawnee, OK; son of Bill (a trucking company manager) and Jane Pitt. Education: Attended University of Missouri.

An actor from the American heartland, Brad Pitt found superstardom in 1995 with the release of the western epic *Legends of the Fall.* Pitt, who was described in *Rolling Stone* as "a good ol' boy with brains," has parlayed his rugged good looks and natural familiarity with the outdoors into a series of roles that have led critics to call him "the next James Dean." Uncomfortable with the trappings of stardom—and frankly bewildered that anyone would particularly care about the details of his private life—Pitt has become an enigma onscreen and off, heightening his appeal in the process. "Pitt is murderously handsome," declared Johanna Schneller in *Vanity Fair.* "As an object, he's as lovingly photographed as any woman or mountain sunrise. As an actor, he's without artifice. . . . In movies, visual is king. Pitt was born for the movies."

Conventional Upbringing

The oldest of three children of a trucking company executive, Pitt was born in Oklahoma and raised in Springfield, Missouri, in a conventional, religious, and close-knit family. Although he was interested in acting from a young age and was encouraged by his parents—especially his mother—Pitt and his family never imagined he would go to California and become a movie star.

After graduating from Kickapoo High School, Pitt entered the University of Missouri in 1983 and majored in journalism with an emphasis on advertising. He joined the Sigma Chi fraternity and began a rebellion against his strict Baptist upbringing. He told *Rolling Stone,* ''I remember one of the most pivotal moments I've had was when I finally couldn't buy the religion I grew up with. That was a big deal. It was a relief in a way that I didn't have to believe that anymore, but then I felt alone. It was this thing I was dependent on.'' Other interests began to awake in Pitt as his college days drew to a close. Just before he was due to graduate, he packed his car, stuffed a little more than $300 in his pocket, and left for Los Angeles. The decision was exhilarating, a final gesture of freedom from Pitt's Midwestern roots.

Pitt told his parents he planned to attend the Art Center College of Design in Pasadena. He never arrived at that establishment's doorstep. Instead, he took a series of odd jobs and tried to establish himself as an actor. He had no acting experience at the time, so he worked with small theater student groups and studied acting with Roy London. To make ends meet he served as a chauffeur for a strip telegram company, delivered refrigerators to college students, and even dressed up as a chicken outside a fast-food restaurant called El Pollo Loco. ''At the time, it was all exciting,'' Pitt told *Rolling Stone,* ''though I wouldn't want to go back and do it now.''

First ''Audition'' a Fluke

Pitt did not languish in obscurity for long. A friend in his acting class needed a scene partner for an audition for an agent. The agent signed Pitt. The fledgling actor quickly began supporting himself by working as a walk-on in movies and television. His first significant appearance came in the television series *Dallas,* in a role he described in *Rolling Stone* as ''an idiot boyfriend who gets caught in the hay.''

Moving from episodic television to movies, Pitt appeared in several low-budget feature films and a tabloid-style NBC movie of the week called *Too Young to Die?* In that 1990 vehicle Pitt portrayed a drug-addicted pimp who preys on a teenaged runaway (played by Juliette Lewis), beating her and selling her for sex. Salacious as the movie was, it still helped Pitt to land a more important role, that of the cowboy drifter J. D. in the big-budget feature film *Thelma and Louise.*

The then-unknown Pitt was the third choice to play J. D. (from 1989 to 1991 Pitt had appeared in four films, none of which received much critical attention). Pitt won the part after a screen test with Geena Davis, and *Thelma and Louise* was the first major domino to topple in his career. Although he was only in the film for a few scenes, Pitt made an impression as the drifter who seduced Davis's character and then stole her money.

After having established himself with *Thelma and Louise,* Pitt received a number of offers for other film projects. In *Johnny Suede* he played a would-be rock star with a pompadour. In *Kalifornia,* again co-starring Juliette Lewis, he portrayed a low-life killer, and in *Cool World* he was faced with the daunting task of acting opposite animated co-stars. *Cool World* was expected to be a major box-office hit, but it failed to find an audience. Pitt, however, had become a prospect for stardom. His next project found him in the wilds of Montana struggling to become an expert fly fisherman.

River Boosted Career

A River Runs Through It, released in 1993, was an adaptation of Norman Maclean's memoir about his family in Montana. Directed by Robert Redford, the film was an ensemble piece that featured Pitt as Paul Maclean, the younger brother who stubbornly refuses to quit gambling and drinking. Pitt knew that the future of his film career was riding on the work he would do in *A River Runs Through It.* ''I felt a bit of pressure,'' he said in *Rolling Stone.* ''And I thought that it was one of my weakest performances. It's so weird that it ended up being the one that I got the most attention for.''

A River Runs Through It earned praise from critics and performed well at the box office. Even though Pitt had been uneasy on the set, his performance was cited by the film's director and others as one of his best. It was then that Pitt's singular good looks became an issue, drawing the comparisons not only to James Dean but also to Robert Redford. The young actor sidestepped the media glare and concentrated on his next two

major film projects, *Legends of the Fall* and *Interview with the Vampire.*

Although it was filmed after *Legends of the Fall, Interview with the Vampire* was released first, in time for the 1994 Christmas season. If Pitt was uncomfortable with his character in *A River Runs Through It,* he was hardly prepared for the challenge of playing Louis, a vampire who longs to die but cannot. Pitt elaborated on his difficulties in *Vanity Fair:* "[The movie] affected me. It messed with my day. . . . Somewhere in the third or fourth week, you respond to things a little differently, like your character would respond. I don't like it. I can't wait to get my own clothes back on."

It would be Pitt's other project, *Legends of the Fall,* that established him once and for all as a Hollywood leading man. *Legends of the Fall,* based on the novel of the same title by Jim Harrison, follows the destiny of the Ludlow family, especially the wild middle son, Tristan, who goes mad after he is unable to save his younger brother from dying in World War I. While some film critics found the finished movie overly melodramatic—with a far-fetched plot—many other

reviewers praised the story for its old-fashioned Hollywood grandeur.

Superstar Status

With *Legends of the Fall* Pitt found fame at last. *People* magazine named him their annual "Sexiest Man Alive" in 1995. He was not entirely happy about all of the attention, however. Hounded by reporters for details about his private life, he often appeared unwilling to disclose his secrets and unable to discuss his craft. "The truth is, I don't want people to know me," he told *Rolling Stone.* "I don't know a thing about my favorite actors. I don't think you should. Then they become personalities." Nevertheless, breathless female fans who can't seem to get enough of Pitt know he has been involved with a number of women, including Gywenth Paltrow and Jennifer Aniston.

It was just prior to the release of *Seven* and Pitt's follow-up film *12 Monkeys,* that *Entertainment Weekly* writer Pat H. Broeske warned: "We're about to see a less-than-picture-perfect Pitt." Shorn of nearly all his hair, the actor plays a young detective paired with a time-hardened Morgan

Freeman to investigate serial murders based on the Seven Deadly Sins. In director Terry Gilliam's *12 Monkeys,* Pitt, who plays a rich eccentric in the time travel adventure, ''worked hard at making himself as unattractive as possible,'' Gilliam stated.

A Variety of Roles

In 1996, Pitt appeared in director Barry Levinson's *Sleepers,* a story of four boys who suffered abuse at reform school. Fifteen years later two of the friends kill their abuser. Pitt portrays Assistant District Attorney Michael Sullivan, one of the now grown boys, who becomes the prosecutor in the murder case of his two childhood friends. Peter Travers commended Pitt's efforts in *Rolling Stone* noting, ''Pitt and [Jason] Patric offer unflinching glimpses into haunted men.'' In *The Devil's Own,* Pitt worked alongside Harrison Ford, playing Frankie McGuire, an IRA activist. In the *New Republic* Stanley Kauffman wrote, ''Pitt, equipped with a Belfast brogue, gives quite a decent account of himself, now that's he's relieved of the need to be another Brando or James Dean.''

Pitt's next project took him to the Andes region of Argentina where he filmed *Seven Years in Tibet,* the true story of Austrian Heinrich Harrer, a mountain climber who is jailed in a British prison camp in 1939 while climbing in the Himalayas. When he escapes, he finds his way to the city of Lhasa, Tibet, and the palace of the Dalai Lama. Harrer and the 14-year-old spiritual leader form a friendship that ends in 1950 when the Chinese attack Tibet and Harrer returns home. Controversy began swirling around the movie before its release when it was discovered that Harrer belonged to the Nazi party and was an active member of the S.S.

In *Vanity Fair* Pitt addressed the pleasures and pains of his career. ''Movies are very complicated,'' he said. ''You don't realize what it takes to get a good movie. Sitting home in Missouri, I

sure didn't. It's fun for a little while. Then I'm ready to get back into my own boxers.'' Asked if he would make the same choice if he could turn back the clock and return to Springfield, Pitt concluded: ''Oh yeah. Sure. It's been a great ride. A very big ride. I think that's what you're looking for, is something big. It just happens, and the happening is big. Good or bad. Good and bad. Hell yes, I would.''

Sources for More Information

Periodicals

Entertainment Weekly, April 11, 1997.

Interview, November, 1997.

People, May 12, 1997; March 8, 1999.

Premiere, November, 1997.

Rolling Stone, April 3, 1997.

On-line

Mr. Showbiz Web site, located at http://mrshowbiz.go.com.

Films
Thelma and Louise, MGM, 1991
A River Runs Through It, Columbia, 1992
Interview with the Vampire, Warner Bros., 1994
Legends of the Fall, TriStar, 1995
Seven, New Line Cinema, 1995
12 Monkeys, Universal, 1996
The Devil's Own, Columbia, 1997
Seven Years in Tibet, TriStar, 1997

Popular Works

Jackson Pollock

Painter
(1912–1956)

"New needs need new techniques. The modern painter cannot express this age in the old forms of the Renaissance or of any other past culture. Each age finds its own technique."

Born January 28, 1912, in Cody, WY; died in an automobile accident, August 11, 1956, in Southhampton, Long Island, NY; married Elizabeth England, 1931 (marriage ended); married Lee Krasner (a painter), 1945. Education: Studied painting under Thomas Hart Benton and sculpture under Robert Laurens at the Art Students League, New York, 1930–33.

The new technique that became painter Jackson Pollock's signature style necessitated putting his canvases on the floor and dripping, splattering, and throwing paint on them. This radical approach—with which the painter hoped to express his energetic vision—won both enthusiastic admirers and heated detractors. His life was cut short by an automobile accident when he was only forty-four years old, but forty years later his work occupies a storied place in modern painting and has been crucial to the development of a number of subsequent styles.

Paul Jackson Pollock was born on January 28, 1912, in Cody, Wyoming. It is central to many of the myths surrounding Pollock's life that he was born in Wyoming, this somehow connecting him to a romantic vision of cowboys and the frontier. In fact, Pollock's family moved from Wyoming to San Diego, California, when he was just a few months old. Paul Jackson Pollock—known as Paul until he was in high school—was the youngest of Stella May McClure and LeRoy Pollock's five sons. During his childhood the poor but close-knit

900

family moved regularly throughout California and Arizona following the demands of LeRoy Pollock's migrant farm work. Stella Pollock, known as a ''capable woman who kept the family on its course,'' loved art and passed this passion on to her brood; all five sons eventually pursued careers in the arts.

Expelled Twice

Pollock began high school in Riverside, California, but his restless, rebellious nature prevented him from finding much of interest there; he was expelled during his first year thanks to an argument with a military recruiting officer. He attended an arts-oriented high school when the family moved to Los Angeles, where he fell under the sway of an art teacher who introduced him to Eastern mysticism, native American beliefs, and vegetarianism. But Pollock was expelled again, along with two friends, this time for publishing a pamphlet criticizing the school for encouraging and rewarding athletics at the expense of academics; nonetheless, he was readmitted the next year.

By this time two of Pollock's older brothers—who were studying art in New York—had begun sending him enticing clippings and academic news. When they came home for a visit in the summer of 1930, Pollock decided to accompany them on their return. He spent two years at the prestigious Art Students League, mostly studying with Thomas Hart Benton, who had gained a sizable reputation for his ''American realism''—depictions of working people, particularly cowboys. Pollock helped mix paints for Benton and posed for some of his works.

Pollock had yet to definitively decide on a career. He felt that he had some talent, but he was uncertain about his technical abilities and the expressive capacity of his work. Fortunately, Benton recognized Pollock's potential and encouraged him; the two corresponded long after the younger artist had moved on. Benton wrote to Pollock, ''You've the stuff old kid—all you have to do is keep it up.''

The 1930s marked an exciting period in art, despite the crushing economic conditions of the Great Depression. In 1934 and 1935 Pollock was earning ten dollars a week working as a school janitor, sharing his meager salary with one of his brothers. In 1935, however, he was accepted into the Federal Art Project, a government aid program, and was paid about ninety dollars a month to turn in a handful of paintings per year. This income was vital to Pollock's development; it enabled him to take classes, in which he met other young artists.

Experimented with New Techniques

In 1936 he worked in the studio of Mexican artist David Siqueiros, renowned for his mural wall paintings. His workshop was the site of considerable experimentation: budding artists investigated new tools like spray-paint guns and airbrushes, as well as innovations in synthetic paint. This open, exploratory atmosphere stimulated Pollock's imagination. He also found inspiration in frequent road trips across the country, sketching the sprawling landscapes of the West during his travels.

Pollock's work from this era betrays a restless search for his signature style. Many of his canvases echo the dark outlines and strong forms of the Mexican style embodied by Siqueiros and Mexican social realist Diego Rivera. Other paintings employed abstract forms reminiscent of Spanish painter and sculptor Pablo Picasso, whose work Pollock studied with great intensity, as he did the creations of Russian master of the abstract Wassily Kandinsky, to whom he was introduced during his tenure as a custodian at New York City's Museum of Non-Objective Painting (later the Solomon R. Guggenheim Museum). Pollock's work appeared in several government-sponsored shows throughout the country, yet despite the comforts of financial aid and some small success, Pollock suffered emotionally. Beginning in the late 1930s, he underwent treatment for alcoholism and psychological difficulties. Though he sporadically controlled his drinking problem, it is widely believed that alcohol played a role in the auto accident that ended his life.

In 1941 Pollock's work formed part of an important New York gallery exhibit, where it was noticed by another young artist, Lee Krasner. Krasner, after discovering that Pollock lived around

Autumn Rhythm by
Jackson Pollock

the corner from her, sought him out; thus began an artistic partnership that led to marriage and lasted until Pollock's death. Krasner introduced Pollock to other artists and provided him with indispensable psychological support. By 1942 he had begun to define the contours of his mature style: his outsized, vividly colored new canvases were strewn with symbols. Paintings like *Male and Female* and *The Moon-Woman* displayed the swirling energy of shapes and lines that became typical of Pollock's work, as well as his celebrated ''alloverness,'' characterized by a rejection of central focus in favor of spreading designs all over the canvas.

The wealthy and powerful collector-exhibitor Peggy Guggenheim took a singular interest in Pollock's work, sponsoring his first solo exhibit at her gallery in 1943 and three more shows from 1945 to 1947. Pollock's efforts were the object of extravagant praise—and stern disapproval from critics who labeled it ''lavish, explosive, and undisciplined.'' An unanswered question in many reviews pertained to the degree of control this firebrand really exercised in his works.

Pollock had bought a house and barn on Long Island with Krasner, using the barn for his studio and tacking his paintings to the floor instead of working on an easel. ''On the floor I am more at ease,'' he wrote in 1947. ''I feel nearer, more a part of the painting, since . . . I can walk around it, work from the four sides and literally be in the painting.'' At this point Pollock began to lay snaking lines of paint over some of the images in his paintings to veil or hide them. He found in this

technique the key to the next phase of his work; he gave up the ''background'' and began painting only the ''veil'' of squiggling, spattering drips and lines.

Pollock made use of a variety of unusual implements to achieve his desired effects, including hardened brushes, trowels, sticks, and even kitchen staples like basters. He used his wrists, arms, and whole body as he whirled thin streams of paint around the canvas. He would drip one color at a time, waiting until the previous one had dried. He tried out different kinds and thicknesses of paint, including metallics. The surface would become interwoven with colored lines, often seeming to explode with its vibrant hues and untrammeled creative verve.

Pollock improvised his canvases, not bothering with sketches or plans and thus inviting the charge that he merely painted chaos. When an interviewer asked him if he had an image in his mind before he began, Pollock replied, ''Well, not exactly . . . because it hasn't been created, you see. . . . I do have a general notion of what I'm about and what the results will be.'' He used the paint to draw—a revolutionary idea at the time given the standard method of using paint to finalize what had first been drawn—since he found in this an appropriate means for manifesting his emotions. ''When I am *in* my painting,'' he wrote, ''I'm not aware of what I am doing. It is only after a sort of 'get acquainted' period that I see what I have been about . . . because the painting has a life of its own.''

Landmark Development or Child's Play?

Critics in the late 1940s were widely divided about the new form that Pollock was spearheading; it became known as abstract expressionism, or action painting. When Pollock's works appeared in exhibitions, some praised them as a landmark development in modern art, while others derided the pieces as empty and merely decorative. Some critics condemned the canvases as too random and argued that any child could drip paint and get similar results. Yet scores of viewers have found meaning in Pollock's creation of space or lack thereof through the use of his drips and lines and the very texture of paint on the canvas. Most of Pollock's works from this time bear only numbers and dates as titles, as he rapidly abandoned descriptive labels. In the 1950s, though, he did bestow a few evocative names, like *Autumn Rhythm* and *Lavender Mist*.

Pollock continued experimenting with his style into the 1950s, working for a time exclusively in black and white. Later, specific faces, figures, and animals began to appear in his paintings. Toward the mid-1950s Pollock even combined his drip technique with traditional brushwork. Works like *Easter and the Totem* and *Ocean Greyness* garnered praise for their variety and inventiveness and demonstrated the artist's capacity to grow and change. Pollock's work appeared in exhibitions throughout the world and powerfully influenced that of other artists. Helen Frankenthaler developed yet another mode of painting, the soak-stain technique, after seeing, and being amazed by, Pollock at work in his studio.

A crash on a curving Long Island road brought an end to this promising career, killing him on August 11, 1956, in the Long Island town of Southampton. A few months before his death, a large show of Pollock's works had opened at an important New York gallery. He had created,

according to one critic, "the most original art among the painters of his generation." Indeed, he would cast a prominent shadow over the artists who followed him. "There was a reviewer a while back who wrote that my pictures didn't have any beginning or any end," Pollock once told a writer for the *New Yorker*. "He didn't mean it as a compliment, but it was . . . a fine compliment." Even four decades after Pollock's death, the story begun by his work goes on.

Sources for More Information

Books

Naifeh, Steven W., *Jackson Pollock: An American Saga,* HarperPerennial, 1991.

Pollock, Jackson, *Pollock,* Hamlyn, 1971.

Soloman, Deborah, *Jackson Pollock: A Biography,* Simon and Schuster, 1987.

Venezia, Mike, *Jackson Pollock,* Children's Press, 1992.

Masterworks

Male and Female, 1942

Composition with Pouring II, 1943

Totem Lesson 1, 1944

Eyes in the Heat, 1946

Number 13A, 1948: Arabesque, 1948

Lavender Mist: Number 1, 1950, 1950

Autumn Rhythm, Number 30, 1950, 1950

Blue Poles: Number 11, 1952, 1952

Easter and the Totem, 1953

Chaim Potok

**Novelist
(1929–)**

"When you write about one person or set of people, if you dig deeply enough, you will ultimately uncover basic humanity."

Born Herman Harold Potok; Hebrew given name, Chaim (pronounced "Hah-yim") Tzvi, February 17, 1929; son of Benjamin Max (a businessman) and Mollie (Friedman) Potok; married Adena Sara Mosevitzky (a psychiatric social worker), June 8, 1958; children: Rena, Naama, Akiva. Education: Yeshiva University, B.A., (summa cum laude), 1950; Jewish Theological Seminary, ordination, M.H.L., 1954; University of Pennsylvania, Ph.D., 1965.

Ordained rabbi Chaim Potok never saw himself in a traditional religious role. He has worked as a writer, rabbi, and professor, often concerning himself with Orthodox and Hasidic Jews and how they merge their beliefs with twentieth-century life. Robert J. Milch wrote in the *Saturday Review:* "Judaism [is] at the center of all [Potok's] works. . . . [It motivates] his characters and provid[es] the basis for their way of looking at themselves, each other, and the world." Potok has often used his rabbinical training to invent a believable world often populated by highly educated Jewish leaders and students. Above all, the writer's "primary concern is the spiritual and intellectual growth of his characters—how and what they come to believe," observed Hugh Nissenson in the *New York Times Book Review.*

Because of his Jewish heritage, Potok is frequently called an American Jewish writer. Although he understands the need for such labels, he prefers to be described as "an American writer writing about a small and particular American

904

world,'' he says in an essay in *Studies in American Jewish Literature.* His vision has enthralled readers of all kinds, due in part, according to *New York Times Book Review* contributor Hugh Nissenson, to Potok's ''talent for evoking the physical details of this world: the tree-lined streets, the apartment filled with books, the cold radiators, the steaming glasses of coffee.'' Potok, however, attributes the success of his novels to the universality of his subject matter. Quoting James Joyce, he explains to Millie Ball in the *Times Picayune:* '''In the particular is contained the universal.' When you write about one person or set of people, if you dig deeply enough, you will ultimately uncover basic humanity.''

Raised in an Orthodox Jewish family, Potok was drawn to the less restrictive doctrine of Conservative Judaism as a young adult and was eventually ordained a Conservative rabbi. While his Judaic background has provided him with a wealth of material for his novels, it was and continues to be a source of conflict as well. Potok's interest in writing and literature, sparked by Evelyn Waugh's *Brideshead Revisited* and James Joyce's *A Portrait of the Artist as a Young Man,* was opposed by both his family and teachers. His mother, for example, when told of his aspiration to write, remarked, '''You want to be a writer? Fine. You be a brain surgeon, on the side [you'll write stories],''' Potok recalls to *Fort Lauderdale News* writer Linda Sherbert. The teachers at his Jewish parochial school responded similarly, disappointed that Potok would want to take time away from studying the Talmud to read and write fiction. Potok commented: ''Scholarship—especially Talmudic scholarship—is the measure of an individual. Fiction, even serious fiction—as far as the religious Jewish tradition is concerned—is at best a frivolity, at worst a menace.'' This conflict between religious and secular commitments is a recurring theme in Potok's novels.

The Chosen

In 1965 Potok completed his best-selling novel, *The Chosen.* The book explores the conflict between the world of the Hasidim and that of Orthodox Jews. Potok portrays Danny Saunders, a young man torn between fulfilling the expectations of his rabbi father and satisfying his own need for secular knowledge. The Saunders belong to the Jewish sect called Hasidim, whose members

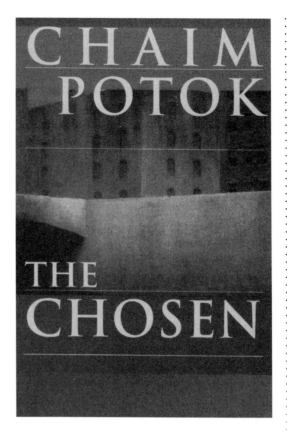

*Cover of **The Chosen***

are ''known for their mystical interpretation of Judaic sources and intense devotion to their spiritual leaders,'' according to S. Lillian Kremer in the *Dictionary of Literary Biography.* When Danny becomes an adult, he is expected to take on his father's role as tzaddik, which Nissenson describes as ''a teacher, spiritual adviser, mediator between his community of followers and God, and living sacrifice who takes the suffering of his people—of all Israel—upon himself.'' To strengthen Danny's soul and thus prepare him ''to assume the burdens of his followers,'' writes Kremer, Rabbi Saunders has raised Danny according to unusual Hasidic tradition which dictates that under certain circumstances a father and son should speak only when discussing religious texts.

In direct contrast to the Saunders are the Malters: Reuven, who becomes Danny's close friend, and Reuven's father, who tutors Danny in secular subjects. As Orthodox Jews, the Malters ''emphasize a rational, intellectual approach to Judaic law and theology,'' explains Kremer. Reuven's father recognizes the importance of Judaic scholarship, but he, unlike Rabbi Saunders, encourages his son to study secular subjects as well. Furthermore, Malter has built his relationship with Reuven on mutual love and respect, not suffering.

Though Danny's problems with his father are crucial to the narrative, *The Chosen* is more than a story of parental and religious conflict, according to Karl Shapiro, who writes in *Book Week—World Journal Tribune:* "The argument of the book concerns the level of survival of Judaism, whether it shall remain clothed in superstition and mysticism, or whether it shall convey the message of humanitarianism, with the secular Jew as the prophet of gentleness and understanding."

One of Potok's strong points in fashioning *The Chosen* is his explanation of Talmudic scholarship. "The elder Malter, patterned after the novelist's beloved father-in-law . . . is the idealized Jewish teacher," wrote Kremer. "Just as he fuses the best in Judaic scholarship with the best in secular culture, Reuven combines intellectual excellence in sacred and secular studies."

The Promise and My Name is Asher Lev

In 1969, the author completed *The Promise,* a sequel to *The Chosen.* Reuven prepares to become a rabbi, but butts heads with apostate scholar Abraham Gordon. Simultaneously Danny—now a student of clinical psychology—treats young Michael Gordon, the scholar's disturbed son. The family achieves unity, however, through Danny Saunders's betrothal and marriage to Rachel Gordon, his young patient's sister. The book's theme, said Kremer, focuses on how "each character defines himself, understands himself, and celebrates himself as a twentieth-century Jew." In the *New York Times Book Review,* Nissenson lauded the novel by writing that "despite an occasional technical lapse, Potok has demonstrated his ability to deal with a more complex conception and to suffuse it with pertinence and vitality."

My Name Is Asher Lev concerns a Hasidic artist. As in his earlier books, Potok relates Asher's experiences in the first-person. Asher's story is "the mature artist's retrospective portrait of his childhood [and] a reexamination of his attitudes," wrote Kremer. Asher's parents dislike his interest in art, often scolding him for his apathy to Biblical scholarship. Asher often dreams of his deceased grandfather, a noted scholar. In the dreams, his grandfather condemns Asher for his devotion to art. Some members of the Hasidic community even consider Asher's gifts demonic, but the Rebbe—who leads the community and also employs Asher's father—unexpectedly champions the boy.

Asher's goal is "how to develop his aesthetic sense through painting," observed Abramson. Like Danny Saunders, Asher is born into the role of heir-apparent. In the latter case, Asher's future position entails working as an international emissary for the Rebbe. The tumult over Asher's studies increases when he begins to paint nudes and crucifixions. Although Asher sees the cross as a non-religious symbol, his father sees it as a figure for anti–Semitism. The crisis comes to a head in Asher's painting called the "Brooklyn Crucifixion." Eventually, Asher must choose between his community and his painting.

In the Beginning and More

During 1973, Potok left the United States with his family to live in Jerusalem. In 1975, he published his next work entitled *In the Beginning.* As with many of his other novels, *In the Beginning* deals with anti-Semitism. "Rarely has the rage of the Jew been so honestly portrayed," remarked Nissenson, who added that "by the power of his own intellect [Potok comes] to grips with the theme implicit in all of his previous work: the problem of sustaining religious faith in a meaningless world. . . . It successfully recreates a time and a place and the journey of a soul." The author goes beyond America's dislike of the Jews and looks at its historical precedence.

The author symbolizes theme through the relationship between David Lurie, a Jewish boy, and Eddie Kulanski, a Gentile. Other main themes in the work revolve around Biblical scholarship and the State of Israel. "The narrator here is a brilliantly gifted Orthodox Jewish boy who eventually accommodates himself to modern life," explained Nissenson. Through David, Potok uses stream-of-consciousness to depict the tragedies endured by the Jews in Europe. When David hears of the losses sustained by Jews during World War II, he enters a dreamland where an imaginary hero fights Nazi oppressors. David deeply loves the Torah, and sees it as a symbol of hope for all Jews. He alienates his family, however, when he adopts the shocking belief that using Gentile scholarship will bridge the gulf separating Jew and Gentile.

Davita's Harp and a Sequel

Much of the impetus for the novelist's sixth work of fiction, *Davita's Harp,* was an experience of sexism his wife suffered while in her teens. The novel takes place in Depression-era New York. Both of Davita's parents—her WASP newspaperman father and Jewish mother—have abandoned religious beliefs for Communism. Seeking security, the girl explores Judaism and attends a yeshiva. Once there, Davita discovers a prejudice against female scholars; when she makes top marks, the young girl is denied the highly coveted school award because she is female. "Davita's commitment to patriarchal Judaism is deeply shaken at her graduation," explains Patty Campbell in the *Wilson Library Bulletin.* The school gives the Akiva award "to a boy to save the school the public shame of a girl as best student."

As a sequel to *My Name Is Asher Lev,* Potok wrote *The Gift of Asher Lev.* The author picks up the narrative many years after the first book. Lev has left New York and the Hasidic world to live with his family on the Cote d'Azur. A funeral brings the Lev family back to Asher's old home. Matters become complicated when Lev's wife and son prefer the tight-knit Hasidic community to life on the Mediterranean. In the end, Lev's father resolves the conflict. As the elderly Rebbe's successor, Lev's father turns his attention to Asher's son, Avrumel. The older man decides that Avrumel shall take his father's place and continue the dynasty. The sad conclusion is that "the price of Lev's restoration to his people is his physical and personal exclusion. Much as Christ was a sacrificed 'missing generation' between God and mankind, Lev's self-sacrificing art is a personal crucifixion. . . . [it also guarantees] that the tradition

The Chosen, Simon & Schuster, 1967

The Promise, Knopf, 1969

My Name Is Asher Lev, Knopf, 1972

In the Beginning, Knopf, 1975

The Gift of Asher Lev, Knopf, 1990

will pass on," described Brian Morton in the *Times Literary Supplement.*

Overall, Potok sees his mission as one that brings meaning to a nonsensical world. He once commented that doing this "specifically . . . is the task of the artist." In his interview with Rothstein, Potok clarified, "You deal with a small and particular world. . . . You dig into that world with as much honesty as you can, and if you do it honestly and skillfully enough, somehow you're going to bridge the gap."

Sources for More Information

Books

Abramson, Edward A., *Chaim Potok,* Twayne, 1986.

Contemporary Literary Criticism, Gale, Volume 2, 1974, Volume 7, 1977, Volume 14, 1980, Volume 26, 1983.

Dictionary of Literary Biography, Gale, Volume 152: *American Novelists since World War II, Fourth Series,* 1995.

Elvis Presley

Singer, songwriter, guitarist, and actor (1935-1977)

". . . a complex figure of American myth: as improbably successful as a Horatio Alger hero, as endearing as Mickey Mouse, as tragically self-destructive as Marilyn Monroe."

—Newsweek

Born January 8, 1935, in Tupelo, MS; died August 16, 1977, in Memphis, TN; son of Vernon Elvis and Gladys Presley; married Priscilla Beaulieu, 1967 (divorced, 1973); children: Lisa Marie.

Admired as one of the most successful recording artists of all time, American singer and guitarist Elvis Presley exploded onto the rock music scene in the mid-1950s. With a sound rooted in rockabilly and rhythm-and-blues, a daringly sexual performing style, and a magnetic charm, Presley became an idol for an entire generation of music enthusiasts. Adoring fans remember him as The Father of Rock 'n' Roll, The King, and Elvis the Pelvis, and he is widely credited with introducing a new era in popular culture. Writing for *Newsweek,* Jim Miller reported that Presley himself has become "a complex figure of American myth: as improbably successful as a Horatio Alger hero, as endearing as Mickey Mouse, as tragically self-destructive as Marilyn Monroe."

Indeed, neither critics nor biographers can find much in the Mississippi-born star's background to presage his rise to fame. The boy spent his earliest years in his hometown of Tupelo, where he and his family shared a two-room house, and as a teen he lived in Memphis, Tennessee, where his family relocated when he was in the eighth grade. Shortly after finishing high school in 1953, the future star began driving a delivery truck

908

for the Crown Electric Company. He fooled around with the guitar in his free time.

Sam Phillips and Sun Records

The year he graduated, however, the young hopeful also made an amateur recording at the Memphis Recording Studio. He followed it with a second in 1954 and captured the attention of Sam Phillips at Sun Records. As a result, Presley created the now-legendary Sun recordings, hailed by many as among his finest. With a musical career in the offing, the future star quit his truck-driving job in 1954 and began performing professionally, mostly in rural areas where he was billed as The Hillbilly Cat. He also saw his first Sun recording, "That's All Right Mama," rise to number three on the Memphis country-and-western charts. Thus, despite some disappointments, including discouraging words from the Grand Ole Opry and rejection by New York City's Arthur Godfrey Talent Scouts, Presley persisted. By the end of 1955, after making a six-state Southern tour with Hank Snow's Jamboree that piqued considerable interest, the up-and-comer had negotiated the agreement with RCA that would bring him stardom.

Presley's first RCA single, "Heartbreak Hotel" (co-written by Presley, Tommy Durden, and Mae Boren Axton, mother of country star Hoyt Axton), was wildly successful and became his first Gold Record. "From the opening notes of the song," opined Miller in another *Newsweek* review, "the air is electric." The air remained electric as the singer scored hit after hit with such tunes as "Don't Be Cruel," "Hound Dog," "Blue Suede Shoes," and "Love Me Tender." His sound, which evolved from his roots in the deep South and combined elements of country-and-western, rhythm-and-blues, and gospel, was new, and it was instantly popular. Though not the inventor of rock and roll, Presley, reflected John Rockwell in the *New York Times,* "defined the style and gave it an indelible image."

Drives Crowds Wild

Voice alone did not comprise the star's appeal. He was also a remarkable showman. Advised by Colonel Tom Parker, whom he signed as his manager early in 1956, Presley began making

films, appearing on television, and otherwise keeping himself in the public eye. Though reportedly shy and disinclined to be interviewed, the upstart musician gave performances that drove audiences mad. His captivating smile, coupled with the pelvic "bump-and-grind" rhythm that earned him the appellation Elvis the Pelvis, projected an exciting sexuality that was unprecedented in the music world. He prompted moral outrage from the older generation and hero worship from the younger to become, in Rockwell's words, an entertainer "parents abhorred, young women adored and young men instantly imitated."

Presley was already a legend by the time he was drafted into the U.S. Army in 1958, and during his two-year hitch, most of it spent in West Germany, his recordings continued to sell well. But by the time he returned from his tour of duty, the music climate in the United States had changed. There was a notable downturn in his career, and The King of Rock and Roll devoted most of the 1960s to making movies that were entertaining but undistinguished. In 1968 the rocker staged a successful, if short-lived, comeback, and during the seventies he concentrated on playing nightclubs.

Self-destructive Life Takes Its Toll

At approximately 2:30 p.m. on August 16, 1977, Presley's body was found in the bathroom at Graceland, his Memphis, Tennessee, home.

Elvis Presley in concert

Although the medical examiner reported that Presley died of heart failure, rumors of the star's amphetamine use flourished. For a number of years prior to his death, in fact, Presley looked as if he had passed his prime. Apparently, though neither a drinker nor a smoker, The King was known as a junk-food addict (reputed to favor fried peanut butter and banana sandwiches) and had gained considerable weight. He also had a history of mild hypertension. As Miller summed it up, Presley, formerly "an icon of glowing youth . . . died tallow-faced and tubby, the victim of too many Dreamsicles and Nutty Buddies, too much Dexedrine, Dilaudid, Demerol, Quaalude, [and] Percodan."

Despite the circumstances, The King continued to grow in stature after his death. Indeed, in a piece for the *Saturday Evening Post,* Jay Stuller even suggested that death "lent [him] a tragic aura." Whatever the reasons, grief-stricken fans remained fiercely devoted and scrambled to preserve their idol's memory. In the process, they spawned an entire industry. More than ten years later, memorabilia abounds and hundreds of new products pay tribute to the Presley legend—everything from slippers and shampoo to porcelain dolls and grandfather clocks. There are some two hundred-odd active Elvis fan clubs, the city of Memphis hosts an annual Elvis Week, and at one time a bill was put before the U.S. Congress that advocated making the recording giant's birthday a national holiday.

The King's achievement has yet to be duplicated. He racked up more than one hundred Top Forty hits as well as more than forty Gold Records, and sales of his recordings exceed one billion copies. He also influenced an entire generation of rock musicians, including Bob Dylan, John Lennon, and Bruce Springsteen. Trying to unravel the mystique, Stuller quoted Graceland Enterprises marketing director, Ken Brixey: ''I guess the best answer is that he was a blue-collar worker who in spirit never tried to rise above his roots. He's the epitome of a man who started out with nothing, became something and never lost his attraction to the masses. He's a true folk hero.''

Sources for More Information

Books

Escott, Colin, and Martin Hawkins, *Catalyst: The Sun Records Story,* Aquarius Books, 1975.

Guralnik, Peter, *Last Train to Memphis: The Rise of Elvis Presley,* Little, Brown, 1994.

Guralnik, Peter, *Careless Love: The Unmaking of Elvis Presley,* Little, Brown, 1999.

Hopkins, Jerry, *Elvis: A Biography,* Warner Books, 1971.

Hopkins, Jerry, *Elvis: The Final Years,* Playboy Publishers, 1981.

Marcus, Greil, *Mystery Train: Images of America in Rock 'N' Roll,* Dutton, 1976.

Marsh, Dave, *Elvis* (photo essay), Rolling Stone Press, 1982.

Presley, Priscilla Beaulieu, with Sandra Harmon, *Elvis and Me,* Putnam's, 1985.

On-line

The *Rolling Stone* Network, located at http://www.rollingstone.com.

Prince

Singer, songwriter, guitarist, arranger, and producer (1958-)

"Can you imagine what I would do if I could do all I can?"

Born Prince Rogers Nelson, June 7, 1958, in Minneapolis, MN; son of John Nelson (a jazz pianist) and Mattie Shaw (a singer); married Mayte Garcia (a dancer); children: one son (deceased).

Pop stars frequently alter their names, but rarely has a change of moniker caused a stir like the one motivated by the artist formerly known as Prince. After signing a lucrative record deal in 1993, the enigmatic multi-instrumentalist bandleader and singer-songwriter announced his retirement and changed his name to an unpronounceable symbol. It later became clear that this "retirement" applied only to the now-defunct Prince and not to the artist reborn as the symbol.

While he was Prince, of course, he was one of the most consistent hitmakers in contemporary music, fusing soul, funk, rock, and power pop into a distinctive, exuberant brew; his unflinchingly erotic (and often simply raunchy) lyrics managed a kind of sacredness, thanks to his apparent sincerity. He displayed an astounding versatility, both in the studio—playing some two dozen instruments, multitracking vocals, and arranging music for his bands—and onstage, where he would participate in elaborate choreography even while peeling off pyrotechnic guitar solos.

As *Guitar Player*'s Chris Gill commented, "Few artists of his stature are as talented in one area as Prince is in many." In his post-Prince existence the symbol-artist quickly embarked on a series of ventures—including a new independent record label (replacing Prince's defunct old one), a musical based on an ancient Greek text, a retail clothing outlet, and an interactive CD-ROM program—and promised that his new music would make the old pale by comparison.

Midwestern Roots

The artist was born Prince Rogers Nelson in Minneapolis, Minnesota, and was named for the Prince Rogers Trio, a jazz group fronted by his father, John Nelson. His mother, Mattie, occasionally sang with the combo, but the Nelsons ultimately found less harmony in their marriage than in the music and went their separate ways. Young Prince's relationship with Mattie's second husband, Hayward Baker, was difficult, but Baker unwittingly helped set his stepson's musical career in motion by taking him to a concert by singer-bandleader and "Godfather of Soul" James Brown. Prince was only ten years old, but Brown's electrifying stew of funk, soul, and energetic showmanship seared itself onto his imagination, as would the fiery guitar of Jimi Hendrix, the communal dance-uplift of Sly & the Family Stone, and the otherworldly funk of George Clinton's Parliament-Funkadelic in the coming years.

By age 12, Prince had begun teaching himself to play the guitar Nelson had given him, but the rockiness of his home life meant that he rarely had a firm address; he stayed with Nelson and with the family of his friend Andre Anderson. The Anderson clan eventually adopted him. Prince would soon master the drums, bass, piano, and saxophone. At age 14 he was the guitarist for Grand Central, a junior-high cover band begun by his cousin, drummer Charles Smith, and featuring Andre (who would later change his last name to Cymone) and Andre's sister Linda on bass and keyboards, respectively.

The following year, the group changed its name to Champagne and underwent various personnel changes; the new lineup included future stars Morris Day and Jimmy Jam—later of the funk band the Time—and Prince took over leadership duties. After various other musical endeavors, he recorded a demo—on which the 16-year-old played all the instruments and sang—that led to a recording contract with Warner Bros.

Megastardom

By 1978 Prince had released his debut, *For You,* which featured the single "Soft and Wet." Working with his band the Revolution, Prince developed his trademark mix of funk workouts, soul balladry, and metallic guitar wailing—overlaid with his silky falsetto vocals—on the subsequent efforts *Prince, Dirty Mind,* and *Controversy.* But he made his first huge splash with *1999,* an ambitious double-length recording that exploded thanks to the apocalyptic dance music of the title track and the crossover sensation "Little Red Corvette." The album remained on the charts for two years, by which time the film and album *Purple Rain* had established Prince as one of pop's megastars.

Though the movie *Purple Rain*—conceived by and starring Prince—was poorly reviewed, it earned nearly ten times what it cost to make. The soundtrack, meanwhile, was a sensation, and featured both his most daring and his most commercially successful work to date. Featuring the enigmatic single "When Doves Cry"—"His shining hour, in terms of a commercially viable artistic statement," according to *Down Beat*—as well as the barnburning "Let's Go Crazy" and the shimmering balladry of the title song, the collection earned Prince an Academy Award for best original song score. It eventually reached the 9 million mark in U.S. sales.

Rhythm and blues siren Chaka Khan scored a huge hit covering Prince's early song "I Feel for You," and several years later Sinead O'Connor sang a smash rendition of his "Nothing Compares 2 U." Yet Prince's artistic restlessness meant that he rarely attempted to emulate past successes, even multiplatinum ones. Thus, the artist recorded the baroque pop and winsome psychedelia of *Around the World in a Day*—with its playful hit "Raspberry Beret"—and the funkified *Parade,* which served as the soundtrack to the coolly received film *Under the Cherry Moon.*

But it was 1987's *Sign O' the Times* that suggested another milestone in Prince's varied career. Once again cramming a panoply of song styles into a double disc, Prince performed a duet with Scottish diva Sheena Easton on the hit "U Got the Look" and scored again with the single "I Could Never Take the Place of Your Man." Though he pulled his now-legendary *Black Album* from circulation because of its allegedly evil qualities—thus making it a sensationally lucrative item

Prince in concert

for bootleggers who got hold of advance copies—he charted again with *Lovesexy* in 1988.

Prince's various proteges—including Apollonia and Vanity—fared poorly on his new record label/production complex, Paisley Park, which opened its doors in 1987. He himself hit what many regard as a fallow period in the next few years. His suite of songs for Tim Burton's film *Batman* sold well but suggested something of a creative letdown to critics, while 1990's *Graffiti Bridge* was a sprawling record that lacked the focus of his mid-1980s work. But he assembled a stellar backup group that he called the New Power Generation and showed them off to fine effect on the 1991 collection *Diamonds and Pearls*.

The Artist Formerly Known As . . .

The following year saw the release of an album bearing only a symbol as its title. The glyph appeared to be a combination of the symbols for male and female, with a hornlike flourish running through the middle. Though the album featured the song "My Name Is Prince," it wasn't long before the unpronounceable symbol became the artist's new moniker. Warner Bros. announced the dissolution of Paisley Park, while the former Prince announced his retirement from music, a proclamation met with some skepticism at his record label and elsewhere; Prince had promised to retire from performing in 1985 for a period of years, only to begin a tour a few months afterward.

In 1993 Prince released his long-awaited greatest hits package, a three-CD set that included favorites from all his albums and a number of B-sides and rarities. Next came what the *Los Angeles Times* called a "musically satisfying but lyrically uneven collection," *Come*. Meanwhile, "The Artist Formerly Known as Prince," or TAFKAP, as he came to be known among bewildered music writers, declared that his new music would surpass all of Prince's output. As if to prove the point, "The Most Beautiful Girl in the World," his first single as the symbol—released on NPG/Bellmark—hit the Number Three position on the U.S. charts.

As Alan Leeds noted in the liner notes to the Prince *Hits* collection, "Prince raced with the times and usually won." Leeds suggested that music historians might someday regard the artist's tenure under his former name as they have the early work of jazz greats Duke Ellington and Miles Davis—as a prelude to greater innovation. "He's 15 years into his career, a time when most stars are kicking back, going through the motions," noted Light. "But he is still rethinking the rules of performance, the idea of how music is released, the basic concepts about how we consume and listen to music, still challenging himself and his audience like an avant-garde artist, not a platinum-selling pop star."

The artist finally released *The Black Album*, recorded around 1987, in 1994, but made it available only for a limited time—two months—amid speculation that it was released by Warner Bros. Records against his wishes. *Time*'s David Thigpen remarked after hearing the long-shrouded album's contents that Prince had "anticipated the decidedly unlovesexy anger and violence in the gangster rap of the 1990s," and added, "In [1987], listeners probably wouldn't have known what to make of its bitter outlook; today it is almost conventional."

New Label, New Life

In the mid-1990s, Prince, now simply called the Artist, found his career shrouded by his unhappy relationship with Warner Bros. The relationship became so strained that the Artist began drawing the word "slave" on his face, and there was some speculation that the poor showing of the 1996 album *Chaos and Disorder* did not offer his best work. The end of his 18-year contract with Warner Bros. inspired the title of his next album, *Emancipation*. The three-disc set, which contains

36 tracks and runs exactly three hours, was greeted by strong reviews. Amy Lindon declared in *People* that although the "album from one of pop's most creative forces breaks no new ground, it is an exhilarating, melodically rich tour de force."

The period surrounding the release of *Emancipation* were pleasant times for the Artist. Besides relishing his new freedom to produce his own music, he became a husband and father. In *Time* the Artist told Christopher John Farley, "My writing has changed immensely. Getting married has really got me focused. Songs come to me a lot easier. This album—I could see the whole thing done in my head. The common thread is love—even the angry songs I tried to resolve positively."

In 1997 the Artist broke new ground again by offering his next album, a four-CD set, first over the Internet. Once again, the Artist embraced a wide range of musical genres, including hip hop, punk, R&B, and even folk. In his *Entertainment Weekly* review, Matt Diehl noted, "While *Crystal Ball* lacks polish, it makes up the difference by offering an astonishing view into the Artist's breadth. . ., capturing sides of him never before exposed."

While much of the entertainment press covered his unorthodox career moves with a combination of cynical gossip and dread, the artist formerly known as Prince simply—and, it seems, fearlessly—went his own way. "[Former pro athlete] Bo Jackson can play baseball and football," he once noted to Light. "Can you imagine what I would do if I could do all I can?"

Sources for More Information

Periodicals

Ebony, January, 1997.

Jet, May, 1997.

Rolling Stone, November 28, 1996.

Time, November 25, 1996.

On-line

Love 4 One Another Web site, located at http://www.love4oneanother.com.

Public Enemy

Rap group

Group formed in 1986. Members include Carlton Ridenhour (Chuck D), William Drayton (Flavor Flav), Norman Rogers (DJ Terminator X), Richard Griffin (Professor Griff), Bill Stephney, Hank Shocklee, Keith Shocklee, Carl Ryder, Eric Sadler, and Sister Souljah. Most members born in Long Island, NY, and educated at Adelphi University.

P ublic Enemy is the vanguard group of the rap/hip-hop world. Both the sound they create and the message they deliver are uniquely intense. These "prophets of rage," as they call themselves, make music that is unquestionably arresting, danceable, and entertaining. At the same time, they constantly exhort the young black men and women in their audience to be proud, to be aware of their culture, to fight the forces of oppression, and to take responsibility for themselves and their race. The group's phenomenal success was summed up by a *New Statesman and Society* contributor who wrote, "Public Enemy have interlocked noise, rage, hype, glamour, and the raising of a new African-American political consciousness more effectively than anyone in the history of popular music."

The band that seems so politically driven began in a casual, party atmosphere at Adelphi University on Long Island—home turf to most of the members. Lead rapper Chuck D was the nucleus around which Public Enemy took shape. He started out at Adelphi as Carlton Ridenhour, a

"When people are asleep, you have to take drastic means to wake them up."

—Hank Shocklee

graphics arts major and the author of *College Madness,* the first comic strip by a black student to appear in the college newspaper *The Delphian.* When Ridenhour began working at WBAU, Adelphi's influential radio station, he adopted the name Chuckie D and began playing the latest rap and hip hop music long before it was anywhere near mainstream airwaves.

In fact, so little of this music was being released that Chuckie D found he was unable to put together a whole show without playing some records twice. In response to that situation, he began contributing his own raps over pre-recorded rhythm tracks. He told Scott Poulson-Bryant in *Spin* magazine that he wasn't political at first, but that as time went on and his confidence increased, "I would say things on the radio and in my raps about the community. As I saw it, I was just being a responsible adult."

A Band of Deejays

Ridenhour didn't guess that the foundations of Public Enemy were being laid when Hank Shocklee, a deejay friend, asked him to emcee a few parties. Their collaboration was so successful that they soon formed a deejay collective known as Spectrum. Other members included rapper William Drayton ("Flavor Flav"), Hank Shocklee's brother Keith, Carl Ryder, Eric Sadler, and Norman Rogers ("DJ Terminator X"). They played countless parties around Long Island, publicizing the events with posters designed by Ridenhour. In 1983 Spectrum took over WBAU's Saturday night airwaves with the Super Spectrum Mixx Show, and they also hosted a local video show, *WORD* (World of Rock and Dance).

Bill Stephney was a peripheral member of Spectrum who had become a record company executive after graduating from Adelphi. He believed that the group could be transformed into a record company's dream—"a combination of Run-D.M.C. and The Clash. Funky beats paired with polemics," he told Poulson-Bryant. He reported the group's potential to entrepreneur Rick Rubin, who had done much to widen rap's popularity by launching the careers of Run-D.M.C. and LL Cool J.

Rubin was convinced after "Public Enemy Number One," a Spectrum creation, became WBAU's most requested song. Chuckie D and the others avoided Rubin's overtures, however, believing that rap artists were targets for victimization by record companies. But Rubin's persistence, coupled with Stephney's reassurances, finally won out. In 1986 Flavor Flav, DJ Terminator X, and Chuckie D (now "Chuck D") signed a contract with Def Jam, Columbia Records' newly created rap division.

Music with a Message

From the first, Public Enemy sought to grab the attention of disenfranchised young blacks and send them a series of pointed messages. Their first album, *Yo! Bum Rush the Show,* attacked the mindless materialism that they saw as the hallmark of the mid-1980s. Their second album, *It Takes a Nation of Millions to Hold Us Back,* was "hittin' hard to make people understand how corrupt the white system is," Chuck D told Poulson-Bryant. And *Fear of a Black Planet* "was about the problems white people have with themselves," while their fourth, *Apocalypse '91: The Enemy Strikes Black* "is the one where we deal with the problems we've got with ourselves. Black accountability."

Each band member's contribution is an integral part of the Public Enemy product, Shocklee once noted: "What you hear, lyrically and musically,... is the sound of a collage of ideas being rejected and accepted." *Detroit Free Press* writer Gary Graff described Public Enemy's "Noise" as "an aural assault of buzzes, sirens, knife-edged guitar riffs, turntable scratches and a bass-drum attack that pummels like uppercuts to the chin." Scott Ian, member of the heavy metal group Anthrax, related to Graff his first reaction to Public Enemy; he was overwhelmed by "Chuck's voice, the heaviness of the beats, all the crazy noises. It wasn't so much musical—just all this stuff going on.... When Public Enemy came out, they just stole the show. There was nothing like it ever before."

Public Enemy's sound may be absolutely original, but many of the ideas expressed in their lyrics are not. Most of the members are students of past and present black leaders and revolutionaries,

Chuck D (left) and Flavor Flav

including Nat Turner, Marcus Garvey, Malcolm X, Huey Newton, and Nation of Islam leader Louis Farrakhan. Their raps echo the rhetoric of the 1960s Black Power movement, and they underscore the parallel between themselves and the Black Panther party with their backup group, S1W (Security of the First World). S1W, which originated as Public Enemy's security force, is a troop of men, clad in military uniforms and toting plastic Uzi machine guns, who stand at attention throughout the performance—except for occasional breaks into martial-arts style moves that Lewis Cole called in *Rolling Stone* "an ironic variation of the synchronized steps of Sixties Motown groups."

Upsetting the Status Quo

Not surprisingly, many people find Public Enemy threatening. The group has been criticized by people of all races for their often violent imagery and their strident opposition to the existing power establishment. Media fire almost forced them to disband in 1989 after member Richard Griffin ("Professor Griff"), leader of S1W and Public Enemy's "minister of information," made anti-Semitic remarks in an interview with the *Washington Times.* The interview contained several other inflammatory remarks—including praise for deposed Ugandan military ruler Idi Amin—and it gained an even wider audience when it was reprinted in the June 20, 1989, issue of the *Village Voice.* Public Enemy came under attack from many quarters, and the Jewish Defense Organization even sent a group armed with chains and clubs to Public Enemy's offices.

Chuck D responded to the furor with a confused series of announcements, stating first that Public Enemy was going to disband, then that it would continue but would refuse to deal with the record industry, and finally, in a press conference, giving notice that Griffin was no longer a part of the group. "The black community is in crisis. Our mission as musicians is to address these problems. Offensive remarks by Professor Griff are not in line with Public Enemy's program. We are not anti-Jewish. We are pro-black, pro-black culture, and pro-human race," *Nation* writer Gene Santoro quoted Chuck D as saying. Following this announcement, he was resolutely silent; but "Fight the Power," the Public Enemy song that served as the theme for Spike Lee's racially charged movie *Do the Right Thing,* climbed the charts and spoke eloquently for the band. Griff eventually returned to the group, and Public Enemy later stirred up more controversy with a single inspired by their media trial, "Welcome to the Terrordome." Far from being apologetic or conciliatory, it brought new charges of anti-Semitism because of the lines "Crucifixion ain't no fiction/so-called chosen frozen/Apology made to whomever pleases/Still they got me like Jesus."

Chuck D philosophized to the *Los Angeles Times:* "We're not liked because never before has the black man or so many black males spoken their opinion on so many things." While decrying the black racism that Public Enemy sometimes seems to encourage, Gene Santoro concurred with Chuck D that the group has been unfairly defamed because of the unpleasant truth they speak; Santoro wrote: "There's no denying that blacks, especially young black males, are stuck at the bottom of the socioeconomic heap. That remains Public Enemy's main point, and it's been validated over recent months by the barely submerged racism in print and television discussions about hip-hop in the wake of the P.E. controversy."

Reunited at Last

In 1994 Public Enemy recorded their first album in almost three years. The reviews for *Muse Sick N Hour Mess Age* were not as strong as the band's earlier albums. However, they maintained their political credibility due to the power of the songs "Give It Up" and "Whatcha Gone Do Now?," which criticize gangsta rap and its violent messages. In 1996, Chuck D released a solo album entitled *The Autobiography of Mistachuck* that attacked the "Big Willie Syndrome" that is so prevalent in the gangsta community. "Big Willie Syndrome" is the nickname for a lifestyle of pursuing wealth and luxuries.

In 1998 the original four members of Public Enemy reunited to record the soundtrack to Spike Lee's drama, *He Got Game.* According to Chuck D, "Having game is being able to deal with whatever is thrown at you." The message delivered in the *He Got Game* soundtrack focuses on the commercialism of sports and the NBA's racial issues. The song "Politics of the Sneaker Pimps," for example, criticizes shoe companies for their exploitation of foreign workers.

The year 1999 brought yet another controversial Public Enemy album into the spotlight. The first four weeks after its release *There's a Poison Going On* was exclusively restricted to mail order and Internet download sales and was priced at more than 40% below the normal retail list price. Chuck D, who is always a proponent of positive change, believes that the Internet can improve the way artists reach fans.

The world portrayed by Public Enemy is not pretty or appealing, but it is reality for many Americans. *Detroit Free Press* writer Graff praised the group for refusing to duck the hard issues: "Public Enemy has walked as dangerous an edge as any rap group has traversed. . . . As [the group] confronts racism, oppression, cultural genocide and self-destruction in the black community—touching on drugs, gangs, education and interracial relationships—Chuck D charges through each topic without apology or diplomacy. . . . [Public Enemy has] brought the Big Picture to modern rap."

Sources for More Information

Periodicals

Entertainment Weekly, May 14, 1999.

Newsweek, May 4, 1998.

People, June 1, 1998.

Rolling Stone, May 28, 1998; May 13, 1999.

On-line

Public Enemy Web site, located at http://www.public-enemy.com/.

Philip Pullman

Author, playwright, and scriptwriter
(1946–)

"I am first and foremost a storyteller."

Born October 19, 1946, in Norwich, England; son of Alfred Outram (an airman) and Audrey (homemaker; maiden name, Merrifield) Pullman; married Judith Speller, August 15, 1970; children: James, Thomas. Education: Oxford University, B.A., 1968.

Philip Pullman is recognized as one of the most talented creators of children's literature to have entered the field in the last twenty years. He is best known for writing fantasy and contemporary and historical fiction for young adults. His historical fiction is usually set in Victorian England, a period that he is credited for recreating with accuracy, and one that he uses to treat themes with strong parallels to contemporary society, including feminism, prejudice, and adjustment to new technology.

Born in Norwich, England, Pullman spent much of his early life traveling with his family, including to locations in Africa and Australia. At age nine, Pullman read his first comic books. He wrote in the *Something about the Author Autobiography Series* (*SAAS*), "When one day my stepfather brought me a *Superman* comic, it changed my life. . . . I adored Batman. What I wanted was to *brood* over the world of Batman and dream actively. It was the first stirring of the storytelling impulse. I couldn't have put it like this, but what I wanted was to take characters, a setting, words, and pictures and weave a pattern out of them; not *be* Batman, but write about him." He added, "I knew instinctively at once, that the telling of stories was delicious, and it all belonged to me.''

As a teenager, Pullman also became enthralled by poetry. After winning a scholarship to Oxford to study English, he became the first person in his family to attend university. Once in college, however, Pullman realized that he was destined to be a storyteller, not a poet. After graduation, he moved to London and worked for a men's clothing store and a library while writing three pages a day—a regime to which he still adheres—in his spare time. After attending Weymouth College of Education, Pullman got his degree and began teaching middle school in Oxford. For twelve years, Pullman taught Greek mythology to his students by telling them stories of the gods and heroes, including oral versions of *The Iliad* and *The Odyssey*. In *SAAS*, the author confirmed that, ''To tell great stories over and over again, testing and refining the language and observing the reaction of the listeners and gradually improving the timing and the rhythm and the pace, was to undergo an apprenticeship that probably wasn't very different, essentially, from the one that Homer himself underwent three thousand years ago.''

Begins Publishing Career

In 1978, Pullman published his first novel, *Galatea,* a book for adult readers that is now considered a cult classic among fans of science fiction and fantasy literature. His first book for young people was *Ancient Civilizations,* a nonfiction title about the cultures of Mediterranean, Eastern, Middle Eastern, and South American countries that R. Baines of *Junior Bookshelf* called ''a lively and informative work.'' Pullman's next book, *Count Karlstein,* was an adaptation of a story that the author had originally written as a play. The book was also published as a graphic novel.

In 1986, Pullman published *The Ruby in the Smoke,* a historical novel for young adults that became the first of his Sally Lockhart series. In *SAAS,* Pullman admitted, ''With *The Ruby in the Smoke* I think I first found my voice as a children's author.'' A thriller set in Victorian London, the novel concerns the whereabouts of a priceless stone that mysteriously disappeared during the Indian mutiny. Sixteen-year-old Sally, a recently orphaned girl who is savvy about such subjects as

business management, military strategy, and firearms, becomes involved in the opium trade when she receives a cryptic note written in a strange hand soon after hearing word of her father's death. David Churchill of the *School Librarian* commented, ''There are not many books that offer such promise of satisfaction to so many children, of both sexes, of secondary age.''

The next volume in the series, *The Shadow in the Plate,* was published in the United Kingdom in 1986, and as *Shadow in the North* in the United States the following year. Pullman introduces readers to such issues as the moral implications of the Industrial Revolution while profiling Sally's growing love for a new detective friend. Writing in *School Librarian,* Dennis Hamley called *The Shadow in the Plate* a ''super read and a story to mull over afterwards for a significance which belies its outward form.''

Continues Writing Sequels

In the third volume of the ''Sally Lockhart'' series, *The Tiger in the Well,* Sally is a successful tycoon as well as a single mother with a two-year-old daughter, Harriet. When Sally receives a court summons informing her that she is being sued for divorce by a man she does not know, the heroine is faced with the prospect of losing her daughter and her property. Pullman outlines Sally's developing social conscience through her experiences, which expose her to an anti-Semitic campaign, while drawing parallels between her treatment and that of the ghetto residents. Writing in *Voice of Youth Advocates,* Joanne Johnson noted that as in his previous books in the series, Pullman ''has recreated 19th century London in good detail. His portrayal of the chauvinism rampant in British law during that time is a lesson to all.'' Marcus Crouch of *Junior Bookshelf* commented, ''Not for the first time in the sequence, but with greater relevance, the name of Dickens comes to mind.''

The final volume of the ''Sally Lockhart'' series, *The Tin Princess,* takes place in Central Europe rather than in Victorian London. A swashbuckling adventure set in the tiny kingdom of Razkavia, the novel introduces two new protagonists, Cockney Adelaide, a former prostitute featured in *The Ruby in the Smoke,* and her friend and translator Becky Winter. Sally Lockhart makes a cameo appearance. Writing in *Booklist,* Ilene Cooper noted that the author's "passion for details gets in the way" and that "too many names and places and plot twists" confuse the readers.

Creates Alternate World

With the popular and critical reaction to "His Dark Materials," a series named for a phrase from John Milton's *Paradise Lost,* Pullman's reputation as a writer for young people became even more secure. In the first volume, published in the United Kingdom in 1995 as *Northern Lights* and in the United States in 1996 as *The Golden Compass,* Pullman describes an alternate world—parallel to our own but featuring technology from a hundred years ago. Julia Eccleshare of *Books for Keeps* commented, "The weaving together of story and morality is what makes *Northern Lights* such an exceptional book. Never for a moment does the story lose ground in the message it carries." While writing the novel, Pullman claims that he knew he was creating a significant work. He told Julie C. Boehning of *Library Journal,* "I felt as if everything I'd read, written, and done in my whole life had been in preparation for this book." *Northern Lights* was awarded the Carnegie Medal in 1996.

About the next novel in the series, *The Subtle Knife,* critic Ann A. Flowers commented in *Horn Book* that Pullman "adds a mythic dimension that inevitably demands even greater things from the finale." Sally Estes of *Booklist* noted, "Often the middle book in a trilogy is the weakest; such is not the case here...." In an interview with Julia

Eccleshare in *Books for Keeps,* Pullman discussed the background of "His Dark Materials": "What I really wanted to do was *Paradise Lost* in 1,200 pages. From the beginning I knew the shape of the story. It's the story of ... how what some would call sin, but I would call consciousness, comes to us. The more I thought about it the clearer it became. It fell naturally into three parts."

In addition to his well-received sets of series, Pullman has enjoyed success with several of his individual titles. *How to Be Cool,* a humorous satire published in 1987, is about a group of teens who expose a government agency that decides which fashions will be hip. The novel was made into a television program by Granada-TV in 1988. *The Broken Bridge,* published in 1990, is considered a major departure for Pullman. The story features Ginny Howard, a sixteen-year-old Haitian/English girl living with her single father in a small Wales town. Anxious to begin her career as a painter, Ginny learns that she is illegitimate, that she has a half-brother, and that her mother, whom she assumed was dead, is actually alive. While seeking out her long-lost mother and learning of her father's abused childhood, Ginny evaluates her own heritage, character, and direction. In a related *New York Times Book Review,* Michael Dorris said, "It's a credit to the storytelling skill of Philip Pullman that this contemporary novel succeeds as well as it does. As the plot tumbles forward, ... the writing remains fresh, the settings original and the central characters compelling."

Pullman returned to nineteenth-century London for the setting of his "New Cut Gang" series, comic mysteries for middle graders that feature a gang of urchins in the 1890s. In a review of the second book in the series, *Thunderbolt's Waxworks,* D. A Young of *Junior Bookshelf* commented that Pullman "creates a convincing picture of his chosen time and place with the lightest of touches." Pullman has also written works that reflect his fascination with folktale and myth, including *The Firework-Maker's Daughter,* a book that won the Smarties Award in 1996.

Pullman once remarked, "I am first and foremost a storyteller. In whatever form I write—whether it's the novel, or the screenplay, or the stage play, or even if I tell stories (as I sometimes do)—I am always the servant of the story that has chosen me to tell it and I have to discover the best way of doing that. I believe there's a pure line that goes through every story and the more closely the telling approaches that pure line, the better the story will be. . . . The story must tell me.''

Sources for More Information

Books

Children's Books and Their Creators, edited by Anita Silvey, Houghton Mifflin, 1995.

Children's Literature Review, Volume 20, Gale, 1990.

Gallo, Donald, editor, *Speaking for Ourselves, Too,* National Council of Teachers of English, 1993.

Sixth Book of Junior Authors and Illustrators, edited by Sally Holmes Holtze, Wilson, 1989.

Something about the Author Autobiography Series, Volume 17, Gale, 1994.

Periodicals

The Lion and the Unicorn, January, 1999.